Beginning DotNetN
Skinning and Desig...

P9-EGN-700

Beginning
DotNetNuke® Skinning and Design

Beginning
DotNetNuke® Skinning and Design

Andrew Hay

Wiley Publishing, Inc.

Beginning DotNetNuke® Skinning and Design

Published by
Wiley Publishing, Inc.
10475 Crosspoint Boulevard
Indianapolis, IN 46256
www.wiley.com

Copyright © 2008 by Wiley Publishing, Inc., Indianapolis, Indiana

Published simultaneously in Canada

ISBN: 978-0-470-10963-2

Manufactured in the United States of America

10 9 8 7 6 5 4 3 2 1

Library of Congress Cataloging-in-Publication Data:

Hay, Andrew, 1973-
    Beginning DotNetNuke : skinning and design / Andrew Hay, Shaun Walker.
       p. cm.
    Includes index.
    ISBN 978-0-470-10963-2 (paper/website)
    1. DotNetNuke (Electronic resource) 2. Active server pages. 3. Web sites--Design. 4. Web site development. I.
Walker, Shaun, 1971- II. Title.
    TK5105.8885.A26H396 2007
    006.7--dc22
                                    2007038099

For general information on our other products and services please contact our Customer Care Department within the
United States at (800) 762-2974, outside the United States at (317) 572-3993
or fax (317) 572-4002.

Trademarks: Wiley, the Wiley logo, Wrox, the Wrox logo, Wrox Programmer to Programmer, and related trade dress are
trademarks or registered trademarks of John Wiley & Sons, Inc. and/or its affiliates, in the United States and other coun-
tries, and may not be used without written permission. DotNetNuke is a registered trademark of Perpetual Motion
Interactive Systems, Inc. All other trademarks are the property of their respective owners. Wiley Publishing, Inc., is not
associated with any product or vendor mentioned in this book.

Wiley also publishes its books in a variety of electronic formats. Some content that appears in print may not be available in electronic books.

About the Author

Andrew Hay is a Microsoft Certified Solution Developer and the Director of Software Development at Pop Art, Inc. After graduating in 1995 with a B.S. from North Central College in Naperville, IL, he started his career at Peoples Energy in Chicago. Here, he wrote and maintained Assembly language code for an IBM OS/360 Mainframe computer. Some of these programs exceeded Andrew's age. In the late 1990s, he was lured into the web development world with everyone else and joined The Information Management Group, Inc., also located in Chicago. As a Microsoft Gold Certified Partner and winner of the Certified Technical Education Center of the Year award, this company was prime spot to witness the first release of the Microsoft .Net Framework. In late 2002, Andrew and his wife Kari moved to Portland, OR where he joined Pop Art, Inc. His current interests include standards-based web development, ASP.Net AJAX, and making the next batch of homebrew beer with his friends.

Credits

Executive Editor
Chris Webb

Development Editor
Christopher J. Rivera

Technical Editor
Robert Bogue

Production Editor
Angela Smith

Copy Editor
Mildred Sanchez

Editorial Manager
Mary Beth Wakefield

Production Manager
Tim Tate

Vice President and Executive Group Publisher
Richard Swadley

Vice President and Executive Publisher
Joseph B. Wikert

Project Coordinator, Cover
Lynsey Osborn

Compositor
Laurie Stewart, Happenstance Type-O-Rama

Proofreader
Amy Rasmussen

Indexer
Jack Lewis

Anniversary Logo Design
Richard Pacifico

Acknowledgments

I'd want to thank my wife, Kari. She knew what I was getting into from the start, gave me tons of encouragement, and did her absolute best to fend off procrastination. You're my little buttercup.

Kelly White and Scott Vandehey were in the trenches with me on a lot of gigs. Thank you for the experience. I also thank Ben Waldron, Justin Garrity, Dave Selden, Ryan Parr, Ben Fogarty, Christina Gonzalez, Thom Schoenborn, Stephen Braitsch, and everyone else at Pop Art, Inc., for their advice and insight into website development and creativity.

Finally, I want to thank Christopher Rivera and Robert Bogue for helping me organize my thoughts in this book. You're two of the nicest guys I've never met.

Contents

Contents

Contents

Contents

Contents

Foreword

For the past four years, DotNetNuke has been quietly rewriting the rules of web development on the Microsoft platform. With more than 450,000 registered users and 3.5 million downloads (as of August 2007), the web application framework has become pervasive in business environments of every size and scope. Licensed under a standard BSD license, the project represents the largest, most active Open Source community on the Microsoft platform. And based on its robust extensibility model, DotNetNuke has cultivated a prosperous business ecosystem for third party products and services.

As the title of this book implies, it is focused on a specific aspect of DotNetNuke — Design. The ability to customize the look and feel is a highly desirable feature in any software application. Sometimes referred to as *templating*, the term *skinning* refers to a software architecture which provides you with a manageable way to separate application logic and content from its presentation. This book focuses on DotNetNuke's superior skinning solution.

If the ability to host multiple websites from a single application was the "killer" feature which provided the initial spark for the DotNetNuke project, the Skinning engine unveiled in March 2004 at VS Live! in San Francisco was certainly the rocket fuel which propelled it forward. Prior to the arrival of DotNetNuke 2.0, web developers on the Microsoft platform were struggling with the design limitations of the ASP.NET 1.1 platform; a platform which offered no native support for separating "form" from "function." DotNetNuke changed all this by providing a flexible portal framework integrated with a sophisticated skinning engine.

As one of the first DotNetNuke platform enhancements which was developed based on public feedback from the open source community, the skinning architecture benefited from a broad range of influences and user requirements. These requirements were distilled down to a number of key criteria which helped guide the development and ongoing evolution of the skinning engine.

Simplicity — the most important item when it comes to skinning is accurately identifying the characteristics of the users who will be creating the skins. In the case of DotNetNuke we recognized that although web developers were the most vocal users of the application, it was actually web designers who would be responsible for creating skins in the majority of cases. Web designers are not comfortable with web development tools, scripting languages, or compilers. As a result, we realized that the optimal skin format must conform to the lowest level web standards; HTML and CSS. By leveraging these basic elements it meant that web designers would be free to design skins in their native environment using their favorite design tools. And to provide the necessary bridge between the static design world and dynamic web application model, we introduced a simple tokenization system which abstracted the all of the complexities from the designers.

Flexibility — web designers are highly artistic by nature; therefore, any solution which seriously restricted their creativity would never gain broad acceptance. This is especially true in terms of page layout, as a rigid structure can quickly become a serious impediment for a professional designer. DotNetNuke introduced the concept of "panes" and placed no restrictions on their usage, resulting in a highly flexible solution.

Foreword

Portability — the ability to combine all skin resources into a single standardized package is a fundamental requirement, as it allows the package to be shared with other users of the platform. This provides the basis of a specialized design community and commercial ecosystem which is now well established in the DotNetNuke project.

Performance — all skinning solutions involve the use of parsing/compilation to merge static design with dynamic elements. Parsing can be an expensive operation, so it is critical that its effects on the run-time behavior of the application are minimized. The skinning engine in DotNetNuke includes a parser which converts static HTML files into dynamic user controls. ASP.NET then takes care of the compilation and caching of these user controls, resulting in a highly efficient skinning architecture.

Even as technology continues to evolve at a rapid pace, the DotNetNuke skinning engine provides a capable solution for professional web designers. Interactive Web 2.0 concepts such JavaScript, AJAX, and Flash can all be seamlessly integrated to provide rich client-side user experiences. The features in the most recent web browsers can be leveraged for advanced design techniques and guidance.

In future releases, we fully expect the skinning engine to evolve to accommodate new use cases. Efforts are currently underway to improve the HTML standards compliance of the core framework. In addition, we expect that the packaging and deployment model for skins will be enhanced to accommodate additional requirements such as versioning, licensing, and advanced installation capabilities.

— Shaun Walker

Introduction

DotNetNuke is an open source framework built on top of the ASP.Net platform. While this system offers an impressive set of out-of-the-box features for public and private sites, it also includes a compelling story for folks who want to present a unique look and feel to visitors.

The skinning engine inside of DotNetNuke has strengthened over the course of several years and hundreds of thousands of registered users. The success of its skin and module developer community is another key indicator of the depth and breadth of this technology. The Core Team responsible for the DotNetNuke brand has gone to great lengths to enable a predictable and positive experience for both the visitors of the site and the developers who build them.

This book takes you through the process of designing a skin for a site. I describe a variety of techniques you can use in your HTML and CSS development as well as coding a few JavaScript, VB.Net, and C# statements. By the final chapter, you will be well versed in the installation, configuration, and customization of a DotNetNuke website.

The practical website design techniques I describe herein provide you with a modern, agile architecture that embraces the features in DotNetNuke and the flexibility of CSS. As a good steward of standards-based development, I show you how to work toward a DotNetNuke solution that successfully passes an HTML validation test. The interactive portions of this book examine how to add personalization, AJAX, Silverlight, and sIFR technology to extend your site.

When you finish this book, you'll have a good idea of your next pursuit. You might choose to stay close to the presentation layer and dive deep into CSS and standards-based web development. Alternatively, this book might have whetted your appetite for DotNetNuke module development, or something in-between including JavaScript, AJAX, or Silverlight technology. I hope you enjoy it!

Whom This Book Is For

The primary audience for this book includes people interested in customizing the look and feel of a DotNetNuke website. Skinning is approachable by developers with a software engineering background as well as HTML and CSS specialists.

Although DotNetNuke expects a Microsoft SQL Server database by default, it's not necessary to have any background in database technology. This book walks you through the database configuration process and quickly moves on to the core focus of the book.

Readers with a little background in website development, regardless of platform, will feel at home here. This book is targeted at showing how to apply web design features to a DotNetNuke site as opposed to teaching individual web development skills like HTML, CSS, and JavaScript. If you have a basic idea of where these technologies fit into the overall spectrum of a website, you'll be able to follow the context of the discussion with ease.

What This Book Covers

This book covers how to create a custom skin for DotNetNuke. As part and parcel of this process, I discuss the steps to install, configure, and construct a website for a specific group of users. The skin helps invoke the appropriate look and feel of the site and augments the content. I show a variety of angles to address this challenge and I present several related technologies including CSS, Silverlight, AJAX, and sIFR that can be used to inspire the right mood for your particular site.

DotNetNuke is under active development and this book focuses on version 4.X of the framework. The skinning development features presented herein are interoperable with all 4.X versions, unless otherwise specified. For example, the chapter on Microsoft ASP.Net AJAX recommends version 4.5.5 or higher.

How This Book Is Structured

This book contains three sections. The first section levels the field and addresses some basic terminology in DotNetNuke skinning. The second section applies the skills of a skin developer to a specific website. The final section explores a few vertical segments that transcend DotNetNuke and offer opportunities for specialized skills in their own right.

Part I: Getting Acquainted

Chapters 1 through 5 get you familiar with installing the system using a variety of techniques and getting acclimated with the files that make up a DotNetNuke skin.

❑ **Chapter 1, "Introducing DotNetNuke Skinning":** In the first chapter, you receive a broad overview of DotNetNuke and learn some key concepts including skins, containers, modules, and panes. If you're new to this open source platform, then this chapter is essential to your success in using the system.

❑ **Chapter 2, "Installing DotNetNuke":** In this chapter, you learn how to get started on the right foot by installing the system through a variety of techniques. DotNetNuke is built on ASP.Net and there are several ways to work with it including IIS, Cassini, Visual Web Developer, and our old friend, Notepad.

❑ **Chapter 3, "Installing Skin Packages":** Chapter 3 starts at the end and shows you how to apply a new skin package to a DotNetNuke site as well as examines the individual parts of a skin package.

❑ **Chapter 4, "Exploring Skins":** After you complete a skin package installation in Chapter 3, you explore the essential parts of a skin file. Chapter 4 discusses the essentials of using panes, skin objects, and containers to augment DotNetNuke modules.

❑ **Chapter 5, "Creating Custom Skins":** Chapter 5 expands on the foundation established in the previous chapter by constructing a custom skin through an HTML file as well as an ASP.Net web user control. I also recommend a couple of tools for developing skins that will help provide some visibility into how the browser renders the page.

Part II: Welcome to the Neighborhood

Chapters 6 through 9 present an opportunity to apply the skills you started to develop in Part I. You'll build a DotNetNuke website for a neighborhood association, including an assortment of custom skins.

❑ **Chapter 6, "The Neighborhood Association Website":** This chapter presents the background and requirements for the neighborhood association website that you will design and build. Here, you apply an appropriate configuration as well as install a set of modules the community will find useful.

❑ **Chapter 7, "Skinning the Neighborhood Association Website":** Chapter 7 goes to work with the process of developing a custom skin for the neighborhood association website. This chapter discusses a process for identifying the number of distinct skins to build and how to architect them for a variety of pages.

❑ **Chapter 8, "Designing the Navigation":** This chapter discusses how to switch the menu navigation feature and apply custom CSS rules to modify the look and feel of the site. As part of the discussion, I show how to install a third-party menu component and work toward a smaller, standards-compliant page.

❑ **Chapter 9, "Leveraging Web User Controls":** The last chapter of Part II shows how to add a little panache to the neighborhood association website with a personalization feature that enables the visitor to make small adjustments to how the website renders in their browser. Web user controls provide an enormous potential and you don't have to be a hard-core developer to utilize them in your site.

Part III: Increasing the Property Value

Chapters 10 through 15 introduce you to a few specialty areas of DotNetNuke, ASP.Net, and general website development. You learn about some compelling new technologies as well as how to maintain consistency in DotNetNuke across several types of browsers.

❑ **Chapter 10, "Exploring Silverlight":** This chapter explores an amazing new client-side feature named Silverlight. It discusses how to add animation and video to the DotNetNuke website you built in Part II.

❑ **Chapter 11, "Using Cascading Style Sheets":** Chapter 11 presents the basic information you should understand about CSS including margins, padding, fonts, backgrounds, and positioning. CSS skills provide you with an agile and search engine–friendly website. This chapter shows you how to modify the various CSS files embedded inside DotNetNuke.

❑ **Chapter 12, "Web Standards and Compliance":** After the fundamentals of CSS are laid out in Chapter 11, I show how to work toward a standard-compliant website in DotNetNuke. I discuss how to swap the menu provider and the HTML Editor provider, too.

❑ **Chapter 13, "Targeting Modules with CSS":** Chapter 13 takes a pragmatic approach to applying CSS to existing DotNetNuke modules without modifying the HTML. The last section builds a web page out of an RSS feed and Extensible Stylesheet Language or XSL.

❑ **Chapter 14, "Exploring AJAX in DotNetNuke":** This chapter takes a look at another hot Microsoft technology, ASP.Net AJAX. The chapter starts with a brief background on AJAX and the DotNetNuke Client API and launches into an example of using AJAX Control Toolkit inside your DotNetNuke page to build an interactive game.

❑ **Chapter 15, "Using sIFR with DotNetNuke":** Chapter 15 rounds out the book with a compelling case for replacing image-text files with a more search engine–friendly component. The technology known as sIFR converts the targeted HTML text into any TrueType font at run time through JavaScript running on the visitor's browser. This feature embraces the work of the copy editor without adding a burden to the graphic designer.

What You Need to Use This Book

To use the samples described in this book, you need the following:

❑ The DotNetNuke installation files

❑ A web server — Internet Information Services or Cassini

❑ A database — Microsoft SQL Server Express, SQL Server 2005, or SQL Server 2000

❑ The Microsoft .Net 2.0 run time

❑ A computer that supports .Net 2.0 — Windows XP/Vista, or Windows Server 2000/2003

❑ Web browsers — Microsoft Internet Explorer 7 and Mozilla Firefox 2

❑ A text editor — Visual Studio, Visual Web Developer Express, or even Notepad

Chapter 2, "Installing DotNetNuke," discusses how to configure these prerequisites on your system so you can download DotNetNuke and execute the installation procedures. All of the essential components, except the Windows operating system, are freely available online.

Conventions

To help you get the most from the text and keep track of what's happening, I've used a number of conventions throughout the book.

Try It Out

The *Try It Out* is an exercise you should work through, following the text in the book.

1. They usually consist of a set of steps.

2. Each step has a number.

3. Follow the steps through with your copy of the database.

How It Works

After each *Try It Out*, the code you've typed will be explained in detail.

> Boxes such as this one hold important, not-to-be forgotten information that is directly relevant to the surrounding text.

Tips, hints, tricks, and asides to the current discussion are offset and placed in italics like this.

As for styles in the text:

- ❑ I *highlight* new terms and important words when we introduce them.
- ❑ I show keyboard strokes like this: Ctrl+A.
- ❑ I show filenames, URLs, and code within the text like so: `persistence.properties`.
- ❑ I present code in two different ways:

```
In code examples I highlight new and important code with a gray background.
The gray highlighting is not used for code that's less important in the present
context, or has been shown before.
```

Source Code

As you work through the examples in this book, you may choose either to type in all the code manually or to use the source code files that accompany the book. All of the source code used in this book is available for download at `www.wrox.com`. Once at the site, simply locate the book's title (either by using the Search box or by using one of the title lists) and click the Download Code link on the book's detail page to obtain all the source code for the book.

Because many books have similar titles, you may find it easiest to search by ISBN; this book's ISBN is 978-0-470-10963-2.

Once you download the code, just decompress it with your favorite compression tool. Alternately, you can go to the main Wrox code download page at `www.wrox.com/dynamic/books/download.aspx` to see the code available for this book and all other Wrox books.

Errata

We make every effort to ensure that there are no errors in the text or in the code. However, no one is perfect, and mistakes do occur. If you find an error in one of our books, like a spelling mistake or faulty piece of code, we would be very grateful for your feedback. By sending in errata you may save another reader hours of frustration and at the same time you will be helping us provide even higher quality information.

To find the errata page for this book, go to www.wrox.com and locate the title using the Search box or one of the title lists. Then, on the book details page, click the Book Errata link. On this page you can view all errata that has been submitted for this book and posted by Wrox editors. A complete book list including links to each book's errata is also available at www.wrox.com/misc-pages/booklist.shtml.

If you don't spot "your" error on the Book Errata page, go to www.wrox.com/contact/techsupport .shtml and complete the form there to send us the error you have found. We'll check the information and, if appropriate, post a message to the book's errata page and fix the problem in subsequent editions of the book.

p2p.wrox.com

For author and peer discussion, join the P2P forums at p2p.wrox.com. The forums are a Web-based system for you to post messages relating to Wrox books and related technologies and interact with other readers and technology users. The forums offer a subscription feature to e-mail you topics of interest of your choosing when new posts are made to the forums. Wrox authors, editors, other industry experts, and your fellow readers are present on these forums.

At http://p2p.wrox.com you will find a number of different forums that will help you not only as you read this book, but also as you develop your own applications. To join the forums, just follow these steps:

1. Go to p2p.wrox.com and click the Register link.

2. Read the terms of use and click Agree.

3. Complete the required information to join as well as any optional information you wish to and click Submit.

4. You will receive an e-mail with information describing how to verify your account and the joining process.

You can read messages in the forums without joining P2P but in order to post your own messages, you must join.

Once you join, you can post new messages and respond to messages other users post. You can read messages at any time on the Web. If you would like to have new messages from a particular forum e-mailed to you, click the Subscribe to this Forum icon by the forum name in the forum listing.

For more information about how to use the Wrox P2P, be sure to read the P2P FAQs for answers to questions about how the forum software works as well as many common questions specific to P2P and Wrox books. To read the FAQs, click the FAQ link on any P2P page.

Beginning
DotNetNuke® Skinning and Design

Part I
Getting Acquainted

Introducing
DotNetNuke Skinning

DotNetNuke (DNN) is a dynamic, database-driven web application that leverages Microsoft ASP.Net to construct a full-featured website in minutes. As an open source product, the barrier to entry is low in terms of dollars; however, the wealth of features can seem daunting at first. DotNetNuke uses Internet Information Services (IIS), the web server included in Windows, and SQL Server 2005 Express Edition, a free database server available for download from Microsoft out of the box. As you migrate a DotNetNuke website out to a hosted web server on the Internet, you'll probably implement a SQL Server 2000 or SQL Server 2005 database for a little more horsepower.

DNN offers plenty of features to solve common business problems. Graphic design and custom module development both have input on the usability and construction of a website. There's a certain balance to strike between beauty, familiarity, and discoverability.

The Origins of DotNetNuke

DotNetNuke's history stems from the IBuySpy Portal that promoted the ASP.Net version 1.0 Framework. Shaun Walker continued the concept over the subsequent years. *Professional DotNetNuke 4: Open Source Web Application Framework for ASP.NET 2.0* (Wiley Publishing, Inc., 2006) is the most recent book written by Shaun and several other folks close to the DotNetNuke Core Team. This book is available at www.wrox.com and is a worthy addition to your web development library. The first chapter provides a firsthand detailed account of the history and evolution of DotNetNuke as both a code base and the people involved.

Why Use DotNetNuke

The web development world of today is very different from its roots. The expectations of a modern, engaging website have leapt since the last turn of the century. Plus, few people possess expert level skills in every technology that touches a feature-rich site, and few have the ability to move a sizeable project from conception to implementation. You can be thankful for the large community of DotNetNuke enthusiasts that support our efforts along the way.

As of July 24, 2007, the DotNetNuke website, www.dotnetnuke.com, listed the following statistics:

- ❑ 6,483 downloads yesterday
- ❑ 440 new members yesterday
- ❑ 459,350 registered users

The community is one of DNN's most valuable assets. As a worldwide project, vast numbers of people contribute to the common storehouse of DNN knowledge and experience. The platform is under active development, and this development shows no signs of slowing. New versions of the core framework are released every few months on average, since version 4.0 was released on November 7, 2005. Ordinarily, this frequent release cycle would be a cause for alarm for any level-headed technologist in charge of maintaining an available system. The core DotNetNuke team addresses this concern by applying lengthy testing procedures prior to a release. Enabling error-free upgrades to the latest version is one of their most heavily protected features.

When a new version is released, visitors access the DotNetNuke site www.dotnetnuke.com, authenticate, and download the latest version as a zip file. This file is unzipped over the top of an existing system. The system discovers the new version and automatically upgrades itself, including any database updates. Of course, responsible administrators make necessary data backups and perform the upgrade in a test environment first.

A company, department, or club can utilize document management and collaboration features in DNN to improve productivity and information availability at an internal level. Externally, this platform is an effective tool for marketing the organization to customers as a public website. DNN can be customized and branded through skinning to reflect the message and nature of the organization.

Public websites are solid candidates for a customized DNN skin. These types of sites have a real need to develop brand equity or carry on an existing brand. Visitors come to the site for its content — the text, photos, and diagrams on the page. Everything else inside the browser helps draw the appropriate mood including fonts, colors, positioning, and background effects. A custom DNN skin is an asset that transforms the website into a unique experience and augments the content, which is the most important aspect of the website. Although the design can be stunning and elegant, the content is what provides the real value to the visitors.

Intranet applications have different priorities from applications available to the public. However, the considerations of each share common ground. The administrator of the DNN website should have a good idea about the desired experience for the visitors to the website.

Intranet applications might share an overall brand for the company and permit a divisional or departmental level sub-brand by emphasizing colors in the brand's color palette or a similar take on a theme.

What Is Skinning?

Skinning is the act of applying a design to the website content. If the various roles for building a website are taken to an extreme, a copy writer produces the words as the core of the page, and a graphic artist develops the mood, textures, tones, and imagery. As you develop a custom DotNetNuke skin, you'll carefully parse each of these inputs and produce a thoughtful web page that balances the ideas of all the stakeholders. DotNetNuke has a well-defined system for separating each of these concerns.

The task of skinning DotNetNuke exists somewhere between a graphic designer role that creates an original idea and a developer role that writes custom code to extend the website. Skinning DNN can be approached by either specialty, or by someone who enjoys wearing both hats.

This book assumes the important tasks of creating website copy and an original graphic design for a skin have already been accomplished, and now the goal of implementing the design inside of DotNetNuke is upon you. You'll learn common patterns and practices for implementing skins over the course of the text. The discussion of creating a graphic composition is outside the scope of this book.

Before you dive into using DNN, it's important to understand some important parts of the system.

DNN Modules

A DotNetNuke module provides a specific feature to the website, such as document management. DotNetNuke has several *modules* included in the default installation. If you can think of an interactive feature for a website, then chances are someone has built a module that does something similar to what you have in mind. If you can't find it commercially or freely available online, then you might have discovered a great niche for selling a new module in the DotNetNuke marketplace as well as some inspiration for building your own component.

A module can be added to any page in the website at any time. A page can hold multiple instances of a module, too. For example, the Documents module allows authorized users to upload documents and tag them with meta information like a title and a description. This module displays the documents as a list in the specified sequence and offers a tracking feature to gauge the popular downloads. A Documents module on the left side of a page might list the training documents for an organization and the right side of the page can hold another Documents module listing supporting information. Security can be configured such that all employees have access to the Documents module on the left side, but only managers have access to the Documents module on the right side.

Many more commercial modules are available online in the $20 to $200 price range. This makes DotNetNuke a worthwhile consideration for a dynamic and feature-rich website with little, if any, out-of-pocket expenses.

The sheer number of out of the box modules in DotNetNuke makes it an excellent option for an instant intranet application. At the end of this chapter, you'll have all the information you'll need to explore around the full installation of a standard DotNetNuke site. Be sure to explore all of the default modules when time permits. There are so many modules that you may find exactly what you're looking for.

Perhaps the most popular module is the Text/HTML module. It displays whatever content was typed into its HTML editor. Although the Text/HTML module is a flexible and familiar component in most DNN installations, it doesn't have any interactive features outside of the HTML editor it displays while in edit mode. The administrator doesn't need to have HTML skills. The editor helps him or her enter content and style it with a wide array of buttons in the toolbar. The Text/HTML module, like any other module in DotNetNuke, can have its own RSS feed and custom print button if it makes sense within the context of the module. You might enable the print button for a Text/HTML module that contains instructions for how to get to your office, but you might disable the print button for a Text/HTML module that just contains hyperlinks to other pages on your site.

Learning About Containers

A DotNetNuke container envelops a module on a one-to-one basis. Every module has a container, although the module can be configured to hide the container that wraps around it. A container traditionally shows the title of the module, common buttons, and the raw content of the given module, whatever that might be.

Imagine you downloaded a free container file online named Roundy. This container draws a nice background with rounded corners around each module that's configured to use it. The Documents and Text/HTML modules on a page are both configured to use the custom container named Roundy. Because each instance of a given container on a page refers to a single physical file named Roundy.ascx, it's easy to make updates cascade across the entire site; you only have to edit a single container file. Later on in this book, you'll build your own custom containers.

Containers help enable consistency around different modules on the same page and across the entire site. Different modules can be configured to have the same container applied to them. It's not uncommon to configure all the modules on a page to use the same container.

Every module has a module settings button. It's the job of the container to show this button to authorized users and hide it when the visitor is not authorized to click it. Administrators can click on the module settings button and navigate to the standard module settings page. This is just one example of the responsibilities assigned to a DotNetNuke container.

Learning About Skins

A DotNetNuke skin is the glue that holds a large number of parts together. Understanding it can be a little rough at the start, but let the information wash over you until the hierarchy begins to make sense.

In DotNetNuke, a given page has only one skin. Different pages can have different skins, and they can all be configured to use the same skin if that is your wish. Skins can be assigned on a page-by-page basis, or they can simply inherit the default skin. If you never assign a skin at a page level, then the site can change dramatically by simply installing a new skin file and making it the default skin. All of the pages that inherit the default skin will instantly take on the look of the new skin. In my experience, most sites use at least three skins: one for the home page layout, one for the landing page layout, and one for the detail page layout. Of course, there are always outliers.

DotNetNuke modules are dropped into panes. The lines around a pane are visible for a viewer logged in as an administrator, but they're invisible for normal users browsing the site. A pane can happily exist without any modules, or it can be overflowing with them; the administrator decides which modules to drop into a pane. The author of the skin merely determines the quantity of panes on a page and where they appear on the page. Panes expand vertically to fit the number of modules inside of them — an important consideration for anyone building their own custom skin.

For example, a landing page that has several detail pages underneath it in the website hierarchy might use a skin with panes arranged in a three-column layout. The detail page might use a skin with panes arranged in a two-column layout. A collection of HTML and CSS rules specify the arrangement of panes on a web page. These arrangement decisions take several roles into account, including the copy writer, the graphic artist, and the DotNetNuke developer.

Developing Skins

DotNetNuke utilizes the Microsoft ASP.Net platform at its foundation, but you have no direct need to compile code, learn object-oriented programming, or launch sophisticated development tools such as Visual Studio.Net 2005.

DNN skin developers spend the majority of their time using their favorite text editor and a web browser. After all, A DNN skin is just a text file. The majority of the work revolves around proper consideration and usage of HTML, CSS, and embedding DotNetNuke components that do interesting things similar to "include" files in Classic ASP or PHP websites. None of this work requires a compiler or two pots of coffee — but it can if that's your thing!

The idea of iterative development lends itself well to the task of skinning DotNetNuke. One of the fundamental tenets of modern software development is the notion of splitting a large task into smaller and smaller chunks. This helps to isolate and identify dependencies as well as reduce the number of things to keep straight in your head, so you can focus on the task at hand.

The sense of accomplishment on a regular basis can go a long way toward problem solving. A task that is allocated several weeks to accomplish might consume several days of pointless thrashing and wasted time before anyone notices. It's easier to spot problems with shorter milestones. They prevent developers from spinning their wheels too long.

When you're building a custom container or designing a unique skin, you shouldn't go too far before checking it in the browser to see if it's behaving as you expect. Start with the smallest file possible, then slowly add to it and check it regularly for errors. If you do this consistently, you'll never get too far along before noticing and correcting a mistake in your files.

Installing Skins

The DotNetNuke administrator has web-based utilities available for installing or updating skins. The various files used to implement a skin are compressed into a single zip file and installed on the DotNetNuke site through a file upload component on a web form.

Once the skins are installed, they can be modified directly by using Windows File Explorer and making file modifications in a text editor. If the DotNetNuke installation is on a remote computer, such as a third-party hosting provider, then an FTP-based approach might suit you better. You learn all about skin installation in Chapter 4, "Exploring Skins."

Browsing the DNN-Blue Skins

A default installation of DNN displays the home page using a skin named *DNN-Blue*. Figure 1-1 shows part of the home page using the DNN-Blue skin.

This skin uses a horizontal menu structure at the top of the page. There are several modules in this page, but Figure 1-1 doesn't give you too much of an idea about where the panes are located. That information is hidden to the normal visitor.

The container around each module applies a consistent blue rectangle. Each container includes the title of the module at the top. The module in the center of the page with the header "Welcome To DotNetNuke®" is an instance of the Text/HTML module. The administrator used the HTML Editor in DotNetNuke to enter the markup into the system so it would render as you see it here.

Figure 1-2 shows the files that make up the DNN-Blue family of skins. It might look like a lot of files to get your head around but there are actually four different skins in this folder. The folder name indicates the family of skins. The files inside a given folder usually have slightly different takes on a common theme. Technically, only one file is required in a given folder to implement a skin. Later on, you'll make your own skin and become very familiar with the contents of a skin folder.

Figure 1-1

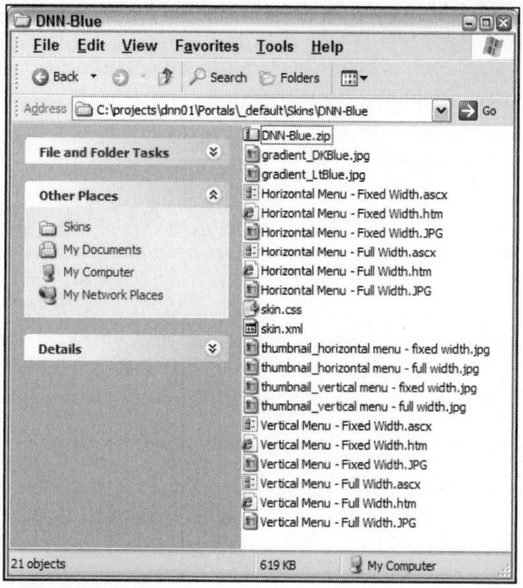

Figure 1-2

You dive deeper into the contents of a skin file in Chapter 4, "Exploring Skins." For now, it's sufficient to know that the DNN-Blue skin comes in four different flavors. By default, DotNetNuke assigns the skin named Horizontal Menu – Fixed Width to a new site. Like the filenames of each skin, the following list describes the characteristics of each distinct skin in the DNN-Blue family:

- ❏ Horizontal menu with a fixed width layout
- ❏ Horizontal menu with a full width layout
- ❏ Vertical menu with a fixed width layout
- ❏ Vertical menu with a full width layout

Feel free to explore these text files and get a glimpse of what's going on to produce the default home page displayed in the browser. As you can see in Figure 1-2, the files are located in `<website root folder>\Portals\_default\Skins\DNN-Blue`.

Cascading Style Sheets

Like other modern websites, DotNetNuke makes extensive use of Cascading Style Sheets, or CSS. This technology provides a great deal of flexibility for site design. Rather than hard-coding presentation instructions directly inside the markup of the content, sites that use CSS can omit presentation instructions altogether or simply label specific blocks of HTML with names. These names are attached to rules in the CSS file, and the rules indicate features such as the color and size of the text.

Before CSS gained the momentum it has today, sites would make extensive use of HTML tables to align and position text. The content would also be littered with instances of the <font> tag to define colors or various font sizes. This type of presentation markup contributes to the difficulty in making site-wide changes. Plus, massive manual changes are prone to error. It's hard for a human to make the same change over and over again in a slightly different context without messing up. Major changes done with CSS are usually limited to just one file. One small change to a single CSS rule can affect the entire site. This single change can be easily tested and reverted if the result was not palatable.

The graphic designers use programs such as Photoshop and Fireworks to create composition as one giant image. The web page is created by applying HTML and images sliced out of the composition. The developer uses tools such as Microsoft Visual Studio.Net to build new modules.

You can become a specialist in skinning with a hybrid of these skills. Developing custom DotNetNuke skins is possible when you have some understanding of HTML and cascading style sheets. Most people have a little more experience on either the creative side or the technical side. Either experience is useful in becoming proficient at skinning.

CSS Zen Garden

The CSS Zen Garden website, www.csszengarden.com/, is an excellent example of how CSS can transform a web page in a radical manner. Figure 1-3 shows the home page.

Figure 1-3

This site celebrates the creative capabilities of cascading style sheets. It's a great place to visit on a regular basis to draw some inspiration. The home page describes the purpose of the site and how to participate. This organization encourages people who are passionate about CSS to submit their cross browser designs to promote the flexibility and creativity of the technology.

The home page of the website renders the content in the default style and the side bar lists recent designs submitted by CSS enthusiasts. You can click on any of the links in the side bar to see the same HTML markup under the guise of a different theme. It's interesting to compare the emphasis applied by different styles and observe what a given designer is signaling as the most important content on the page. This is the crux of website development: the creative integration of design and content to produce a compelling web page.

These designers create customized CSS files and image files that transform the display of the standard HTML content into prolific representations of a particular style. The CSS file renders the image files as background images. Few sites can demonstrate the creative capabilities of cascading style sheets in such a succinct manner. Take a look at the HTML source for any of the designs and get a look at the HTML tags that can be targeted through CSS.

The most grueling part of this process is arriving at an idea for an interesting website theme. Once the idea is solidified, the follow through is accompanied with several options for achieving the same goal. As with most things in software development, myriad ways exist to accomplish a given task. The array of web browsers and their varied HTML rendering capabilities add a special multiplier to the complexity you'll encounter.

CSS and Web Browsers

Modern web browsers have now reached a respectable level of consistency. Each popular browser continues to have its own unique traits, but to the credit of browsers as a group, they're good stewards in the implementation of established web standards. The list of specific differences in how various browsers render the same HTML and CSS has been reduced enough to allow a respectable amount of authoring by folks who don't eat, sleep, and breathe the cascading style sheet lifestyle.

Internet Explorer 7 is a major leap forward from its predecessor. Firefox 2 is also popular in the tech savvy circles. Macintosh users enjoy the experience of Safari as the default browser. Most browser development teams have a blog that demonstrates their passion as well as the challenges they face in building a great product. You would do well to keep a couple of them on your radar to stay abreast of the current developments.

There are many more browsers. For the purposes of this book, I'll limit the discussion to the aforementioned three. You should know that the vast majority of your users will have a great experience, and a tiny percentage of your visitors might have a near-great experience in other web browsers. You can now feel relieved that the days of Internet Explorer 3 and Netscape Navigator 4 are long behind us, and get on with building great looking sites.

Building a Website with DNN

In this section, you'll briefly cover some common steps in configuring a DotNetNuke website. Figure 1-4 shows a standard Documents module added to a page with a DNN-Blue skin.

The module displayed in Figure 1-4 applied the default container. Containers are just text files, so after a few minutes of editing this file in your favorite text editor, it can look like the page shown in Figure 1-5.

The header has a rounded background, and the printer icon has moved to the top. Notice the two palm trees in front of the header, but behind the table, just to snaz it up a bit. You'll work toward a more comprehensive set of goals to create a customized skin for DNN throughout the remainder of the book.

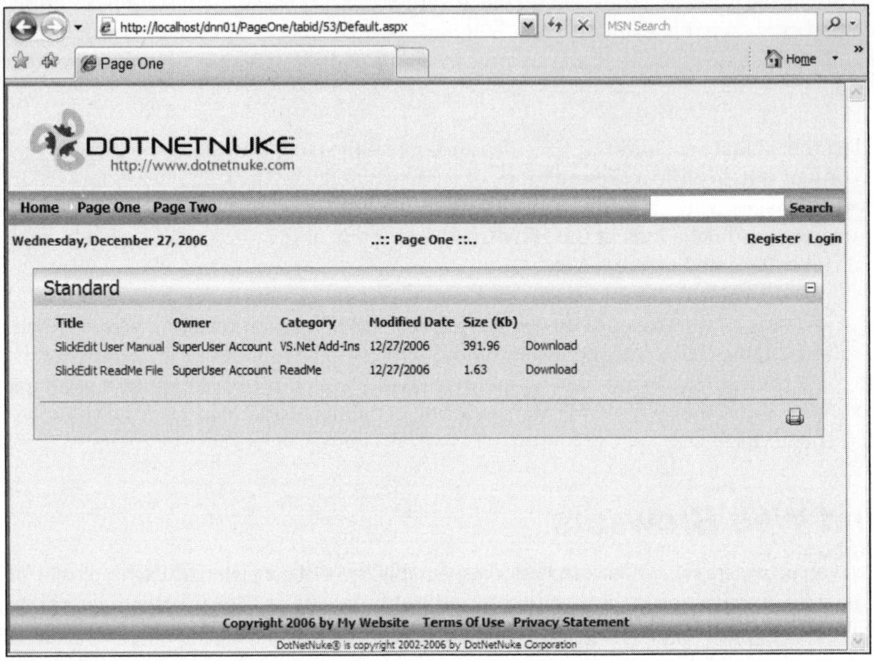

Figure 1-4

Skinning Made Easy

Custom module developers are proficient in a .Net language. Most choose Visual Basic.Net or C#, and they can create a custom DNN module that solves a particular need for a DotNetNuke installation. Similar to the challenge facing a graphic designer, the module developer has the burden of identifying the next great idea. As DotNetNuke skin designers, you don't need to learn a programming language or work with complex business logic, but you still need to keep reaching for that next great idea for a site.

Recent additions to the default set of modules in the current DNN release include the Gallery, Blog, and Store modules. These are excellent additions to the default installation package available on the www .DotNetNuke.com website. These modules were once just ideas. When they became real, they were deemed useful enough by the DNN core team to be included in the default installation. It's hard to think of a greater compliment than to have your skin or module included in the default installation of such a widely used platform.

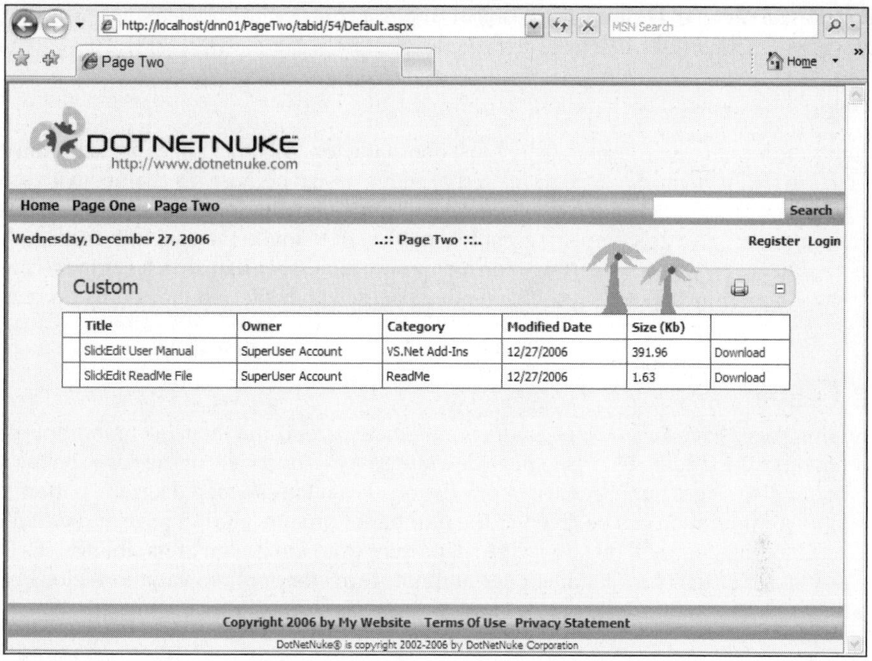

Figure 1-5

Site Map Diagram

When you are building a new site, it's helpful to create a site map diagram that lists all of the web pages in a simple hierarchy. There might be several pages that are cross-linked throughout the website. For the purposes of this discussion, the site map has a simple hierarchy where each subpage is limited to only one parent page. Figure 1-6 is an example of a site map that clearly projects the depth and breadth of the website to be constructed.

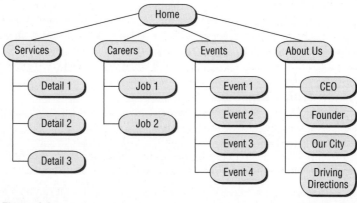

Figure 1-6

Each page in the site map is classified as one of three basic types: the home page, a landing page, or a detail page.

Home Page

The home page is pretty easy to spot; there's just one at the top. All other pages are subordinate to the home page. The skin for the home page can have a very unique design because it's charged with setting the mood for the entire site. It also has to advertise the content under all of the pages. To that end, it might have very few panes and rely on wide, compelling photos in the skin to invite the user into the site. Although this might sound like a great task to start with on a new site, remember that search engines scan for keywords on your site. These keywords are probably on other pages in your site and they oddly become the first page visitors see on your site.

Landing Pages

Most landing pages have the home page as an immediate parent, and they link to multiple child pages. The general notion of the landing page is to provide a summary or overview of the pages below it. Depending on the site, landing pages might come in a few flavors. From the site map diagram, patterns will begin to emerge, and consideration can be given to the number of unique landing page and detail page designs. Unless each landing page will make a radical departure from the design of its siblings, it's OK just to have one graphic composition of the landing page and note the color or photo variations along each branch in the site map.

Detail Pages

Detail pages have a very narrow focus by design. They usually require a wide pane in the skin for a table of documents or lots and lots of text. Because the visitor is deep within the site when they arrive at a detail page, a breadcrumb is a nice navigation feature to give them some context about their location in the site map.

If you're building a public website and not an internal business application, you can assume visitors are coming to the site to read content. Detail pages make up the majority of the site, followed by landing pages and the one home page, so you would do well to spend the majority of your time building a solid detail page, and then working backward.

I've seen an enormous amount of time spent on the home page, which has precious little content. At the same time very little conscious effort was given to the detail page layout and the voice of the content. The content on the detail pages supplies the real value to the website. Because public sites are scanned by search engines and visitors are linked to detail pages with the matching keywords instead of the home page, it seems odd to spend any time on the home page until the rest of the site is fully baked.

Parent-Child Page Relationships

Parent-child relationships are interesting in DNN. On a typical static website, where every page is represented by a unique file on the hard drive, the landing page is special. By convention, it's the default file in the directory. For example, if the URL www.company.com/services/ were typed into an address bar, the default file in the directory would appear in the browser.

It's the job of the web server to know the default file in the directory so it can be served up when no specific file is requested. The Windows web server, IIS, has an editable list of default files. When no specific file is requested, IIS traverses the list in top-down order and serves up the first matching file it discovers in the directory. By convention, the file is named default.aspx in an ASP.NET environment.

In DNN, the parent-child relationship is virtual, not physical. Suppose a website has the following URL that displays information about the company:

```
www.company.com/about-us/default.aspx
```

If this were a DNN site, the web server would not have a physical file named `default.aspx`; in fact, it would not even have a physical directory named about-us. This is the magic of DotNetNuke and its URL rewriting feature.

ASP.Net supports a feature that allows the web server to intercept a web request, perform and look up in the database, and potentially redirect the web request to another page on the site without ever telling the visitor. This can be a very powerful and valuable feature, and DotNetNuke takes full advantage of it. In fact, there's basically only one web page in the entire site. Its name is `default.aspx` and it's located in the root directory. All of the modules and various features are loaded dynamically into this page and the URL rewriting feature makes it appear as though a site might have hundreds of pages.

Setting the Parent and Child Pages

On the plus side, the URL rewriting feature allows pages to move around on the site with ease. The relationship can be redefined at any time because the change occurs in the database, where DNN stores most of its information. Figure 1-7 shows a portion of the DotNetNuke administration page that indicates the parent of the given page. Changing this value will move the location of the page in the navigation. Because the field is in a drop-down list, there's a chance you'll pick the wrong parent, but you won't mistype it.

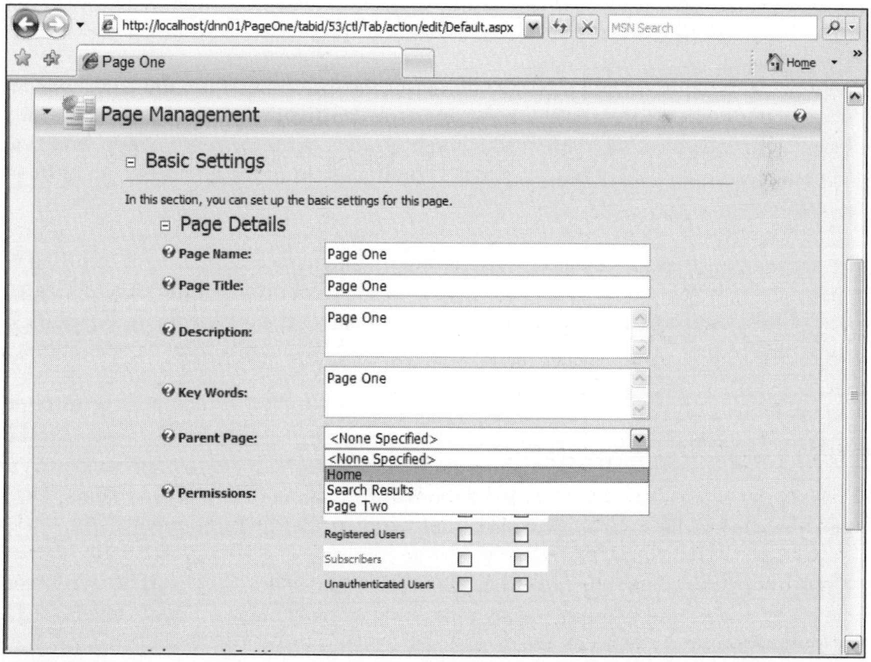

Figure 1-7

This dynamic parent-child association feature takes a burden off the shoulders of the build team. During the course of website development it's common to move pages around much like furniture in a new apartment. Because all of the relationships are managed through a web-based interface, there is less risk of losing a file, misnaming the file, or other oversights.

Installing DNN Automatically

Provided you have all of the prerequisite software available, DotNetNuke can install itself. Presuming the web server and database server are already on a computer, these are the basic steps to install DotNetNuke:

1. Download and unzip the bits from www.dotnetnuke.com into a folder.

2. Inside IIS, the web server in Microsoft Windows, create a new website that points to the folder in Step 1.

3. DotNetNuke will create and modify files on disk, so verify the appropriate file permissions are set on the folder.

4. As with most other ASP.Net web applications that use a database, verify that the database connection in the web.config file is pointed at the appropriate database — in this case, a new (empty) database that you created or one created for you on the corporate network.

5. Launch a web browser, and answer a few questions in the DotNetNuke Installation Wizard.

    These installation steps are covered in much greater detail in Chapter 2, "Installing DotNetNuke." For now, just keep the basic installation concepts in mind.

Upon the initial web request, DotNetNuke will detect the need to execute the auto-installation process. As DNN traverses the list of installation tasks, the browser displays the growing list of completed steps. The system first installs the core framework, then upgrades to the current version, and finally extends itself by installing a default set of modules. Based on the speed of the computer, all of this takes place in just a few minutes.

Figure 1-8 shows a page displayed after a successful installation. The middle of this long web page has been cropped to show the starting and ending messages. The bottom of the page indicates the entire installation process took just over a minute to execute locally on a run-of-the-mill laptop. Clicking the bottom hyperlink will navigate to the default home page of the DotNetNuke installation.

Several installation options and considerations can be exercised before installation and post-launch, yet the basic software package remains approachable to people just starting their exploration of web-based systems. When the situation calls for it, the system has enough layers to peel back and customize in order to satisfy the extensibility and customization requirements of complex systems. The last chapters of this book examine some complex scenarios that you'll gradually build toward.

DotNetNuke has matured into a feature-rich application that spans the needs of many scenarios. At the same time it has stayed true to its origins by remaining approachable on many levels, including custom designs through skinning.

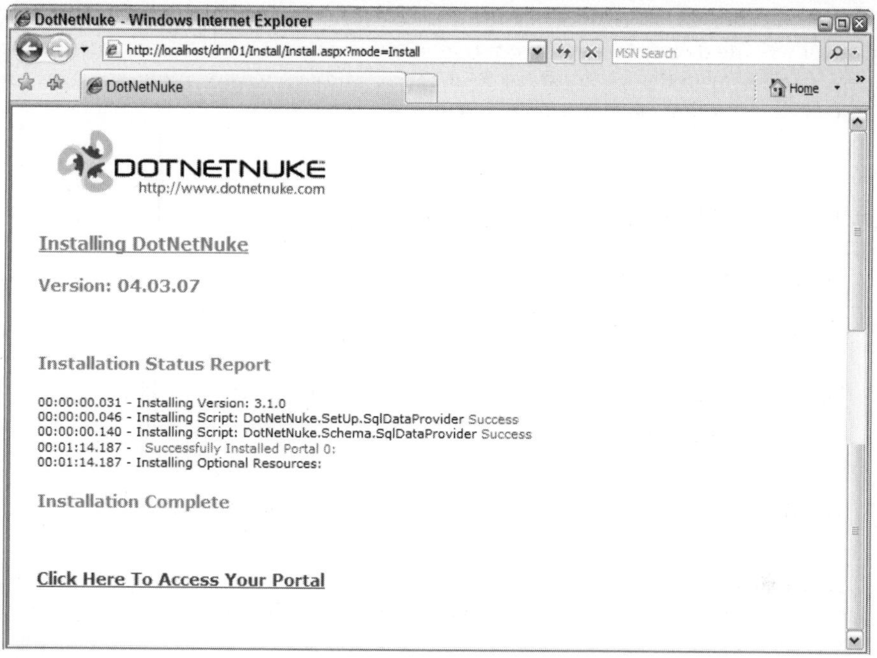

Figure 1-8

Summary

This chapter discussed a broad overview of the DotNetNuke framework and the tangential aspects of creating a database-driven ASP.Net website. The following chapters are much narrower in scope. This chapter introduced you to the following items:

- ❑ The roots of DotNetNuke and its popularity statistics
- ❑ What skinning DotNetNuke is and how it relates to graphic design and custom module development
- ❑ Modules, containers, and skins as the components of DotNetNuke
- ❑ The installation process

2

Installing DotNetNuke

The goal of this chapter is to make you comfortable with installing DotNetNuke. If you're new to web development and databases, this can seem daunting the first few times. You should practice installing the software a couple of times to get familiar with the experience.

DotNetNuke v4.5.0, released April 6, 2007, included a fantastic new feature for installation — a set of web pages that manage the installation on your behalf and greatly reduce the complexity of the process. Prior to this version, the installation process involved a couple of key edits that were a little tricky to the uninitiated.

If there is a list of things that contribute to the drag on adoption of DotNetNuke technology, the manual installation process is on that list. As of DotNetNuke v4.5.0, this drag has been nearly eliminated. If you have the ambition to install a great ASP.Net technology, there's little that will get in your way of seeing the default home page of fresh DotNetNuke installation today. That's not to say the manual installation process doesn't still have a valid place. This chapter covers a couple of different installation techniques, starting with the prerequisite software, then manual installation procedures, and finally using the shiny new installation wizard.

If you already have some experience with ASP.Net, there's a good chance you have the prerequisite software installed on your local development computer. DotNetNuke is built on the ASP.Net Framework and will feel very natural to folks who edit web user controls and `web.config` files on a daily basis. For the benefit of those who are just starting to explore this area, the chapter begins with the assumption that you have a modern computer in front of you running Microsoft Windows, and that's about it.

Installing Prerequisites

DotNetNuke uses a Windows web server; therefore, one of the following Windows operating systems is required to get started:

- ❏ Microsoft Windows 2000 Professional
- ❏ Microsoft Windows 2000 Server

- ❑ Microsoft Windows XP

- ❑ Microsoft Windows Server 2003

- ❑ Microsoft Windows Vista

The following list includes the components you'll need to install on your system before DotNetNuke. Some of these programs leverage or depend on the existence of prior installations, so the order in which you install is important.

1. Internet Information Services (IIS)

2. Microsoft .Net Framework 2.0

3. Microsoft SQL Server 2005

4. Microsoft SQL Server Management Studio

5. Windows Updates

The easiest way to deal with these prerequisites is to have someone else install them for you. A friend with a server in his basement, your IT department at work, or a hosting provider that you pay monthly or annually may all provide this service. Hosting providers rent space on their servers and manage all of the installation and maintenance of the server software. Some of them even install DotNetNuke for you. Fees for providers capable of hosting DotNetNuke can be less than $10 per month, if you keep an eye out for a deal. The banner ads on www.dotnetnuke.com are a good place to start looking for hosting providers.

Keep an eye out for hosting providers and ask about customer support experiences from people you already know. I consider myself to be reasonably tech savvy and I've always had to call a hosting provider for one reason or another. Believe me, there's a wide range of quality in the customer support metric.

Installing a Web Server

Internet Information Services, or IIS, is the Microsoft web server, and ASP.Net runs on top of this as an extension. ASP.Net is supported on the following platforms:

- ❑ Microsoft Windows 2000 Professional

- ❑ Microsoft Windows 2000 Server

- ❑ Microsoft Windows XP Professional

- ❑ Microsoft Windows Server 2003

- ❑ Microsoft Windows Vista

IIS is recommended, but it is not technically required. An alternative web server named Cassini is also available for local development. If you are new to web development in general, Cassini might provide an easier entrance to the world of DotNetNuke. Cassini is discussed in the section following the IIS installation instructions.

Installing IIS on Windows XP Professional

The following steps describe installing IIS on a machine running Windows XP Professional. You might be prompted for the Windows XP installation media during the steps, so keep it handy. The process for installing IIS on the other supported operating systems is similar to the following:

1. Launch the Control Panel by clicking Start, Control Panel.

2. Double-click Add or Remove Programs.

3. Click Add/Remove Windows Components.

4. Select Internet Information Services.

5. Click the OK button to accept the component selection.

6. Click the Next button to finish the installation.

Using Cassini

You'll start with some background information to help understand the technology at play here, and de-clutter the instructions on how to use the technology later on in this chapter. You may have heard about Cassini, the lightweight Windows web server for local development. It's a reasonable alternative to IIS on your development machine. You'll learn how to use both types of web servers with DotNetNuke in this chapter. You don't have to choose now; both can be installed side by side on a development machine and you can pick which server to use later.

One of the scenarios where Cassini might be a good choice is if you're using Windows XP Home Edition. This operating system does not support IIS. Cassini, as a lightweight web server, makes ASP.Net web development more accessible to folks with Windows machines outside of the typical developer spectrum.

If you decide to use Cassini as your web server, you'll need to be mindful of the port used to communicate with the web server. By default, Cassini uses a random port number, which can cause problems with DotNetNuke. Given this issue, I'll back up a second and give you a basic understanding of how ports apply to web servers.

In a networked environment, information flows into and out of your computer through ports. Ports are numbered so they can be identified and managed. Port 80 is the standard port used for traffic on web servers and messages are sent through this port using the HTTP protocol. Most of your normal web browsing experience is done over port 80. Port 443 is the standard port used for secure transmissions using the HTTPS protocol. This is all by convention, so there's nothing particularly special about these two ports; any numbered port will do the job.

URLs can specify the port by adding a colon and a number after the domain name. The following two URLs are equivalent because port 80 is the default:

```
http://www.company.com
http://www.company.com:80
```

A lot of folks who have Cassini installed on their development machine also have IIS installed. Having both servers running can potentially cause problems as only one service can be listening to a given port for requests at a time. IIS uses port 80 by default. Therefore, Cassini opens a random port on your computer in lieu of port 80.

Most web applications don't care which port is used to transport messages on a web server, as long as the result is successful. DotNetNuke is not one of those programs; it likes to know where it lives. The DotNetNuke database has a table identifying where the website exists, including the port number and any application folder name.

The following example URL is typical for a local ASP.Net solution using IIS:

```
http://localhost/MyASPNetSolution
```

The `localhost` part is a keyword that indicates the web server exists on the local computer. The `MyASPNetSolution` part is the virtual application folder on the web server. This virtual folder can be pointed to any physical folder on the computer. The virtual folder abstracts where the physical web pages exist on the computer.

The following example URL is typical for a local ASP.Net solution running on Cassini:

```
http://localhost/MyASPNetSolution:4672
```

If you access an existing DotNetNuke website through a URL that is technically equivalent, DotNetNuke will redirect to the URL that it knows about, the one inside its database table. Hence, if the port is random upon each start of Cassini, you'll have a hard time running the DotNetNuke application.

You can work around the issue created by this random port feature by disabling the dynamic port in Visual Web Developer Express. The steps to do this are coming up shortly in the installation instructions. At this point, it's important to know that Visual Web Developer Express launches Cassini to render the website and closes down Cassini when Visual Web Developer Express closes. To see the site in Cassini, you need to launch the site through Visual Web Developer Express each time.

If you decide to use IIS as your web server, you can simply launch your web browser to view the website locally. If you use Cassini, you might as well use Visual Web Developer Express as your text editor, because it will have to be running anyway. There are ways to launch Cassini without Visual Web Developer Express, but they'll be out of scope for this book. Here, you're just interested in getting a web server that's capable of running ASP.Net 2.0 applications as simple as possible.

Installing ASP.Net 2.0

ASP.Net runs on top of IIS as an extension of the web server. When IIS receives a request, it looks at the file extension. Under normal conditions, files ending with `.gif`, `.jpg`, `.js`, or `.html` are sent back immediately to the browser. Files ending with the extension `.aspx` are passed off to the ASP.Net engine for processing. IIS knows to do this because `.aspx` files are *mapped* to the ASP.Net engine.

The file mapping inside IIS is just a simple list of filename extensions linked to a list of processing engines. You could add your own name as a new file extension inside IIS, if you wanted, and map it to the ASP.Net processing engine. Files ending with `.andrew`, for example, might raise some quality and maintenance concerns around the office.

The Microsoft .Net 2.0 Framework is the foundation of the DotNetNuke website. ASP.Net is included in the framework and you will need to install it if you don't already have it. The .Net Framework 2.0 is a free download from Microsoft. You can find a link to the download on the ASP.Net website at www.asp.net.

If you plan to use IIS, please make sure that you have installed the IIS web server before installing the .Net 2.0 Framework. During the .Net 2.0 installation, IIS will be discovered, and the ASP.Net mappings will automatically happen; otherwise, you'll have more work on your hands than you want.

If you find yourself in a situation where the .Net 2.0 Framework is already installed prior to IIS, you'll need to run the command-line program named aspnet_regiis.exe. It comes with the .Net 2.0 files and is probably located in the following folder on your computer:

```
C:\windows\microsoft.net\framework\v2.0.50727\aspnet_regiis.exe
```

You can run the aspnet_regiis.exe program with the /? argument from the command line to see all of the switches. Running the program with the -i switch will install the script maps for ASP.Net 2.0 into IIS and update all of your existing web applications to use version 2.0 of the ASP.Net Framework. If you don't have any ASP.Net web applications installed, then the -i switch is a no-brainer.

You may have heard about the .Net 3.0 Framework and be wondering if that should be used instead. Windows Vista ships with version 3.0 of the .Net Framework installed by default. Version 3.0 has many new features but they are just extensions of the 2.0 release. The .Net 3.0 Framework includes the following four pillars:

❑ Windows Presentation Foundation for building client applications

❑ Windows Workflow Foundation for building systems with complex business rules

❑ Windows Communication Foundation for building systems that make calls to external services

❑ Windows CardSpace for improving security and identity concerns

The Microsoft .Net 3.0 Framework does not include much for ASP.Net as it applies to DotNetNuke. Therefore, version 2.0 of the .Net Framework will suit us just fine.

It's worth mentioning that ASP.Net 2.0 is packaged with the third major release of .Net technology from Microsoft. The initial foray into web-based development with .Net technology came with ASP.Net version 1.0 released in early 2002, and version 1.1 followed in 2003. ASP.Net 2.0 was released with several new enhancements in late 2005.

Using Microsoft SQL Server

DotNetNuke is a data driven web application. This opens up another large area of specialization, database administration. The default DotNetNuke installation uses Microsoft SQL Server 2005 Express Edition as the database.

This book uses Microsoft SQL Server Express Edition as the reference point. If you're using another Microsoft SQL Server database, then chances are you're already a pro and don't need any help in that department. DotNetNuke can be easily installed on SQL Server 2000, or any edition of the SQL Server 2005 family except the Everywhere edition, which wasn't intended for web application use.

Understanding Abstraction and the Provider Model

Before beginning the installation, there are a few key points to discuss. While the goal of this book is to help you gain an insight into DotNetNuke skinning, you'll be well served by a high-level understanding of how DotNetNuke operates under the hood. You won't need to explore inside the database at a low level, but you will make some configuration changes. In later chapters, you'll swap out components and make your own customizations, so learning a few technical concepts here will go a long way later on.

The DotNetNuke database is the place where most people begin to learn about two key concepts in DNN: *abstraction* and the *provider model*. Abstraction in software is where the consumer of a service doesn't care or even want to know how the service is actually done. It just cares that when a request or a command is performed, it's performed successfully in a timely manner. This idea is put to good use in DotNetNuke. You might prefer the user experience of one component over another. Abstraction in DotNetNuke helps components such as HTML editors to be swapped out easily for different editors that perform the same core service.

A related concept is implemented into DotNetNuke as the *provider model*. The provider model starts with a list of features, which can also be described as a type of contract. There are two parties to this contract. One party is the consumer of the services, such as the DotNetNuke Documents module. The second party is the provider. The contract requires the provider to perform specific services that are clearly defined in the contract. Therefore, any number of providers can fill the role of the second party as long as they provide the specified services. Figure 2-1 is a conceptual view of the provider model.

In Figure 2-1, the data provider box is the contract. The business logic exists as a consumer of the service and the SQL provider exists to implement the service. The SQL provider in turn knows how to communicate with the SQL Server database. If the Access provider is available, it can be easily swapped and the information will be placed inside an Access database. Just to drive the point home, I also included the notion of an XML provider, where all of the information is stored in a series of XML files. Keep in mind, the business logic doesn't care which provider is used.

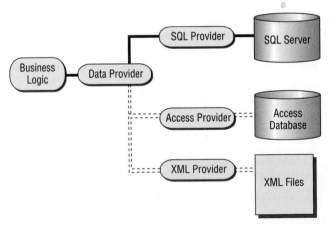

Figure 2-1

The provider model is not unique to DotNetNuke. It exists in many forms across all types of modern software development. ASP.Net 2.0 is one such technology that embraces this concept and makes it easy for developers to build their own provider modules. If you're curious about the providers used in your DotNetNuke installation, use your favorite text editor to view the `web.config` file in your web root folder and check out the list of providers.

Installing Microsoft SQL Server Express Edition, Service Pack 1

Microsoft SQL Server Express Edition can be downloaded for free from the following URL. There is a version of SQL on this web page that includes Advanced Services, but you don't need it.

```
http://msdn.microsoft.com/vstudio/express/sql/download/
```

The installation process is a typical, wizard-based installation program. The default options in the installation process are fine for first-time users, except for one potential "gotcha," the authentication mode. Be careful to choose the right authentication mode. There are two choices:

1. Windows Authentication Mode
2. Mixed Mode (Windows Authentication and SQL Server Authentication)

Windows Authentication mode only allows authorized Windows accounts to access the database. Although this is the most secure mode, it may create more headaches than it solves for beginning users.

Mixed mode permits both Windows Authentication and SQL Server Authentication. This feature stems from SQL Server's long legacy as a popular database before being integrated into Windows. SQL Server has its own private repository of users and passwords, which is still in popular use today. Selecting an authentication mode is an important security issue and should not be overlooked in a business or public Internet environment. Windows Authentication mode is more secure because the credentials used to access the database are more obfuscated than Mixed Mode. However, Mixed Mode will work just fine for your local development database needs.

When you select Mixed Mode, enter the System Administrator password for this instance of SQL Server Express Edition. Don't forget this password!

Installing SQL Server Management Studio Express

Microsoft SQL Server Express is a small and efficient database engine that is used throughout this book. Just like its bigger siblings, SQL Server Express is a respectable database engine, but it does not include a graphical user interface for visualizing and manipulating the database. This tool can simplify some of the steps you see later on during the DotNetNuke installation process. The installation process for SQL Server Management Studio Express is simple, and the default installation options are fine for most people.

The download link to the Management Studio is on the same page as the link to download SQL Server Express.

Installing Microsoft Visual Studio 2005

You can use your favorite text editor for the skinning work. Visual Studio 2005 is my choice editor, but it doesn't have to be yours. Notepad will work just fine. The screenshots in this book use Visual Studio 2005 Professional Edition. You can download Visual Web Developer 2005 Express Edition for free and have the same HTML and CSS editing experience as the Professional Edition.

You can find the free download link for Visual Web Developer Express Edition on the Downloads page of the ASP site at `http://msdn.microsoft.com/vstudio/express/downloads/`

One of the installation packages for DotNetNuke is a solution template for Visual Studio. You can choose from a few DotNetNuke packages, so you're not out of luck if you have an affinity for another editor.

Checking Microsoft Update

Before you begin installing the software for DotNetNuke, you should make sure Windows is up to date with the latest software patches. Microsoft has made this really easy. Unless you have a good reason not to, you should be using the Automatic Updates feature in Windows. This feature allows Windows to search for and install updates to the operating system on its own, periodically. Folks who are contractually obligated to maintain systems that require more than 99.999% up-time have a good reason, but most of us should just turn it on and forget about it.

Launch Internet Explorer, and then click Tools, Windows Update item in the menu bar. First, Microsoft Update scans the computer, which could take a few minutes. Then, you are presented with a choice of either selecting the express option or the custom option. Either choice is fine; the custom option provides more detail. Depending on the particular software patch, multiple items might be installed at once or just one at a time. If the computer hasn't been updated in a while, it's a good idea to run the Windows Update feature several times until it reports that no outstanding high priority updates exist.

Installing DotNetNuke

Now that your computer has all of the required software, it's time to turn your attention to the main attraction: DotNetNuke.

As mentioned in Chapter 1, DotNetNuke is under active development. The team is churning out revisions at a good clip. They're using a popular practice of small incremental stabilization releases. Every once in a while a large release is pushed out.

As someone who enjoys the notion of having the very latest software, I can find it a little discouraging to fire up my RSS reader and learn that my DotNetNuke installation is one or more versions from the front of the line. Not to worry though, the upgrade path for DotNetNuke has been well planned. For information on upgrading your installation of DotNetNuke, you should look at *Professional DotNetNuke 4: Open Source Web Application Framework for ASP.NET 2.0* by Shaun Walker, et al. (Wiley Publishing, Inc., 2006).

Getting the Latest Release

Navigate to www.dotnetnuke.com, create an account, and navigate to the Downloads section at the following URL:

```
www.dotnetnuke.com/tabid/125/default.aspx
```

Choose a package to download. DotNetNuke is offered in several packages for a given version:

❑ **Install Package:** This download contains the files necessary to get a DotNetNuke site up and running. This package has no source code, just the essential files to run the system.

❑ **Starter Kit Package:** This download contains templates used by Visual Studio 2005 and Visual Web Developer Express. Developers can use these to create a new DotNetNuke installation by launching Visual Studio 2005 and clicking File, New Website and selecting the DotNetNuke Starter Kit.

❑ **Upgrade Package:** This download is useful if you already have a prior version of DotNetNuke installed and you're interested in upgrading it to the current version.

❑ **Source Package:** This download puts the "source" in open source development. Custom module developers will be interested in this version to learn how the existing modules were built. This source code compiles into the same files used by the Install package.

❑ **Docs:** This download includes a laundry list of PDF documents describing detailed aspects of the system.

For our purposes in this chapter, you need only download the Install and Starter Kit packages to your computer.

Experimenting with Installation Approaches

Welcome! I'm glad you made it to the fun part of the process. Don't let your guard down though; you need to remain cautious and methodical until you have several installations under your belt.

I'm pretty savvy when it comes to websites and databases, particularly Microsoft tools. When I waded into DotNetNuke a few years ago, I encountered several problems. Looking back, I now realize that the problem was my own failure to follow the documentation or to find a proficient mentor. This book will provide you with the guidance I lacked during my first experiences with DotNetNuke and will make your first experience with DNN pleasurable. The installation is key and can be tricky. If you master this, however, your future with DNN will be a happy one.

As mentioned earlier, two types of web servers are available: Cassini and IIS. There are also three database versions: SQL Server 2000, SQL Server 2005, and its agile sibling SQL Server 2005 Express Edition. There are even two ways to use the Express edition, so you can calculate the permutations of possible configurations, and that's not even counting the versions of the Windows operating systems. This section covers some of the popular configurations, and hopefully you'll find one that appeals to you. I recommend you try every combination at least once to come to understand the process thoroughly.

Using Visual Web Developer and Cassini

This path involving Visual Web Developer and Cassini will bypass some steps related to configuring IIS and creating a database. It's a good way to learn the manual process of installing DotNetNuke if you don't have a lot of web development experience.

Starter Kit Installation

The starter kit needs to be installed only once on your computer. Then it will be available from Visual Web Developer to create as many new DotNetNuke sites as you like.

1.   Unzip the DotNetNuke Starter Kit package into a folder on your computer.

2.   Double-click the Visual Studio Community Content Installer file named `DotNetNuke .vscontent`. It's the only file in the directory that's not a zip file.

3.   Click the Next button to install all of the templates and starter kits.

If you only have Visual Web Developer installed, you might receive a warning on the DotNetNuke Compiled Module, but that's OK; you don't really need it. That template requires a feature of Visual Studio that's not included in this free edition.

DotNetNuke File Installation

Now that the DotNetNuke Starter Kit is installed on your computer, you can utilize its features inside Visual Web Developer. The following steps create a new instance of DotNetNuke running in your web browser:

1.   Launch Visual Web Developer.

2.   In the menu bar, click File, and then New Web Site.

3.   In the New Web Site window, set the following fields as instructed:

  a.   In the Location drop-down list, select the item named File System. This tells the system to use Cassini for the web server.

  b.   In the text box to the right of the Location drop-down list, enter the path of the new solution. I put all of my solutions in a folder named projects, so I might enter `c:\projects\ MyDNNSolution01` in the text box.

  c.   Select Visual Basic from the Language drop-down list.

  d.   In the Templates box at the top of the window, click the item named DotNetNuke Web Application Framework.

4.   Click OK.

Figure 2-2 shows the correct values of the New Web Site window.

Your computer will chug along for a while as Visual Web Developer copies the template files into this new solution. It might take a minute or two depending on your machine.

When the process is complete, you will see all of the DotNetNuke files in the Solution Explorer window and a single open file containing a welcome message and some documentation. The template has inserted the name of your project into the documentation file. Read the welcome message, too; it has some good information.

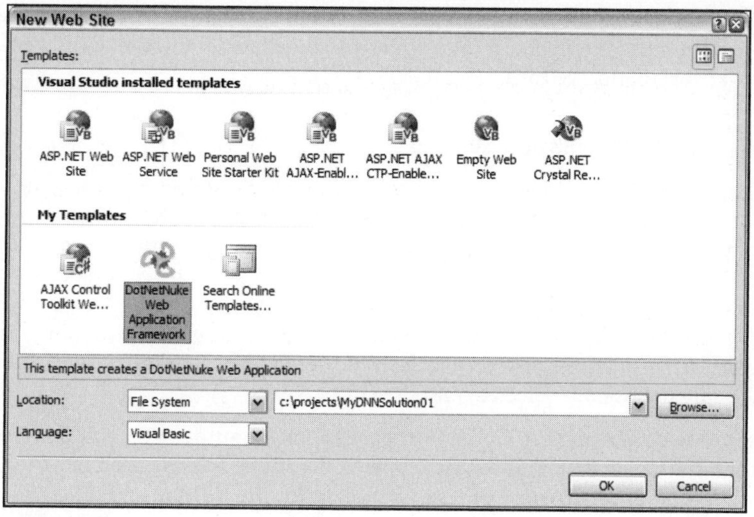

Figure 2-2

Controlling Ports in Cassini

You need to do just one more thing before launching the site: Disable the dynamic port feature of Cassini so this instance of DotNetNuke will continue to work each time Cassini is started. Remember, DotNetNuke likes to know where it lives, and the port is part of the address; the port value must be controlled.

With the project loaded in Visual Web Developer, follow these steps to disable the dynamic port feature:

1. Click the top node in the Solution Explorer tree. (This node displays the folder path of the solution.)

2. Press F4 to view the Properties window for the solution. (Note that the contents of the Properties window depend on which node is selected in the Solution Explorer. Make sure the top node is selected.)

3. In the Properties window, change the value of the field Use Dynamic Ports from True to False.

4. Change the four-digit number in the Port Number field to an arbitrary port number of 8080.

Figure 2-3 shows the values of the Properties window with values that disable the dynamic port feature and specify an arbitrary port value.

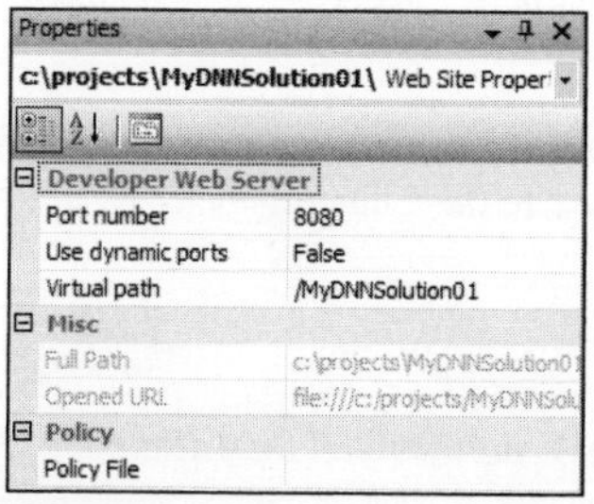

Figure 2-3

Now it's time to launch the site! In the menu bar of Visual Web Developer, click Debug, Start without Debugging. Your computer will churn for a while and then launch Internet Explorer. The first screen is the DotNetNuke Installation Wizard.

Using the DotNetNuke Installation Wizard

The DotNetNuke Installation Wizard helps you configure the right settings for your installation. Even though the URL is showing a web page, the DotNetNuke system really isn't installed, yet. The next set of seven screens walk you through the process of selecting the right settings for your installation and help minimize the risk of mistakes during the process. It's a fantastic new feature available since DotNetNuke 4.5.0.

1. The first screen includes just three radio buttons. The item labeled Typical is fine for your purposes. Make sure that item is selected, and then click Next.

2. The next wizard item verifies the file permissions are sufficient. Click the Test Permissions link to confirm the file system is set up properly. If you see an error, you need to grant the ASPNET account Modify permissions on the root folder for the website and all of the child files and folders. After you've confirmed the necessary file permissions are in place, click the Next button.

3. The next page helps configure the database for the system. Because you're using the default database settings for DotNetNuke, the default field values on this page are sufficient. If you were using SQL Server 2005, you would make the necessary changes here and enter the database credentials for that type of database.

4. The next screen shows the actual installation of the database. After all of the installations have completed, click the Next button.

5. The Configure Host User form prompts you to enter the credentials for the Host account. This account can do anything in DotNetNuke, so make sure the credentials you create here are secure and hard to guess.

6. The following Host Portal form configures the Portal Administrator account. Again, the Admin has a lot of authority in the system so make sure the account has a good password. Click the Next button when the credentials are entered.

7. This is the final step in the Installation Wizard. It confirms all of the values have been entered. Click the Finished button to go to your new website.

Figure 2-4 shows the default installation loaded inside the browser.

While working with SQL Server 2005 Express Edition, you may get the following message:

"Failed to generate a user instance of SQL Server due to a failure in starting the process for the user instance. The connection will be closed."

This is a known problem that sometimes occurs when temporary files on your computer are corrupted. The work-around solution is to delete the following folder on your computer:

```
c:\Documents and Settings\<Your Account Name>\Local Settings\Application
Data\Microsoft\Microsoft SQL Server Data\SQLEXPRESS
```

If the folder is locked, reboot your computer, and then delete the folder.

Figure 2-4

Using Internet Information Server

With this installation, you won't rely on Visual Web Developer or the Starter Kit package. Instead, you'll use just IIS and the Install Package. This installation might be appealing if you're fond of another text editor, or if you're using a central server in your office to host the DotNetNuke website and you're accessing it over the network.

DotNetNuke File Installation

These are the steps for installing the DotNetNuke files with IIS and your bare hands:

1. Using Windows Explorer, create the folder path `c:\projects\MyDNN`.

2. Copy the contents of the unzipped Install package into the new folder named `MyDNN`.

3. You need to indicate to the web server that the new folder `MyDNN` is a Web Share, and you must grant sufficient permissions to the web server account to access this folder on behalf of the visitors to the website. Using Windows Explorer, right-click on the new folder named `MyDNNSolution03`. Select the menu item named Properties from the pop-up menu.

4. In the Properties window, click the tab labeled Web Sharing.

5. On this tab, select the bottom radio button labeled Share this folder to display the Edit Alias window.

6. In the Edit Alias window, accept the default values. Click OK.

7. In the Properties Window, select the tab labeled Security.

8. Click Add under the list of usernames to display the Select Users window.

9. In the Select Users window, enter the name of the account that will be running the ASP.Net on the web server. Windows XP and Windows Server 2003 use different accounts to run ASP.Net. (For example, in Windows XP, the account is named ASPNET and my Windows XP laptop is named ANDREW-M, so I would enter the value `ANDREW-M\ASPNET`. In Windows Server 2003, the default account assigned to the application pool is named Network Service and my Windows Server 2003 laptop is named HOME2, so I would enter the value `HOME2\NETWORK SERVICE`.)

10. After entering the name, click the Check Names button to verify you've typed it correctly.

11. Click the OK button to close the Select Users window.

12. In the Properties window, with the ASPNET account selected in the User Names list box, make sure the following checkboxes are selected in the Allow column and none is selected in the Deny column: Modify, Read & Execute, List Folder Contents, Read, Write.

13. In the Properties window, click OK to apply the changes and close the window. It might take a moment for the computer to apply all of the file permission changes.

Confirm ASP.Net 2.0 Mapping

These steps assume that ASP.Net 2.0 is the default mapping in IIS. This might not be the case if you have installed a prior version of the .Net Framework on your machine. If you have multiple versions of ASP.Net running on your machine, you should check the version.

These are the steps to check the version of ASP.Net mapped to your web application:

1. Click Start, Control Panel; double-click Administration Tools.

2. Double-click the Internet Information Services Console.

3. Locate your new application in the tree.

4. Right-click the web application, and select Properties from the pop-up window.

5. Click the tab labeled ASP.Net.

6. Confirm that version 2.0 is selected in the drop-down list.

7. Click OK to close the Properties window and apply any changes.

If you don't see the ASP.Net tab inside the properties window of IIS, then you should check to see whether .Net 2.0 is installed and possibly run the `aspnet_regiis.exe` file discussed earlier in this chapter to make sure the ASP.Net Script Mappings are in place.

Figure 2-5 displays the ASP.Net tab of the Properties window within IIS.

To recap your progress, you've taken the following actions:

❑ Copied the Installation package to a new directory

❑ Created a Web Share on the directory

❑ Granted sufficient permissions to the ASPNET account

❑ Confirmed that IIS is mapped to the correct version of ASP.Net

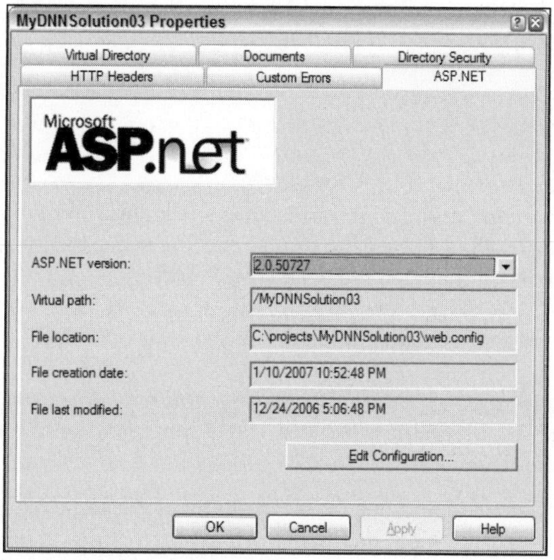

Figure 2-5

DotNetNuke Database Installation

If you've been following along the book and installing each permutation of DotNetNuke, then you might have correctly anticipated that it's time to create the database. Because you won't be using Visual Web Developer's database features to create the database, you'll call upon another utility, the Microsoft SQL Server Management Studio. You'll use SQL Server Management Studio to connect to a running instance of SQL Server Express Edition, create a new database, and create accounts to log in to the database.

These are the steps to create a new database with SQL Server Management Studio:

1. Launch SQL Server Management Studio.

2. When prompted, connect to your local instance of SQL Server Express on your computer using Windows Authentication.

3. Click the New Query button in the toolbar in the top left corner of the window. This launches a new window in the body of Management Studio for running T-SQL queries.

4. Enter the following six T-SQL commands into the query window. Take special care to make sure the text is exactly right. Each command is followed by a GO statement on the following line. For improved readability, place a blank line after each GO statement. You can also find this SQL code in the code download for this book if you don't want to type it directly.

```
USE Master
GO

CREATE DATABASE MyDNN
GO

EXEC sp_addlogin 'MyDNN', 'abc123', 'MyDNN'
GO

USE MyDNN
GO

EXEC sp_grantdbaccess 'MyDNN', 'MyDNN'
GO

EXEC sp_addrolemember 'db_owner', 'MyDNN'
GO
```

After you have carefully typed in the commands and verified the single quote marks and commas, click the Execute button in the toolbar. The query should execute successfully. If you get an error in the message window, confirm the commands have been typed correctly.

In the series of commands just executed, the following events occurred:

❑   A new database named MyDNN was created. You may change this. Database names must be unique. It does simplify matters for local development when the website name, database name, and the login name match.

❑   The sp_addlogin command created a new login of the same name as the database and a simple password of abc123. The login and password are for your local development computer, only; the database will not contain any sensitive information. You should have a more secure login and password when you deploy it in the real world.

❑   You created a database user that matches to the SQL Server login. The sp_grantdbaccess command linked the login to the database user.

❑   The sp_addrolemember command gave the login sufficient authorization to the database. DotNetNuke creates tables and other database objects on the fly, so it needs a heaping amount of database security. The DBO, or database owner role, is the most authority you can have over a single database.

There are many ways to create a database. If you're new to SQL Server, then I hope the preceding method I've selected is easy and clear. Also, I hope that it whetted your appetite for exploring other capabilities within this powerful database. You would do well to repeat this process several times and to explore the changes you make to the Object Explorer window inside SQL Server Management Studio Express. You'll be well on your way to creating several DotNetNuke websites and becoming very comfortable with the installation process.

Edit the Database Connection

Now that you've prepared the web server and created an empty database, you need to tell DotNetNuke where to find the database. This information is stored in a special file named web.config that is located in the root directory of the website.

The database connection string has had a long life in software; many programming languages make use of it. It's called a "string" because that is how programming languages refer to a piece of text or a given sequence of alphanumeric characters. The database connection string stores the information necessary to locate a database and log in to it. It is formatted in a special way. The following is an example of a database connection string:

```
Server=andrew-m\SQLExpress;Database=MyDatabase;UID=MyLogin;PWD=MyPassword;
```

Each segment is delimited by a semi-colon. Each segment is composed of a name and a value. The name and value are delimited by the equal sign. There are several valid formats for a connection string. The format shown previously is quite common.

- ❏ Server: identifies the machine name or IP address of the computer with the database instance
- ❏ Database: identifies the unique name of the database within the server
- ❏ UID: User Identifier; the login used to authenticate to the server
- ❏ PWD: Password; the password used to authenticate to the server

The database connection string can be stored in the web.config file of a website. The web.config file is just an XML file, and you can edit it with your favorite text editor. In this case, you want to modify the database connection string. This is where DotNetNuke can begin to show some signs of its age. It has been around long enough to require backward compatibility. Several modules are built for DotNetNuke 3.x that expect the database connection information to exist in a specific location. That location was moved with the release of DotNetNuke 4.x, so now there are two locations for the database connection information to reside.

These are the steps for editing the database connection specified in web.config:

1. Back up the web.config file in the root folder of your web application in case you make a mistake during this process and need to restart.

2. Open the web.config file with your favorite text editor.

3. Locate the XML node named connectionStrings.

4. Replace the existing values in the node with this:

```
<connectionStrings>
    <add name="SiteSqlServer"
      connectionString="Server=.\SQLExpress;Database=MyDNN;uid= MyDNN;pwd=abc123;"
      providerName="System.Data.SqlClient" />
  </connectionStrings>
```

5. Now locate the element named appSettings, and find the element within it named SiteSqlServer.

6. Copy the same connection string value to this element.

```
<add key="SiteSqlServer"
   value="Server=.\SQLExpress;Database=MyDNN;uid=MyDNN; pwd=abc123;"/>
```

7. Notice the first element you changed stores the connection string in an attribute named `connectionstring` and the second element you changed stores the connection string in an attribute named `value`. This is understandably confusing, but hopefully you'll get the gist of it after a little practice.

8. Save the changes to your text file and close your editor.

The aforementioned long connection string values have been wrapped to fit within the pages of this book. It should be apparent from other values in `web.config` that line breaks are not permitted between two quotes. If you encounter problems, anyone familiar with XML should be able to help you.

Launch the Website

Since the last recap, you've created a new database using SQL Server Management Studio, created an account to access the database, and informed DotNetNuke where to find the database.

Now it's time to launch the site! Because the site was manually created, you need to launch Internet Explorer on your own and navigate to this URL:

```
http://localhost/MyDNN
```

Once the Installation Wizard appears, fill out the forms the same as the previous. Then your installation will be in the same position as the other installation, except this solution is running on top of IIS. Congratulations!

Installing DotNetNuke on IIS Remotely

The final installation option explored in this chapter considers a hosted solution where a third party has provided an ASP.Net 2.0 website, FTP credentials to the root directory of the website, and a set of SQL Server credentials to access the database.

This option closely follows Option 3, where only IIS was used. Also, this option assumes that the website is configured for ASP.Net 2.0 and the ASPNET account has read/write access to the root folder. Therefore, there is much less work than in the other options.

DotNetNuke File Installation

Use your favorite FTP client to copy the contents of the Install package to your website. The only file you'll need to change is the `web.config` file, but you'll overwrite that in just a bit.

DotNetNuke Database Installation

One of the many benefits of a hosted solution is someone else does all the heavy lifting for you. As part of your hosting package, someone has already created a database and given you the credentials to access it. Assume that the credentials have sufficient permission to install the database objects or you'll have your first opportunity to contact customer support!

Edit the Database Connection

Follow the same steps as in Option 3 to edit the `web.config` file. Use the database credentials provided to you by the hosting provider. You should have a database server name, a database name, a login, and a password.

After you've edited the `web.config` file, send it to the website using your favorite FTP client.

Launch the Website

Well, that was fast. Let's recap the steps to make sure you handled everything. You did the following:

❑ Copied the DotNetNuke Install package to the existing website that someone else created for you, along with setting the appropriate file permissions

❑ Edited the `web.config` file to include the proper database connection string values that someone else created for you

Now it's time to initiate your first request to the website and watch it execute the auto installation procedures. Launch your web browser and enter the URL provided by the third-party hosting provider. Congratulations!

A Brief Tour

Now that you've installed DotNetNuke, it's time to take a walk around the shop. It's a fun place to tinker because it can always be reinstalled. That's not true for existing installations that have valuable assets, so make sure any new components are thoroughly tested before you add them to an existing site.

The following steps set the stage for the activities that you'll do throughout the book. If you're new to DotNetNuke, practice these items until they become comfortable and familiar.

Host and Admin Accounts

DotNetNuke has two accounts available by default: Host and Admin. Deeper explanations are available in *Professional DotNetNuke 4*, but a brief description is sufficient for your needs here.

The host account has all the rights and privileges of the system. DotNetNuke is capable of hosting multiple *portals*.

For example, imagine the following URLs, which might have two very different websites:

```
http://www.CompanyOne.com
http://www.CompanyTwo.com
```

Imagine that these websites serve different audiences and the visitor would have no indication of their relationship. They *could* be running off the DotNetNuke installation by making use of the portal feature. If this were the case, the DotNetNuke installation would have one Host account and two Admin accounts. The Host account has access to everything, and the Admin account has access to a specific portal.

Try It Out   Log in as Host and Admin

Launch a web browser and navigate to the default DotNetNuke installation. At this point, you are not authenticated and you see the content available to anonymous users. You might have noticed the login information on the home page of the default DotNetNuke installation.

1. Click the Login hyperlink located in the top right corner of the web page, under the search field. The browser navigates to the User Log In form.

2. In the Login form, enter a username of **Host** and the password you created during the site installation, and then click the Login button. Notice the menu bar has changed with the addition of two new menu items, Admin and Host.

3. Click the Logout hyperlink on the right side under the menu bar.

4. Click the Login hyperlink again, and this time, enter a username of Admin and the password you created during the installation procedures, and then click the Login button. Notice the menu bar now has the Admin menu item and it does not have the Host menu item.

Figure 2-6 shows the Control Panel that appears at the top of the page while logged in as the Host or Admin account.

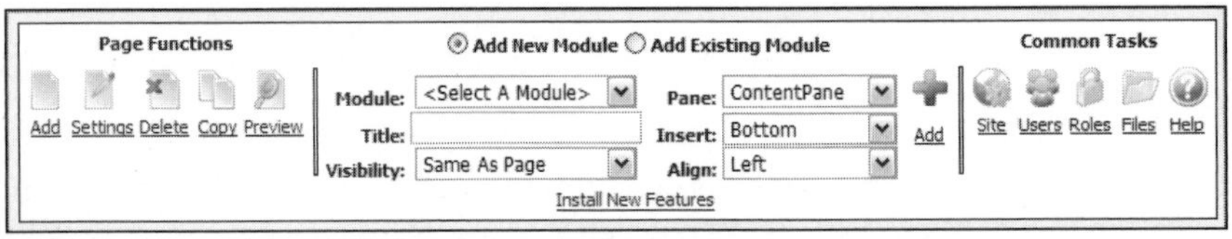

Figure 2-6

How It Works

Upon authenticating, the home page is transformed into a view appropriate for the user's permission level. A section of controls has been injected at the top of the page; this is called the *Control Panel*. It contains links for common functions, such as editing a page and adding modules to a page. An enhanced view of the page, as displayed to anonymous visitors, is located below the Control Panel.

The *panes* for this page are also highlighted in this view. A pane is a structural element of the page. Panes provide a way to organize modules. Modules are added to panes or moved from one pane to another. Subsequent chapters provide a thorough explanation of how panes work.

Notice the triangle icon at the top left corner of each module. This triangle provides access to the module menu. Hover your cursor over the icon, and a pop-up menu will appear with a series of actions that can be taken on the module. The list of actions in the pop-up menu is specific to the module. Some of the actions in the Links module located in the left pane are different from those in the module titled Open Source in the right pane.

Try It Out   Create a Page

Creating a new page in DotNetNuke is an easy task, and its ease undoubtedly played a large role in the popularity of the platform.

1. Log in as the Host or Admin.

2. Click Add on the left side of the Control Panel to navigate to the Page Management form.

3. In the Page Details section of the form, enter a value in the Page Name field.

4. Click Update at the bottom of the page. The browser navigates to the new page you just created. You should be able to see the name of the page in the navigation bar.

5. Click Log Out on the right side of the page under the navigation bar. The Control Panel should disappear from the top, and your new page should disappear from the menu bar.

How It Works

Inside DotNetNuke, a page is just a row of data inside a database table. Creating a new page inserts a new row of data into that table. Several other tables depend on the primary table, for example, the table defining the list of roles that have permission to view the page, or the table defining the list of modules that exist inside the page. All of this complex business logic has been abstracted away from you and simplified by an intuitive web based administration system.

Because of the default permission values, this new page is only visible to the Host or the Admin. You have not authorized any other role to view this page.

Try It Out   **Change Modules**

The system has automatically added a Text/HTML module to the page. You will be using this particular module extensively in subsequent chapters. For now, let's get some practice in the area of adding and deleting modules on a page.

1. Log in as the Host and navigate to your new page.

2. Hover over the triangle icon on the left side of the module header.

3. Select Delete, and then click OK on the confirmation window. Your browser should display your new page without any modules inside.

4. In the Control Panel at the top of the page, select Links in the Module field.

5. Click Add in the middle section of the Control Panel and the Links module will be injected into a pane in the new page.

You'll be adding and skinning modules in later chapters, so for now, tidy up the page for the remaining activities in this chapter by deleting the Links module using the same technique used for the Text/HTML module starting in Step 1.

How It Works

DotNetNuke maintains a list of all the modules on a given page and keeps track of which panes contain them. There are easy mechanisms to add modules to a page, move modules around in a page, or delete modules from a page. There's even a Recycle Bin in the Admin menu in case you're overzealous in your module deletion. You can restore a module to its original page in the Recycle Bin page.

Try It Out **Change Page-Level Permissions**

DotNetNuke maintains a list of who is permitted to view a page and the modules within a page. In this exercise, you change the permissions for the page so it is visible to all users.

1. Log in again as the Host.

2. Navigate to your new page by clicking the item in the menu bar.

3. In the Control Panel at the top of your page, click Settings.

4. On the Page Management form find the series of checkbox controls that define permissions inside the page details section. There are two columns of checkboxes. The left column controls view permissions and the right column controls edit permissions. Each row is a different group of users. Click the checkbox in the All Users row and the View Page column.

5. Click Update at the bottom of the page. (The browser navigates to your new page with no visible changes while logged in under this account.)

6. Click the Logout hyperlink under the menu bar and this time, the browser will stay on this page.

How It Works

The business logic inside DotNetNuke looked at who was requesting the web page, analyzed their permissions, and made a determination on the request. When you logged out, DotNetNuke determined that it was OK for you to stay on this page because it was available to anonymous visitors. The menu bar continues to display the link to the new page.

Browsing the Modules

When you are logged in as the Host or Admin, the Control Panel is visible at the top of the page. The center of the Control Panel provides a way to add modules to any page in the portal. By default, DotNetNuke 4.4.0 has just seven modules installed. The Text/HTML and Links modules are typical self-contained features, while the other five are much more tightly coupled to the DotNetNuke infrastructure.

The number of modules installed by default in DotNetNuke 4.4.0 has been dramatically reduced from prior versions. The other modules are still "in the box," just not available for immediate use. Decreasing the number of components loaded into memory improves performance.

While logged in as the Host, navigate to the Host, Module Definitions page. On this page, you see a section labeled Available Modules. You should install every one of these modules on your development installation and play around with them. Quite a few are in the box and many more are available online.

Try It Out **Browse the Skin Administration Pages**

The skin administration pages provide a way for authorized users to browse the skins currently installed, preview the skins on the site, and upload new skins into the system. These pages make it easy to quickly change the look and feel of a site by implementing the deliverables created by a custom skin designer. Later on in the book, you use these pages to install your own custom skins.

1. While logged in as the Host, click Host, Skins in the menu bar and examine the Skins administration page.

2. Filter the skins on this page by selecting different items in the Skins list and the Containers list.

3. Click on the thumbnail of the skins to see a larger image.

4. Click the Preview link to see a temporary application of the skin to the site.

5. Click the Apply link to select the permanent skin for the site. Don't worry, you can always return to this page and change your selection later.

How It Works

After you provided sufficient authentication to DotNetNuke, the system displayed the Admin and Host menu items — one important administrative page manages skins. The skin management pages contain logic that will scan specific locations in the file system and show the skin and container files available on the system.

The filters at the top of the page help you manage a large assortment of the skins installed on a given site. When you preview a skin, a small parameter is loaded into the query string of the URL. This value tells DotNetNuke that a temporary skin file should be applied to the current web request. In turn, DotNetNuke processes the request using this temporary skin only for the administrator. Any other user on the system will see the normal skin applied to the site. Once the Apply link is clicked, a database level change forces all users to see the selected skin.

Summary

In this chapter, you learned how to install DotNetNuke in a number of different configurations. Hopefully, you took the opportunity to install the bits at least ten times to get familiar with the process. DotNetNuke can take advantage of many databases and be manipulated by an endless set of tools. Visual Web Developer can include a set of templates that makes creating new DotNetNuke sites as easy as clicking File, New Website in the menu bar. SQL Server can present its own set of challenges, but there are a number of paths through this specialization.

Finally, you took a brief tour around DotNetNuke, including the administration pages. You'll spend a good deal of time in the administration pages and in your favorite text editor for the remainder of the book. Fire up your web server because you're about to create some great looking websites!

The following chapters conclude with exercises that help internalize and expand your understanding of the technology. So far, you've been presented with an introduction to the DotNetNuke Framework and performed some rote, yet essential, tasks in order to confirm that you are all on the same page (pardon the pun) and working with the same bits.

3

Installing Skin Packages

Adding a new DotNetNuke skin you found online is one of the easiest ways to customize a portal and give a site a new look. It's also a way to draw some inspiration from fellow designers and learn how they accomplished a particular design. Analyzing how other designers have architected their skins provides a good background for modifying an existing skin in Chapter 4, "Exploring Skins" and developing your own skin in Chapter 5, "Creating Custom Skins."

This chapter covers the following:

- ❑ Obtaining DotNetNuke skins online
- ❑ Reviewing the contents of a skin package
- ❑ Installing a skin using the DotNetNuke administration pages
- ❑ Installing a skin using the Install folder
- ❑ Controlling access to a skin

A good way to learn what's possible with skinning DotNetNuke is to see what others have done. A simple search for "DNN skins" on the Internet will return a large number of sites. Some skins are freely available online, and others charge a small fee. First, you'll poke around and see exactly what files are inside a skin package, and then you'll apply some skin pages in a couple of different scenarios.

What Is a Skin Package?

A skin package consists of one zip file. It contains all of the resources necessary to implement a skin on a DotNetNuke page. Chapter 1 introduces the concept of a skin and a container — two key DotNetNuke design elements. These two types of files are bundled into a skin package along with images and CSS files so the skin can be installed elsewhere. You can find skin packages online or build them yourself with a local installation of DotNetNuke, and then import them into another instance of DotNetNuke for a department in your company or the site for your child's youth soccer league.

In a typical scenario, you will create a skin on your local development computer. When it's completed, it's packaged up and deployed to your real DotNetNuke site on the Internet or your corporate network. Packaging your skins in a zip file also enables a method of archiving your work and versioning the files if you don't have Subversion, or another version control system in place yet.

From a technical perspective, a skin package is a zip file that has a specific file structure. Once a skin is designed and packaged it can be installed on any DotNetNuke website. Let's examine the skin package named `DNN-Blue.zip`. This package contains the default skin applied to DotNetNuke out of the box. It's a good example of the types of things found in a skin package. The file is located in the following directory:

```
<install folder>\Portals\_default\Skins\DNN-Blue\DNN-Blue.zip
```

You can browse around this zip file by double-clicking it in Windows Explorer or your favorite zip file utility. Inside this zip file, you'll find two more zip files: `Containers.zip` and `Skins.zip`. This particular package contains both containers and skins. In just one simple skin upload procedure, both the containers and skins for a given design can be installed onto a portal. Although convenient and practical, it's not a technical requirement to include both skins and containers in a package.

Containers.zip File

Figure 3-1 shows the contents of the `containers.zip` file for the `DNN-Blue.zip` skin package.

This package has four containers. Each container has the `.ascx` extension, which identifies these files as ASP.Net web user controls. A web user control is a technology that can encapsulate a given feature on a web page. For example, a newsletter sign-up form is usually a small rectangle in the side column of a page. This newsletter sign-up form might include a few text box fields, some checkboxes, and a submit button. Several pages on the website might show the same newsletter sign-up form. This is a textbook case for a web user control. Each web page can include a reference to the same web user control instead of including duplicate code on several pages. Then, the effect of any edits to the web user control will be seen by all of the pages that use it.

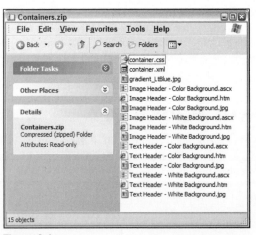

Figure 3-1

An ASP.Net page can include multiple web user controls on a single page, as well as multiple instances of the same web user control. These controls can even contain other web user controls. Therefore, this ASP.Net technology is well suited for DotNetNuke containers.

Any resource used by the container should exist in this same directory or subdirectory. This includes CSS files, images, or other types of media files used by the container. The resources for the DNN-Blue containers consist of five image files and one CSS file. The CSS file is dynamically loaded by DotNetNuke only when a module uses one of the containers in this package.

As with most areas in software, DotNetNuke provides a couple of ways of doing the same task. One method of creating containers starts with creating a text file with an `.htm` extension containing HTML tags and some *tokens*. Tokens are placeholders for controls that will be injected later. The DotNetNuke menu control is an example of a feature that can be represented by a token in an `.htm` container file. A file named `container.xml` holds the configuration values for the token in an XML format. The XML file configures the menu control to render in either a horizontal or vertical format. The `.htm` file method has the benefit of not requiring ASP.Net programming skills and might be an easier way for nondevelopers to enter the skinning role.

Building containers out of `.htm` files gives you some visibility into the niche utilities baked inside DotNetNuke, one of which is the automatic conversion of `.htm` files into `.ascx` files for containers. When a container displays on a web page, it's running as a web user control. If the container wasn't originally developed as an `.ascx` file, it was converted into an `.ascx` file during the upload process into the portal.

Although enticing, the `.htm` file technique can become a complicated burden. A lengthy XML file that contains all of the configuration values for the tokens has to sync up with the tokens used in the `.htm` file. It takes more time to make incremental edits to a container under development with this process. General software development best practices tell us to make small incremental changes as you work. In this case, you should apply just a few edits to the skin during development, and then view the result emitted from the DotNetNuke site in the browser. This iterative approach requires the `.htm` file to be packaged in a zip file and uploaded to the portal in order to see the effect of each modification.

A simpler way embraces the notion that a DotNetNuke is a website built on top of ASP.Net. A little time spent learning the "Hello World" of ASP.Net web user controls can go a long way toward simplifying design changes and debugging problems. Once the container has been installed on a portal, you can open the `.ascx` file in your favorite text editor, make some small changes, save the file, and refresh the browser to evaluate the results. There's no need to repackage the container or reinstall it on the portal.

Note that the `.ascx` files already exist in the DNN-Blue zip file. It wasn't necessary to include the `.htm` files or the `container.xml` file in the package; they are simply here for completeness and comparison for folks interested in learning more about skinning DotNetNuke.

Skins.zip File

The skins file follows a similar pattern to the container zip file. The contents of the `skins.zip` file are shown in Figure 3-2.

This package has four skins inside. Like the `containers.zip` file, this skin package contains both `.ascx` and `.htm` versions of each skin. The file named `skin.xml` contains the token values for the `.htm` files. The file named `skin.css` contains the CSS selectors and associated rule set for displaying the skins.

Figure 3-2

Searching for DotNetNuke Skins

Although it's easy to search for skins online, it might not be so easy is to find a quality design that complements a DotNetNuke portal and appeals to your sense of style.

Especially if skinning DotNetNuke is completely new to you, it's worth a few days of searching online for some inspirational designs. Keep a log of the sites visited and the skins that make an impact. Send an e-mail to the creator if something really stands out. After all, they were created by people who share your interests. It's always worthwhile to spend a little time networking.

Here are some sites with some interesting skins that work well for your purposes in this chapter. Take a moment to browse these and other sites that are available online.

❑   www.xhtmlskins.com

❑   www.dnnskin.com

❑   www.ninasfreeskins.com

The forums on the DotNetNuke website at www.DotNetNuke.com are another great place to learn about new ideas and issues and solutions that other people like you are experiencing with DotNetNuke. I encourage you to spend some time mining for some juicy nuggets of information there.

A proficiency in creating skins can be a good way to enter the thriving DotNetNuke commercial space. The only prerequisites are a notion of what makes a good-looking website and a space to sell third-party DotNetNuke skins. The folks who made the skins available online applied what you're learning right now!

Uploading a Skin

Uploading a new skin to an existing DotNetNuke site is an easy process that you'll perform several times throughout the course of this book. In this first opportunity, the browser-based file upload technique is used. Later on in this chapter, you will use a special DotNetNuke folder to install the skin, and you will get a glimpse of some of the advanced features available in the system.

Figure 3-3 shows the Skin administration page. This is the management tool to upload, preview, apply, and delete skin packages on a system.

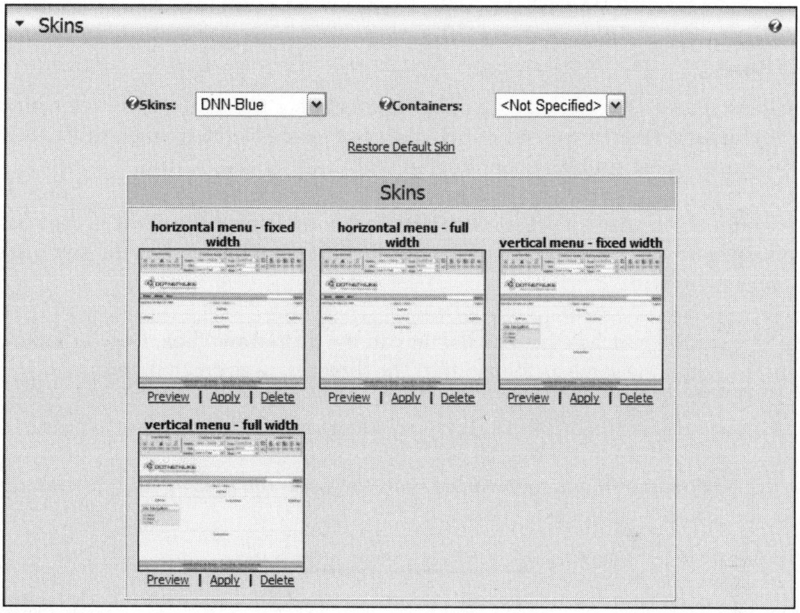

Figure 3-3

Try It Out   **Apply a Skin Package**

Before getting started, go ahead and download the files for this chapter onto your computer. In this section, you upload a sample skin file available with the code online for this chapter. This is an exercise in uploading a new skin, so any of the DotNetNuke installations you have on your local computer from Chapter 2 will suit you fine.

1.   Find the skin package named `autumn.zip` located in the code available online for this chapter.

2.   Open a web browser to an existing DotNetNuke portal on your computer, and log in using the host account you created during the installation process.

3.   Within the Host menu select the item named Skins to display the skin page.

4. Click the link named Upload Skin in the bottom left side of the page. This navigates to the File Upload ⇨ Install Skin Package page.

5. Click the Browse button and locate the skin package on your computer identified in the first step.

6. After selecting skin package, click the link named Save File. This uploads the package to the web server and installs it onto the portal.

7. Examine the system messages displayed on the page. Confirm that no messages appear red and that no errors have occurred.

8. Click the link named Return at the bottom of the page. This returns the browser to the Skin page. The new skin is displayed in the drop-down control labeled Skins at the top of the page.

How It Works

This example installed a set of skins and a complementary set of containers onto the portal. The web form accepted a zip file, and when it was submitted, the code inside DotNetNuke extracted the contents and placed the resources in the appropriate folder.

Skin creators normally provide a set of containers that complement the skins in the package. So most of the time you'll just upload one zip file and let DotNetNuke unzip the contents and install both the skins and the containers for you.

The name of the zip file matches the new list item in the drop-down box. DotNetNuke created a new directory and named it the same as the zip file. The directory was created here:

```
<install folder>/Portals/_default/Skins/Autumn/
```

If you want to see how the skin is constructed, you can open the files inside this skin directory with your favorite text editor and take a peek.

Applying Skins to Pages

Now that a custom DotNetNuke skin has been uploaded to the DotNetNuke website, it's time to try it out. At the end of these steps, you will see the new skin applied to a new page in your website.

Try It Out   Preview and Apply a Skin

1. Launch one of the DotNetNuke sites that you created in Chapter 2 in your browser.

2. Log in as the host account and navigate to the Skin Administration page by selecting Host, Skins in the menu bar.

3. Locate the thumbnail for the Autumn skin on the Skins Administration page.

4. Click the Autumn thumbnail image to see a full-size example of what the skin might look like in this portal. Clicking the thumbnail image launches a new browser window with a full-size image.

5.   Click the preview link under the thumbnail. Because DotNetNuke is a dynamic web platform, it has the ability to apply this skin temporarily and demonstrate how the skin will actually look on this site. The preview link opens a new browser window and applies the Autumn skin to the portal. Navigating to another page while in preview mode reverts the portal to the original skin.

6.   Click the Apply link under the thumbnail. This applies the Autumn skin to all pages in the portal.

7.   Over the course of uploading several skins to the portal in an effort to discover one that truly fits your sense of style, you are bound to create clutter. Tidy up. Click the apply link for any skin other than the Autumn skin. Then click the delete link under the thumbnail for the Autumn skin to delete the skin package from the DotNetNuke portal.

How It Works

Notice the address bar of the browser when the preview skin is applied to the page. The last part of the URL should resemble this:

```
/default.aspx?SkinSrc=[G]%2fskins%2fseasons%2fautumn
```

The question mark character signifies the end of the path to the ASP.Net web page and the start of the query string parameters. The query string is everything after the question mark. It's a very common method of passing parameters to the web server so it can take some action and works well for the skin preview feature.

In this case, the web page indicates that the value of the SkinSrc parameter is [G]%2fskins%2fseasons%2fautumn. The parameter name and the parameter value are separated by an equal sign. The forward slash character has been escaped with its hexadecimal equivalent notation of "%2F".

Upon the page request, the code inside DotNetNuke knows to look for this parameter. If it's present, it will use the value of the parameter to evaluate which skin to use for the page. This is how the preview method works. It passes a parameter in the query string that requests a specific skin be used to render the page in the browser.

When the browser navigates away from the preview page by clicking a link in the navigation, the query string is not used, and the site reverts to the current skin. Now you have a trick for previewing the skin on any page in DotNetNuke. Simply copy the entire query string parameter, including the question mark, and append it to any page in the portal.

Using Portals

In DotNetNuke terms, a portal is a single website with its own set of user accounts. DotNetNuke creates the first portal by default during installation. You can create additional portals by using the online tools in DotNetNuke. Hosting multiple portals inside the same DotNetNuke installation is just a technique to segment pages, users, skins, and other DotNetNuke objects.

With the exception of the host account, the login credentials for one portal will not work in another portal. The host account can access any portal in the given DotNetNuke installation. Of course, you can create identical login credentials in two portals, but that raises the question of why another portal is necessary.

Considering an example, you might want to create a portal for a youth sports league. Each team might have their own portal where all the players, coaches, and parents create accounts and share information. Some pages might be public and other pages might be available only to team members. Each team might have a very different looking website from the others, too, but all of the pages within a given portal are consistent and well polished.

All of this can be accomplished with a single installation of DotNetNuke. The system contains administration pages for creating additional portals. Technically, there's no upper limit on the number of portals, but you should keep it to a number that you can reasonably manage as the administrator.

Parent and Child Portals

DotNetNuke has two types of portals. A *parent* portal has a unique domain name. The default installation of DotNetNuke creates a single parent portal. A *child* portal shares the same domain name as its parent and has a unique folder name as a suffix. When DotNetNuke is installed on a local development machine, the URL to the parent portal might resemble this:

```
http://localhost/DotNetNuke
```

By convention, a child portal shares some visual elements with its parent portal. Two parent portals in the same DotNetNuke installation might look very different and serve unrelated needs. The aforementioned youth sports league example transfers well to the idea of a company with a couple of departments. Each department can have a child portal and visually share the same banner as the parent portal at the company level. The company might have a sister company that serves different clients in a different way. The sister company would use its own separate parent portal, and create its own child portals as it grows.

Figure 3-4 identifies key parts of the URL for DotNetNuke Portals.

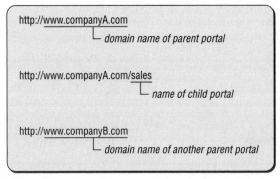

Figure 3-4

In Figure 3-4, the first URL could be the default portal created by DotNetNuke during the installation process. It's an ordinary domain name. The next URL in the figure shows the domain name followed by a folder name. This folder can map to a child portal in DotNetNuke. Again, by convention, the child portal is expected to share some visual characteristics with its parent. The last URL is a simple example of another parent portal. Because the domain name is different, you expect no connection between the two parent portals. All of these URLs can be served from a single installation of DotNetNuke.

There are a couple of ways to add portals to the DotNetNuke installation and create multiple websites. To stir your curiosity about the vast feature set in DotNetNuke, I'll limit this discussion to child portals.

For now, it's sufficient to know the only differences between parent and child portals are the domain names and the website relationships implied by the URL.

Figure 3-5 shows the DotNetNuke management utility for creating child portals. You'll use this now to create your own child portal.

Figure 3-5

Try It Out   Create a Child Portal

These are the steps to create a child portal. By creating a child portal, you'll be able to experiment with skins installed in different locations.

At the end of these steps, another website will be running parallel to the default parent portal in the same DotNetNuke installation. As a prerequisite, the default DotNetNuke installation must already be installed and running on your computer.

1. Navigate to one of the test DotNetNuke installations on your computer that you created in Chapter 2.

2. Log in with the credentials for the host account.

3. In the menu bar, select Host, Portals. The browser navigates to the portal administration page.

4. The first table on this page lists the existing portals. Only one row should appear in this table now. To add a second row, click the hyperlink labeled Add New Portal in the lower left corner of this table. The browser navigates to the Portal Setup page.

5. In the Portal Setup section, enter the following values. Each field includes a question mark icon that you can click to see a little more context about each field.

   a. Portal Type: Click the Child radio button.

   b. Portal Alias: Enter the URL of the child portal by adding a suffix to the URL already in the text box. The suffix should follow the standard URL conventions. Only use letters, numbers, and dashes. Don't use spaces in the URL.

   c. Title: Enter **Marketing** as the title of the child portal.

   d. Description: Enter **This child portal contains private online resources for the marketing department.**

   e. Keywords: Enter **marketing, intranet**.

   f. Template: Select the item named DotNetNuke in the drop-down list.

6. In the Security Settings section, enter the credentials for the admin account; these should be the same as for the parent portal:

   a. First Name: Enter your first name.

   b. Last Name: Enter your last name.

   c. Username: Enter **MarketingAdmin**. This will both clarify the name of the admin account and allow you to create your own non-admin account to keep the two nicely separated.

   d. Password: Enter a secret password in this field. Don't forget this password!

   e. Confirm: Re-enter the password in this field.

   f. Email: Enter your e-mail address so you can receive administrator notifications.

7. Click the hyperlink Create Portal. The system creates the portal as specified and navigates to the home page.

   If you haven't made any changes to the parent portal, then it might be difficult to distinguish between the two websites.

8. Make a noticeable change; click the button labeled Settings in the control panel at the top of the page.

9. Expand the Advanced Settings section and change the Page Skin field to the item named `DNN-Gray - Vertical Menu - Fixed Width`.

10. Click the Update hyperlink at the bottom of the page.

11. Click the Log out hyperlink in the top right corner of the page.

12. Now, navigate to your new child portal by typing the address in your browser. This portal should look just like your original portal.

How It Works

These steps create a child portal in the same DotNetNuke installation as the original portal. The two portals currently lack any links between them, so you have to type the URLs in the address bar of your browser manually. Toggle between the two URLs and confirm that the sites really are different.

```
http://localhost/dnn - the parent portal
http://localhost/dnn/marketing - the child portal
```

My installation is named dnn, as shown in the preceding example. You might choose a different website name while you are practicing the DotNetNuke installation procedures.

The Portal Setup pages stored the new configuration data in the DotNetNuke database. This new information allows DotNetNuke to map the new URL of `http://localhost/dnn/marketing` to the new child portal named `marketing`.

DotNetNuke has also created a new *portal root folder* on the hard drive of the web server to store assets specific to this new portal, like images, documents, and skins. Other portals cannot access files stored in this portal root folder. This is another reason you might consider creating child portals. It's an easy, broad stroke technique of securing access files through a browser for a particular group of users.

Take a look at the current contents of the portal root folder by logging into the child portal as the administrator account established on the Portal Setup form. After you are logged in, click the Files icon in the top right corner of the control panel. This navigates the browser to the File Manager page.

The folder hierarchy is displayed in the left column, and the contents of the selected folder are displayed in the main column. DotNetNuke has added some default files to the portal root folder. Most DotNetNuke modules provide their own methods of uploading files to the web server if necessary, but every so often, you'll need to come here for a specific file management task. Figure 3-6 shows the web-based file manager.

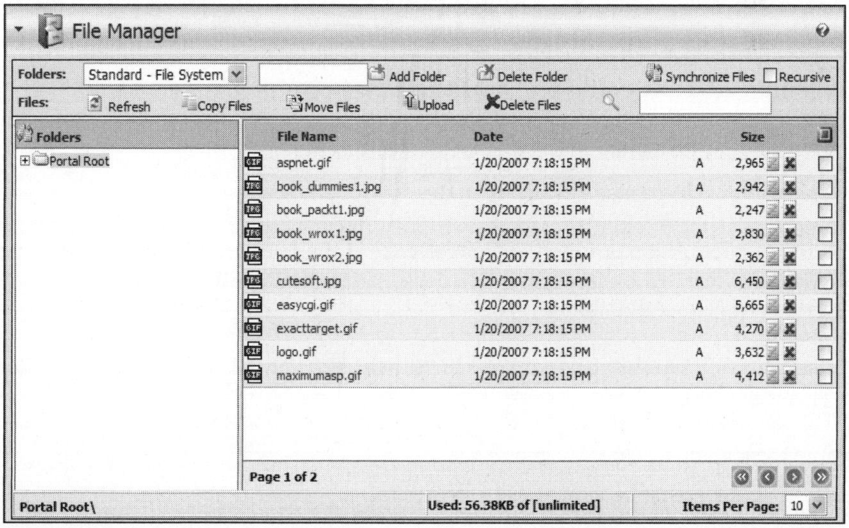

Figure 3-6

Of course, having physical access to the machine and using Windows Explorer to navigate the file structure bypasses all of the security mechanisms of DotNetNuke portals and implies a much higher level of security clearance. Examine the contents of the portal root folders on the machine by launching Windows Explorer and navigating to the place where DotNetNuke is installed on the computer. Inside that folder is a child folder named Portals. In my installation, the portals folder is located here:

```
c:\projects\dnn\portals
```

The Portals folder contains all of the portal root folders installed on DotNetNuke. The first portal created by the DotNetNuke installation process is the folder named 0 and your new portal is the folder named 1.

> *In later chapters, you'll be accessing these portal folders quite a bit. It's not a bad idea to create a shortcut for it on your desktop. You can right-click and drag the folder to your desktop. When you release it, one of the options in the context menu is "Create Shortcuts Here."*

The folder named _default contains the files shared by all portals. This is where the skins for the parent portal and the new child portal are located. That's worth a few minutes of browsing before you start diving deeper.

Discover Skins in Host and Portal Skins

Earlier in this chapter, you uploaded a skin at the host level. Skins installed at the host level are available to all portals in the installation. Skins installed at the portal level are available only to the given portal.

Only the host account is permitted to install new skins. Both the host and administrator accounts can browse the skins installed at the host level and the given portal level, as well as apply a selected skin to the site.

Try It Out   Install a Portal Level Skin

As a prerequisite, these steps make use of the following items:

- ❏ The child portal named marketing created earlier in the chapter
- ❏ The Winter skin package available in the downloads section

In the following steps, a skin is added to DotNetNuke at the portal level. Then, another portal in the same DotNetNuke installation is examined to demonstrate how the skin administration page handles multiple skins installed at different levels.

1. Launch a web browser, and navigate to the marketing portal website created earlier in the chapter. This is the URL:

```
http://localhost/dnn/marketing
```

2. The home page of this portal site uses the vertical menu in the left column while the original parent portal uses the horizontal menu. Log in to the portal website using the host account credentials.

3. From the home page of the portal website, expand the Admin menu item in the left column, and click the Skins menu item. The browser navigates to the Skins administration page.

4. Upload the Winter skin package to this portal. Refer to "Uploading a Skin" for instructions from earlier in this chapter and perform the same steps to upload the skin to this portal.

5. The Winter skin should be visible in the Skins drop-down list control in the Skins administration page.

6. In the Skin Type field, uncheck the checkbox labeled Site. The web page will post back and redraw the page.

7. Examine the contents of the Skins drop-down list control. It should not contain the Winter skin now because clearing the checkbox field filtered out portal level skins.

8. Log out of this marketing portal site, and navigate to the original website located at this URL:

```
http://localhost/dnn
```

9. Log in with the administrator account credentials.

10. In the menu bar, select Admin, Skins. The browser navigates to the Skin administration page.

11. With both the Host checkbox and the Site checkbox selected in the Skin Type field, examine the contents of the Skins drop-down list. The item named Winter is not visible here because it was installed at the portal level for a different site.

How It Works

DotNetNuke tracks who is using the site and which URL is being requested. Based on these two pieces of information, it can separate skins at a portal level and isolate different sets of users.

You should have a pretty good understanding of how portals operate in DotNetNuke at this point. As with most things in software development, you can always dive deeper into portals. You've explored a wide swath of technology that should get you well on your way to understanding how to skin DotNetNuke sites.

Using the Install Folder

Another technique of installing items in DotNetNuke involves the use of the folder named Install. Sometimes you might be working with a remote instance of DotNetNuke and you won't be able to launch Windows Explorer and manipulate the files, but you probably have FTP access to the website. This special DotNetNuke folder is located in the topmost directory of the installation; it's a sibling to the Portals folder discussed in the last section.

DotNetNuke examines the contents of this folder for installable items when it is prompted to do so. This folder contains a set of files and seven folders. The seven folders represent the categorization of items available for installation with this technique. Take a peek at this folder in your system now using Windows Explorer.

Try It Out   Use the Install Folder

This technique is a quick and simple method of installing a skin. In the following steps, you will install a new skin on DotNetNuke. It's slightly more technical than the browser-based method because you must enter a specific URL into your web browser; however you don't need to log in with the Host account.

1. Find the Summer skin in the downloads section for this chapter.

2. Using Windows Explorer, open the Install folder.

3. Copy the Summer skin to the Skin folder located inside the Install folder.

4. Enter the following URL in your web browser. This prompts DotNetNuke to process the contents of the Install folder.

```
http://localhost/dnn/Install/Install.aspx?mode=InstallResources
```

5. The system discovers the new skin package and executes the process to install it. The system also reports the status through a series of messages in the browser.

6. Log in as the host account and navigate to the Skin administration page by selecting Host, Skins in the menu bar. The Summer skin item should appear in the Skins drop-down list control.

How It Works

DotNetNuke was prompted to examine the contents of the Install folder when you accessed this special URL. When it discovered the skin package, it performed the skin installation at the host level and removed the package from the Skin folder. The end result is indistinguishable from the browser-based upload method.

This process works well for folks using an FTP client to access the files on their site instead of Windows Explorer. You can FTP the files to the appropriate folder and launch the special URL in your browser to perform the installation in a similar manner. You can upload the same skin repeatedly, too. The system will overwrite the files without a complaint, which is conducive to an iterative development environment when you're using an FTP client.

Remember that you did not have to log in as the host account to perform this installation. That fact might make a few of your security hairs stand up on end; however, you did have to access the Install folder from Windows Explorer, so there are still some security mechanisms in place.

DotNetNuke makes use of this powerful feature during the initial system installation, too. If you examine the Install folder before the system has been installed on your computer, you'll see quite a few files in the Module folder. This is how the modules are initially installed on your system.

As you get more advanced, you might want to customize which modules are initially installed in DotNetNuke. Version 4.4.0 of the system took a step back from this common practice of prior versions. Only two modules are installed by default in version 4.4.0 of DotNetNuke. Earlier versions had many more modules installed during the initial setup. If you want to install some or all of the modules in the box, just remove the .resources filename extension that is currently preventing the automatic installation of the modules. Alternatively, you can just check the available modules in the Modules administration page while logged in under the host account.

Summary

Installing and configuring a skin package is intuitive and fast thanks to the many niche utilities provided by DotNetNuke. A package containing multiple skins and containers can be uploaded in one simple procedure. Each visual skin and container in the package can be previewed and managed independently once installed. Sometimes, it's beneficial to limit access to a skin or provide global access throughout the portal.

In this chapter you learned the following:

❑   What the contents of a DotNetNuke skin package are

❑   How to install a skin package onto a DotNetNuke portal using the administration pages and the install folder techniques

❑   How to limit access to a skin for just one portal or broaden access to all portals

Chapter 4, "Exploring Skins," dives into the contents of a skin file in order to make some customizations before and after uploading the skin to a portal.

Exercises

1. What types of files will you find in a skin package?

2. Which DotNetNuke accounts are permitted to upload skin packages?

3. Which DotNetNuke accounts are permitted to browse and apply skin packages?

4. If a page is not displaying a skin set at the portal level, what might be the reason?

5. What is the difference between a parent portal and a child portal?

6. How can a skin be installed in DotNetNuke without using the credentials for the host account?

4

Exploring Skins

From their control of the HTML structures to their ability to select from a series of controls that expose powerful features in DotNetNuke, skin designers, of all the users of DotNetNuke, have the most granular level of control over page layout. After all, the DNN skin determines the entire page layout. Administrators also have a say in the look of a page, because they can elect to enable or disable skin features through the online tools in the system.

This chapter focuses on the core of the book: understanding DotNetNuke skins. It starts with a detailed exploration of skins, panes, and containers. Skin objects and other controls within these files are covered, too.

Editing skin files is a developer-oriented task where text editors are used nearly as often as the web browser. There's a certain balance to strike in your mind between aesthetic interpretation and technical know-how. Therefore, this is a good time to discuss some developer practices that professionals use every day to protect their work and to be as productive as possible with their time.

The task of designing a skin has a fair number of considerations. One is the structure of the HTML output. The layout of the HTML can help or hinder search engine indexes as well as the design agility of the page. Search engines traverse the *Document Object Model*, or DOM, of web pages. This is the structure that starts with the opening <html> tag and branches out to every tag in the page in a hierarchical format.

Consider two pages that display the same content. In this contrived example, the first page uses a series of nested tables, font tags, and style attributes that contribute to a complex DOM. The second page uses only header tags, paragraph tags, and ordered list tags to produce the equivalent page. If you were writing a search engine, how could you calculate the value of the jumbled mess on the first page? You probably couldn't. Which page would your search engine rank higher? The second page, because it clearly identifies section titles and detailed content. The search engine wants to learn the intent of the content on the web page. Web page designers have a choice of giving good hints about content up front or burying those hints deep within the DOM. I suggest you provide the hints up front.

Another great reason to concern yourself with the HTML output is the agility of the design. If CSS files are used to control the margins, padding, and positioning, then massive updates to all the pages of the site are considerably less work. Only one or two files can be edited and affect all of the pages in the website. You can also be much more certain of consistency throughout the site. If all of the <h1> tags use the same CSS rules, then you don't have to worry about some pages using the wrong font or size. This would not be the case if the presentation rules were hardcoded into each page. If you decide to use a series of nested tables and their friend, the spacer.gif file, then the file size of the page is increased and the DOM is more complex.

A classy brochure site that touts a product or service company's offerings to the public has different needs from a structured portal for an information worker who uses the site to perform his job for three hours out of the day. When you create your own custom skin, you need to consider the intended audience and continuously evaluate the website copy. In this chapter, you start with a finished product and analyze it. In Chapter 5, "Creating Custom Skins," you start with a clean slate and design a skin of your own.

Examining Skins and Containers

This section examines the actual contents of a skin and a container. Both skins and containers are ASP.Net web user controls used to describe the layout and aesthetics of a web page in DotNetNuke. A ton of extensible features are available to skins. *Skin objects* extend the capabilities of a skin or container by injecting into them a small piece of functionality such as a menu navigation display or a button that helps visitors rate content. Skin objects are covered later on in this chapter.

Examining the Skin File

You can learn a lot about the structure of skins by examining existing skins. Start by looking at the default skin file for DotNetNuke. Using your favorite text editor, open the file named Horizontal Menu - Fixed Width.ascx in this folder:

```
<install folder>\Portals\_default\Skins\DNN-Blue\
```

Using Directives

This .ascx file starts with a *control directive*. This line informs ASP.Net that the file is a web user control so that ASP.Net knows how to handle the file when it's loaded into a page.

```
<%@ Control Language="vb" Codebehind="~/admin/Skins/skin.vb"
    AutoEventWireup="false" Explicit="True" Inherits="DotNetNuke.UI.Skins.Skin" %>
```

Every ASP.Net web user control must include a control directive. A couple of attributes embedded in the control directive wire up the .ascx file to other ASP.Net and DotNetNuke specific code. At this point, it's just necessary to understand that this file is an ASP.Net web user control, and the first line is an instance of the mandatory control directive.

The next series of lines in the skin file contain the *register directives*. These lines inform ASP.Net that this web user control will make use of other web user controls. This is a powerful feature: web user controls can contain other web user controls. You might be familiar with "include files" in Classic ASP, PHP, or similar web technologies — a technique to embed the contents of one file in another file and refer to those contents. This is similar in concept. To use a web user control, the file must include a register directive that identifies the location of that web user control, as shown in the following example:

```
<%@ Register TagPrefix="dnn" TagName="LOGO" Src="~/Admin/Skins/Logo.ascx" %>

<%@ Register TagPrefix="dnn" TagName="BANNER" Src="~/Admin/Skins/Banner.ascx" %>

<%@ Register TagPrefix="dnn" TagName="MENU" Src="~/Admin/Skins/SolPartMenu.ascx" %>

<%@ Register TagPrefix="dnn" TagName="SEARCH" Src="~/Admin/Skins/Search.ascx" %>

<%@ Register TagPrefix="dnn" TagName="CURRENTDATE"
     Src="~/Admin/Skins/CurrentDate.ascx" %>

<%@ Register TagPrefix="dnn" TagName="BREADCRUMB"
     Src="~/Admin/Skins/BreadCrumb.ascx" %>

<%@ Register TagPrefix="dnn" TagName="USER" Src="~/Admin/Skins/User.ascx" %>

<%@ Register TagPrefix="dnn" TagName="LOGIN" Src="~/Admin/Skins/Login.ascx" %>

<%@ Register TagPrefix="dnn" TagName="COPYRIGHT"
     Src="~/Admin/Skins/Copyright.ascx" %>

<%@ Register TagPrefix="dnn" TagName="TERMS" Src="~/Admin/Skins/Terms.ascx" %>

<%@ Register TagPrefix="dnn" TagName="PRIVACY" Src="~/Admin/Skins/Privacy.ascx" %>

<%@ Register TagPrefix="dnn" TagName="DOTNETNUKE"
     Src="~/Admin/Skins/DotNetNuke.ascx" %>

<%@ Register TagPrefix="dnn" TagName="LANGUAGE"
     Src="~/Admin/Skins/Language.ascx" %>
```

Chapter 3 discusses web user controls at a high level. In this chapter they are in action. Remember, web user controls can contain other web user controls. The code shown previously lists 13 register directives that help wire up other web user controls nested inside this user control. In DotNetNuke terms, these are classified as *skin objects*. These skin objects are small pieces of DotNetNuke functionality that are embedded in a skin file. There are several to choose from, and you can build your own if you also have a developer hat in your closet. Skin objects will be examined a little closer later on in this chapter.

Using the HTML and Skin Objects

The remainder of the skin file is the actual DotNetNuke skin. In this particular skin, the outer layer is an HTML table that has a CSS class set to pagemaster. The vast majority of the section below the register directives is just standard HTML. This book focuses on applying HTML and CSS to DotNetNuke skins as opposed to teaching it. If you need a little brush-up on authoring HTML and CSS files, then grab a copy of *Beginning CSS: Cascading Style Sheets for Web Design*, 2nd Edition by Richard York (Wiley Publishing, Inc., 2007) to get back in the flow.

Aside from clever HTML structures, the interesting things you'll find inside a skin file include instances of skin objects and panes. Remember, *skin objects* is simply a DotNetNuke term for web user controls. The first instance of web user controls in this skin appears in the form of an HTML table having a CSS class of `skinheader`.

```
<table class="skinheader" cellspacing="0" cellpadding="3"
    width="100%" border="0">
    <tr>
        <td valign="middle" align="left">
            <dnn:LOGO runat="server" ID="dnnLOGO" />
        </td>
        <td valign="middle" align="right">
            <dnn:BANNER runat="server" ID="dnnBANNER" />
        </td>
    </tr>
</table>
```

The preceding code shows a single-row, two-column HTML table. Both cells in the HTML table contain an instance of a skin object. The first skin object displays the logo configured for this portal, and the second skin object displays the configured banner.

Using the Logo Skin Object

The job of the logo skin object is to display the image specified by the administrator or host accounts. These accounts can use the menu bar to click Admin, Site Settings to access the Appearance section of the Site Settings page. Figure 4-1 displays Logo field located in the Site Settings page.

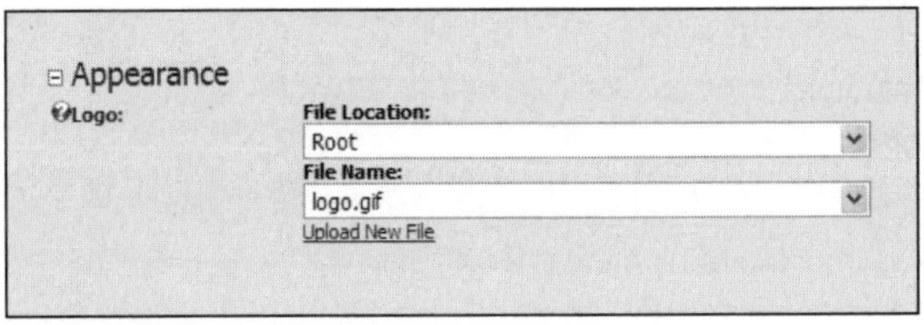

Figure 4-1

This field contains the familiar file selection control for DotNetNuke. The top drop-down list selects the folder of the image, and the bottom drop-down list selects the image file within the given folder. Most image selection tasks in DotNetNuke use this control to perform the work. New image files can also be uploaded through this control by clicking the hyperlink at the bottom of the control.

The logo skin object becomes very useful for a DotNetNuke installation that has multiple portals using the same skin. This skin object provides one additional layer of abstraction over the website. For example, in the case of a collection of team portals for a youth sports league on a single instance of DotNetNuke, the team logo can be injected into the web page to give it just a touch of personalization while still adhering to the overall branding of the league. Someone can change the logo of the web page by just using the online management tools. They do not require extensive knowledge of DotNetNuke skins in order to change the look of the site. It's an inexpensive and efficient method of branding a website with a specific logo.

Most skin objects, including this one, are not mandatory. A single DotNetNuke portal with a custom skin can omit this skin object from the design with no ill effects. It's simply a matter of choosing which features to leverage in your portal.

Try It Out   Upload a New Logo

Here is an easy exercise to get started. In this section, you'll customize the default skin in DotNetNuke with your own logo. To get started, you need a default installation of DotNetNuke.

1. Use your favorite graphics program to create an image file to use as a logo on the site. The file should be roughly 280px wide and 80px tall.

2. Log in to the DotNetNuke portal as the Admin or Host account.

3. In the menu bar, select Admin, Site Settings.

4. In the Appearance section under Basic Settings, click the Upload New File hyperlink for the Logo field.

5. Use the browse button to locate the image file you created in step 1.

6. Click the Upload Selected File hyperlink. The graphics file is uploaded to the web server that is running DotNetNuke, and the filename should be selected in the File Name drop-down list control.

7. Click the Update hyperlink at the bottom of the page to save the changes. The browser should stay on the site settings page, and you should see your new logo at the top.

How It Works

The default installation of DotNetNuke uses a skin that contains the logo skin object. When this skin object is processed, it looks up the value of the logo field in the system and displays the image wherever it is positioned in the skin as an HTML <img> tag. These series of steps modified the existing logo to use your own custom-made image. This is how the skin designer delegates a little bit of control to the portal administrator to provide some minor customizations to the page design.

Using the Banner Skin Object

The banner skin object handles the task of displaying a rotating collection of advertisements. This skin object has its roots in the early days of DotNetNuke and touts a full set of tools for managing banners.

A youth sports league might find funding for a few items by seeking advertising placement from local sports equipment stores, pizza places, or shoe stores. The skin object displays the various banner images according to the requested parameters and tracks the number of times the banner is displayed, known as impressions, as well as the number of times the banner is clicked.

In its simplest form, the banner object exists in a skin, as shown in the prior block of code. A portal can display banners configured at the host level or at the portal level. If all of the portals on a DotNetNuke installation are related, it makes sense to configure banners in one place at the host level instead of repeating the same banner configuration steps for each portal.

Banners are configured at the host level by logging in as the host account and selecting Host, Vendors in the menu bar. The Vendor administration page lists all of the configured vendors for the DotNetNuke installation. In the spirit of reusing familiar tools in DotNetNuke, the Vendor administration page closely resembles the User administration page located at Admin, User Accounts in the menu bar.

The Vendor administration page contains a link to add a new vendor. This link leads to a page that contains a form for entering vendor detail information, such as address and website. After the preliminary information is entered here, the vendor is added to the list on the Vendor administration page.

It's common for vendors to have multiple banners on a website. Banners are added by selecting the vendor on the Vendor administration page. This navigates the browser to the Edit Vendors administration page. This page resembles the form used to enter the vendor into the system with some additional sections at the bottom of the page, including Banner Advertising and Affiliate Referrals, as shown in Figure 4-2.

The banner advertising section lists all of the ads for the selected vendor. Skin objects can be configured to show the following types of banners: Banner, MicroButton, Button, Block, Skyscraper, Text, and Script. These values are found in the Banner Type drop-down list on the Edit Banner administration page. This field categorizes the type of advertisement. Banners are the most common type and are characterized by a wide rectangular box usually positioned near the top of the page. Skyscrapers are tall and skinny, which makes them a good fit for the right column of a page. Figure 4-3 shows the portion of the Edit Banner administration page that identifies the banner type.

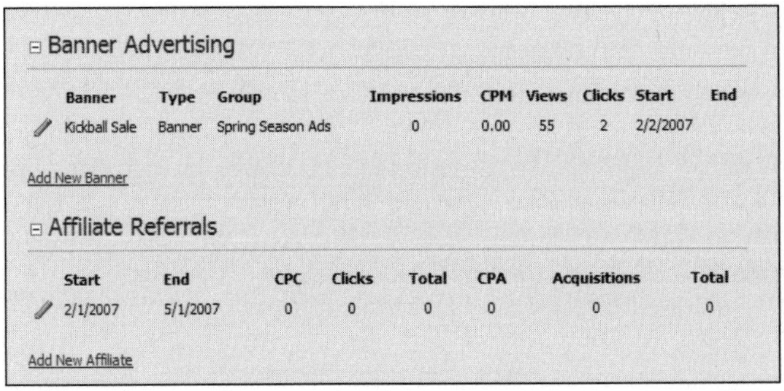

Figure 4-2

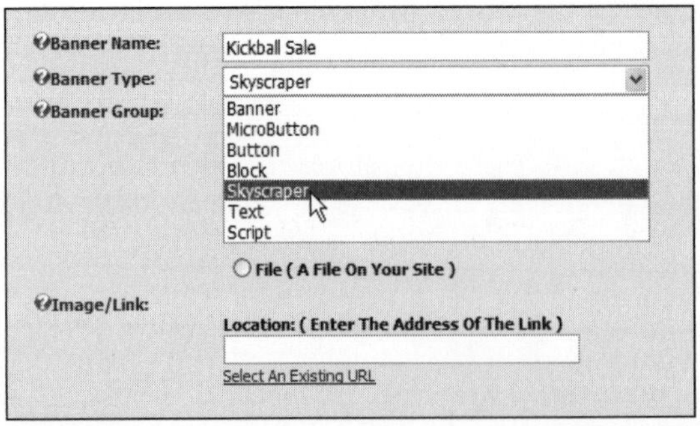

Figure 4-3

The banner skin object can only show one type of banner. By default, it shows ads set to the Banner Type value of Banner. To configure the skin object to display another type of banner, set the `BannerTypeId` attribute of the skin object to the matching index number of the item in the Banner Type drop-down list. The following code shows the banner skin object configured to display banners classified as Skyscraper advertisements:

```
<dnn:BANNER runat="server" ID="dnnBANNER" BannerTypeId="5" />
```

The Skyscraper type is the fifth item in the list, so in order to show these types of banner ads in a skin, the banner skin object must have a `BannerTypeId` attribute set to `"5"`.

The logo and banner skin objects provide a nice introduction to the task of wiring up configuration settings inside DotNetNuke to the skin file and to what is eventually rendered in the browser. Skin objects are like a sealed DotNetNuke module. They might have some configuration options available to modify indirectly the output in the DotNetNuke administration pages, but the skin object itself is sealed inside the skin. To modify the skin object, you must open the skin file and manually adjust it. DotNetNuke modules have special web-based interfaces for making modifications directly to the module.

Understanding Panes

The final part of a skin file is the simplest and most powerful feature: the pane. A pane is a special location in a skin file that serves as a placeholder. Panes enable administrators to drop any type of DotNetNuke module into a page. Administrators drop modules into the pane(s) of a skin. Remember that a page has a one-to-one relationship with a skin file and multiple pages can all display the same skin.

The person designing the skin might have some good guesses but he or she has no control over what the administrator might drop into the pane. The pane might be left empty or it might have ten or more modules added to it. It's up to the skin designer to construct a quality skin that serves the needs of the DotNetNuke website administrator, whether that's the person two cubicles down or the person who purchased your custom skin in Tokyo, Japan.

A skin can have any number of panes. The following code is the world's simplest DotNetNuke skin file. It has everything necessary to be a fully functional, albeit boring, skin in three easy lines.

```
<%@ Control Inherits="DotNetNuke.UI.Skins.Skin" %>
<div id="ControlPanel" runat="server"></div>
<div id="ContentPane" runat="server"></div>
```

The first line is the control directive discussed earlier in the chapter. The next two lines are ASP.Net HTML server controls with a special `id` attribute value. Without the two attributes, the `<div>` tags would be normal HTML elements.

When a page is configured to use the skin shown previously and it's populated with modules, a flurry of events happens when a visitor requests the page in their browser. The following list is a simplified version of the activities that take place:

1. At this early point, the web page in DotNetNuke is nearly void of all content.
2. DotNetNuke looks up the skin assigned to the page in the database.
3. DotNetNuke looks up the modules assigned to the page in the database.

4. DotNetNuke injects the modules inside the pane(s) of the skin.

5. DotNetNuke injects the skin into the web page.

6. Any skin objects embedded in the skin generate their HTML content.

7. The fully populated page is sent down to the visitor's browser.

In ASP.Net, tags having an attribute of `runat="server"` are classified as *server controls*. Server controls are accessible for manipulation by the code running on the server before the page is rendered on the browser. HTML elements are not accessible by the code running on the server, so they're treated as regular text. The following tags are commonly converted into server controls as panes with the `id` and `runat` attributes:

❑ Division tag, `<div>`

❑ Paragraph tag, `<p>`

❑ Table cell tag, `<td>`

These are block elements that contain other elements, unlike self-closing elements that do not contain child elements such as the line break tag, `<br />`, and the horizontal rule tag, `<hr />`.

As a matter of convention, you should add the Pane suffix to all of your panes, such as LeftPane, RightPane, or TopPane. This makes it obvious to someone maintaining your design later as well as administrators who are dropping modules inside panes labeled on the page.

Using the ControlPanel

The first server control in the code shown previously has the special name of ControlPanel. DotNetNuke looks for this control when an administrator or host account user is logged into the site. This is where the familiar control panel is injected into the skin. If you forget this server control in your skin, DotNetNuke version 4.4.1 is forgiving and will automatically inject the control panel at the top of the page. It's better to declare the location of this important item directly in your skin file. Because it's declared, the skin designer has complete control of the position in the skin. By convention, the control panel appears at the top of the page. It can work well at the bottom of the page, too, especially if administrative users are logged into the site frequently and the control panel takes up a large portion of the screen on a laptop.

Using the ContentPane

The second server control in the code shown previously is the pane. This pane is special because its name is ContentPane. You can add as many panes as you like and name them anything you like, but you must include a pane named ContentPane.

When an administrator creates a new page in DotNetNuke, he or she has the option of specifying a skin for the page. Suppose he or she selects a skin that has three vertical columns with one pane in each column. Then, the administrator can add modules to each pane in the page. Now, what would happen if the administrator returns to the Settings page and changes the skin from a three-column layout to a two-column layout that has only two panes? Fortunately, the fine developers of DotNetNuke have your backs.

When DotNetNuke prepares to render the page, it attempts to honor the pane assignments for each module. If the module is assigned to a pane that doesn't exist in the current skin, then the module is added to the ContentPane by default. Thus, you are always required to include a pane named ContentPane in every skin. If you are developing a skin with multiple panes; it makes sense to name one pane that will hold the body of the page as ContentPane.

Some advanced text editors have an auto-format feature that can convert an HTML file from an unreadable mess into a clean file with ample line breaks, white space, and proper indentation (so it's easy to see structures and parent-child relationships). If you have that feature, congrats! If not, you might want to keep searching for an editor that can perform this valuable cleaning service.

Examine the skin file named `Horizontal Menu - Fixed Width.ascx`, and identify all of the panes in the file. You should find five panes in a central block of code in the file. The HTML table holding all of the panes has three rows. The top and bottom rows have all of the columns merged into one cell. The middle row has three columns, as shown in the following example:

```
<table cellspacing="3" cellpadding="3" width="100%" border="0">
   <tr>
      <td class="toppane" colspan="3" id="TopPane" runat="server"
         valign="top" align="center"></td>
   </tr>
   <tr valign="top">
      <td class="leftpane" id="LeftPane" runat="server"
         valign="top" align="center"></td>
      <td class="contentpane" id="ContentPane" runat="server"
         valign="top" align="center"></td>
      <td class="rightpane" id="RightPane" runat="server"
         valign="top" align="center"></td>
   </tr>
   <tr>
      <td class="bottompane" colspan="3" id="BottomPane"
         runat="server" valign="top" align="center"></td>
   </tr>
</table>
```

Try It Out   Change a Pane

These steps involve some changes to an ASP.Net web user control. So, fire up your favorite text editor and open the file named `Horizontal Menu - Fixed Width.ascx`. The file is located in the following directory:

```
<install folder>\Portals\_default\Skins\DNN-Blue\
```

In this exercise, you'll modify panes in the default skin to create a slightly different layout. The default skin has header and footer panes. Between those panes, it has a left, right, and center pane. These steps will change the layout to a wide content pane in the middle and a narrow pane on the right for promotions. You'll also modify the CSS file to give the skin a slight change to suit your needs.

1. In the skin file, locate the <table> tag that has the class attribute value of `skinmaster`. Remove the width attribute and the align attribute from this <table> tag. You'll specify these values and a few more in the CSS file.

2. Find the <table> tag that is the immediate parent of the five panes in this skin. Change the `cellpadding` and `cellspacing` attribute values to zero. Delete the width attribute entirely from this <table> tag; you'll specify these settings in the CSS file.

3. In this same HTML table, delete every `valign` and `align` attribute that exists in the cells of this table. In the three rows of this table, there are currently five table cell tags. When you are finished with your backspace frenzy, this HTML table will only contain the following attributes: `cellspacing`, `cellpadding`, `border`, `class`, `colspan`, `id`, and `runat`.

4. Find the `<td>` server control that has the `id` attribute value of LeftPane. This control is not needed for your structure so delete the entire table cell server control, including the closing tag. The structure is now sufficient for the design, so the next step is to modify the CSS file.

5. Open the file named `Skin.css` located in the same folder as the web user control.

6. Find the CSS rules for the class pagemaster in the CSS file. Add a rule that will center the content inside this class:

```
text-align:center;
```

7. Find the CSS rules for the class `skinmaster`. Add a width assignment of 770 pixels to the class `width:770px;`.

8. Find the CSS rules for the class contentpane. Change the width assignment to 500 pixels and change the background color to blue. Also, set the vertical alignment to the top as follows:

```
width:500px;
background-color: #006699;
vertical-align:top;
```

9. Find the CSS rules for the class rightpane. Change the width assignment to 180 pixels and change the background color to a light grey. Also, set the vertical alignment to the top as follows:

```
width:180px;
background-color: #CCC;
vertical-align:top;
```

10. Load the home page of the default DotNetNuke website, and observe the changes to the skin file and the CSS file in your browser.

The following snippets of code show the skin file and the CSS file after the edits are applied. This HTML code is considerably cleaner and easier to read now that the presentation rules have been moved to the CSS file.

Horizontal Menu - Fixed Width.ascx

```
...
<table class="skinmaster" border="0" cellspacing="0" cellpadding="0">
...
    <table cellspacing="0" cellpadding="0" border="0">
      <tr>
          <td class="toppane" colspan="3" id="TopPane" runat="server"></td>
      </tr>
      <tr>
          <td class="contentpane" id="ContentPane" runat="server"></td>
          <td class="rightpane" id="RightPane" runat="server"></td>
      </tr>
```

```
        <tr>
            <td class="bottompane" colspan="3" id="BottomPane" runat="server"></td>
        </tr>
    </table>

...
```

Skin.css

```
...
.pagemaster
{
    width: 100%;
    height: 100%;
    background-color: #fefefe;
    text-align:center;
}
.skinmaster
{
    width: 770px;
    height: 100%;
    background-color: #f3f5fa;
    border-right: #7994cb 1px solid;
    border-top: #7994cb 1px solid;
    border-left: #7994cb 1px solid;
    border-bottom: #7994cb 1px solid;
    moz-border-radius-bottomleft: 15px;
    moz-border-radius-bottomright: 15px;
    moz-border-radius-topleft: 3px;
    moz-border-radius-topright: 3px;
}

...
.contentpane
{
    width: 500px;
    vertical-align:top;
    background-color: #006699;
    padding-left: 6px;
    padding-right: 4px;
    padding-top: 6px;
}
.rightpane
{
    width: 250px;
    vertical-align:top;
    background-color: #CCC;
    padding-left: 6px;
    padding-right: 4px;
    padding-top: 6px;
}
...
```

How It Works

The two panes should be distinguishable by their background colors. Note that the books and links modules have moved into the default ContentPane since you deleted the left pane from the skin. DotNetNuke won't complain if you drop a module in the pane of one skin, and then assign a new skin to the page that doesn't have panes with the same name. It will happily dump any orphaned modules into the default ContentPane.

DotNetNuke served up the new structure in the skin and the updated CSS file to your browser, and the default skin was converted into a two-column structure in just a few minutes. Figure 4-4 shows the page after edits have been applied.

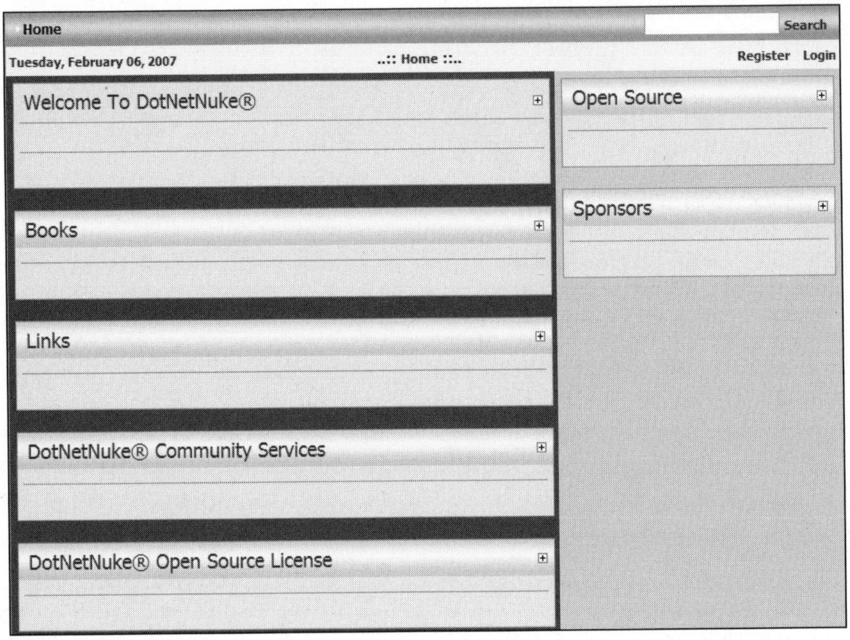

Home				Search
Tuesday, February 06, 2007		..:: Home ::..		Register Login

Welcome To DotNetNuke®   ⊞   Open Source   ⊞

Books   ⊞   Sponsors   ⊞

Links   ⊞

DotNetNuke® Community Services   ⊞

DotNetNuke® Open Source License   ⊞

Figure 4-4

DotNetNuke had no idea what it would find in the skin file the second before you requested the page. During the request, it processed the skin file, assigned modules to the assigned panes, and handled the case where the modules were assigned to unknown panes. The system also found the CSS file used by this skin and created a link to it in the HTML source so the browser would use it.

These are the exact skills you'll develop by working with DotNetNuke skins. A clear design direction is important to understanding what changes in the skin file are necessary. Skin developers also need to consider support for different types of browsers for the HTML and CSS designs they create. Future ease of maintenance should also be considered. In this example, you moved some presentation rules to the CSS file to clean up the HTML file and to make future design changes easier to execute.

Examining the Container File

A container's job is to wrap around a single DotNetNuke module. A module has only one container. Similar to skins, the same container file can decorate multiple modules. If a given container displays a green box with rounded corners around the module, then you can set every module in the site to use the same container and see lovely green boxes with rounded corners everywhere. On the other hand, you can also configure each module to display its own unique container. Most sites settle on just a few containers for consistency.

This terminology can be a little confusing to start, especially with the names. When a "skin package" is installed in DotNetNuke, it usually includes one or more "skin files" and one or more "container files."

Let's examine a container file now. Using your favorite text editor, open the file named Image Header - Color Background.ascx in this folder:

```
<install folder>\Portals\_default\Containers\DNN-Blue\
```

Using Directives

Like the skin file, the container file is also an ASP.Net web user control. Therefore, the .ascx file starts with a control directive, as shown in the following example:

```
<%@ Control language="vb" CodeBehind="~/admin/Containers/container.vb"
    AutoEventWireup="false" Explicit="True"
    Inherits="DotNetNuke.UI.Containers.Container" %>
```

This control directive is slightly different from the directive in the skin file. It points to a different file for the CodeBehind attribute, and it inherits from a different class in DotNetNuke. This line doesn't concern us much as DotNetNuke skin developers. If you're interested in more ASP.Net programming related items you can research the purpose of these attributes more on your own but they are outside the scope of this book.

This web user control refers to other web user controls just like the control in the skin file. Therefore, it must include a series of register directives to tell ASP.Net where to look for these external resources. The following code lists nine register directives that allow the container file to make use of these other features:

```
<%@ Register TagPrefix="dnn" TagName="ACTIONS"
    Src="~/Admin/Containers/SolPartActions.ascx" %>
<%@ Register TagPrefix="dnn" TagName="ICON"
    Src="~/Admin/Containers/Icon.ascx" %>
<%@ Register TagPrefix="dnn" TagName="TITLE"
    Src="~/Admin/Containers/Title.ascx" %>
<%@ Register TagPrefix="dnn" TagName="VISIBILITY"
    Src="~/Admin/Containers/Visibility.ascx" %>
<%@ Register TagPrefix="dnn" TagName="ACTIONBUTTON1"
    Src="~/Admin/Containers/ActionButton.ascx" %>
<%@ Register TagPrefix="dnn" TagName="ACTIONBUTTON2"
    Src="~/Admin/Containers/ActionButton.ascx" %>
```

```
<%@ Register TagPrefix="dnn" TagName="ACTIONBUTTON3"
    Src="~/Admin/Containers/ActionButton.ascx" %>
<%@ Register TagPrefix="dnn" TagName="ACTIONBUTTON4"
    Src="~/Admin/Containers/ActionButton.ascx" %>
<%@ Register TagPrefix="dnn" TagName="ACTIONBUTTON5"
    Src="~/Admin/Containers/ActionButton.ascx" %>
```

Using HTML and Skin Objects

Like the skin file, the remainder of this container file includes standard HTML code and some specialized skin objects. You'll examine those items now.

Using the Actions Menu Control

This control creates the menu pinned to the familiar triangle that becomes visible when the administrator host account is logged in.

```
<dnn:ACTIONS runat="server" id="dnnACTIONS" />
```

The default pop-up displays a contextual menu that applies to the given DotNetNuke module. The home page displays a couple of instances of the Text/HTML module and one instance of the Links module by default upon a new installation. Compare the items in the actions menu between the Text/HTML module and the Links module. Figure 4-5 shows the contents of the action menu for the Text/HTML module.

When the administrator is logged into the system and hovers over the triangle, the pop-up menu over the module appears. The action menu control in the container file is responsible for injecting the appropriate HTML and JavaScript necessary to render the menu.

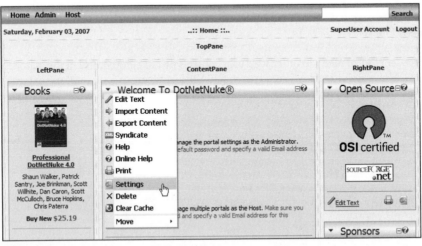

Figure 4-5

Using the Icon Control

The icon control renders an HTML <img> tag to display the icon configured for the given DotNetNuke module.

```
<dnn:ICON runat="server" id="dnnICON" />
```

If the given module does not have an icon configured, the control is smart enough to render nothing and avoid making a kludge of the HTML sent to the browser. Similar to the logo skin object, the icon control gives administrators a small portion of customization ability without requiring them to have HTML or DotNetNuke skills.

Figure 4-6 shows the location within the module settings where the icon is specified. As with the logo skin object, this field uses the familiar image file selection control to configure the value.

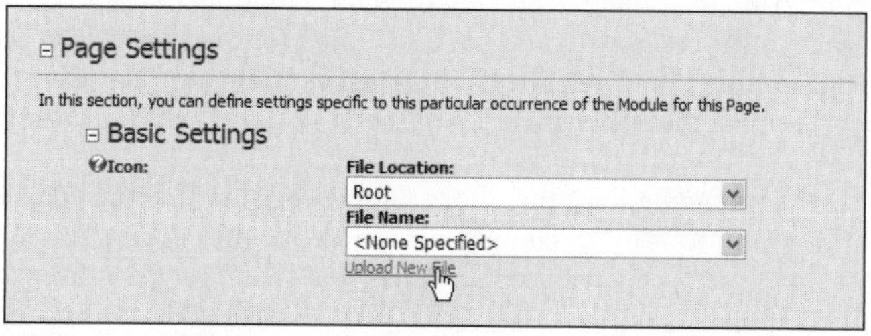

Figure 4-6

Using the Title Control

The title control displays the module title text of the given module.

```
<dnn:TITLE runat="server" id="dnnTITLE" />
```

By default, this control renders the title wrapped by an HTML <span> tag that has the CSS class name of head. This control also enables a little extra editing ability. When an administrator is logged into the system, the title control can swap to edit mode by clicking on the title text. A red box will surround the title text and it can be edited in place without switching to the module settings view. Clicking anywhere outside the red box will return the title control to its normal display mode.

Using the Visibility Control

The visibility control is responsible for the traditional portal feature of expanding and collapsing modules; this feature provides the user with the ability to see information he deems important while minimizing the rest.

```
<dnn:VISIBILITY runat="server" id="dnnVISIBILITY" />
```

Among other features, the speed of the expand/collapse animation can be modified by customizing the `AnimationFrames` property; by default this property is set to 5. You can slow the animation by adding the following attribute to the control:

```
<dnn:VISIBILITY runat="server" id="dnnVISIBILITY"
    AnimationFrames="50"
/>
```

Using the Module Help Control

The module help control displays the module help icon when the administrator user is logged in.

```
<dnn:ACTIONBUTTON5 runat="server" id="dnnACTIONBUTTON5"
    CommandName="ModuleHelp.Action" DisplayIcon="True" DisplayLink="False" />
```

Module developers can provide online documentation for a module that's just one click away. Because the documentation usually describes how to add or edit content for the system, the documentation icon is hidden when the given user does not have editorial privileges for the module. The icon can be exchanged for a text hyperlink by swapping the Boolean values of the `DisplayIcon` and the `DisplayLink` attributes.

An astute ASP.Net developer will notice that the matching register directive for this control shares the same src attribute as four other controls in the container file. The only important difference between this control and the others is the `CommandName` attribute that determines what function the control will perform.

Using the Add Content Control

DotNetNuke modules have three traditional display types: View, Settings, and Edit. Most visitors will only use the View display type to see the information in the module, such as a formatted list of links. Administrators use the Edit display type to modify the information contained in the module. This control produces a hyperlink that helps the administrator navigate from the View display type to the Edit display type.

```
<dnn:ACTIONBUTTON1 runat="server" id="dnnACTIONBUTTON1"
    CommandName="AddContent.Action" DisplayIcon="True" DisplayLink="True" />
```

The module developer has control over the actual name of the hyperlink produced by this control. The field in the Links module is named Add Link, and the field in the Text/HTML module is named Edit Text. They both do the same thing: Switch to the module's Edit display type. DotNetNuke also has the capability of localizing this hyperlink text so it appears in the administrator's preferred language. By convention, this control shows both the icon and the text hyperlink.

Using the Syndicate Content Control

DotNetNuke was an early adopter of RSS feeds. It provides support for feeds at a module level. Every module in DotNetNuke can have its own distinct RSS feed. This service is provided inside the container file through the following web user control:

```
<dnn:ACTIONBUTTON2 runat="server" id="dnnACTIONBUTTON2"
    CommandName="SyndicateModule.Action" DisplayIcon="True"
    DisplayLink="False" />
```

Some modules, depending on their context, are great candidates for syndication through an RSS feed. The syndicate content control displays an icon or a text hyperlink that directs the user to a dynamic XML file that contains a summary of the content in the module. RSS feeds are just XML files that conform to a particular format. DotNetNuke can generate the XML file and place a link on the page next to the module just by using this control.

Using the Print Content Control

The print content control displays a printer icon or a text hyperlink that directs the user to a page that provides a printer-friendly view of the content in the module.

```
<dnn:ACTIONBUTTON3 runat="server" id="dnnACTIONBUTTON3"
   CommandName="PrintModule.Action" DisplayIcon="True" DisplayLink="False" />
```

If the visitor wanted a hard copy of the page as it appears in the web browser, he would click File, Print in the menu bar of their browser. The hard copy might not look exactly the same. By default, most browsers have the "print background colors and images" setting turned off to save on ink and laser toner. This is a key point to understand. You should be well aware of how your page looks as a printed document. I've seen very expensive sites launch with a near laughable experience at the printer station. I've also seen corporations have strict approval procedures that call for every page to be printed out and reviewed by committee before the site can launch. It's pretty tough to get sign off if the site looks horrible on paper.

In some cases, the visitor just wants the content on a piece of paper in an easy-to-read format. He is not concerned about the copy in the side bar or the rounded edges of the website design. This control gives the user the printer-friendly view of just the content in this module.

Using the Module Settings Control

The module settings control provides an alternative method of navigating to the module settings page.

```
<dnn:ACTIONBUTTON4 runat="server" id="dnnACTIONBUTTON4"
   CommandName="ModuleSettings.Action" DisplayIcon="True" DisplayLink="False" />
```

This control can display an icon or a text hyperlink to the module settings page. Another way of accessing the module settings page is to hover over the triangle in the top left corner of the module and select the Settings item from the action menu in the pop-up window.

Using the Content Pane

There is only one content pane for each container file, and the content pane has a special id attribute value.

```
<TR>
   <TD id="ContentPane" runat="server" align="center"></TD>
</TR>
```

DotNetNuke is expecting to find this pane in order to drop in the associated module. This markup should make it really clear that the container is a wrapper around only one module. In turn, the container and module are dropped into a pane on a skin file. A pane in a skin file may hold multiple modules.

Configuring Containers

The Basic Settings section is under the Page Settings section of this Module administration page. The contents of a container file used by a module play a large role in determining the potential of the HTML output. Containers have configuration options available on the module settings page in DotNetNuke. To view the module settings page, hover over the action menu icon and select Settings in the action menu pop-up.

Figure 4-7 shows some configurable fields in the Basic Settings section.

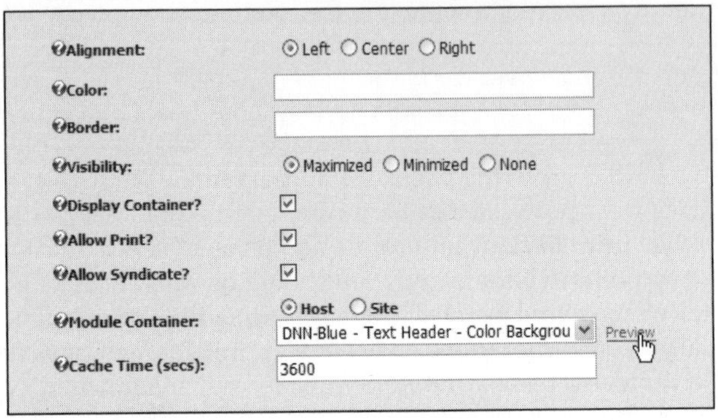

Figure 4-7

❑ **Alignment, Color, and Border.** These fields are fairly self-explanatory. I recommend this level of control be left to the skin designer instead of the module administrator. Keeping design level decisions to the skin files and the CSS files can help simplify the inevitable maintenance tasks that follow the launch of a site.

❑ **Visibility.** These radio buttons control the state of the expand/collapse feature available for each module. If the administrator suspects that a module is necessary on a page, but that it should not immediately occupy its full height on the screen, the value of Minimized will start the module in the collapsed state until the visitor manually expands it. The value of "None" removes the expand/collapse feature from the screen, regardless of the contents of the container control. If a set of containers should not have the expand/collapse feature, it's better to omit the control from the container than to set the Visibility field for each module to none, manually.

❑ **Display Container.** This checkbox is powerful. The container and the module render as expected in the browser when this checkbox is selected. When this checkbox is cleared, the anonymous visitor will not see the controls that are embedded in the container file. The administrator will continue to see the controls since they contain essential elements for working with the module. A custom brochure website might work best without the portal style feature of clear rectangular borders and collapsible sections, and this checkbox is one way to help implement such a design.

❑ **Allow Print.** This checkbox controls the display of the print icon, the icon created by the print control found in the container file. When the printer icon is clicked, DotNetNuke displays the printer-friendly view of the content in the module.

❑ **Allow Syndicate.** This checkbox controls the display of the icon for the RSS feed for the module. When the icon is clicked, DotNetNuke displays the RSS feed for this module. The URL of this feed is targeted by a visitor's RSS reader so that they are notified when new content is posted to the module. Internet Explorer 7 has an integrated subscription feature where visitors can view an RSS feed and click a button on the same page in the browser to subscribe to the feed.

❑ **Module Container.** This drop-down list displays the name of the container that is configured for the given module. You can use this field to change the assigned container.

If the module does not have a container specified, DotNetNuke uses a specific hierarchy to determine which container should be used to wrap a module. DotNetNuke examines the Module Container field in each of the following locations using this order to identify the appropriate container:

1. Module Settings

2. Page Settings

3. Site Settings

4. Host Settings

5. `Image Header - Color Background.ascx` of the DNN-Blue skin

Therefore, if no container is specified at any level, the container is set to the `Image Header - Color Background.ascx` container, as this is a hard-coded value in DotNetNuke. If a container is specified at both the Page Settings level and the Site Settings level, then the Page Settings container specification will take precedence and display on the page.

Similar to the skin administration page, this field also contains a hyperlink to preview the selected container file before it is actually applied. When the preview hyperlink is clicked, DotNetNuke launches another browser window and includes the name of the container to preview in the query string portion of the URL. You can see this value in the address bar of your browser.

Try It Out   Modernize the Default Container

In this exercise, you'll convert the default container to a slightly more standards compliant structure. These steps will improve the readability of the structure, make future changes easier, and simplify the Document Object Model.

Break out your favorite text editor. These steps will modify the default container file named `Image Header - Color Background.ascx` located in the following directory:

```
<install folder> \Portals\_default\Containers\DNN-Blue
```

1. Sometimes it's best just to start cutting. Open up this container file in your text editor, and launch another text editor window to hold some temporary text.

2. Find the following HTML table; it contains five controls near the top of the page. Copy these lines of text to your temporary window. Call this block #1.

```
<table width="100%" border="0" cellpadding="0" cellspacing="0">
    <tr>
        <td valign="middle" nowrap>
            <dnn:ACTIONS runat="server" id="dnnACTIONS" /></td>
        <td valign="middle" nowrap>
            <dnn:ICON runat="server" id="dnnICON" /></td>
```

```
                <td valign="middle" width="100%" nowrap> 
                   <dnn:TITLE runat="server" id="dnnTITLE" /></td>
                <td valign="middle" nowrap>
                   <dnn:VISIBILITY runat="server" id="dnnVISIBILITY" />
                   <dnn:ACTIONBUTTON5 runat="server" id="dnnACTIONBUTTON5"
                      CommandName="ModuleHelp.Action" DisplayIcon="True"
                      DisplayLink="False" /></td>
             </tr>
          </table>
```

3. Find the following HTML table; it holds the four action button controls near the bottom of the file. Copy these lines to the temporary window. Call this block #2.

```
<table width="100%" border="0" cellpadding="0" cellspacing="0">
    <tr>
        <td align="left" valign="middle" nowrap>
           <dnn:ACTIONBUTTON1 runat="server" id="dnnACTIONBUTTON1"
              CommandName="AddContent.Action" DisplayIcon="True"
              DisplayLink="True" /></td>
        <td align="right" valign="middle" nowrap>
           <dnn:ACTIONBUTTON2 runat="server" id="dnnACTIONBUTTON2"
              CommandName="SyndicateModule.Action" DisplayIcon="True"
              DisplayLink="False" /> 
           <dnn:ACTIONBUTTON3 runat="server" id="dnnACTIONBUTTON3"
              CommandName="PrintModule.Action" DisplayIcon="True"
              DisplayLink="False" /> 
           <dnn:ACTIONBUTTON4 runat="server" id="dnnACTIONBUTTON4"
             CommandName="ModuleSettings.Action" DisplayIcon="True"
                DisplayLink="False" /></td>
    </tr>
</table>
```

4. Now that you've copied the necessary elements from the container, delete all of the lines following the last register directive.

5. Enter the following HTML structure in the container file:

```
<div class="containermaster_blue">

    <!-- block 1 -->

    <!-- content pane -->
    <div id="ContentPane" runat="server" class="MyContentPane">
    </div>

    <hr class="containermaster_blue" />

    <!-- block 2 -->

</div>
```

6. Paste block #1 under the HTML comment identifying its position in the previous HTML structure.

7. Paste block #2 under the HTML comment identifying its position in the previous HTML structure.

8. Add a CSS class attribute to the HTML table tag in block #1. Give it the value of `containerrow1_blue`.

9. Open the file named `container.css` located in the same folder as the container. Find the CSS rules for the class named `containerrow1_blue`. Add a rule that sets the height to 32 pixels.

```
height:32px;
```

10. In the CSS file, create a new rule for the class named `MyContentPane`, and set the padding to zero pixels on the top and bottom and 6 pixels on the left and right.

```
.MyContentPane
{
    padding:0 6px;
}
```

11. Load the home page in the browser, and view the results of your changes.

Here is the entire container file after the changes have been applied:

```
<%@ Control language="vb" CodeBehind="~/admin/Containers/container.vb"
    AutoEventWireup="false" Explicit="True"
    Inherits="DotNetNuke.UI.Containers.Container" %>
<%@ Register TagPrefix="dnn" TagName="ACTIONS"
    Src="~/Admin/Containers/SolPartActions.ascx" %>
<%@ Register TagPrefix="dnn" TagName="ICON" Src="~/Admin/Containers/Icon.ascx" %>
<%@ Register TagPrefix="dnn" TagName="TITLE" Src="~/Admin/Containers/Title.ascx" %>
<%@ Register TagPrefix="dnn" TagName="VISIBILITY"
    Src="~/Admin/Containers/Visibility.ascx" %>
<%@ Register TagPrefix="dnn" TagName="ACTIONBUTTON1"
    Src="~/Admin/Containers/ActionButton.ascx" %>
<%@ Register TagPrefix="dnn" TagName="ACTIONBUTTON2"
    Src="~/Admin/Containers/ActionButton.ascx" %>
<%@ Register TagPrefix="dnn" TagName="ACTIONBUTTON3"
    Src="~/Admin/Containers/ActionButton.ascx" %>
<%@ Register TagPrefix="dnn" TagName="ACTIONBUTTON4"
    Src="~/Admin/Containers/ActionButton.ascx" %>
<%@ Register TagPrefix="dnn" TagName="ACTIONBUTTON5"
    Src="~/Admin/Containers/ActionButton.ascx" %>

<div class="containermaster_blue">

    <!-- block 1 -->
    <table width="100%" border="0" cellpadding="0" cellspacing="0"
        class="containerrow1_blue">
        <tr>
            <td valign="middle" nowrap>
                <dnn:ACTIONS runat="server" id="dnnACTIONS" /></td>
            <td valign="middle" nowrap>
                <dnn:ICON runat="server" id="dnnICON" /></td>
            <td valign="middle" width="100%" nowrap> 
                <dnn:TITLE runat="server" id="dnnTITLE" /></td>
            <td valign="middle" nowrap>
```

```
              <dnn:VISIBILITY runat="server" id="dnnVISIBILITY" />
              <dnn:ACTIONBUTTON5 runat="server" id="dnnACTIONBUTTON5"
                 CommandName="ModuleHelp.Action" DisplayIcon="True"
                 DisplayLink="False" /></td>
       </tr>
   </table>

   <!-- content pane -->
   <div id="ContentPane" runat="server" class="MyContentPane">
   </div>

   <hr class="containermaster_blue" />

   <!-- block 2 -->
   <table width="100%" border="0" cellpadding="0" cellspacing="0">
       <tr>
          <td align="left" valign="middle" nowrap>
             <dnn:ACTIONBUTTON1 runat="server" id="dnnACTIONBUTTON1"
                CommandName="AddContent.Action" DisplayIcon="True"
                DisplayLink="True" /></td>
          <td align="right" valign="middle" nowrap>
             <dnn:ACTIONBUTTON2 runat="server" id="dnnACTIONBUTTON2"
                CommandName="SyndicateModule.Action" DisplayIcon="True"
                DisplayLink="False" /> 
             <dnn:ACTIONBUTTON3 runat="server" id="dnnACTIONBUTTON3"
                CommandName="PrintModule.Action" DisplayIcon="True"
                DisplayLink="False" /> 
             <dnn:ACTIONBUTTON4 runat="server" id="dnnACTIONBUTTON4"
               CommandName="ModuleSettings.Action" DisplayIcon="True"
                  DisplayLink="False" /></td>
       </tr>
   </table>
</div>
```

How It Works

The page rendered in your browser should be very similar to the original file. You've managed to remove three table rows from the container and taken some steps to remove clutter from the HTML.

Of course some XHTML purists can spot some inconsistencies in the prior block of code, but the point of the exercise is to get you thinking about methods to move HTML into a standards compliance mode, not to beat you into submission over it. Now, hopefully, you've a good idea of the opportunities you'll find to edit containers and the types of skills that are involved.

A Look at the Pros

If you're building a DotNetNuke site as a hobby or a small community project, you might not be aware of some helpful tools and tips that web professionals use every day. Because you'll soon be in the thick of it, this is a good place to make you aware of some great tools that provide a ton of value, regardless of the project size.

From a high-level perspective, you're about to enter a place where several files will be edited. This may be a short project or it may take several days to complete a design that fits your mood. You also might like to work in parallel with several skins under design at once, instead of completing one before moving to the next. A couple of methodologies and tool sets are available to you to keep you productive and provide a nice safety net.

Providing Proper Formatting

I find that it's easier to work with a file when its elements are properly nested under each parent. I use a standard of three blank characters for each level of indentation for my HTML files, web user controls, and even my C# code. Use whatever makes you happy; just be consistent.

You might open a file and discover a jumbled mess of HTML tags with few line breaks or inconsistent nesting. This is difficult to read. The file can be quickly formatted through a feature available in most popular text editors. In the menu bar of Visual Web Developer, click Edit, Advanced, Format Document to format a file automatically. Do this with every file you create or review. Each file has to be formatted properly. If it is not, you'll waste your time trying to discover the intent of the developer instead of focusing on the real challenge.

As a nice extra feature in Visual Web Developer, you can specify that `<td>` tags be followed by two line breaks instead of one. This makes a long page with a couple of nested tables much easier to read. Play around with the Text Editor settings available under the Tools, Options menu item in Visual Web Developer. Use what works for your eye.

Using Version Control

If you're doing any kind of useful software development for your business, hobby, or community you should be versioning your files. If anyone is depending on the software and websites you modify, you need a way to track changes. While file versioning software is well outside the scope of this book, I encourage you to explore methods to find a system that works for you.

If this topic of version control is completely new to you, I recommend you check out Subversion, a free, open source file versioning system available at `http://subversion.tigris.org/`. It's a great program that can run on your laptop or on a central server and provide easy file versioning for your project. It's an amazing tool, and it deserves some of your attention (unless you already have a version control tool in place).

Comparing File Comparison Utilities

The need for file comparison happens frequently, especially on multiperson teams. Even if you work alone, you'll want to know what changes were made to a file three weeks ago. There are some great utilities to solve this challenge, and I'll recommend two if you don't already have a favorite.

TortoiseSVN is a free Windows client program that provides a graphical user interface to a Subversion file repository. Bundled with the program is a great file comparison utility. It shows both files on the screen and highlights rows and characters that don't match. It's simple and fast. The download can be found at `http://tortoisesvn.tigris.org`.

If you want to take it up a notch, Scooter Software offers an inexpensive file comparison utility named BeyondCompare. This application has a ton of features, and is one of the best I've seen for this task. It can compare files, directories, and FTP sites. This download can be found at www.scootersoftware.com.

Exploring Skin Objects

Earlier in this chapter, you took a look at the logo and banner skin objects. There are plenty more in the default installation of DotNetNuke and oodles more available online for free or a small fee. In this section, you'll see more of the skin objects that come in the box.

Exploring Standard Skin Objects

The following table lists some interesting skin objects that are installed with DotNetNuke. You can try them out by adding the register directive to the top of a skin file, and then adding an instance of the web user control to the page. This is similar to how the other skin objects are used in a file.

Skin Object	Description
Breadcrumb.ascx	Displays a series of hyperlinks that form a breadcrumb to the current page. This is a common method of informing users where they are, especially if a search engine dropped them in the middle of a large site.
Copyright.ascx	Displays the text in the Copyright field on the Site Settings page. This field is in the Other Settings section.
CurrentDate.ascx	Displays the current date, which is helpful for applications where users have questions about the data on the screen. This field can help pinpoint issues with data that depend on the time of day.
DotNetNuke.ascx	Displays the DotNetNuke copyright along with a link back to www.DotNetNuke.com.
Help.ascx	Displays a mailto: hyperlink on a page. Visitors can click this and quickly send an e-mail to the portal administrator if they have questions or issues with a particular page on the site.
HostName.ascx	Displays a hyperlink to the configured URL in the Host Details section of the Hosting Settings page. This is useful to inform visitors of the parent portal when they're browsing a child portal in DotnetNuke.
Language.ascx	Displays a drop-down list control of the languages installed on DotNetNuke. If only one language is installed, then the control is not visible. Additional language packs are available on the DotNetNuke website. The language packs can be installed on the Admin, Languages page or the Host, Languages pages.

Skin Object	Description
Links.ascx	By default, this skin object shows a list of links at the same level as the given page. This is a helpful control to place opposite of the primary navigation, such as the bottom of the page, to give visitors an easy method of finding other pages after they are done reading content on the current page.
Login.ascx	Displays a login hyperlink if the visitor is not authenticated; otherwise it displays a logout hyperlink.
Privacy.ascx	Displays the localized hyperlink text to the privacy statement. The hyperlink text is defined in the language editor available from the menu bar by selecting Admin, Languages and clicking the Language Editor hyperlink at the bottom of the page. On the language editor page, expand the nodes for Local Resources, Admin, Skins, App_LocalResources, Privacy.ascx to see the form that allows the text of the hyperlink to be edited. This is the technology that allows the word "Privacy Statement" to be translated to another language. The actual privacy statement is stored in the Global Resources node on this page.
Terms.ascx	This skin object operates much like the Privacy skin object to display the terms and conditions for use of the website.
TreeViewMenu.ascx	This control can be exchanged for the SolPartMenu skin object in order to display the menu vertically in a hierarchical format. This menu format works well for larger sites that need expansion for an unknown number of pages such as a corporate intranet.
User.ascx	Displays a hyperlink to the Register page if the visitor is not authenticated, otherwise it displays a link to the profile page for the user.

Using House of Nuke Skin Objects

One of my favorite DotNetNuke skin objects, available for free online, is the HouseMenu Module available on the House of Nuke website, located at http://houseofnuke.com. The default menu in DotNetNuke is a table that adds a lot of HTML tags and complexity to the Document Object Model. This control produces the same labels and hyperlinks, but as an unordered list. This list is easy to style with CSS and has a small footprint on the web page. Try downloading the skin object menu and installing it on a test portal to see how you like it.

Try It Out   Insert the TreeViewMenu Skin Object

As a prerequisite, create a default installation of the DotNetNuke system. Rather than simply selecting the skin file with the vertical menu in the DNN-Blue skin, you will make it by hand. It's not too much harder than selecting the skin from the drop-down list. This exercise will edit the file named `Horizontal Menu - Fixed Width.ascx` located in the following directory:

```
<install folder>\Portals\_default\Skins\DNN-Blue
```

1. Open the skin file `Horizontal Menu - Fixed Width.ascx` in your favorite text editor.

2. Locate the menu skin object in the file:

```
<dnn:MENU runat="server" id="dnnMENU" />
```

3. Remove the skin object from the file by pressing Ctrl+X to cut the text and place it in your clipboard. Enter a nonbreaking space entity reference in its place to preserve the skin's format:

```
 
```

4. Paste the menu skin object after the opening table cell tag of the LeftPane and insert an attribute named level with a value of root.

```
<td class="leftpane" id="leftpane" runat="server" valign="top" align="center">
    <dnn:MENU runat="server" id="dnnMENU" level="root" />
</td>
```

5. Now that the instance skin object is in place, change the source of the web user control by editing the register directive. Find the register directive for the menu skin object at the top of the file.

```
<%@ Register TagPrefix="dnn" TagName="MENU"
    Src="~/Admin/Skins/SolPartMenu.ascx" %>
```

6. Modify the attribute `Src` to point to the treeview skin object.

```
<%@ Register TagPrefix="dnn" TagName="MENU"
    Src="~/Admin/Skins/treeviewmenu.ascx" %>
```

7. Refresh your browser and view the results.

How It Works

The skin is referring to the treeview skin object, and the control has been configured to display pages at the root level. Figure 4-8 shows the contents of the hierarchical menu structure when you are logged in as the host account.

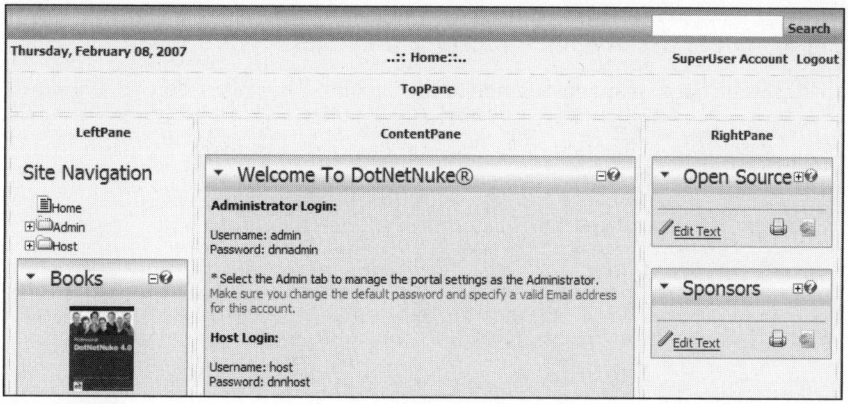

Figure 4-8

Summary

This chapter provided a detailed look at the physical makeup of a skin file and its constituent parts. A skin displayed on a DotNetNuke web page comprises a physical skin file, known as a web user control in ASP.Net terms, and a physical container file, which is also a web user control.

Both the skin file and the container file have their own CSS file that holds presentation rules for how to render various tags and classes within the given page. You took a few steps toward a standards based design and explained some benefits that come out of such an effort. Skin files on their own are simply HTML markup and panes. Interesting additions can be skin objects that are installed by default or are downloaded from the Internet.

You covered a lot of ground in this chapter, and you're well on your way to creating custom skin files. In the next chapter, you do exactly that. You also take a longer look at some HTML and CSS features that can enable some slick designs and keep the maintenance hassles to a minimum (when the inevitable changes are requested).

Exercises

1. What's the difference between a control directive and a register directive?

2. What tags are commonly used as panes in a skin?

3. What changes are necessary to convert an ordinary HTML `<div>` tag into a server control?

4. How could you insert all hyperlinks to sibling pages which share the same parent page and never worry about broken links were the site map to change over time?

5. What benefits are derived from standards compliant HTML markup?

6. If the Module Settings object were omitted from a container, how might an administrator still access the module settings page?

5

Creating Custom Skins

Now that the preliminary items have been addressed, it's time to discuss the steps for developing a custom skin from the ground up. In the last chapter, the components of an existing skin were examined and modified to see some of the moving parts. Now you'll create one of your own.

The first prerequisite for creating a custom skin is an idea for a design. This can take the form of a large JPG file that mocks up the entire page in the browser, or something less sophisticated like a piece of paper with some scribbling. The important thing is to identify a goal for the skin to achieve with an acceptable level of risk. If your client has to approve the site before they cut the final check, you're probably less willing to accept risk in the design.

The design is the inspiration for constructing the skin and container files, as well as the CSS files used by both items. This chapter outlines a couple of approaches for constructing each element of a skin and discusses some tools useful for solving problems that are bound to spring up along the way.

Considering Design

The process starts with the idea for a web page. Give some thought to what the website should look like before you get knee-deep in HTML and CSS. The design isn't likely to consider every possible feature on a web page, but it is beneficial to spend some time in creative space before you get your angle bracket hammer and start pounding out some HTML.

In this chapter, you work with a custom graphic composition that I constructed with my favorite graphics program, `Paint.Net`. This Windows application is available for free at `www.getpaint.net`.

> *If you use this application on a regular basis, as I do, then I recommend you click the Donate item in the Help menu and let this team know how much you appreciate them.*

I usually spend my time building databases, business logic, and web controls and implementing web designs, so this is about as close as I get to pure graphic design in my daily pursuits. I'm fortunate enough to work with some excellent graphic artists. They work with the client and arrive at a graphic composition after a professional consultation. Then, I sit with them to discuss how the web design should flow and articulate any special considerations for dynamic content or interactive behavior. Figure 5-1 is the composition.

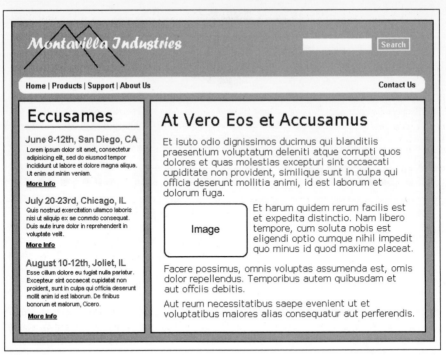

Figure 5-1

The roles of a copy writer and a graphic designer are distinct and intricately connected at the same time. Often, these roles are performed by the same person. In more specialized companies, these roles are separated, and two (or more) people collaborate on the project.

Graphic compositions created by a designer often use "Lorem ipsum" text as a substitute for copy. It provides the illusion of actual text because it exhibits a similarity to English, but it keeps the reader focused on the design. If actual content were used, and it weren't fully baked, the reviewer might be distracted by copy instead of giving feedback on the web page layout, font, and color choices. The website `http://lipsum.com/` gives an interesting story of how this usage came about.

Figure 5-1 shows a simple design, but it has the quality of bearing little resemblance to the familiar DNN-Blue skin. It displays a logo in the top left and a search feature in the top right. This particular website has few top-level pages, and they are listed in the primary navigation bar. The Contact Us hyperlink is separated from the rest of the menu items. This design is implemented in two panes. On this particular page, an Event module, Announcement module, or Text/HTML module could produce the content in the narrow column. The wide column is probably best implemented with a Text/HTML module.

How to Build Skin Files

In this section, you'll implement the design in Figure 5-1 a couple of ways. First, you'll use a plain HTML file as the skin. This technique might be more approachable for folks who are using ASP.Net for the first time. Then, you'll make another pass at the skin by implementing it as an ASP.Net web user control. In either case, the skin will become an `.ascx` file when it's used on a page; it's just a matter of deciding when to make the leap.

Building an HTML Skin

Creating skins from HTML files was introduced in Chapter 3. This method combines an HTML file, a CSS file, and an XML file. The XML file contains values for the embedded tokens found in the HTML file. You'll learn all about where to put these files in just a bit. Using the HTML file methodology for building skins can produce a trim and easy-to-read HTML file, which are attractive qualities, to be sure.

Remember that skins use skin objects to provide core DotNetNuke features. Skin objects are references to ASP.Net web user controls that provide small, independent features for a skin. Because an HTML file is not as powerful as an ASP.Net web user control, the skin developer uses an XML file to bridge this gap and to provide all of the attributes, or parameters, of the skin objects to DotNetNuke.

The following parts of this section explain the process of creating an HTML skin, including the `.html` file, the `.xml` file and the `.css` file. At the end, you'll build your own HTML skin in the Try It Out section.

Creating the HTML File

The tactical steps of building an HTML skin start with creating an empty file with an `.html` extension. The name of this file is also the name that will appear in the drop-down list in the DotNetNuke Skin administration system.

The following HTML block shows a simple table-based structure that implements the design presented at the start of this chapter. I've chosen to use HTML tables in the following skin to set the focus on the skin creation process as a whole instead of getting sidetracked by features specific to CSS and table-free designs. An electronic version of this HTML can also be found in the download section for this book.

```html
<table cellpadding="0" cellspacing="0" id="MySimpleTableSkin">
    <tr>
        <td id="ControlPanel" runat="server"></td>
    </tr>
    <tr>
        <td>

            <table cellpadding="0" cellspacing="0" id="bannerTable">
                <tr>
                    <td id="logoCell">[LOGO]</td>
                    <td id="searchCell">[SEARCH]</td>
                </tr>
            </table>

        </td>
    </tr>
    <tr>
        <td id="menuTableWrapperCell">

            <table cellpadding="0" cellspacing="0" id="menuTable">
                <tr>
                    <td id="menuWrapper">[MENU]</td>
```

```
                <td id="contactUsWrapper">
                    <a href="#" id="ContactUsLink">Contact Us</a>
                </td>
            </tr>
        </table>
    </td>
</tr>
<tr>
    <td id="contentTableWrapperCell">

        <table cellpadding="0" cellspacing="0" id="contentTable">
            <tr>
                <td id="PromoPane" runat="server" class="PromoPane"></td>
                <td class="SpacerPane"> </td>
                <td id="ContentPane" runat="server" class="ContentPane"></td>
            </tr>
        </table>
    </td>
</tr>
<tr>
    <td id="footerTableWrapperCell">
        <table cellpadding="0" cellspacing="0" id="footerTable">
            <tr>
                <td id="copyrightCell">
                    [COPYRIGHT]
                    [TERMS]
                    [PRIVACY]
                </td>
                <td id="userCell">
                    [USER]
                    [LOGIN]
                </td>
            </tr>
            <tr>
                <td colspan="2">
                    [DOTNETNUKE]
                </td>
            </tr>
        </table>
    </td>
</tr>
</table>
```

The outermost layer of this simple table-based structure is a series of five table rows that each have only one table cell. Some of the cells in the outer table hold nested HTML tables with multiple columns. The keywords surrounded by square brackets are tokens that refer to DotNetNuke skin objects. Any configurable values for these tokens are found in the skin.xml file located in the same folder as the .html file.

There are several ways to implement this design in HTML. This approach uses a single-column layout in the outer table because there is no clear shared column boundary among the rows. The column widths of the top row, with the logo and the search field, are different from the column widths of the PromoPane and ContentPane fields. Therefore, a multicolumn layout in the outer table would give more grief than relief.

The tenth line of the skin file makes use of the Logo skin object discussed in Chapter 4. The downloadable code for this chapter contains a sample logo of a fictional company named Montavilla Industries. This logo can be uploaded to a DotNetNuke installation using the Site Settings administration page. Once the logo is set for the site, any skin using the logo skin object will display the configured logo image.

Given the constraint of using an HTML table to implement the design, the structure and style are separated as much as possible. While the table-based layout creates a more complex Document Object Model than the <div> tag-based layouts that are popular with many design folks today, the table-based approach does limit the markup to the HTML table tag family such as <table>, <tr>, and <td> and simple attributes such as id, border, cellpadding, cellspacing, class, and colspan. This layout relies on the CSS file to provide the design elements for the font, color, width, padding, margin, and background image choices. The HTML code is easier to read than files with unnecessary HTML attributes that go beyond the task of providing a simple structure. The content exists in DotNetNuke modules wrapped by containers. Therefore, a skin file is focused on providing only structure for a page. There are few opportunities for a skin file to contain <h1> tags and <p> tags.

Creating the XML File

For the most part, the table-based skin implementation uses the default skin object parameters. In order to show how the parameter configuration technique works, one customization is provided in the skin.xml file. So far, you've heard how this file contains the configuration values for the tokens; now you'll see how it's really done. Take a look at the following XML file; you'll dissect it next. The goal of the following XML file is to assign an attribute to the HTML emitted by a particular skin object. This attribute can be targeted with CSS and thereby enable customization through any number of CSS rules added to the CSS file.

```
<Objects>
    <Object>
        <Token>[USER]</Token>
        <Settings>
            <Setting>
                <Name>CssClass</Name>
                <Value>MyUserSkinObjectCssClass</Value>
            </Setting>
        </Settings>
    </Object>
</Objects>
```

The previous XML block has a simple format. The <Objects> element is the root node of this XML document. It contains one or more <Object> elements. In this case, you're only customizing one skin object; therefore only one <Object> element is in the XML file.

The <Object> element has two child elements: the <Token> element and the <Settings> element. The <Token> element maps the given <Object> element to the token embedded in the .html skin file. The <Settings> element contains all of the configuration values in a series of one or more <Setting> elements. In this case, there is only one setting named CssClass, which maps to a property of the same name in the User skin object. This property is set to a value of MyUserSkinObjectCssClass.

If the previous XML configuration file did not include a setting for the CssClass property, the User skin object would emit a default CSS class of SkinObject. The previous XML configuration value overrides this default value and applies a custom CSS class.

Creating the CSS File

If you view the HTML source code of any DotNetNuke page in your browser, you'll see a couple of references to CSS files there. The topmost `<link>` tag in the HTML source code refers to the `default.css` file.

A basic characteristic of CSS gives a subsequent CSS rule the opportunity to override any CSS rule that preceded it. The overridden CSS rule could be in the same CSS file or another file — so long as it physically exists above the CSS rule that is overriding it.

Therefore, in your effort to customize the presentation of this skin object, you could simply insert a rule for the `SkinObject` class in the CSS file for your skin and eliminate the need for a `skin.xml` file to modify the CSS class used by the skin object. You don't want to override every instance of the `SkinObject` CSS class in the page. The goal is only to modify the display of this skin object. Other skin objects on the page might use the same CSS class. Therefore, it makes sense to change the CSS class applied to the User skin object. The CSS file for this skin contains a CSS rule for the custom class named `MyUserSkinObjectCssClass`. The XML file assigns this class to the User skin object.

The following CSS file contains the rules for `SkinObject` CSS class. Open it up in your favorite text editor and take a look at it.

```
<install folder>\Portals\_default\default.css
```

When you open the previous CSS file, look for the CSS selector that targets HTML tags having a class attribute of `SkinObject`. The following CSS block shows the default rules for this class:

```
.SkinObject
{
    font-weight: bold;
    font-size: 8.5pt;
    color: #003366;
    font-family: Tahoma, Arial, Helvetica;
    text-decoration: none;
}
```

The following CSS block contains the CSS rules for your customized User skin object. This rule belongs in the CSS file for your skin. You can see the previous default CSS rules use the longer format for specifying CSS font properties. The CSS properties in the subsequent CSS block use the shorter format where several space-delimited values appear in a single line to modify the font. For more info on the shorthand technique, take a look at *Beginning CSS: Cascading Style Sheets for Web Design*, 2nd Edition by Richard York (Wiley Publishing, Inc., 2007).

```
a.MyUserSkinObjectCssClass
{
    font:normal normal bold 8pt verdana;
    color:#EEE;
}
```

The following CSS block includes the complete CSS file for this skin. The HTML skin file that you looked at earlier contains several targetable locations including id attributes and class attributes. The hash character in the following CSS selectors refers to id attributes in the HTML. The id attribute values of HTML elements should be unique on a page. A period character identifies class attribute values in the HTML.

Multiple HTML elements on a page can have the same class attribute value. Flip between the following CSS block and the previous HTML block and match up the CSS rules with the target location in the HTML.

```
*
{
    margin:0;
    padding:0;
}
table#MySimpleTableSkin
{
    width:780px;
    background-color:#8794E7;
    margin:8px;
}
table#bannerTable
{
    width:100%;
}
td#logoCell
{
    padding:6px 0 0 6px;
}
td#searchCell
{
    text-align:right;
    vertical-align:top;
    padding:20px 30px 0 0;
}
td#searchCell a
{
    border:solid 2px #FFF;
    padding:0 10px 0 10px;
    font:normal normal small-caps 10pt Arial;
    color:#FFF;
}

td#menuTableWrapperCell
{
    padding:10px 0 10px 10px;
}

table#menuTable
{
    background:transparent url(menu-background.jpg) no-repeat;
    width:750px;
    height:36px;
}

td#contentTableWrapperCell
{
    padding:10px 0 10px 10px;
}
td#contactUsWrapper
{
```

```
        text-align:right;
        padding:0 20px 0 0;
}

table#contentTable
{
        width:750px;
}
td.PromoPane
{
        width:240px;
        vertical-align:top;
}
td.SpacerPane
{
        width:10px;
}
td.ContentPane
{
        width:500px;
        vertical-align:top;
}
td#footerTableWrapperCell
{
        padding:10px 0 10px 10px;
}
table#footerTable
{
        width:750px;
        margin:6px 0;
}

td#userCell
{
        text-align:right;
}

a.MyUserSkinObjectCssClass
{
        font:normal normal bold 8pt verdana;
        color:#EEE;
}
/* -----------
    MENU Styles
    ----------- */

.MainMenu_MenuBar
{
            cursor: pointer;
            cursor: hand;
            background-color: Transparent;
}
.MainMenu_MenuItem, .MainMenu_MenuItemSel, a#ContactUsLink
```

```
{
    border: #cad5ea 0px solid;
    cursor: pointer;
    cursor: hand;
    color: #000000;
    font:normal normal bold 100% Arial;
    background-color: Transparent;
    text-decoration:none;
}
.MainMenu_MenuItemSel, a#ContactUsLink:hover
{
    color:#DDD;
}
```

The CSS rules in the previous code block start by declaring all elements to have a common margin and padding value of zero with the asterisk selector. Various browsers can have their own idea of an appropriate default margin for an element so it's best to zero out this value early so each browser can display a uniform value. The next batch of lines provides some ordinary style settings such as width, margins, padding, colors, font treatments, and a background image. The last batch of CSS rules modifies the default DotNetNuke menu control.

It is safe for the skin file to use ID attributes, and the CSS file can use ID attributes as selectors because a page can have only one skin. A page can have multiple containers, so containers must use CSS classes as selectors instead of the ID attribute.

Try It Out   Install a Custom HTML Skin

Now that you have a good understanding of the contents of the files for this simple table-based skin, try packaging the custom skin into a zip file and uploading it into your DotNetNuke installation.

Start by downloading the files for this chapter if you haven't already done so. Find the collection of files for the HTML version of the skin. For this exercise, you should have the following files in a single folder on your computer visible in Windows Explorer:

- ❑   menu-background.jpg
- ❑   SimpleTableSkin.html
- ❑   SimpleTableSkin.jpg
- ❑   skin.css
- ❑   skin.xml
- ❑   thumbnail_SimpleTableSkin.jpg

1. Create a new zip file in this folder. Right-click on a blank space in Windows Explorer and select New, New Compressed (zipped) Folder from the pop-up window. Name this zip file `skins.zip`.

2. Drag all of the files listed in Step 1 into the zip file named `skins.zip`.

3. Create another zip file. Right-click on a blank space in Windows Explorer and select New, New Compressed (zipped) Folder from the pop-up window. Name this new zip file `MyHtmlSkin.zip`.

4. Drag the `skins.zip` file into the `MyHtmlSkin.zip` file. The skin package is now complete and you're ready to upload it into DotNetNuke.

5. Log into your DotNetNuke installation using the Host account.

6. On the menu bar, select Host, Skins. The browser navigates to the Skin Administration page.

7. Click Upload Skin located at the bottom of the page. This navigates the browser to the Install Skin Package page.

8. Click the Browse button on the Install Skin Package page and locate the zip file you created in Step 4 named `MyHtmlSkin.zip`.

9. Click the Save File hyperlink next to the Browse button to install the skin. You should see a series of progress statements flash by in your browser. Click Return located at the top or the bottom of the page to return to the Skin administration page.

10. In the Skins drop-down list, select the item named `MyHtmlSkin`. This will load the thumbnail image of the new skin you uploaded into the Skins box.

11. Create a new test page in your DotNetNuke installation and configure the page to use the new skin. When you create the page, set the Page Skin field to the item named `MyHtmlSkin - SimpleTableSkin`.

12. Drop a Text/HTML module into the PromoPane and the ContentPane of your test page to get a feel for the structure of the skin.

Figure 5-2 shows the partial implementation of the skin. This DotNetNuke site has a custom logo set on the Site Settings administration page. Each skin that uses the Logo skin object will show the custom logo. You haven't defined the custom containers yet, so the default containers look a bit out of place with this custom skin.

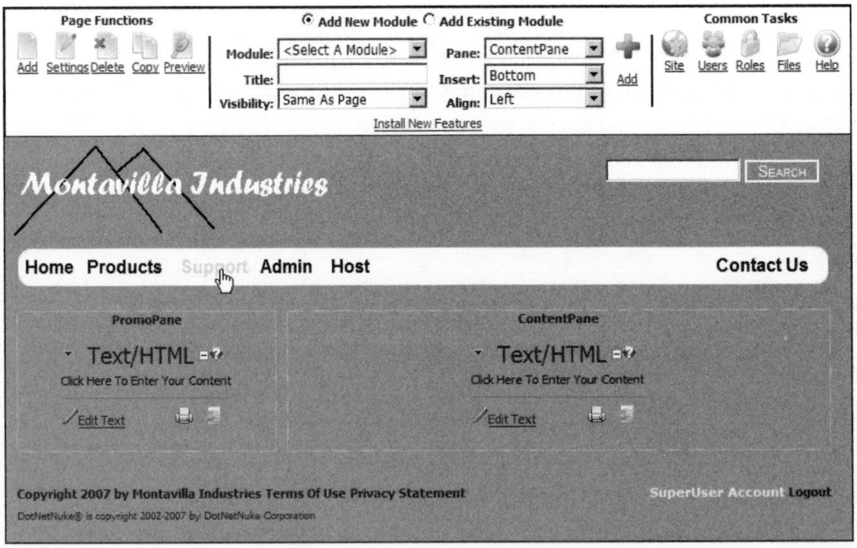

Figure 5-2

How It Works

Looking at the HTML source of a page in your browser makes it easy to see where the skin leveraged some HTML tricks to implement some parts of the design. The design called for a Contact Us link to appear way out to the right. Therefore, the skin takes the liberty of a hardcoded menu item in the skin with a specific ID attribute to target with CSS. You'll modify the `href` attribute of the hyperlink, later. The rest of the items function as expected in the menu bar. The skin also uses a shortcut to implement the rounded edges of the menu bar. The design established a firm width, so the skin uses a background image created with the rounded corner tool in `Paint.Net` and wires it up to the menu using CSS.

When the skin file was uploaded to DotNetNuke, the `.html` file was converted into an ASP.Net web user control. Open up the folder containing the skin in DotNetNuke and examine it for yourself. You should see a file named `SimpleTableSkin.ascx` next to the original `.html` file of the same name. Open up this new web user control in your favorite text editor and compare it with the `.html` file. Each of the tokens is expanded into instances of web user controls. Figure 5-3 shows the contents of the new skin folder in DotNetNuke.

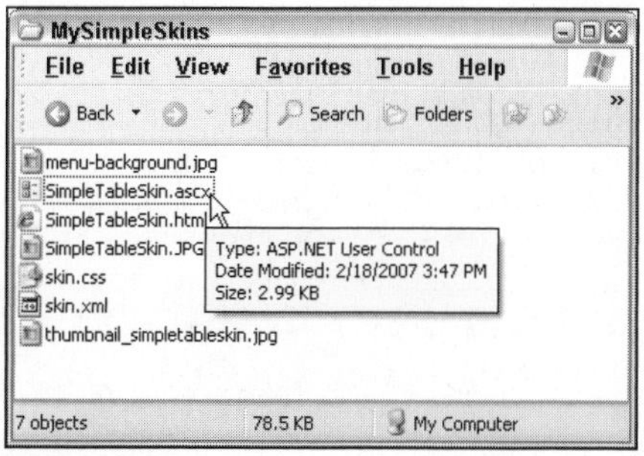

Figure 5-3

This activity helps shed some light on how HTML skin files with tokens are converted into their equivalent web user control files for use in DotNetNuke. The original XML file and HTML file are still there for evaluation and comparison, just as they are in the default DNN-Blue skin.

Now that the skin has been converted into an `.ascx` file, any changes to the `.html` file inside DotNetNuke will be ignored. There is no persistent connection between the `.html` file and the `.ascx` file. If any changes to the skin are required, the developer has the choice of making additional changes to the `.html` file on his or her local computer, and then repackaging the files and uploading them again into DotNetNuke. The developer can also simply open the `.ascx` file directly in his or her favorite text editor and start making the changes immediately.

DotNetNuke can be installed and used with a variety of tools on Windows as described in Chapter 2. Because it is an ASP.Net application and the skin makes use of dynamic features in ASP.Net, I recommend that you learn the `.html` file technique of making skins, but adopt the web user control method as your primary technique. If you're new to ASP.Net development, it might take a few minutes to understand the subtle differences between the two types of development, but you'll be better off in the long run because it's easier to edit the files as `.ascx` files than to package and install them over and over.

As in real life, the previous graphic composition omitted a few points that had to be dealt with in the web page. This is likely to happen when the graphic designer role and the DotNetNuke developer role are executed by different people or when one person does the same job days apart, which is what happened to me. The design did not indicate where the login and username feature should appear. Plus, it omitted the copyright and privacy policy that is customary in the footer. If you're working with a graphic artist, it helps to have a protocol for dealing with issues like this before you start. It'll help smooth out any hard feelings about implementing their design later on.

Building an ASCX Skin

Take a look at the differences in the web user control version of the skin file. Web user controls have a file type extension of .ascx. The XML file is not used in this technique because parameters for the skin objects can be written directly inside the .ascx file.

The following code displays the .ascx version of the same skin created in the previous section:

```
<%@ Control language="vb" CodeBehind="~/admin/Skins/skin.vb"
    AutoEventWireup="false" Explicit="True"
Inherits="DotNetNuke.UI.Skins.Skin" %>
<%@ Register TagPrefix="dnn" TagName="LOGO" Src="~/Admin/Skins/Logo.ascx" %>
<%@ Register TagPrefix="dnn" TagName="SEARCH" Src="~/Admin/Skins/Search.ascx" %>
<%@ Register TagPrefix="dnn" TagName="MENU" Src="~/Admin/Skins/SolPartMenu.ascx" %>
<%@ Register TagPrefix="dnn" TagName="COPYRIGHT"
    Src="~/Admin/Skins/Copyright.ascx" %>
<%@ Register TagPrefix="dnn" TagName="TERMS" Src="~/Admin/Skins/Terms.ascx" %>
<%@ Register TagPrefix="dnn" TagName="PRIVACY" Src="~/Admin/Skins/Privacy.ascx" %>
<%@ Register TagPrefix="dnn" TagName="USER" Src="~/Admin/Skins/User.ascx" %>
<%@ Register TagPrefix="dnn" TagName="LOGIN" Src="~/Admin/Skins/Login.ascx" %>
<%@ Register TagPrefix="dnn" TagName="DOTNETNUKE"
    src="~/Admin/Skins/DotNetNuke.ascx" %>
<table border="0" cellpadding="0" cellspacing="0" id="MySimpleTableSkin">
    <tr>
        <td id="ControlPanel" runat="server"></td>
    </tr>
    <tr>
        <td>

            <table border="0" cellpadding="0" cellspacing="0" id="bannerTable">
                <tr>
                    <td id="logoCell"><dnn:LOGO runat="server" id="dnnLOGO" /></td>
                    <td id="searchCell"><dnn:SEARCH runat="server" id="dnnSEARCH"/></td>
                </tr>
            </table>

        </td>
    </tr>
    <tr>
        <td id="menuTableWrapperCell">
```

```
            <table border="0" cellpadding="0" cellspacing="0" id="menuTable">
                <tr>
                    <td id="menuWrapper"><dnn:MENU runat="server" id="dnnMENU" /></td>
                    <td id="contactUsWrapper">
                        <a href="<%= SkinPath %>#" id="ContactUsLink">Contact Us</a>
                    </td>
                </tr>
            </table>


        </td>
    </tr>
    <tr>
        <td id="contentTableWrapperCell">
            <table border="0" cellpadding="0" cellspacing="0" id="contentTable">
                <tr>
                    <td id="PromoPane" runat="server" class="PromoPane"></td>
                    <td class="SpacerPane"> </td>
                    <td id="ContentPane" runat="server" class="ContentPane"></td>
                </tr>
            </table>


        </td>
    </tr>
    <tr>
        <td id="footerTableWrapperCell">

            <table border="0" cellpadding="0" cellspacing="0" id="footerTable">
                <tr>
                    <td id="copyrightCell">
                        <dnn:COPYRIGHT runat="server" id="dnnCOPYRIGHT" />
                        <dnn:TERMS runat="server" id="dnnTERMS" />
                        <dnn:PRIVACY runat="server" id="dnnPRIVACY" />
                    </td>
                    <td id="userCell">
                        <dnn:USER runat="server" id="dnnUSER"
                            CssClass="MyUserSkinObjectCssClass" />
                        <dnn:LOGIN runat="server" id="dnnLOGIN" />
                    </td>
                </tr>
                <tr>
                    <td colspan="2">
                        <dnn:DOTNETNUKE runat="server" id="dnnDOTNETNUKE" />
                    </td>
                </tr>
            </table>


        </td>
    </tr>
</table>
```

This version of the skin is similar to the HTML version. This web user control version includes register directives at the top so it can embed instances of external web user controls. I find it easier to deal with skin object customizations when they're specified directly in the skin file, as opposed to an XML file. You can see the assignment of the property named CssClass on the User skin object near the bottom code, about 14 lines up from the end of the file, as shown in the following code block:

```
<dnn:USER runat="server" id="dnnUSER"
    CssClass="MyUserSkinObjectCssClass" />
```

Try It Out   Install a Custom Web User Control Skin

Find the collection of files for the ascx version of the simple table skin. For this exercise, you should have the following files in a single folder on your computer visible in Windows Explorer:

❑   menu-background.jpg

❑   SimpleTableSkin.ascx

❑   SimpleTableSkin.jpg

❑   skin.css

❑   thumbnail_SimpleTableSkin.jpg

1.   In the same folder, create a new zip file named skins.zip.

2.   Drag all of the files listed into the skins.zip file.

3.   Create a new zip file named MyASCXSkin.zip.

4.   Drag the skins.zip file into the MyASCXSkin.zip file.

5.   Log into your DotNetNuke installation using the Host account.

6.   On the menu bar, select Host, Skins. The browser navigates to the Skin Administration page.

7.   Click Upload Skin located at the bottom of the page. This navigates the browser to the Install Skin Package page.

8.   Click the Browse button on the Install Skin Package page and locate the zip folder you created named MyASCXSkin.zip.

9.   Click Save File next to the Browse button to install the skin. You should see a series of progress statements flash by in your browser. Click Return located at the top or the bottom of the page to return to the Skin administration page.

10.   In the Skins drop-down list, select the item named MyASCXSkin. This will load the thumbnail image of the new skin you uploaded into the Skins box.

11.   Create a new test page in your DotNetNuke installation and configure the page to use the new skin named MyASCXSkin - SimpleTableSkin in the Page Skin field.

12.   Drop a Text/HTML module into each pane on the page to get a feel for the structure of the skin.

How It Works

This method created and installed a skin that is identical to the skin from the last exercise. This time, you created the web user control yourself instead of using an HTML file with an XML file. This skin was applied to a test page on a local DotNetNuke instance used for testing.

Creating a skin in your favorite text editor and installing it in DotNetNuke will rarely be the end of the process, if ever. This task is just too complex to get right the first time. Creating custom skins will always involve some iteration. You might not see the parts that look wrong until a page is loaded up with real DotNetNuke modules. Once the problems are fixed, you'll be able to move onto aesthetic modifications to the skin.

It's important to include the CSS file in the initial skin package, even if it's currently sparse. DotNetNuke maintains an inventory of skin packages. If the CSS file is not present in the skin during the installation, DotNetNuke will ignore any CSS file dropped into the skin folder after installation. You can omit other types of files from the initial installation such as the full skin image file, the thumbnail version, as well as images used by the skin or the CSS file. Just make sure the skin installation package includes the web user control and the CSS file at a bare minimum.

Setting the Document Type Definition

Hopefully, it's becoming clear that the skin is the wrapper for a web page, and that the modules on a page are wrapped by containers. Modern skins and containers use CSS files for customizations of the font, color, position, and other aspects. One important item that has a big influence on how well a browser can apply CSS rules to the HTML is the Document Type Definition, also known as the DTD or *doctype*.

If a doctype exists in a page, it's found in the first line of text. The following doctype indicates the page is written in the HTML 4.01 Transitional format:

```
<!DOCTYPE html PUBLIC "-//W3C//DTD HTML 4.01 Transitional//EN"
    "http://www.w3.org/TR/html4/loose.dtd">
```

The doctype is often overlooked by developers. It seems like sites are frequently built with just one browser in mind — the developer's browser. It takes a good deal of time and discipline to verify that each page of the website renders well in four or five browsers. A program that tests for valid hyperlinks is easy to automate. The program scans a website for links, follows them, and reports any invalid links. Because the doctype affects the visual output of the page, testing it is a difficult task to automate.

The importance of the doctype becomes clear when you look at all of the versions of HTML, including HTML 3.2, HTML 4.01, and XHTML 1.0. Some versions also have specific flavors such as Strict, Transitional, and Frameset. Each one has a slightly different application of HTML rules.

When the doctype is explicitly stated, the browser renders a page in *Standards Compliance mode*. When the doctype is not explicitly stated, the browser goes into *Quirks mode* (an appropriate name). This is one reason modern browsers might display a page slightly distorted. For example, the margin around a `<div>` tag might be inconsistent in Internet Explorer and Firefox while these two are in Quirks mode. It's easier for a browser to render a page correctly if the web page developer actually tells the browser what type to use — clever, eh?

Figure 5-4 shows the Firefox browser reporting a page in Quirks mode. Figure 5-5 shows the same browser reporting a page in Standards Compliance mode. You can check the render mode of any page in Firefox by selecting Tools, Page Info in the browser's menu bar.

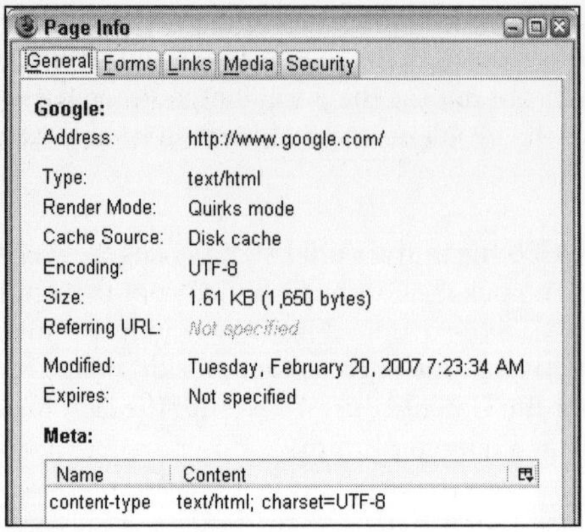

Figure 5-4

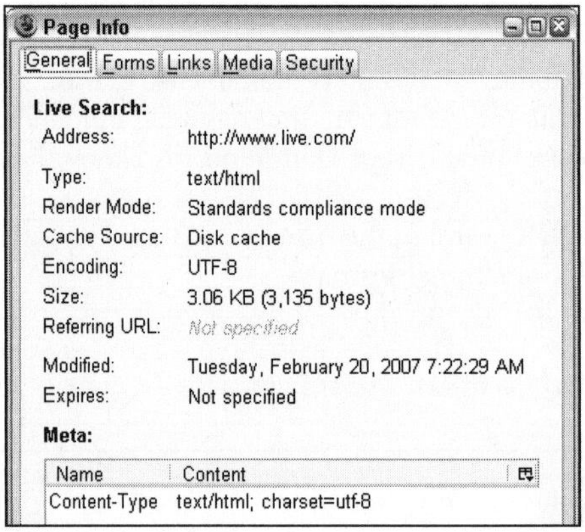

Figure 5-5

The standards organization that manages the various HTML specifications, the World Wide Web Consortium (W3C), has a great explanation of the doctype at this url: `www.w3.org/QA/Tips/Doctype`. Here's a brief excerpt from that web page:

> *Why specify a doctype? Because it defines which version of (X)HTML your document is actually using, and this is a critical piece of information needed by browsers or other tools processing the document.*
>
> *For example, specifying the doctype of your document allows you to use tools such as the Markup Validator to check the syntax of your (X)HTML (and hence discovers errors that may affect the way your page is rendered by various browsers). Such tools won't be able to work if they do not know what kind of document you are using.*
>
> *But the most important thing is that with most families of browsers, a doctype declaration will make a lot of guessing unnecessary, and will thus trigger a "standard" parsing mode, where the understanding (and, as a result, the display) of the document is not only faster, it is also consistent and free of any bad surprise that documents without doctype will create.*

DotNetNuke v4.4.0 included a new feature that permits the doctype to be specified with the skin file. In earlier versions, the `default.aspx` file in the web application root defined the doctype for the entire DotNetNuke installation. You were allowed to overwrite the existing doctype in `default.aspx` or replace it with a custom ASP.Net web user control. DotNetNuke v4.4.0 now has a web user control for this feature baked into the core.

The DotNetNuke change log that accounts for every change to the core system describes this feature briefly in Issue ID DNN-3623. It was reported and implemented by Cathal Connolly, a DotNetNuke Core Team Trustee and Security Manager.

The process for adding a skin specific doctype to DotNetNuke has a few simple steps. First, create a new file with your favorite text editor. Type a small bit of XML and the doctype to use. Then, save the XML file to your skin folder with a name that matches the skin and ends with `doctype.xml`. For example, if a skin were named `autumn.ascx`, the XML file should be named `autumn.doctype.xml`.

Now you have most of the information necessary to create the doctype XML file. This XML file containing the doctype value contains just one element, the root node, named `SkinDocType`. The content of this root node is the doctype to be used with the matching skin.

There's just one more facet of XML to cover. XML uses the angle bracket characters, < and >, to define elements and XML elements that have specific rules. What happens when the data enveloped by an XML element also contain angle bracket characters, such as doctype? The program parsing an XML file can't tell the difference between a doctype value and invalid XML; the parsing program will just throw an error when it encounters invalid XML. XML is a packaging methodology for data, and it includes a simple technique for dealing with data containing characters that would otherwise violate the XML rules.

An XML *character data section* contains — wait for it — character data, in an XML document. These character data do not need to adhere to the XML rules; therefore, they are good for holding nearly any set of characters. The XML parser ignores the content of the character data section. This feature is valuable for your needs to encapsulate the doctype inside an XML file. The doctype is not XML friendly because it contains angle brackets.

In an XML document, the character data section opens with `<![CDATA[` and ends with the characters `]]>`. The doctype goes inside these characters, and the entire CDATA section is ignored by the XML parser. The XML parser can retrieve the content of the CDATA section as one big chunk, but it doesn't try to validate it or do anything fancy. The following code is an example of an XML document that a skin can use to set the doctype to HTML 4.01 Transitional:

```
<SkinDocType><![CDATA[<!DOCTYPE html PUBLIC "-//W3C//DTD HTML 4.01
Transitional//EN" "http://www.w3.org/TR/html4/loose.dtd">]]></SkinDocType>
```

The previous XML document starts with a root node named `SkinDocType` and is immediately followed by a CDATA section. The content of the CDATA section is the doctype. Then, the CDATA section closes and the root node closes, too. The previous XML block wraps lines in this book, but your XML file should be a single-line file to ensure that you don't have any invalid line break characters in the doctype value.

The following code blocks show five common doctype values in use today. The syntax is a little cryptic, but you can easily identify the flavor of each doctype by examining the text after the letters DTD in each doctype value. For a time reference, the HTML 4.01 specification became a W3C recommendation December 24, 1999, and the XHTML 1.1 specification reached working draft status February 16, 2007.

```
<!DOCTYPE html PUBLIC "-//W3C//DTD HTML 4.01 Transitional//EN"
   "http://www.w3.org/TR/html4/loose.dtd">
```

```
<!DOCTYPE html PUBLIC "-//W3C//DTD HTML 4.01//EN"
   "http://www.w3.org/TR/html4/strict.dtd">
```

```
<!DOCTYPE html PUBLIC "-//W3C//DTD XHTML 1.0 Transitional//EN"
   "http://www.w3.org/TR/xhtml1/DTD/xhtml1-transitional.dtd">
```

```
<!DOCTYPE html PUBLIC "-//W3C//DTD XHTML 1.0 Strict//EN"
   "http://www.w3.org/TR/xhtml1/DTD/xhtml1-strict.dtd">
```

```
<!DOCTYPE html PUBLIC "-//W3C//DTD XHTML 1.1//EN"
   "http://www.w3.org/TR/xhtml11/DTD/xhtml11.dtd">
```

The three XHTML doctype values shown previously assert the HTML on the web page as a well-formed XML document; it obeys the basic XML rules, such as all elements having opening and closing tags. The long and the short of it is that you just need to pick one and do your best to build web pages that adhere to the given specification.

A web page can include doctype at the top of the page and then use HTML that does not comply with the declared specification. Sometimes this will result in an obviously broken page, and other times the issues will be much more subtle, if they're visible at all. You might also find invalid markup emitted from a DotNetNuke module or typed in using an HTML editor control. All of these challenges are par for the course and will need your consideration when developing a custom DotNetNuke skin.

Try It Out   Configure a Skin Doctype

In this exercise, you will apply a skin specific doctype to a skin and observe any changes in the browser for the public web page. You should view the changes in Firefox and Internet Explorer. You'll also use the Page Info window in Firefox to tell you when the page is in Quirks mode or Standards Compliance mode.

1. Launch the home page of a default installation of DotNetNuke using Firefox and Internet Explorer.

2. In the Firefox menu bar, click Tools, Page Info. The Page Info window will appear and present a tabbed interface for browsing information about this page.

3. Examine the Render Mode field in the Firefox Page Info window. It should tell you the page is rendering in Quirks mode.

4. Close the Firefox Page Info window.

5. Launch your favorite text editor, and create a new file. Enter the following XML into your new file. It's best if you type the opening and closing tags of the root element and paste in the actual doctype from the W3C website discussed earlier in this section. Make sure the file is only one line and doesn't contain any line break characters.

```
<SkinDocType><![CDATA[<!DOCTYPE html PUBLIC "-//W3C//DTD HTML 4.01
Transitional//EN" "http://www.w3.org/TR/html4/loose.dtd">]]></SkinDocType>
```

6. Save this new file as Horizontal Menu - Fixed Width.doctype.xml in the DNN-Blue skin folder located here:

```
<install folder>\Portals\_default\Skins\DNN-Blue
```

7. Refresh the pages in the Firefox and Internet Explorer browsers. When you click the Refresh button, pay close attention to the page to observe any change in the way the page renders.

8. Launch the Page Info window in the Firefox browser again.

9. This time, the Render Mode field should indicate the page is rendering in Standards Compliance mode.

How It Works

When you toggled the page between Quirks mode and Standards Compliance mode, you probably noticed a slight shift in the layout of the page. This is the difference that an individual browser will make while attempting to display a page that doesn't declare its doctype. Go back and toggle the doctype a couple of times by moving the XML file into and out of the skin folder.

Now that you've declared the doctype, you can run the page through an HTML validation utility. The website `http://validator.w3.org/` is a free markup validation service provided by W3C. It uses the doctype to identify the validation rules that apply to a given page.

You might be surprised to learn that the default DotNetNuke web page doesn't validate under any of the doctype values listed earlier. There are little bits and pieces of HTML emitted by this large web application framework that violate the given HTML specification in one way or another. Such is the life of a web developer — there's always another task ahead of you.

Implementing Container Files

Now that you've created a custom skin from scratch, it's time to finish off an iteration of your skin with a custom container file. This process is similar in concept to creating a custom skin file. In this section you'll walk through the steps of creating a custom container from the ground up. First, you'll learn the HTML file technique, and then you'll branch over to the web user control technique.

Building an HTML Container

Start by using the HTML method to create the container and insert the necessary tokens to customize the web user controls. This process is similar to the skin creation process because it uses an HTML file, a CSS file, and an XML file to hold skin object parameter values. The folder for this container will also hold any assets used by the container, like custom icons or background images.

Creating the HTML File

The following code takes a few steps toward a standards based DotNetNuke container with fewer tables than the DNN-Blue container. The HTML tables work really well for the header and footer elements when the admin or host account is logged in. This layout implements the page design presented at the start of the chapter.

```
<div class="containerWrapper">

    <table border="0" cellpadding="0" cellspacing="0" class="titleContainer">
```

```
        <tr>
            <td class="actionCell">[ACTIONS]</td>
            <td class="titleCell">[TITLE]</td>
            <td class="helpCell">[ACTIONBUTTON:1]</td>
        </tr>
    </table>

    <div id="ContentPane" runat="server" class="ContainerContentPane"></div>

    <table border="0" cellpadding="0" cellspacing="0" class="footerContainer">
        <tr>
            <td class="addActionCell">[ACTIONBUTTON:2]</td>
            <td class="settingsActionCell">[ACTIONBUTTON:3]</td>
        </tr>
    </table>

</div>
```

The previous code block is a basic DotNetNuke container that wraps the content in an HTML `<div>` tag and uses a CSS class to target the content. The container has a good probability of being used multiple times on a single page, so it's best to omit ID attributes from normal HTML elements; otherwise, duplicate ID attributes could appear on the same page and the HTML would be out of compliance.

ID attributes should be unique on a given web page. The same class attribute values can appear as many times as needed on a single page. The `<div>` tag with the ID attribute of ContentPane is actually an ASP.Net server control because it has an attribute of `runat="server"` included in the element definition. The ASP.Net framework handles the task of making this ID attribute unique in the HTML content sent to the browser. Therefore, it's not recommended that ID attribute values for ASP.Net server controls be used as selectors in a CSS file.

Because this is an HTML container, any references to skin objects must be "tokenized" with a square bracket surrounding the name of the token. This container file includes five tokens. It's hard to decipher what each token is used for just by looking at the HTML file. You'll look at the XML file that contains the appropriate values for each token next.

Creating the XML File

Similar to the HTML skin file, the HTML container file is paired with an XML file that holds all of the skin object customizations. You load these up with the familiar values to harness the typical container features in the following code block:

```
<Objects>
    <Object>
        <Token>[ACTIONBUTTON:1]</Token>
        <Settings>
            <Setting>
                <Name>CommandName</Name>
                <Value>ModuleHelp.Action</Value>
            </Setting>
            <Setting>
                <Name>DisplayIcon</Name>
                <Value>True</Value>
```

```
            </Setting>
            <Setting>
                <Name>DisplayLink</Name>
                <Value>False</Value>
            </Setting>
        </Settings>
    </Object>
    <Object>
        <Token>[ACTIONBUTTON:2]</Token>
        <Settings>
            <Setting>
                <Name>CommandName</Name>
                <Value>AddContent.Action</Value>
            </Setting>
            <Setting>
                <Name>DisplayIcon</Name>
                <Value>True</Value>
            </Setting>
            <Setting>
                <Name>DisplayLink</Name>
                <Value>True</Value>
            </Setting>
        </Settings>
    </Object>
    <Object>
        <Token>[ACTIONBUTTON:3]</Token>
            <Settings>
            <Setting>
                <Name>CommandName</Name>
                <Value>ModuleSettings.Action</Value>
            </Setting>
            <Setting>
                <Name>DisplayIcon</Name>
                <Value>True</Value>
            </Setting>
            <Setting>
                <Name>DisplayLink</Name>
                <Value>False</Value>
            </Setting>
        </Settings>
    </Object>
</Objects>
```

Only the ActionButton controls required customization in the HTML container file. The `container.xml` file shown in the previous code block gives a unique command name to each control and indicates if the icon or the text hyperlink should be displayed. Each token in the XML file matches a corresponding token in the HTML file. It can be challenging to get a lengthy XML file configured properly, so just move in a slow and methodical manner.

The final portion to cover is the CSS file used to style the contents of the container. While the HTML structure in the container is less complex than the skin file, the CSS file can be as verbose as the CSS file for the skin. The container CSS file has to anticipate and manage the style for the various modules it might contain.

This important realization will spark ideas for containers that are customized or intended for use with specific DotNetNuke modules. The container designer might plan to use this module only with the Text/HTML module, and enter specific classes in the CSS file that target the content of that module.

The following code block is the CSS file for the container that implements the design presented at the start of this chapter. Each selector is composed of only elements and classes found in the previous HTML container. As I mentioned earlier, targeting ID attributes can be problematic.

```
div.containerWrapper
{
    background-color:#FFF;
    border:solid 2px #666;
    padding:10px 0 0 0;
}

div.containerWrapper div.ContainerContentPane
{
    margin:10px;
}

table.titleContainer, table.footerContainer
{
    width:99%;
}

td.titleCell
{
    width:100%;
    padding:0 0 0 8px;
}

td.titleCell hr
{
    margin:4px 0 0 0;
    width:98%;
}

td.helpCell, td.settingsActionCell
{
    text-align:right;
}

table.footerContainer td a.CommandButton
{
    font:normal normal bold 8pt verdana;
    display:inline-block;
    margin:0 0 4px 6px;
    color:#AAA;
}

table.footerContainer td a.CommandButton:hover
{
    color:#FF0000;
}
```

```
div.ContainerContentPane p
{
    font:normal normal normal 12pt verdana;
    margin:0 0 12px 0;
}

div.ContainerContentPane p img
{
    padding:0 10px 10px 0;
}

div.ContainerContentPane h2
{
    font:normal small-caps bold 12pt verdana;
}

div.ContainerContentPane .promoText
{
    font:normal normal normal 8pt verdana;
    color:#666;
}

div.ContainerContentPane a.promoLink
{
    margin:6px 0 0 0;
    display:block;
    font:normal small-caps bold 8pt verdana;
    color:#AAA;
}
```

Adding Sample Content

Just to round things out, the following two code blocks show the sample HTML content inside the Text/HTML modules. The following *semantic markup* consists of paragraph tags, headline tags, anchor tags, and an image tag. Semantic markup means the HTML used to mark up the content can help identify the purpose of the content. Header tags are used to identify headline text, paragraphs are used to identify detailed content related to the headline, and so on. The use of one table cell to hold the header and another table cell to hold the detail content does not provide any semantic value.

You can see there are no fancy parlor tricks going on inside this markup, yet the CSS file displays the two blocks of content in a custom manner that's easy to read and consistent with the skin. One pane uses a class attribute to enable CSS to target the content. The following block of HTML is from the ContentPane:

```
<p>In reprehenderit in voluptate velit esse cillum dolore eu fugiat nulla pariatur.
Excepteur sint occaecat cupidatat non proident, sunt in culpa qui officia deserunt
mollit anim id est laborum.</p>
<p><img alt="aspnet.gif" src="/dnn441/Portals/0/aspnet.gif" align="left">Sed ut
perspiciatis unde omnis iste natus error sit voluptatem accusantium doloremque
laudantium, totam rem aperiam, eaque ipsa quae ab illo inventore veritatis et quasi
architecto beatae vitae dicta.</p>
<p>Ut labore et dolore magnam aliquam quaerat voluptatem. Ut enim ad minima veniam,
quis nostrum exercitationem ullam corporis suscipit laboriosam.</p>
```

This next block of HTML is from the PromoPane:

```
<h2>Sept 3rd, Portland</h2>
<p class="promoText">Sit amet, consectetur adipisicing elit, sed do eiusmod tempor
incididunt ut labore et dolore magna aliqua. <a href="#">More Info</a></p>
<h2>Jan 8th, Chicago</h2>
<p class=promoText>Ut enim ad minim veniam, quis nostrud exercitation ullamco
laboris nisi ut aliquip ex ea commodo consequat.. <a href="#">More Info</a></p>
```

Try It Out   Install a Custom HTML Container

This is the final piece necessary to implement the design started in this chapter. Take it for a spin by loading it up into DotNetNuke in this exercise!

Find the collection of files for the simple HTML container. For this exercise, you should have the following files in a single folder on your computer visible in Windows Explorer:

- ❏ container.css
- ❏ container.xml
- ❏ SimpleTableContainer.html
- ❏ SimpleTableContainer.jpg
- ❏ thumbnail_SimpleTableContainer.jpg

1. Create a new zip file by right-clicking on a blank space in Windows Explorer to bring up the context menu. Select New, New Compressed (zipped) Folder. Name the file containers.zip.

2. Drag all of the files listed in Step 1 into containers.zip.

3. Create another zip file named MyHtmlContainer.zip.

4. Drag the containers.zip file into MyHtmlContainer.zip. Now you're ready to upload the package into DotNetNuke.

5. Log into your DotNetNuke installation using the Host account.

6. On the menu bar, select Host, Skins. The browser navigates to the Skin Administration page.

7. Click Upload Skin located at the bottom of the page. This navigates the browser to the Install Skin Package page.

8. Click the Browse button on the Install Skin Package page and locate the zip folder you created in Step 4 named MyHtmlContainer.zip.

9. Click Save File next to the Browse button to install the skin. You should see a series of progress statements flash by in your browser. Click Return located at the top or the bottom of the page to return to the Skin Administration page.

10. In the Containers drop-down list, select the item named MyHtmlContainer. This loads the thumbnail image of the new container in the Containers box.

11. Navigate to the page that is displaying the custom skin you uploaded earlier in this chapter. Then navigate to the module settings for each Text/HTML module on the page and configure the Module Container field to your new container named `MyHtmlContainer - SimpleTableContainer`.

12. Finally, if you haven't already done so, add some content to the Text/HTML modules that's consistent with the example content presented just before this exercise. Simple header tags and paragraph tags will suffice.

Figure 5-6 shows the complete page with the custom skin, custom container, and sample text inside some Text/HTML modules.

Figure 5-6

How It Works

This exercise brought all of the pieces together to form a custom web page using several design features available in DotNetNuke. This final step converted the HTML container file into an ASP.Net web user control as it was installed in DotNetNuke. When a module is configured to use this container, DotNetNuke loads this web user control, as well as all of the items encapsulated by this container. The web user control also contains the configuration set in the XML file for hiding or showing the module action item icons or text hyperlinks. DotNetNuke evaluates these settings each time it loads the page and processes the instructions.

Building an ASCX Container

Just as skin files can be constructed directly as web user controls, the same is true for container files. One advantage of creating a custom skin or container as an ASP.Net web user control, instead of an HTML file, is the ability to use the DotNetNuke application programming interface, or API. This book is focused on skinning DotNetNuke, so I won't be taking any long excursions into the VB.Net or C# programming languages, but there is some low hanging fruit that you can pick to serve your needs.

If you put on your HTML purist hat and review the HTML version of the container file in the previous section, you'll notice that the HTML table for the DotNetNuke module administration controls above and below the content pane is always present in the HTML source code, even when you are not authenticated as the admin or host account. You can leverage the DotNetNuke API and choose to hide the HTML table from all but the administrator. This will clean up the HTML in the page for a non-administrative visitor, reduce the download size, and improve the content-to-markup ratio on the page for search engine indexing.

The following block of code is a web user control that contains the structure for implementing the container design presented at the start of the chapter. Remember, web user controls can embed references to other web user controls, too. Immediately following the control directive, this container includes three register directives that refer to other web user controls.

```
<%@ Control language="vb" AutoEventWireup="false" Explicit="True"
      Inherits="DotNetNuke.UI.Containers.Container" %>
<%@ Register TagPrefix="dnn" TagName="ACTIONS"
      Src="~/Admin/Containers/SolPartActions.ascx" %>
<%@ Register TagPrefix="dnn" TagName="TITLE"
      Src="~/Admin/Containers/Title.ascx" %>
<%@ Register TagPrefix="dnn" TagName="ACTIONBUTTON"
      Src="~/Admin/Containers/ActionButton.ascx" %>

<div class="containerWrapper">

<% If PortalSecurity.IsInRoles( _
      PortalController.GetCurrentPortalSettings.AdministratorRoleName ) Then %>

    <table border="0" cellpadding="0" cellspacing="0" class="titleContainer">
        <tr>
            <td class="actionCell">
                <dnn:ACTIONS runat="server" id="dnnACTIONS" /></td>
            <td class="helpCell">
                <dnn:ACTIONBUTTON runat="server" id="dnnACTIONBUTTON1"
                    CommandName="ModuleHelp.Action"
                    DisplayIcon="True"
                    DisplayLink="False" /></td>
        </tr>
    </table>

<% End If %>
    <h1><dnn:TITLE runat="server" id="dnnTITLE" /></h1>

    <div id="ContentPane" runat="server" class="ContainerContentPane"></div>

<% If PortalSecurity.IsInRoles( _
      PortalController.GetCurrentPortalSettings.AdministratorRoleName ) Then %>
```

```
        <table border="0" cellpadding="0" cellspacing="0" class="footerContainer">
            <tr>
                <td class="addActionCell">
                    <dnn:ACTIONBUTTON runat="server" id="dnnACTIONBUTTON2"
                        CommandName="AddContent.Action"
                        DisplayIcon="True"
                        DisplayLink="True" /></td>
                <td class="settingsActionCell">
                    <dnn:ACTIONBUTTON runat="server" id="dnnACTIONBUTTON3"
                        CommandName="ModuleSettings.Action"
                        DisplayIcon="True"
                        DisplayLink="False" /></td>
            </tr>
        </table>

    <% End If %>

    </div>
```

The characters <% and %> in the previous code block indicate where the code begins and ends. The page directive at the top of the file includes an attribute that indicates the language found between these symbols. It can be VB.Net, C#, or any other managed language. ASP.Net uses these markers to identify and execute the embedded code as it processes a page request. This "HTML mixed with code" technique is a carry-over from a predecessor web technology, now called Classic ASP. It's easy to see how too much of this on one page can lead to confusing spaghetti code, but just a little bit in the container file serves our needs well.

The prior container code block conditionally shows the HTML tables that contain the DotNetNuke module controls. The VB.Net code in this container file is just a simple statement that basically says, "if one of the current user's roles is an administrator role, then output the enclosed content." Therefore, when the user is logged out of the system, DotNetNuke will skip over the HTML table tags. When the user is logged in as the admin or host account, the HTML table tags will appear in the browser.

This VB.Net customization will work for your purposes on this site, but it's not for every situation. Containers can hold any module, and DotNetNuke has a flexible security model. While it might seem slick, this customization permits only the administrator and host accounts to access the module settings and other management features on modules that use this container. That might be OK for a fair number of cases, but it's not true for all. Keep these types of things in mind, and know your audience when making these types of customizations.

Try It Out   Install a Custom Web User Control Container

In this section, you'll install the custom web user control version of the container file that only shows the HTML table tags when the current user is an administrator.

Find the collection of files for the simple HTML container. For this exercise, you should have the following files in a single folder on your computer visible in Windows Explorer:

❑   ConditionalTableContainer.ascx

❑   ConditionalTableContainer.jpg

❏   `container.css`

❏   `thumbnail_ConditionalTableContainer.jpg`

1.   Create a new zip file named `containers.zip`.

2.   Drag all of the files listed into `containers.zip`.

3.   Create another zip file named `MyASCXContainer.zip`.

4.   Drag the `containers.zip` file into `MyASCXContainer.zip`. Now you're ready to upload the package into DotNetNuke.

5.   Log into your DotNetNuke installation using the Host account.

6.   On the menu bar, select Host, Skins. The browser navigates to the Skin Administration page.

7.   Click Upload Skin located at the bottom of the page. This navigates the browser to the Install Skin Package page.

8.   Click the Browse button on the Install Skin Package page and locate the zip folder you created in Step 4 named `MyASCXContainer.zip`.

9.   Click Save File next to the Browse button to install the skin. You should see a series of progress statements flash by in your browser. Click Return located at the top or the bottom of the page to return to the Skin Administration page.

10.   In the Containers drop-down list, select the item named MyASCXContainer. This loads the thumbnail image of the new container in the Containers box.

11.   Navigate to a page displaying a custom skin you uploaded earlier in this chapter. Change just one of the Text/Html modules to use this new container named `MyASCXContainer – ConditionalTableContainer`. Now you can compare the results with the HTML container on the same page.

How It Works

When you visit the web page without logging in, the container omits the HTML table tags inside the container. Right-click on the web browser to view the HTML source of the page. View it while you're an anonymous visitor and while you're logged in as the host account. You should see cleaner HTML markup around the container when you're not logged into DotNetNuke.

The following two code blocks show a snippet of HTML and content from the two container file implementations while viewing the page as an anonymous visitor. The first code block is a from the web user control version around the Text/HTML module in the main content pane:

```
<h1>
    <span id="dnn_ctr376_dnnTITLE_lblTitle" class="Head">Lorem ipsum dolor</span>
</h1>
```

The next code block is from the HTML version of the container file surrounding the Text/HTML module in the left promo pane. This container used an HTML table to show the title as well as position the module administration controls. Consequently, the markup is a bit more verbose:

```
<table border="0" cellpadding="0" cellspacing="0" class="titleContainer">
    <tr>
```

```
      <td class="actionCell"></td>
      <td class="titleCell">
         <span id="dnn_ctr375_dnnTITLE_lblTitle" class="Head">
            Duis aute irure dolor</span></td>
      <td class="helpCell"></td>
   </tr>
</table>
```

Remember, the customization used in the web user control version also included some constraints that limit the scenarios of its effectiveness. These are the types of things that DotNetNuke skin designers must think about when developing custom skins.

Selecting Tools for Analyzing Skins

The iterative process works well for creating custom DotNetNuke skins. The skin developer can create a very basic skin that implements the design at the most abstract level and view the skin in a DotNetNuke installation. Next, the skin developer can iterate the skin many times by applying small changes to a file, and viewing the results of the changes in a browser. Each developer can find his or her own comfort level for the size of an iteration.

It's inevitable that complex issues will be uncovered, and mistakes will happen during development. By keeping the iterations small, the source of the problem stays small and easy to debug. The process you use to develop a skin can either trim or create a good deal of trouble; regardless, the developer needs tools to gain visibility into the problems when they do happen.

Many utilities expose the HTML information in the Document Object Model (DOM) for developers. I'll call out two that I use on a regular basis to get you started on your own toolkit.

Microsoft Internet Explorer Developer Toolbar

When a problem happens during skin development, you need tools that help assert your assumptions and give you some insight into the scenario. The Internet Explorer Developer Toolbar inspects the content sitting inside the browser and enables detailed analysis. This plug-in for Internet Explorer can be downloaded for free on the `Microsoft.com` website. Figure 5-7 shows the Developer Toolbar docked inside of Internet Explorer.

The Developer Toolbar is configured to outline HTML tables with a rectangular border in the previous figure. You can see that the custom web user control container on the left does not have an outline around the header. The other container does have a rectangular border indicating a table has been used to encapsulate the header.

Here's a partial list of other items the Developer Toolbar can expose:

❑   **Color Picker:** This tool identifies the hexadecimal color of the pixel currently under the mouse, a useful tool when the background color of a section must match a color in an embedded image.

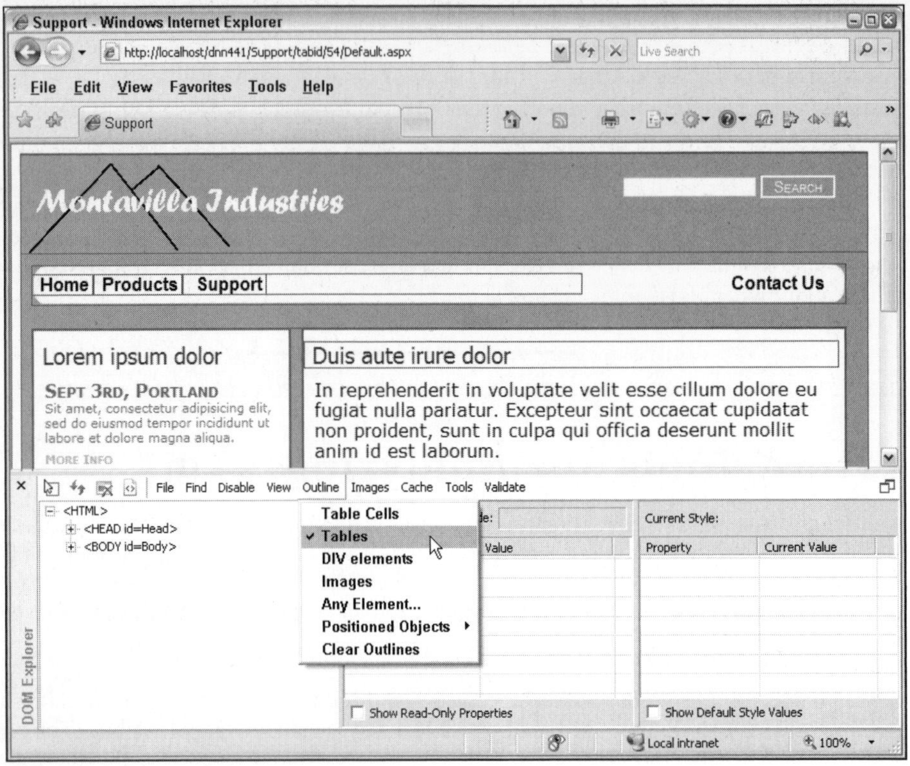

Figure 5-7

❑ **CSS Classes:** A complex HTML page has several nested HTML elements. CSS classes are assigned at several levels in this nested structure, sometimes overlapping each other. You could fish through the HTML source to find a CSS class assigned to a specific element, or you could simply click on the location in the browser and just look at the list of properties for that location inside the Developer Toolbar.

❑ **Div Sections:** Outlining the div sections of a skin is helpful for getting a quick overview of a new skin before you dive in to change it. If you see a lot of positioned or aligned content in the browser and the div section outline shows nothing, you can bet that the table outline feature will light up the browser like a Christmas tree.

❑ **Positioned Elements:** Modern skins usually take advantage of some absolute or relative positioning in the layout through CSS. The Developer Toolbar can light up these elements and give you some insight into how the skin was structured.

❑ **Disable Options:** The Developer Toolbar can temporarily turn off the effects of JavaScript and CSS on a web page. A good web page uses semantic HTML and continues to be readable without any CSS by using simple header tags, paragraph tags, and lists. If the page becomes a jumbled mess without any CSS, then at least you have a good idea of what the search engines are seeing, too.

❑ **Validation:** Validity and doctype values were discussed earlier in the chapter. The Developer Toolbar makes validating HTML, CSS, and hyperlinks on a web page just a click away.

Firefox Add-Ons

Firefox has an amazing level of pluggable add-ons available from third parties, because they've made the process for creating them so easy. One can draw parallels to the DotNetNuke skin and module marketplace.

Using View Source Chart

One of my favorite Firefox add-ons was created by Jennifer Madden and is called View Source Chart. This add-on provides a way to see the current HTML source code. By default, the View Source feature in a browser shows the HTML as it was originally received from the web server. JavaScript has the ability to modify the HTML from the web server by using the Document Object Model. The add-on called View Source Chart gives the developer insight into the current state of the HTML source code, including any changes made through JavaScript. This add-on is available at the following URL: http://jennifermadden.com.

At the time of this writing, version 2.5.02 is available for free, and version 2.6 is available for $3.00 and comes with custom CSS files. I highly recommend this component, and if you end up using it regularly, you really ought to show your appreciation to the developer.

Figure 5-8 shows an example view of the Source Chart for the skin created in this chapter. Each parent element nests its child elements so the relationships are clearly understood. The borders around each element block help to visualize the page structure. The add-on varies the border style between solid, dashed, and dotted as well as using consistent background colors to highlight special element blocks.

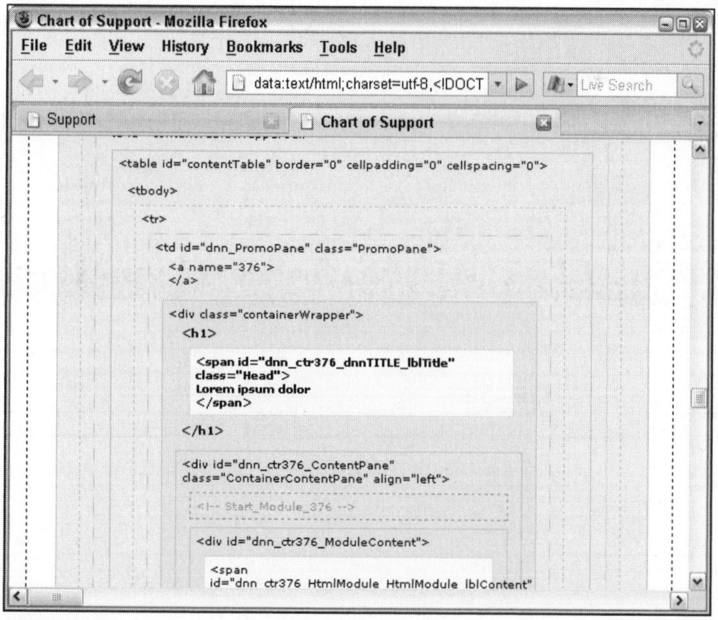

Figure 5-8

Using Firebug

Another solid Firefox tool that I reach for is called Firebug. This add-on is similar to the Developer Toolbar in Internet Explorer. You can download this add-on from the following URL:

```
https://addons.mozilla.org/en-US/firefox/addon/1843
```

Figure 5-9 shows Firebug in action.

Firebug can attach itself to the bottom of the Firefox browser and show detailed information about the current state of the HTML, CSS, and JavaScript operating inside a page. Figure 5-9 shows the collapsible HTML on the left column of Firebug while the right column shows the current property values in a scrollable list. It's well worth your time to learn the ins and outs of this tool.

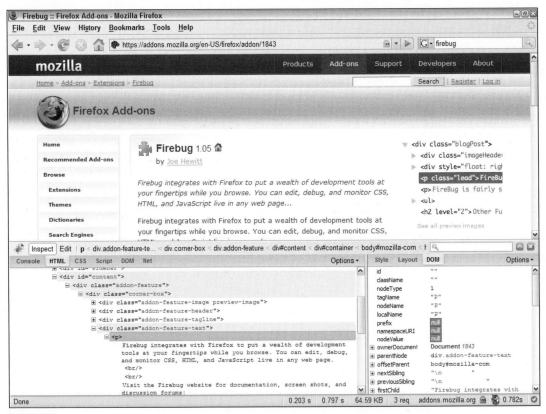

Figure 5-9

Summary

This chapter got to the heart of the book and exposed you to the process of writing custom skins for DotNetNuke. Each part of the process has its own considerations and plenty of room for creativity. An HTML skin file is less verbose than an .ascx skin, but they come with the extra baggage of an XML file for matching up embedded tokens with parameters. Plus, you need to re-import your HTML skin file every time you make a change.

Building containers is largely about writing HTML and CSS that envelop DotNetNuke modules. Skin files exist at a page level, and container files exist at a module level. HTML itself has several different versions, and the version is specified in the first line in the HTML file, called the doctype. Browsers have the best chance of rendering the HTML well when they're informed of the doctype value and the HTML actually conforms to the given specification.

This chapter presented some considerations important to skin developers as they implement a design. There is a certain balance to strike between elegant HTML and the type that constrains the layout but can be achieved in little time. There's no shame in meeting your current deadlines with your current abilities and continuing to improve your skill level over time. You also took a look at some ways to use the DotNetNuke API and bridge the gap between semantic HTML and going home at five o'clock.

Exercises

1. If the name of a skin file is MyCustomSkin.ascx, what is the name of the XML file that will inject a skin specific doctype value at the top of the page, and where should the file be placed?

2. What types of files are you likely to find in a skin package?

3. What happens when a browser doesn't find a doctype at the top of a web page?

4. Write a few lines of HTML as semantic markup; then write the same content using a nonsemantic markup.

Part II
Welcome to the Neighborhood

The Neighborhood
Association Website

This chapter lays the foundation for constructing a website for a neighborhood association. The first five chapters covered the principles of developing custom DotNetNuke skins from an academic and forensic perspective. This chapter begins a series that will apply these skills to develop a complete website with custom skins and selected modules that fulfill the needs for the audience of the specific website.

The idea of a neighborhood association website has broad applications because it deals with many types of users, serves several purposes, and has distinct branding requirements. The site must reflect the character of the people in the neighborhood and present the information in a compelling and understandable manner. This setting is a good incubator for the skills you've covered in earlier chapters. Now, you'll apply them to a website for a group of people with specific needs.

In this chapter, you design, construct, and configure a fictional neighborhood association website starting from a default DotNetNuke installation. You're taking a step back from the angle brackets and CSS rules used to design a single skin and getting a feel for the overall needs of a website. This activity will help to advise and inform decisions that you will make later on when you dive back into the raw HTML. It's important to understand the intended audience and the capabilities of the core DotNetNuke modules. So, you take a look at both factors throughout this chapter to gain some valuable insight for an effective set of skins.

About the Neighborhood Association

This neighborhood association is like many others across the country; some of the people have been members for 30+ years and a new person will occasionally appear at the general meeting held monthly in the community building. The board consists of young and old members from various socioeconomic backgrounds. They all have at least one quality in common — the desire to maintain a good neighborhood.

The Neighborhood Association has an existing website. It contains some pages with the history of the neighborhood going back to the founding of the city. There's some basic contact information and a schedule of the upcoming meetings. One of the long time members has maintained the static website on behalf of the neighborhood association for a couple of years.

An idea surfaced at the general meeting two months ago; a little research and some encouragement from the current volunteer webmaster have brought you to this point. The organization would value the ability to delegate website updates instead of asking just one volunteer to make every change. Each board member will be able to edit the site, and other community members will be granted access as deemed appropriate by the board. The neighborhood has reached consensus on the desired features of the new site and their current hosting provider has a good plan for ASP.Net 2.0 and SQL Server hosting.

Because the current website is just static HTML, it won't be too difficult to recreate the same content on your local server. Over time, the site will be enhanced with additional features as needs are discussed and evaluated. The initial launch will migrate the existing content to the new site and address some other immediate needs. Additional skins and modules will extend the usefulness of the site over time.

Planning a DotNetNuke Site

Based on the current understanding, the pages on the site will be available to anonymous visitors. Some of these pages will be standard HTML, such as the page that describes the history of the neighborhood association. Other pages can make use of more interesting DotNetNuke modules to provide some extra content management features. In this chapter, you'll focus on applying a few of those modules to the needs of this website. You'll configure them and get some general familiarity, and then apply some customized skins to this site in the following chapter.

You just need a few DotNetNuke modules to deliver good value, without getting too complicated, for the initial release. The page that lists upcoming events can use the Announcements module instead of the standard Text/HTML module. The Announcements module gives more structure to the content by using a consistent Title and Description field for each announcement. The list can automatically show items according to their published date as well as trim the list of old announcements after a specified number of days.

The board is interested in sharing their thoughts with the community on a regular basis. The DotNetNuke Blog module is a great tool for this need. Among other features, the Blog module has a simple interface for adding new blog posts, visitors can search posts, see a calendar view of the archives, as well as the familiar DotNetNuke RSS feed that goes hand-in-hand with blogging.

While the Blog module is targeted at expressing opinions from a few select people, the board also needs a simple, managed process for soliciting feedback from the community. The aesthetics of a forum module are more closely suited to this need. Anyone can create a new thread under an appropriate topic instead of simply commenting on an existing blog entry. The surface area for forum topics is greater than for blogs. The number of potential forum contributors vastly outnumbers the count of blog authors. You'll need to give some thought to what type of moderation is appropriate for the forum on the association website.

Finally, the board has a lower priority item involving document sharing. Although it's not urgent, the need can be quickly addressed by dropping a DotNetNuke Documents module onto a page that is only available to authorized users. The board can log in to the system and gain access to the list of documents to share with the other board members, yet avoid publishing them on the public Internet.

Getting Started

The local website hosting company is providing some technical services to help the Neighborhood Association move to the new website. The hosting company provisioned a new website on a Windows IIS web server. They provided an FTP account for access to the files on the web server, and they provided credentials for accessing the SQL Server 2005 database.

The hosting company also made this new ASP.Net 2.0 website publicly available through an IP address so it can be previewed by the board members before launch. The board can access the website through this special IP address and watch the site evolve from a default installation to a customized system. When the hosting company gets the word from the Neighborhood Association, they'll change the DNS settings so that their existing domain name points to the new IP address and all the website visitors will see the new site, too.

There are a couple of valid ways to get started. Because you will build custom skins from the ground up for this site, plus some mistakes along the way, it's a good idea to proceed along a route that lets you iterate as fast as possible. You'll install a new instance of DotNetNuke on a local development computer so that you have fast access to the files on disk using Windows Explorer, and you'll minimize the response time by moving the developer, the web server, and the database as close together as possible.

Because you'll develop parts of the site locally in Chapter 7, "Skinning the Neighborhood Association Website," you need to move your work onto the web server located at the Host's data center. One option for migrating your customizations is to copy the finished website and database to the remote servers. There are many FTP client programs to choose from that will copy the local files on disk to a remote server. Moving the database is a little more complex.

One tool that should be in your belt is the Database Publishing Wizard. In some instances, you might work on your local development machine for the duration of the build, and then deploy the completed web application and database to another server for either review or the final launch. The Database Publishing Wizard is a free utility that can help reduce the hassle of moving a database. This utility is available for free at the following URL:

```
www.codeplex.com/sqlhost
```

The Database Publishing Wizard converts a given database into a file containing a long list of T-SQL commands that represent a snapshot of the database. It doesn't modify the source database, so it's safe to run it against production databases, too, providing you have permission from the database administrator. You can configure the utility to include the schema, the data, or both in the T-SQL file it generates. After the script is generated, you can use the SQL Server Management Studio discussed in Chapter 2 to run the script against the destination database.

In the case of the Neighborhood Association website, you know the following things to be true:

1. The current site consists of static HTML files. None of the files contains server-side code.

2. The DotNetNuke site will be launched with the same content as the current site, plus a few new features.

3. The site will be enhanced over time by adding pages, modules, and more skins.

These facts put you into a position where you can install DotNetNuke locally and work on a skin. Then, you can install DotNetNuke a second time on the server at the hosting company. You can upload your skin package to the remote instance of DotNetNuke. In this case, there's not a lot of value in creating all of the pages for the initial site on your local computer. It only creates the need to migrate that content, specifically the database, to the server. Although it's possible to migrate the database with tools such as the Database Publishing Wizard, it's better to avoid this particular hassle when you can.

Try It Out   Install Two Instances of DotNetNuke

For this website build, you'll use two instances of DotNetNuke. The first instance is installed on the local development computer. It will be used for developing custom skin packages and testing ideas. The second instance is the version that will eventually become the live site — it lives in the data center of your fictional hosting company. For clarity, in this chapter I'll refer to the second instance of DotNetNuke installed on the server at the hosting company as the *remote site*. I'll refer to the one on your PC as the *local development site*.

> *If you don't have access to a second computer at home, a spare server at your company, or a site at a real hosting company, it's perfectly acceptable to create two instances of DotNetNuke on one computer and simulate one installation as the local development site and the other installation as the remote site, sans the joy of FTP, of course.*

In these steps you will install two separate instances of DotNetNuke to create the local development site and the remote site.

1. Download the latest installation package from www.DotNetNuke.com.

2. Using the skills you learned in Chapter 2, install an instance of DotNetNuke on your local development computer.

3. If you have access to a hosted website, use FTP to copy the DotNetNuke installation package to that location. Otherwise, use Windows Explorer to copy the bits from the installation package to the remote server. If you're using the same computer as the "remote server," then the process is the same as Step 2. Make sure the web.config file contains the appropriate database connection string information, and install the remote DotNetNuke site as you learned in Chapter 2.

4. Assign a valid administrator e-mail address to the remote site so it can send messages to the given administrator. Log in to the remote site as the Host account. Navigate to the Host Settings page and expand the Basic Settings section. Under the Host Details section, enter your e-mail address in the Host Email field. Click the Update link at the bottom of the page to save the change.

5. Configure the SMTP server for DotNetNuke so that it can send e-mail messages. Expand the Advanced Settings section in the Host Settings page. Here, you'll find the SMTP Server field. Enter a value of **localhost** in the SMTP Server text box unless you know of a different value provided by your IT professional. Click the Update hyperlink to save the change.

6. Now you can test the SMTP Server setting by sending an e-mail to the address you configured in Step 4. Click the Test hyperlink next to the SMTP Server field. DotNetNuke displays a warning if it could not find the given SMTP Server. If the page indicates the message was sent successfully, you should see the message in the inbox of the e-mail account you configured in Step 4.

How It Works

These steps create your local development environment to use as a workbench and a remote environment that will eventually become the live website. This gives you a fair amount of room for making mistakes, should you need it.

Aside from the SMTP server configuration, most of this was familiar territory. As a DotNetNuke developer, it's important to become familiar with the installation process. There are a number of steps along the way, and as a resident expert with many installations under your belt, you'll be in a position to come in to resolve any problem.

Planning the Sitemap

The primary audiences for this website are the residents of the neighborhood and the people who are actively involved in the association's activities. The goals of the website are to inform visitors of the current association activities, provide an archive of past actions, and document a history of the community.

The neighborhood association board members have outlined specific requirements for the website that will help them communicate ideas to other committee members. For example, they need a repository for basic operational documents, such as a list of who has opening and closing duties for the community room when it's used for official board activities.

People outside of the neighborhood will use the site, as well. The city employees and officials have an interest in this website. The association has regular contact with the city in which it resides and their active cooperation goes a long way toward smooth operations for both organizations.

After the initial DotNetNuke installation is prepared, the next step is to build out the site by creating a set of pages that conforms to the current site. This isn't an enormous website. It's just a few pages that provide an online identity for the neighborhood association. The organization has chosen quality over quantity.

This site will replace an existing set of static HTML pages and include a few pages for specific DotNetNuke modules that make use of the talent and wisdom of the active community members.

Try It Out   Create the Public Web Pages

In this step of the site building process, you'll create the pages of the website using the normal web-based tools inside DotNetNuke. This chapter concentrates on establishing the functionality for the site, so don't specify a Page Skin setting for any pages; you cover that in the next chapter when the site is given a custom look and feel.

Some of the pages are at the top level, and others appear under a landing page, so make sure to set the Parent Page value appropriately. These pages should be visible to all users.

Use the Add New Page feature in DotNetNuke to create the following pages on the remote server:

1. **Home:** This page is created by default when DotNetNuke is installed. Make sure the page is visible to all users.

2. **Sharing Ideas:** This page will be the landing page for the Blog and Forum pages. This page will explain the intended use of the detail pages to the visitors, and it lives at the top level, so it has no Parent Page.

3. **Blog:** This page will hold the Blog module. Its Parent Page setting is set to the Sharing Ideas page.

4. **Forum:** This page will hold the Forum module. Its Parent Page setting is set to the Sharing Ideas page.

5. **The Board:** This page will contain basic information about the board members, such as their name or position on the board. It lives at the top level, so it has no Parent Page.

6. **History:** This page will contain some history about the neighborhood and the city. It lives at the top level, so it has no Parent Page.

How It Works

These steps created the initial six-page structure of the website. By default, DotNetNuke also added a Text/HTML module to each new page. For some pages, that saved a step, but for others, you'll just end up deleting it and choosing another module.

If you're interested in viewing or possibly changing the values of the default page template, take a look at the following file where the values are stored:

```
<install folder>\Portals\_default\Templates\Default.page.template
```

If you want to create a new page void of any modules, then set the Page Template field to <Not Specified> when you create the page and it won't use any template defined in the previous folder.

Configuring User Registration

The vast majority of the content on this website is available to the anonymous visitor. The board has determined that the forum should be available to anonymous visitors, but that they must authenticate before starting a new thread or commenting on an existing discussion. This requirement is the basis for the user registration feature. DotNetNuke can be configured to provision new user accounts in a few ways. In your case, you want the site to create accounts automatically for visitors so they can authenticate and participate in the community discussion. You don't need to have an administrator create each account manually.

DotNetNuke has account registration baked into the core feature set. You just need to configure it to your particular needs. Out of the box, there are four options for user registration.

1. **None:** User registration is disabled for the site. Visitors cannot request an account online.

2. **Private:** Users can register for their own accounts, but they must be granted by an administrator before they are enabled.

3. **Public:** Users can register and receive an account for the website by completing the online registration process.

4. **Verified:** This is the same as Public, but the accounts are not valid until the users enter a secret code that is sent to the given e-mail addresses. This is a way of validating the e-mail addresses of your users when they register.

For this site, the Verified User Registration setting is the most appropriate. You are choosing to require valid e-mail addresses when visitors sign up for an account. This is a good way to make sure the user list is valid and not mixed with bogus accounts. You can set a policy later for purging unverified accounts that exceed a given age.

Try It Out   **Configure User Registration**

You tested the e-mail server connectivity earlier in this chapter, so you should be confident that changing the User Registration setting to Verified should go smoothly.

1. Log in to the remote server as the Host account.

2. Select Admin, Site Settings in the menu to navigate to the Site Settings page.

3. Expand the Advanced Settings section and find the Security Settings section.

4. Select the item named Verified in the User Registration field. Then, click the Update hyperlink at the bottom of the page to save your changes.

5. Log out of the system, and click the Register hyperlink next to the Login hyperlink.

6. Complete the registration form to create a test account. Use a valid e-mail address that you can access. Click the Register hyperlink at the bottom of the page to submit the registration request.

7. You should receive an e-mail message from DotNetNuke at the given address. The message contains a code for verifying the account. Verify the account.

How It Works

When you log in with the new account, you are prompted to enter the verification code. After you enter the verification code sent in the e-mail message, the account will be authorized and automatically added to the Registered Users security role.

These steps changed the entire user registration system for the website. The login skin object that you put in your custom skin during the earlier chapters inspects the User Registration setting before rendering the two links. If the setting is None, then the control changes its output to omit the Registration hyperlink. When the setting is configured to any other value, the login skin object displays both the Register and the Login hyperlinks. Just one radio button setting can take a large burden off the shoulders of the site administrators by allowing visitors to provision their own accounts.

Securing Pages for Selected Roles

Earlier in this chapter you noted the need for the lower priority feature of a shared document library that only board members can access. You can implement this feature without much work and get a lot of value back — a worthwhile effort by any metric.

By default, anyone with a valid account is a member of the Registered Users security role, so you should create a custom role specifically for board member accounts. Then, as board members register for their accounts, the administrator or Host account can add these selected accounts to the Board Member role.

You've created several pages in DotNetNuke and so far you've always granted access to all users. This time, you need a new page that is only visible to members of the custom Board Member role. Then, any module you drop on this page will only be visible to board members, as they will be the only group that can access the page.

Try It Out   Secure a Page Using a Custom Security Role

In this section, you'll create a custom security role, add a user to the role, and secure a web page so it's only available to members of that role.

1. Log in to the remote site as the Host or Admin account; both accounts have sufficient permission to do the work.

2. Select Admin, Security Roles to navigate to the Security Roles page.

3. Click the Add New Role hyperlink at the bottom of the page. This takes you to the Edit Security Roles page.

4. In the Edit Security Roles page, enter the following values:

    Role Name: **Board Member Role**

    Description: **This is a role for board member accounts.**

    Role Group: **Global Roles**

    Public Role: **No**

    Auto Assignment: **No**

5. Click the Update hyperlink at the bottom of the page to save the form values. The browser should return to the Security Roles page and display the new custom security role.

6. In the row for the Board Member Role, there are two icons on the left side of the role name. The Edit icon looks like a pencil and takes you to the Edit Security Roles page. You were just on this page in Step 5. The Manage Users icon looks like two people and navigates to a page for managing the members of the given role. Click on the Manage Users icon.

7. On the User Roles page, locate the User Name drop-down list. It contains all of the user accounts in the system. You should see the test account you created earlier in the chapter; go ahead and select it.

8. Click the Add User hyperlink on the right side of the page. This adds the selected user to the role.

9.   Create a new page on the remote server. Name the page Shared Documents and configure the Parent Page as The Board. In the View Page column of the Permissions field of this new page, select the Board Member Role. Keep the All Users checkbox clear.

10.   After the new page is created, log off and confirm that anonymous visitors cannot access the page. Then, log in as a test account member of the Board Member Role to confirm that that account can access the page.

How It Works

DotNetNuke confirms the authorization for each request. The menu is trimmed to show only the pages that the current user has permission to see. This is why the test account can see the Shared Documents page and anonymous users cannot see it. In fact, if an anonymous user typed in the exact URL to the page, the system would reject the request and indicate the visitor does not have authorization to view the page.

Take special care when securing sensitive information. This technique is sufficient for the board members, but it's not perfect for all cases. While an out of the box installation of DotNetNuke enables password protection for individual web pages, you cannot secure files such as Word, Excel, and PowerPoint on an individual file level.

ASP.Net and DotNetNuke manage security for requests to .ASPX pages; however, if the visitor requests an image or a document directly in the address bar of the browser, the web server will not pass the request to ASP.Net or DotNetNuke for processing. Instead, IIS will process the request on its own, which could bypass the intended security mechanisms.

Selecting DotNetNuke Modules

So far you've installed a default instance of DotNetNuke, added some pages to the site, created a custom security role, and added another web page that is only accessible by members of that custom security role. As each page was added, DotNetNuke automatically included an instance of the Text/HTML module in the default pane. This default module works for some pages of the site, but you'll want to utilize some functionality of other core modules, too.

The neighborhood association website will make use of the Announcements module, Blog module, Forum module, and the Documents module. This section will cover a general overview of these module features and how to configure them for your specific scenario.

Installing Available Modules

By default, DotNetNuke does not install all of the core modules along with the core system installation. Before version 4.4.0, DotNetNuke would install several modules on its own. Although this provided a great deal of potential out of the box, it also made the system a little slower, which is bad news if the installation isn't making use of the modules.

To strike a balance between performance and ease of use, DotNetNuke 4.4.0 included a hyperlink in the Control Panel labeled Install New Features. The Host user can click this hyperlink and navigate to the Module Definitions page. The Available Modules section of the page contains a checkbox list of modules that are available, but not yet installed. You should only install modules that you intend to use, which is smart from a security perspective as well as a performance viewpoint.

Depending on the version of DotNetNuke that you're working on, you might need to install an available core module using this checkbox list. For example, the following section makes use of the Announcements module, which is not installed by default. To drop this module into a pane on a page, you need to install it first.

Try It Out   Install an Available Module

In this section, you will practice installing the Announcement module in your system. This is one of the core modules in DotNetNuke, but it stays in-the-box until you explicitly request the installation. This assumes you are using DotNetNuke version 4.4.0 or later because that's when this feature was introduced.

1. On the remote server, log in as the Host account.

2. In the Control Panel, confirm the Announcements module does not exist in the modules drop-down list field.

3. Click the Install New Features hyperlink in the Control Panel. This takes you to the Module Definitions page.

4. Scroll down to the Available Modules section and select the checkbox for the Announcements module.

5. Click the Install Selected Modules checkbox, and the system will process the request. The Announcements module should now exist in the modules drop-down list field inside the Control Panel.

How It Works

The system accesses the package on the file system of the remote server and installs the module. This process is similar to installing a skin or a module from a zip file. Because the core module already exists inside the DotNetNuke file system, the file upload step is not required. It can immediately go to work on unzipping the contents of the module zip file and execute the installation process. This new process in DotNetNuke 4.4.0 keeps the core modules accessible by installing them as requested, with just a few clicks, while keeping the system performance in mind by only loading up the necessary modules into memory.

Using the Announcements Module

This module provides a good way to structure the content on a page by using a list. Each item in the list consists of a title and a description. The item can optionally include a standard hyperlink to more information; the description field doesn't need to contain a manually inserted hyperlink. It's valuable to have a standard method of linking to additional information for each item in the list. It avoids confusion for the readers, and it provides a consistent visual aesthetic on the page.

The module shown in Figure 6-1 displays the Announcements module while the administrator is logged in. The module has a hyperlink labeled Add New Announcement at the bottom and a pencil icon for editing each existing item in the module.

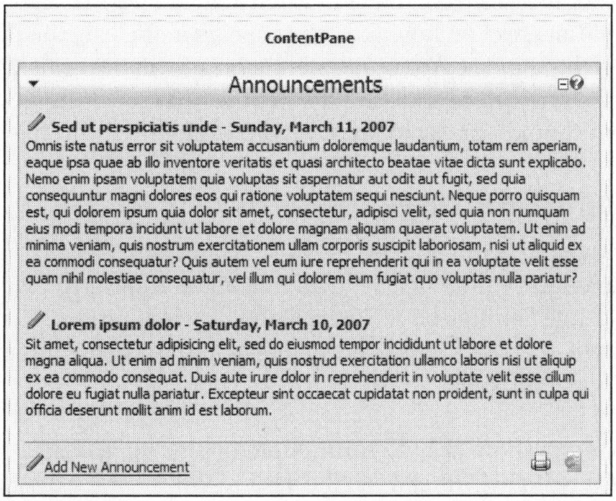

Figure 6-1

Adding an Announcement

The Add New Announcement hyperlink takes you to the Edit Announcements page. Here, the title field is a simple HTML text box field, which does a good job of keeping titles short and to the point. The description field is implemented by the familiar HTML Editor component.

Each item in the list also has a Link Type property. This property can be configured as a link to an external resource, a page on your site, a file on your site, or "none," which disables the link feature for the given item. If the Link Type is enabled, a hyperlink with the text Read more... will appear after the description.

The Link field will change depending on the selected value of the Link Type property. If the Link Type property is set to URL, the Link field changes to accept a fully qualified URL such as www.wrox.com. That setting is broad enough to allow any type of URL. If the goal is simply to link to another page on the same DotNetNuke site, then the Link Type of "Page" is a better choice. This setting changes the Link field to a drop-down list of all the pages in the site. Selecting an item in a list box is much easier to get right than typing or pasting a URL into a text box.

The last Link Type is File, which is similar to Page because it displays a drop-down list of choices. In this case, two drop-down lists are displayed. The top drop-down list selects a folder in the site, and the bottom drop-down list selects a file in the given folder. This is a good way to link to a PDF document from an item in the announcement list.

The next set of configurable properties for an item in the Announcement module includes a few items relating to the Read more hyperlink. The system can track the number of times this link is clicked at an aggregate level. Depending on the context, it might be useful to track exactly who clicked the link and when they clicked it. If the link is to an external URL or a document on the site, it's good to open the link in a new browser window. Unless you have a specific reason to do otherwise, you'll want visitors to remain on this site after they click the link.

The last two properties for the Announcement module item are the Publish Date and View Order. Both of these properties can have an effect on how the item appears in the list. The Publish Date is the official date the item is published on the site. The Announcement module can be configured to show future-dated items or wait until the Publish Date before showing the item. The View Order is a number that can be used to indicate where this item should appear in relation to the other items in the list.

Announcement Module Settings

This module has three custom settings: History, Description Length, and Template. These go beyond the normal Title, Permissions, and Container Settings that all modules utilize. These three settings are listed at the bottom of the Module Settings page — the standard location for all module specific settings. These configurations control when future-dated items appear, a limit on the number of characters, and a very powerful setting, the item template.

The list can be configured to show or hide future-dated items via a checkbox. If this feature is selected, the list will show all future items. Otherwise, the system will wait for the Publish Date of a given item before displaying it in the list. This setting applies to administrators, too. The administrator will not see the future-dated item in the list after he or she enters the information and clicks Update. This might be a little disconcerting, so a quick toggle of the Display Future Items setting to make sure the information is correct might put your mind at ease.

The History setting indicates the number of days a given item should appear in the list beyond the Publish Date. This value can go a long way toward automating a policy that keeps the website fresh and trimmed of obsolete information. Of course, this setting can be disabled by clearing the field so the list will show all of the items. This might be necessary if the Publish Date was incorrect for a new item that does not appear in the list after the Update hyperlink was clicked.

The Template field gives you a great deal of control over the display of the items in the list — a topic that should be near and dear to your heart. When the Announcement module goes to work, it retrieves a list of items from the database. Then the module iterates over the list, processing one announcement item at a time to build up a collection of HTML content. Finally, the collection of HTML content is rendered in the browser. Each time the module processes an item, the HTML content is derived from the specified template. The following code block is the default Template setting for the Announcement module:

```
<span class="SubHead">[TITLE] - [PUBLISHDATE]</span>
<div class="Normal DNN_ANN_Description">
    [DESCRIPTION] <a href="[URL]" target="[NEWWINDOW]">[MORE]</a>
</div>
<br>
```

Notice the tokens; the notion of tokens permeates much of the DotNetNuke world. In the previous code block, you can see the familiar fields for a given announcement item. Each token is replaced with the real value for the item and surrounded by the HTML code specified in the template. This elegant solution gives enormous flexibility to the DotNetNuke developer. You can easily change the CSS class for a given item or insert a horizontal rule tag after each item in the list through this template field.

Try It Out   **Add an Announcement Module**

In this section, you will add an Announcement module to the home page of the neighborhood association website and apply the appropriate configuration settings.

1. On the remote server, log in as the Host account.

2. Navigate to the home page. Clear the page of any default modules that appear in the panes. You'll add your own later; right now, you're just interested in adding the Announcements module.

3. On the home page, add an instance of the Announcement module to the ContentPane. If this module doesn't appear in the module drop-down list, then you must install it using the instructions in the previous Try It Out section.

4. Add two test announcements to the module by clicking the Add New Announcement hyperlink. Just enter a title and description for the items. At this point you can accept the default values for the other fields.

5. Just for fun, make one small change to the Template field in the Module Settings page. Navigate to the Module Settings page and remove the line break HTML tag from the Template code. It's the last HTML element listed in the Template field.

6. Click the Update link at the bottom of the Module Settings page to save your changes.

7. View the HTML source in your browser and confirm that the HTML line break tag is now omitted from the code for each item in the Announcements list.

How It Works

When the Announcements module prepares to show the list of items to a visitor, each item is inspected for its Publish Date and View Order to determine the sequence. The system parses the template and replaces the tokens with the actual data values. The template is a clever device to use here because it gives the developer control over what the resulting HTML will look like, including CSS classes and surrounding HTML code. Depending on the context of its use, the list can be dynamic and show a new set of items each day, or it can be used in a more static manner and display the same list everyday to all visitors.

Using the Blog Module

Blogs have exploded on the Internet, and they've also managed to find a way into the core set of DotNetNuke modules. The Blog module is a large component that comprises several smaller pieces. They work together to form a complete set of features one would expect in any blog engine.

If you don't see the Blog module in the modules drop-down list in the Control Panel, you need to install it just like the Announcements module. When the Blog module is dropped on a page, you might be surprised to see five distinct modules load into the pane. Instead of adding each module one by one, the system just drops all of them into the pane at once and assumes you'll organize the modules as you see fit. You can browse the physical web user controls that make up the Blog module by browsing the following folder:

```
<install folder>\DesktopModules\Blog
```

These related web user controls provide the familiar features that folks ordinarily see on blog sites. The following list describes what you'll see after selecting the Blog module and clicking the Add button in the Control Panel. For the sake of clarity, the default names of the modules will be used as identifiers in the following list:

❑ **Most Recent Blog Entries:** As its default title suggests, this module shows recent blog posts. By convention, a blog page shows some recent posts and includes other utilities to find older posts or a collection of posts with a given keyword. This module usually occupies the largest pane and consumes the most space on the page.

❑ **Blog_List:** This module provides a type of navigation to specific posts on the blog. Clicking links in this module changes the posts displayed in the Most Recent Blog Entries module.

❑ **New_Blog:** This module contains two important administrative hyperlinks. The Blog Settings hyperlink navigates to an uber-Module Settings page. The Blog module comprises several web user controls that work together; therefore, the Blog Settings page contains properties that would otherwise be configured in the Module Settings page of a less complex module. The New_Blog module is for administrative purposes only, so most sites will change the permissions so that it is only visible to the blog author(s). In that case, this module can exist on the public page, but it will not be displayed to anonymous visitors.

❑ **Search_Blog:** This module provides typical keyword search functionality that is specific to the blog. By default, this search feature and the core DotNetNuke site search feature are independent. Visitors searching for a keyword in a blog don't want to see a search result for another page in the website.

❑ **Blog_Archive:** Blogs usually include a date-based search feature. This module shows a calendar view for scanning blog posts by a given day as well as a list of monthly hyperlinks for a more coarse grained search.

Figure 6-2 is an example of the Blog module on a page. This screenshot was taken while logged in under the Host account. The five web user controls that play a part in this module have been spread out into three panes to provide some visual clarity; they can be arranged in any order. The box and warning text in the New_Blog control give an indication of the permission settings for that module.

Several configuration settings are available in the Blog module, but you've already covered the essential items that will get you started. You'll learn more along the way. For now, you'll add the Blog module into the neighborhood association website and get moving.

Try It Out   Add a Blog Module

In this section, you'll install and configure the DotNetNuke Blog module on the neighborhood association website. By the end of these steps, the website will have a fully functional blog, sans any custom skinning, of course.

1. Log in to the remote server as the Host account.

2. If you haven't already done so, install the Blog module on the remote server using the same steps as you used to install the Announcements module.

3. Navigate to the Blog page of the website.

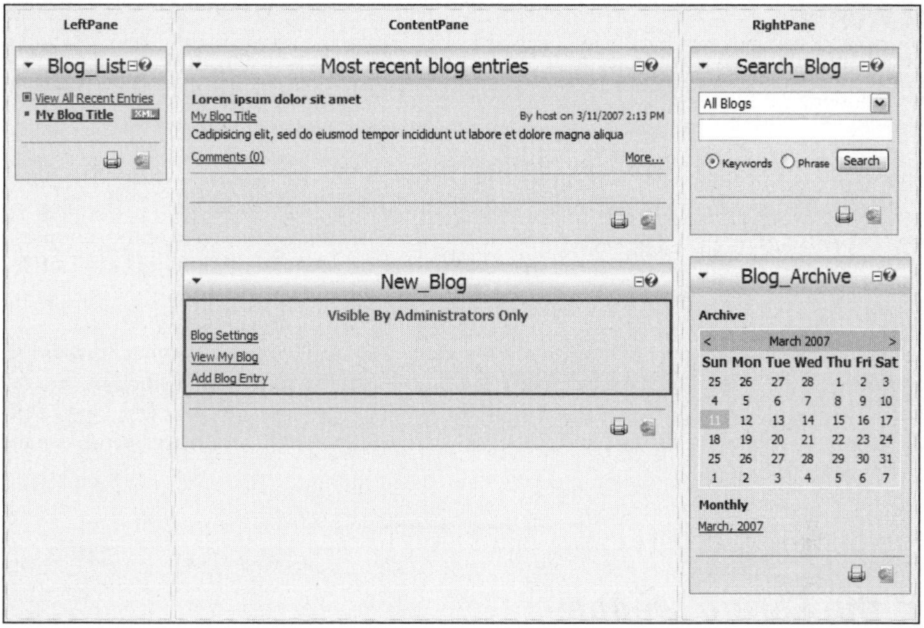

Figure 6-2

4. Add the Blog module to the ContentPane of the Blog page by selecting the Blog item in the module drop-down list field and clicking the Add hyperlink in the Control Panel.

5. Position the components of the Blog module as shown in Figure 6-2. Use the Action Menu in each module to move them. For example, to move the Blog_List module to the LeftPane, hover over the Action Menu icon and select Move, Move To LeftPane.

6. Navigate to the Module Settings page for the New_Blog module by clicking the Module Settings icon in the lower right corner of that module.

7. The New_Blog module should be hidden from all users except the administrator. In the Module Settings page, clear the checkbox for Inherit View Permissions from Page. All of the enabled checkboxes in the Permissions field should be cleared. This ensures that the module is only visible to and editable by the administrative users.

8. Click the Update link in the Module Settings page to save the changes. This navigates back to the Blog page.

9. In the New_Blog module, click the hyperlink labeled Create My Blog. This navigates to the Create New Blog page.

10. Enter a title and a description for the blog. Click the checkbox for the Blog Option labeled Make this blog public. You'll accept the default values for the remaining fields. Click the Update hyperlink at the bottom of the page to save the changes.

11. In the New_Blog module, click the hyperlink labeled Add Blog Entry, which takes you to the Add Blog Entry page.

12. Create a sample blog post by entering some "lorem ipsum" text in each of the fields, and then click the Update hyperlink at the bottom of the page to save your changes.

How It Works

At first glance, the Blog module seems large and complex; however, as you've just seen, it's easy to add blogging functionality to a DotNetNuke site. The five modules work together to provide a complete blogging solution.

The previous steps installed the Blog module in DotNetNuke with just a few clicks. The Blog module was added to a page and organized by placing the modules in the various panes. The Blog module has no idea about the skin that it's dropped into, so it makes no attempt to organize the modules on its own. The modules were customized by changing permissions just like any other module in DotNetNuke. Finally, a sample blog post was added to see how the content flows.

The Blog module abstracts a lot of new database activity and business logic for you; however, the fundamentals are still the same. You have the ability to assign a skin to a page and position the modules in panes as you see fit. Containers can be assigned to modules to change their look and feel. Good DotNetNuke modules follow a common pattern, and once you learn the pattern it becomes easier to use modules that you've never seen before.

Using the Forum Module

Forums have long been a staple of the Internet. Even before the World Wide Web, users were posting comments and having threaded discussions on text-based bulletin boards. The Forum module is the opposite of the Blog module in terms of custom layout opportunities. Although it's more complex than the Blog module, the Forum module is neatly bundled into a single module. You cannot move parts of the forum into different panes the way you can with the blog module; it's just one big rectangle. By necessity, this module consumes a large part, if not all, of the web page, as it has a lot of information to convey.

Like the Announcement module and the Blog module, the Forum module must be installed onto DotNetNuke before it is available for use. Figure 6-3 shows an instance of the Forum module on a page while logged in as the Host account.

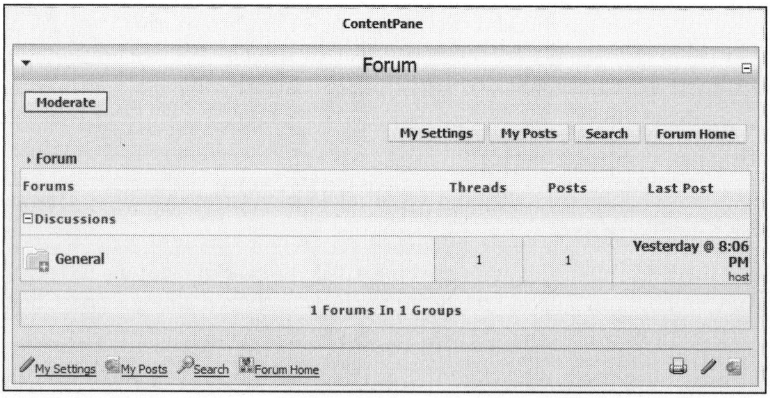

Figure 6-3

Describing the functionality of the Forum component fully could easily consume an entire chapter. The Forum includes an impressive set of features for managing users, forum groups, word filters, and statistics. As the documentation in this open source platform describes, the forum module was ported from the TTT Forums. To keep marching toward your initial release milestone, you'll get the module configured to an acceptable level without getting too deep.

<table>
<tr><td>Try It Out</td><td>Add a Forum Module</td></tr>
</table>

In this section, you'll add the Forum module to the neighborhood association website and perform some initial configuration. At the end of the steps, you'll have a functional forum system in which visitors can have threaded discussions on various topics. As with most public forums, the content must be moderated. The neighborhood association does not want inappropriate posts on the website, nor does it want to be vulnerable to spam messages. These requirements will be implemented with a simple configuration setting.

1. Log in to the remote server using the Host account.

2. If you haven't already done so, install the Forum module onto the DotNetNuke system.

3. Navigate to the Forum page and add the Forum module to the ContentPane using the Control Panel.

4. By default, the module contains one forum group named Discussions, and one forum named General. This is sufficient for your current needs, but you need to ensure that the posts to the forum are moderated. Hover over the icon for the Action Menu and select the item named Forum Administration. This takes you to the Forum Administration page.

5. On the Forum Administration page, select the icon for the item named Manage Forums/Groups. This takes you to the Manage Forums page.

6. Expand the Discussions forum group and click the pencil icon in the General forum row. This takes you to the Edit Forum page.

7. In the Edit Forum page, expand the General Settings section. In this section, select the checkbox for the item labeled "Is Moderated." Selecting this checkbox will require each post to be reviewed before it is visible to the public on the Forum page. Click the Update hyperlink on the Edit Forum page to save the change.

8. You've ensured that the posts to the forum are moderated, but you haven't specified a forum moderator, yet. For now, assign that job to the Host account. In the Action Menu for the Forum module, select the item named My Settings. This takes you to the User Settings page.

9. Expand the Admin Settings section and select the checkbox for Is Moderator. The page will post back and show another item named Is Global Moderator. Select that checkbox, too, and click the Update hyperlink at the bottom of the page. Now the Host account can moderate discussions in the forum.

10. Click the Forum Home link at the bottom of the module to return to the main forum view.

11. You have established a moderator, but only the Host account may post discussions to the forum. You want all registered users to be able to post ideas to the forum. Use the Action Menu to navigate to the Module Settings page. In the Permissions field of the Basic Settings section, grant the Registered Users group permission to edit the module by selecting the checkbox that intersects the Edit Module column and the Registered Users row. Click the Update hyperlink at the bottom of the page to save your changes.

12. Now create a test post to the forum. Log out of the Host account, and log in as any registered test account that you created in an earlier section. Navigate to the General forum, and click the New Thread button at the top of the page. Enter the subject and details of the thread and click the Update hyperlink at the bottom of the page to submit the forum post. The post will not be immediately visible because the forum is moderated.

13. Log out of the test account, and log in again as the Host account. Navigate to the Forum page, and click the button labeled Moderate in the top left corner of the module. This navigates to a view that displays a list of forums and the number of posts to moderate in each forum.

14. Click the forum named General, and then click the Approve button next to the test post. This marks the post as being approved so visitors on the website can see the discussion unfold. If the post doesn't follow the policy of the forum, the Delete button is nearby. Use due diligence when moderating forum posts on your own. Your own policy might require forum moderators to notify the group when deleting a forum post or to save a copy of a post in a private location for further review.

How It Works

The Forum module contains a great deal of functionality. The module can hold multiple forums and even organize them into groups of forums. Users can be granted a special status of "Moderator" or "Trusted" so that their posts do not need to be approved by moderators. This is an elaborate module that still adheres to the fundamentals of the DotNetNuke framework.

The New Thread button starts a new conversation in a given forum. DotNetNuke hides this button unless the visitor is authorized to edit the module. That's why we granted the Registered Users access to edit this module. Every module in DotNetNuke has a security setting for edit access. The Admin and Host accounts have this privilege implicitly. You can grant any role in DotNetNuke the ability to edit the Forum module, the Text/HTML module, or any other. When a visitor has edit access, you're giving them permission to modify the content of your website.

Using the Documents Module

The final module you'll install in this release of the neighborhood association website is the Documents module. This module will exist on a page that is only visible to the members of the custom Board Member Role. This page will help the organization share private documents. For example, the module will hold the current phone tree sheet. It will also contain a checklist for the rotating assignment of opening and closing the meeting room in the community center.

In a previous section, you created a custom security Board Member role and a page that is only visible to members of that role. The next step is to create an instance of the Documents module on this page and configure it so that board members can read documents as well as post.

The Documents module shows a simple list of the documents that it has been given. By default, the list displays the following columns:

❏ Title: This is the title of the document. The title can be different from the name of the file.

❑ Owner: This column tracks the name of the account that added the document to this instance of the Documents module.

❑ Category: The document owner can enter a category value to provide some context for a given document. Categories might include General, Human Resources, Draft, or anything that helps provide context to a subset of the documents in the module.

❑ Modified Date: This is the date the item in the module was last modified.

❑ Size: This decimal value indicates the size of the file in kilobytes. Visitors using slow Internet connections will pay attention to this column.

❑ Download – This is a hyperlink used to download the physical file from DotNetNuke to your computer.

Figure 6-4 shows an example of the Documents module while logged in as the Host account. The module contains two documents.

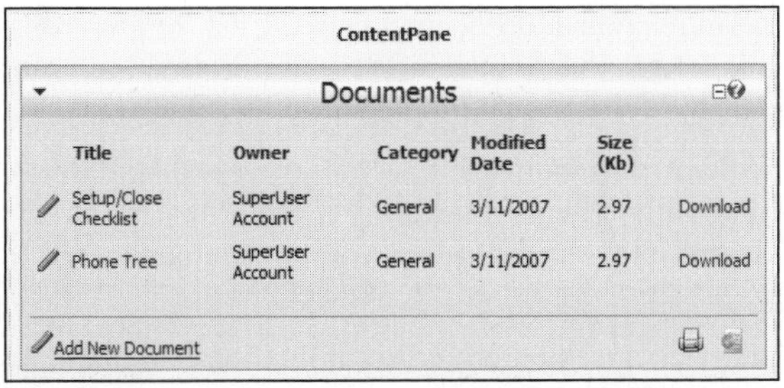

Figure 6-4

The Module Settings page for the Documents module contains the following fields:

❑ Use Categories List: This checkbox controls the information contained in the categories column for the document entry. If left unchecked, then any value can be entered in the category text box when a new document is added to the module. If this checkbox is selected, then the text box for the category field is replaced with a list box, and only the values in the list box are permitted. You can navigate to the Lists page in the Host menu to edit the values displayed in the list box. Select this checkbox when you want to tightly control the category values.

❑ Show Title Link: When this checkbox is selected, the title of the document becomes a hyperlink and operates the same as the download hyperlink. If the page is too crowded, the download link can be removed from the display, and the title column can serve the dual purpose of indicating the name of the document as well as providing a link to the document.

❑ Display Columns: This field shows a collection of all the columns in the document module. Select the checkbox next to each column name that should appear in the main view of the Documents module. To adjust the sequence of the selected fields in the main view, click the up or down arrows.

❑ Sorting: This field configures the sort order for the Documents module. To sort the list, select a field in the drop-down list and click the Add Sort Order hyperlink. Select another field in the drop-down list and click the Add Sort Order hyperlink again to configure the list to sort by multiple columns.

Try It Out   **Add a Documents Module**

In this section you'll add a Documents module to the password-protected page on the remote server named Shared Documents.

1. Log in as the Host account on the remote server.

2. Navigate to the page named Shared Documents that exists under the page named The Board. The page might have a default Text/HTML module inside the ContentPane. Delete this module if it exists.

3. If the Documents module isn't already installed, go ahead and install it just as you've done with the previous modules in this chapter.

4. Drop an instance of the Documents module into the ContentPane on the Shared Documents page.

5. Navigate to the Module Settings page for the Documents module. You'll accept the default values in the Documents Module Settings section, but you will need to grant members of the Board Member Role permission to add documents to the list. To grant this permission, select the checkbox in the Permissions field that intersects the Edit Module column and the Board Member Role row. Click Update to save the changes to the Module Settings page.

6. Members of the Board Member Role now have access to add items to the list in the Documents module, but they still don't have the ability to read files or upload files in the repository in DotNetNuke. To grant this access, select Admin, File Manager in the menu to navigate to the File Manager page.

7. On the File Manager page, you need to grant the Board Member Role permission to view and write to the Portal Root folder. To do this, select both checkboxes on the row for the Board Member Role in the Permissions field at the bottom of the page. Click the Update link at the bottom of the page to save the changes to the File Manager permissions.

8. Log out of the Host account, and log in as a test account that is a member of the Board Member Role.

9. Navigate to the Shared Documents page and click the Add New Document hyperlink to navigate to the Edit Documents page.

10. Enter a test document by completing the form. Don't worry about selecting a real PDF file; it's fine just to select an image file in the Root folder for testing purposes. Click the Update hyperlink at the bottom to insert the new item in the Documents module.

How It Works

You configured the Documents module to grant members of a custom security role permission to view and edit a specific module using the Module Settings page. This was necessary, but not sufficient. You also had to grant the custom security role permission to view and write files to a folder in the File Manager. When an authorized user uploads a new document from a computer and adds it to the Documents module, the physical file is saved to a folder under the Portal Root folder. This folder is visible in the File Manager page as well as the Documents module.

If the Documents module reaches a state where it's holding a large number of documents, then you can tune it by making better use of the Category field, perhaps converting the field into a drop-down list instead of a text box. You can also make use of the inherent sorting features of the module to organize a lengthy list of documents. All of the documents exist in the Portal Root folder in the File Manager, but you can install a couple of instances of the Documents module on a page, or a collection of pages, to segment the documents even further. The Documents module is just a specific view of files inside the Portal Root folder along with some meta information such as the title and owner fields.

Summary

This chapter took a step back from studying skins and examined the high-level needs of a website for a neighborhood association. The scenario gives a real world feel to the skills that have been developed in the previous chapters. It's insufficient just to know how a particular technology works — the full value lies in the appropriate application or informed restraint of using a given technology.

The scenario of the Neighborhood Association website set the groundwork for replacing a static HTML website with a dynamic system that enables multiple users to access content value on the pages. This chapter discussed some basic concepts of other popular modules in the core system. Most modules in the recent releases of DotNetNuke will need to be installed manually before they are dropped into a pane. Many of the configuration skills that applied to the familiar Text/HTML module also apply across the board to other modules.

The Announcements, Blog, Forum, and Documents modules all have their unique traits on a page while sharing a common bond as DotNetNuke modules. Skinning a DotNetNuke system requires a certain level of familiarity with several modules. When a new module is encountered, the developer will be able to draw upon past experiences and apply a common set of techniques to the custom skin that envelops the page.

The next chapter returns to the raw HTML and CSS to build a custom skin for the Montavilla Neighborhood Association website. The audience and the initial modules for the system have been established. You can leverage this information to apply a skin that is specifically targeted for the members of the association.

Exercises

1. What is the name of the Microsoft tool that helps migrate a database from one computer to another?

2. What are the steps to securing a page so only members of a specific security role can see it?

3. How can you switch the order of the Title and the Publish Date fields for all items in the Announcement module?

4. What are the steps necessary to regulate the posts on a forum so they can be reviewed for conformance to the website policy?

5. After a role has been given edit authority on a Documents module, what must be configured before they can upload documents into the module?

Skinning the Neighborhood Association Website

Chapter 6 set the stage for building an appropriate website for the Neighborhood Association. The modules were installed on the remote server and the essential pages were created. The remote server is currently in a usable state, but it doesn't have any custom skins, yet. The site is displaying the default DNN-Blue skin for all pages.

You haven't done too much with the local development server, but now its time has come. The custom skin will be developed and revised on your local machine. Then, the skin will get bundled up and installed on the remote server. If any skin problems are encountered on the remote site, you can work out the kinks on your local machine, bundle up the skin again, and reinstall it on the remote server.

The first five chapters described the fundamental parts of a skin and how to create a custom design from scratch. This chapter goes deeper and applies the prior skills to several types of pages. First, you'll use the information about the content of the neighborhood association website to plan some custom skins. Next, you'll cover some common ways custom skins can go awry. Finally, you'll use this information to construct and apply a custom set of skins to several pages in the site.

Designing the Site

As you create your own custom skins, you'll find a design technique that suits you. Chapter 5 used a graphical composition of a web page as a starting point for the skin. Designing a giant image file can clear up a lot of ambiguities during a site build, but it requires some decent skills with your favorite graphics program.

Folks who are new to graphic design might get more traction by creating a simple wire frame sketch for each distinct layout. A couple of sheets of paper and a number 2 pencil is all you need. The goal of a wire frame sketch is loosely to identify regions of a web page in a simple manner; it's just a sketch of nested rectangles. In this section, you'll use the wire frame technique as a sort of middle ground in the spectrum of web design planning techniques.

Wire frames make little, if any, attempt at articulating the actual look and feel of the website. Their elegance lies in the simplicity of the information they convey. A wire frame layout contains a series of positioned frames (rectangles) to indicate space allocation. In your case, the concept of frames will translate nicely into a series of DotNetNuke panes in a skin. Figure 7-1 illustrates the general idea for the layout of this skin. It was made with a graphics program, but the same job could be done with just paper and pencil. The following sections will look at three wire frame layouts for the site.

Defining the Home Page Layout

Public informational and marketing websites commonly have a layout on the home page unique to the site. As the most general page on the site, the home page has the job of advertising all other pages. Figure 7-1 illustrates the general idea for the layout of the neighborhood association home page.

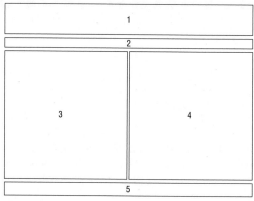

Figure 7-1

For this site, the Announcements module is planned for frame 3, and a Text/HTML module will be dropped into frame 4. Both of these frames will expand or collapse vertically with the content, and frame 5 will always be under the longer frame above it.

All of the pages of the website share a common header and footer component that occupy frames 1 and 5, respectively. This website will have a horizontal menu structure that occupies frame 2 in all of the wire frame plans.

The actual web page might not give exactly equal space to the left and right panes, but you're not too concerned about that level of detail in a wire frame. This diagram presents the layout at a glance, which will facilitate discussions with stakeholders, in this case, with Board Members.

If both people understand this as the layout for the home page and one person has an idea for a rotating set of promotions for their upcoming event, a tactical discussion would answer questions such as which position number is most appropriate, what are the heights and widths of the promotions, or if this layout is even appropriate for such a presentation. Perhaps it's necessary to modify the wire frame by adding an additional position under 2 and above 3 and 4. These are the types of challenges that are simplified by using a wire frame.

Defining the Wide Layout

A wide layout will be used for the forum page and detail pages with lots of text. This layout grants the most amount of space for modules to occupy. Figure 7-2 illustrates this layout.

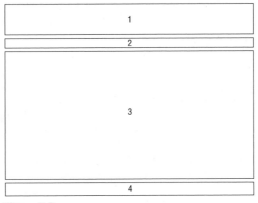

Figure 7-2

Based on your experiences in Chapter 6, you know the Forum module is a bulky object that consumes a lot of space on the page. Therefore, you need a layout like this to accommodate large modules that will exist in frame 3. Detail pages with paragraphs of text and an occasional embedded image work well in this layout, too. The HTML author can insert the appropriate headers in the paragraphs of text to break up the flow and make the online document easier to comprehend. Nearly every site needs a wide layout.

Websites sometimes use a narrow promotional pane on the right or left of the primary content pane for detail pages. There hasn't been a need identified for that style yet, so the wide layout will be your standard layout for detail pages until something else is called for.

Defining the Blog Layout

Figure 7-3 shows the layout for the blog skin. Several modules are in play to produce the blog, so a layout with some astutely placed panes will go a long way toward creating an intuitive space for the readers.

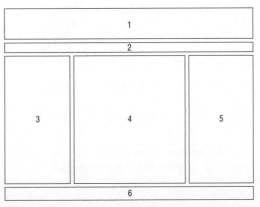

Figure 7-3

You know the Blog module consists of five modules that provide features for searching and listing blog entries. The largest of these modules displays the full blog post.

The Blog page gives us some room for creativity. You could implement the five modules in a single frame, but the look would be dull and difficult to read. You could implement the large module in a larger frame and the other modules in a narrower pane on the side. That's a common format and certainly usable. You're interested in using some slick HTML and CSS for this page though, so go for it; implement three adjacent frames.

Avoiding Traps

Right from the start, this book led you down the primrose path of defining skins for pages using a standards compliant approach that leverages the flexibility of CSS. In my experience with DotNetNuke, understanding the purpose and capabilities of panes inside a skin can be equally difficult for new developers and masters. The hurdle is accepting the facts that a pane can hold any type of module and that adjacent panes can affect each other by the amount of HTML content they hold.

Hopefully, this book has provided you with some solid examples as a reference, and now you can take a look at some common misunderstandings in the arrangement of panes in a skin. I sought to help you understand a healthy object before progressing into the study of abnormalities. After all, the abnormalities are what give us the most headaches, and learning to identify them is the first step in solving the problems they create.

Allowing for Control Panel Injection

The Control Panel is a mandatory element of a DotNetNuke skin. The skins for the neighborhood association website have implemented this element with the following code:

```
<div id="ControlPanel" runat="server"></div>
```

The Control Panel can exist nearly anywhere in the DotNetNuke skin, but is commonly placed at the top of the page. In its default implementation, the Control Panel element is a wide rectangle of controls used to modify a page or execute common tasks. If the designer really wants to buck tradition, it can be inserted at the bottom of the skin so the portion of the website above the fold always looks the same.

Developers highly proficient in CSS but new to DotNetNuke may overlook this injection of the Control Panel into the page. When an anonymous user visits the site, the Control Panel exists as an empty <div> tag in the HTML source. HTML zealots might even request that the empty <div> tag be removed from the source. When an admin or host user is authenticated on the site, the <div> tag is filled with the HTML content that produces the controls that the admin or host uses to modify the modules on a page or to add new pages to the site.

Developers who are fluent in CSS will make regular use of the *position* property in their CSS files. Its value affects where an element appears on a page. The position property can take four values:

1. static: This is the default value for all elements in a web page. The static setting makes an element appear as it would without any CSS treatment.

2. `relative`: This value indicates the element should be positioned relative to where it would have been positioned if its value were set to static. For example, the position of an element can be set to 10 pixels to the right of where it would have been positioned without any treatment. If you apply the notion of X and Y coordinates, X would be +10 and Y would be 0. The element is offset 10 pixels to the right of its 0,0 coordinate.

3. `absolute`: This position setting is similar to relative positioning — it places a given element somewhere on a page using an X,Y coordinate structure. With relative positioning, the 0,0 coordinate is where the element would appear in the normal flow of the web page. Absolute positioning is a little more complex — but not much. It implies that the element using absolute positioning is contained by another element using relative positioning.

The 0,0 coordinate for this absolutely positioned element is the top left corner of the relatively positioned element. Just remember that absolutely positioned elements are always contained by relatively positioned elements. A `<div>` tag that contains a `<p>` tag is a good example. When the `<p>` tag uses absolute positioning, it looks to the `<div>` tag with relative positioning for its 0,0 coordinate.

4. `Fixed`: This setting holds an HTML element in the same position of the browser, even as you scroll it. For example, a rectangle with the name of the current user can appear 20 pixels from the top right corner of the web browser. With fixed positioning, the rectangle remains at this exact position, even when the browser page is scrolled vertically. Although this might make sense in very specific cases, visitors are generally more annoyed with this feature than appreciative.

Obviously, absolute positioning is the most complex of the three commonly used values. However, understanding just a few simple principles can clear up the entire matter. Examine the following hierarchy of HTML elements:

```
<body>
   <div>
      <h1>Lorem Ipsum</h1>
      <p>
         <img src="/folder/image.jpg" alt="Consectetur" />
         Sed do eiusmod tempor incididunt ut labore et
         dolore magna aliqua.
      </p>
   </div>
</body>
```

The previous block of HTML contains a hierarchy. The ancestors of the `<img>` tag include the `<p>` tag, the `<div>` tag, and the `<body>` tag. If the `<img>` tag were configured to use absolute positioning in the CSS file, then it would look to the first ancestor that implemented relative positioning to identify its 0,0 coordinate. The CSS file could be configured to use relative positioning on any combination of the ancestor tags. The `<p>` tag can use relative positioning at the same time as the `<div>` tag. The 0,0 coordinate for the `<img>` tag will be the nearest ancestor to implement relative positioning. The term "nearest" in this sense refers to the hierarchical chain of ancestor elements. If none of the ancestors implemented relative positioning, the 0,0 coordinate of the `<body>` tag is used by default.

Now consider what would happen if a developer used absolute positioning on a `<div>` tag that contained the menu skin object — a perfectly legitimate design scenario. If the developer didn't account for the potential height of the Control Panel, then the menu and the Control Panel might collide and make the page unusable. A simple solution to this problem is to envelop the skin in a single `<div>` tag and place the Control

Panel outside of this `<div>` tag, either above or below. Then, the `<div>` tag that wraps the skin can be configured to use relative positioning with no offset, so it's not really positioned differently from a static setting. However, any absolutely positioned elements within it will use its position as the 0,0 coordinate. The Control Panel is free to expand and collapse as admin and host users log in to the site.

This solution to positioning problems accounts for the dynamic nature of a DotNetNuke web page. There are things that can happen on a data driven website that don't exist on a static HTML page. Developers need to review their skins as the anonymous user as well as the host user to make sure the positioning rules are adequate.

Solving Pains with Panes

Risk averse folks who understand that non-technical users will be updating the website might go to extra lengths to "protect the design" as they begin to create custom DotNetNuke skins. Armed with the knowledge that modules can be dropped into panes and Text/HTML modules are good for entering content, one might be compelled to create the following skin in Figure 7-4. The rectangles around the content indicate the developer's intended allocation of panes.

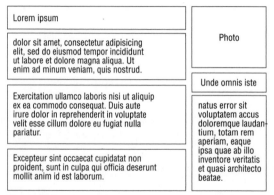

Figure 7-4

There are seven panes on this skin that contain header, paragraph, and image elements. The top left pane contains an HTML `<h1>` tag and the headline text of the document. The three panes below it "help" the user maintain three paragraphs of content on this page. The top right pane isolates the photo on the page, and the two panes below the photo are allocated for an HTML `<h2>` tag and a single paragraph. This type of skin design is overkill for this web page.

The problem with too many panes is akin to the problem of an HTML table-based layout. A table-based layout can structure the web page so tightly that it prohibits things that CSS does well. An HTML page should semantically describe the content and not go much farther. HTML tables excel at displaying tabular data, but it's easy to go overboard. Panes provide a way to structure modules on a page, and a developer can go too far in this area, too.

You should implement a better balance of panes to modules than the one shown in Figure 7-4. The allocation of a pane solely for the use of a photo is certainly within reason. A single Text/HTML module can easily handle both header and paragraph content. The layout shown in Figure 7-4 would be more balanced if the left side became a single pane and the right side contained two panes stacked on top of each other.

Creating Custom Skins

You've addressed the high-level plans for the website and designed some wire frames that will inform the custom skin development process. The previous section covered some key problems novices might encounter with DotNetNuke. Existing HTML and CSS skills are great assets when beginning to learn this dynamic platform, but you're still bound to run into subtle issues. The only way to overcome them is to get more DotNetNuke experience creating skins — so here's another batch!

Three types of skins that need to be constructed for the initial release of this site are listed in the following table.

Skin Name	Pages Using Skin
Home Page Skin	Home Page
Wide Skin	Sharing Ideas page Board page History page Forum page Shared Documents page (for board members only)
Blog Skin	Blog page

The site will initially contain seven pages and is certain to grow over time. Therefore, it's important to allow for growth in the skin design. A beautiful skin design can be hampered by the lack of potential for growth. For example, the menu structure might be implemented in such a way that prohibits new top-level pages. Make sure that your custom skins leave sufficient room for the site to grow after their initial release.

Creating the Initial Skin

The local development server will serve as your workbench for creating the collection of custom skins. You'll build out various parts of it in stages. First, you have to create a space to work inside DotNetNuke. In the last chapter, you installed an instance of DotNetNuke on the local development server, and that's about it. All of the page creation work occurred on the remote server. You don't really need a perfect set of matching pages on the development server and the remote server. Just one page that lets you view each type of skin is sufficient.

Try It Out   Initialize the Skin

In this section, you'll create the folder structure and set of files that will help you get started. This section assumes you have a default instance of DotNetNuke installed on your local development server. At the end of these steps, you will have a place to start building custom skins.

1. Launch Windows Explorer and navigate to the following folder inside the DotNetNuke installation on your local development server:

```
<install folder> \Portals\_default\Skins
```

2. Under the Skins folder, create a new folder named Autumn. This is the group name for the new set of custom skins.

3. Now create a user control for the first skin and a set of CSS files to augment it. Navigate to the new skin folder named Autumn and create the following empty text files by right-clicking in the folder and selecting New, Text Document in the context menu:

   a. homepage.ascx

   b. skin.css

   c. skin-global.css

   d. skin-homepage.css

4. The first skin has been initialized; do the same for the container. Use Windows Explorer to navigate to the following folder inside the DotNetNuke installation on your local development server:

```
<install folder>\Portals\_default\Containers
```

5. Under the Containers folder, create a new folder named Autumn. This is the group name for the new set of custom containers.

6. Now create a user control for the custom container and a CSS file. Navigate to the new container folder named Autumn and create the following empty text files by right-clicking in the folder and selecting New, Text Document in the context menu:

   a. standard.ascx

   b. container.css

   c. container-global.css

   d. container-standard.css

How It Works

These steps created the initial structure to use for the custom skins. They're just empty files at the moment, so they won't do much right now. I hope it's becoming increasingly clear that skins are composed of simple text files and can exist at a specific level inside DotNetNuke.

If you were creating custom skins all on your own, you would now open each of these text files in your favorite text editor, start writing code, and be on your merry way. Fortunately for you, you're reading this book, and this code is already done for you. So, make sure you check out the code for this chapter that's available for download online.

In an upcoming section, you're going to split out the CSS rules into a series of files so that it's more manageable. That's why you've initially created three CSS files here. The primary CSS file that's automatically injected into the page by DotNetNuke will refer to the other CSS files. It's a good technique for keeping the scope of any one CSS file from getting too large.

Building the Home Page Skin

The structure for the skin file is created. Now, you're ready to author the HTML inside the web user control for the home page skin. Because you're leveraging CSS, the HTML in this skin file is minimal. The following code block shows the contents of the home page skin:

```
<%@ Control language="vb" Inherits="DotNetNuke.UI.Skins.Skin" %>
<%@ Register TagPrefix="dnn" TagName="MENU" Src="~/Admin/Skins/SolPartMenu.ascx" %>
<%@ Register TagPrefix="dnn" TagName="USER" Src="~/Admin/Skins/User.ascx" %>
<%@ Register TagPrefix="dnn" TagName="LOGIN" Src="~/Admin/Skins/Login.ascx" %>
<%@ Register TagPrefix="dnn" TagName="COPYRIGHT"
    Src="~/Admin/Skins/Copyright.ascx" %>
<%@ Register TagPrefix="dnn" TagName="TERMS" Src="~/Admin/Skins/Terms.ascx" %>
<%@ Register TagPrefix="dnn" TagName="PRIVACY" Src="~/Admin/Skins/Privacy.ascx" %>
<%@ Register TagPrefix="dnn" TagName="DOTNETNUKE"
    Src="~/Admin/Skins/DotNetNuke.ascx" %>
<div id="ControlPanel" runat="server"></div>
<div id="homePageSkinContainer" class="skinContainer">
    <div id="headerContainer">
        <p>Montavilla Neighborhood Association</p>
    </div>
    <div id="contentContainer">
        <div id="LeftPane" runat="server" class="leftPane"></div>
        <div id="RightPane" runat="server" class="rightPane"></div>
        <div id="ContentPane" runat="server" class="contentPane"></div>
    </div>
    <div id="footerContainer">
        <dnn:COPYRIGHT runat="server" id="dnnCOPYRIGHT" />
        <dnn:TERMS runat="server" id="dnnTERMS" />
        <dnn:PRIVACY runat="server" id="dnnPRIVACY" /><br />
        <dnn:DOTNETNUKE runat="server" id="dnnDOTNETNUKE" />
    </div>
    <div id="userContainer">
        <dnn:USER runat="server" id="dnnUSER" />
        <dnn:LOGIN runat="server" id="dnnLOGIN" />
    </div>
    <div id="menuContainer">
        <div id="theMenu">
            <dnn:MENU runat="server" id="dnnMENU" />
        </div>
    </div>
</div>
```

The home page skin file starts with the familiar ASP.Net declarations and places the Control Panel at the top of the file. A single HTML <div> tag wraps the contents of the skin. The header, content, and footer sections are in familiar places, too. Two interesting aspects of this skin are the positions of the login and menu sections — they're at the bottom of the page!

This skin is utilizing some CSS goodness to move the menu structure and the user login skin objects to the top of the page in the browser. This allows the primary content on the page to exist higher in the physical file, which is an important point for search engine indexing. The verbose HTML that creates the menu can exist at the bottom of the page. There, it is appropriately given lower priority by the search engine index.

This home page skin actually contains three panes, and the wire frame you drew up earlier contained only two. So, what's the reason for the third pane? Either the left or the right pane could have been omitted, and the mandatory content pane would have happily taken its place. The choice to include three panes is linked to the experience a user will have while logging into the system. The login form will appear in the content pane by default. If the content pane were positioned on the left or right side of the page, it would look a little off balance. As the host user, you'll make sure that you don't actually drop any modules into the content pane. The login form will look better centered on the page, so you can make the appropriate CSS rules to implement that effect.

The CSS rules for this skin start with the file named skin.css. The following two-line block of code shows the contents of this file that are automatically injected into the page by DotNetNuke.

```
@import url("skin-global.css");
@import url("skin-homepage.css");
```

Even if you've used CSS for years, you might not be familiar with the @import statement in CSS. This statement allows the developer to use just a single <link> tag in the HTML source for a page, and literally import other external CSS files to style the content. The HTML source is less complex because only one <link> tag is needed and the CSS developer gains the benefit of segmenting CSS rules into distinct files.

You'll place all of the global CSS rules that affect every skin in the group named Autumn inside the file named skin-global.css. The CSS rules that only apply to the home page will exist in the file named skin-homepage.css.

Placing rules in a single file is beneficial for a couple of reasons. It's easier to spot rules that ought to live in another file. The HTML <div> tag that envelops the home page skin has an id attribute value of homePageSkinContainer and a class attribute value of skinContainer. So, rules that are specific to the home page skin will use the id attribute selector, and general CSS rules will use the class attribute selector. When the rules are split up into several files, it also makes them easier (but still not easy) to edit. A file with fewer lines is easier to maintain over time. An omitted bracket character can break the entire set of CSS rules. Would you prefer to hunt down the bug in a 1,000-line file, or a 100-line file?

The following code block contains the contents of the skin-homepage.css file:

```
div#homePageSkinContainer div.leftPane
{
    width:300px;
    float:left;
}
```

```
div#homePageSkinContainer div.rightPane
{
    width:450px;
    float:right;
}
```

The styles specific to the home page use a selector that refers to the id attribute of the HTML <div> tag that envelops the skin. The two other skins you'll create will use different id attribute values for their HTML <div> tag.

You don't need to go through all the CSS for this skin on a line-by-line level in this chapter. I encourage you to examine the code for this chapter, available online. You focus on CSS rules in a subsequent chapter. For now, you'll set your sights on the HTML aspects of building a series of skins for the neighborhood association website.

Try It Out   **Create the Home Page Skin**

In this section, you'll construct the skin that will give you the custom home page look for the neighborhood association website. You'll need the code available online for this chapter to complete the steps.

1. This step populates the skin folder with some files. Copy the following files from the code available online into the new skin folder you just created in the previous Try It Out section. Some are new files and others overwrite existing (empty) files created in the last step.

    a. `homepage.ascx`

    b. `homepage.jpg`

    c. `skin.css`

    d. `skin-global.css`

    e. `skin-homepage.css`

    f. `thumbnail_homepage.jpg`

    g. `hdr-house.jpg`

2. Copy the files for the custom container, too. This step populates the container folder with some files. Locate the container files in the code available online for this chapter and copy the following files into the new container folder you created earlier:

    a. `container.css`

    b. `container-global.css`

    c. `container-standard.css`

    d. `standard.ascx`

    e. `standard.jpg`

    f. `thumbnail_standard.jpg`

    g. `fade.jpg`

3. Now, it's time to load up the skin. Open your browser, and navigate to the home page of the DotNetNuke website on your local development server.

4. Log in as the Host account, and click on the Settings icon in the Control Panel to navigate to the settings page for the home page.

5. Expand the Advanced Settings section, and set the Page Skin field to the item named `Autumn - Homepage`.

6. Set the Page Container field to the item named `Autumn - Standard`.

7. Click the Update hyperlink to save your changes. The browser navigates back to the home page and displays the new skin.

8. Make sure the page contains one instance of the Announcements module and one instance of the Text/HTML module. Create the module instances if they don't already exist.

9. Move the Announcements module to the left pane and the Text/HTML module to the right pane. Enter some sample content in each module to fill out the page.

How It Works

This section used two additional CSS files that were imported by the familiar `skin.css` file. Because you had access to the development server, you could operate directly on the files — you didn't have to zip up a skin package in order to install it.

If you view the HTML source in your browser, you can confirm that the menu content is at the bottom of the page, although CSS positions this content just under the page banner. When you log in as the Host account, the form is centered on the page and occupies the entire available width. This is made possible by using two custom panes for the actual page content and leaving the required content pane empty, except for system level functions, such as logging in.

You assigned the module containers at the page level instead of doing this twice at the module level. By default, modules use the containers assigned at the page level. In turn, the page assigns the containers configured at the site level. Finally, the site uses the containers assigned at the host level. You could have assigned the single container at the site level or host level, but you're leaving a little room for some fun later on.

Building the Wide Skin

The next skin you'll construct is the typical wide skin that most developers include in their repertoire. Again, because you're counting on CSS to do most of the styling, there's not much to this skin.

```
<%@ Control language="vb" Inherits="DotNetNuke.UI.Skins.Skin" %>
<%@ Register TagPrefix="dnn" TagName="MENU" Src="~/Admin/Skins/SolPartMenu.ascx" %>
<%@ Register TagPrefix="dnn" TagName="USER" Src="~/Admin/Skins/User.ascx" %>
<%@ Register TagPrefix="dnn" TagName="LOGIN" Src="~/Admin/Skins/Login.ascx" %>
<%@ Register TagPrefix="dnn" TagName="COPYRIGHT"
   Src="~/Admin/Skins/Copyright.ascx" %>
<%@ Register TagPrefix="dnn" TagName="TERMS" Src="~/Admin/Skins/Terms.ascx" %>
<%@ Register TagPrefix="dnn" TagName="PRIVACY" Src="~/Admin/Skins/Privacy.ascx" %>
<%@ Register TagPrefix="dnn" TagName="DOTNETNUKE"
   Src="~/Admin/Skins/DotNetNuke.ascx" %>
<div id="ControlPanel" runat="server"></div>
```

```
<div id="wideSkinContainer" class="skinContainer">
    <div id="headerContainer">
        <p>Montavilla Neighborhood Association</p>
    </div>
    <div id="contentContainer">
        <div id="ContentPane" runat="server" class="contentPane"></div>
    </div>
    <div id="footerContainer">
        <dnn:COPYRIGHT runat="server" id="dnnCOPYRIGHT" />
        <dnn:TERMS runat="server" id="dnnTERMS" />
        <dnn:PRIVACY runat="server" id="dnnPRIVACY" /><br />
        <dnn:DOTNETNUKE runat="server" id="dnnDOTNETNUKE" />
    </div>
    <div id="userContainer">
        <dnn:USER runat="server" id="dnnUSER" />
        <dnn:LOGIN runat="server" id="dnnLOGIN" />
    </div>
    <div id="menuContainer">
        <div id="theMenu">
            <dnn:MENU runat="server" id="dnnMENU" />
        </div>
    </div>
</div>
```

The wide skin is nearly identical to the home page skin, which is a good thing. A related set of skins usually share a common theme and differ only in small parts. In your case, most of the differences are expressed in CSS instead of the HTML. After the first skin is built, the remaining skins usually go up pretty quickly.

The parts that make this skin file unique include the id attribute of the HTML <div> tag that surrounds the skin and the use of only one pane, the mandatory content pane. The rest of this file is identical to the home page skin. The savvy developer will start to think of ways to reduce the amount of redundant code in the skin files. Put that notion on the back burner for now; you'll come back to it in a later chapter. Rest assured that hard drives are cheap, and you don't actually have to write this skin, because it's available for download with the code for this book.

Try It Out   Create the Wide Skin

In this section, you'll build the wide skin that's used by several pages on the neighborhood association website. This will build on the previous section that created the home page skin.

1.   Use the files available online for this chapter, and copy the following files to the new skin folder you just created:

   a.   wide.ascx

   b.   wide.jpg

   c.   skin-wide.css

   d.   thumbnail_wide.jpg

   e.   hdr-pans.jpg

2. The page named Sharing Ideas will use this skin, so create that page in DotNetNuke if you haven't already done so. This page exists at the top level and is viewable by all users.

3. While logged in as the Host account, navigate to the Sharing Ideas page in DotNetNuke and click on the Settings icon in the Control Panel. This takes you to the Settings page.

4. Set the Page Skin field to the item named Autumn – Wide.

5. Set the Page Container field to the item named Autumn – Standard.

6. Click the Update hyperlink to save your changes. The browser navigates back to the Sharing Ideas page and displays the new skin.

7. Make sure the page contains one instance of the Text/HTML module. Create the module instance if it doesn't already exist. Enter some sample content in each module to fill out the page.

How It Works

This skin works much like the home page skin. The mandatory content pane serves dual purposes here. It displays the Text/HTML module, or any other module you drop into it. Furthermore, if the user chooses to log in on this page, the login form will replace any modules in the content pane and continue to display the polished look of your custom site.

Building the Blog Skin

Constructing this skin is a little trickier because of the five modules that provide all of the features. Nevertheless, you shouldn't be too shocked to see a skin file below that is nearly identical to the home page skin.

```
<%@ Control language="vb" AutoEventWireup="false" Explicit="True"
Inherits="DotNetNuke.UI.Skins.Skin" %>
<%@ Register TagPrefix="dnn" TagName="MENU" Src="~/Admin/Skins/SolPartMenu.ascx" %>
<%@ Register TagPrefix="dnn" TagName="USER" Src="~/Admin/Skins/User.ascx" %>
<%@ Register TagPrefix="dnn" TagName="LOGIN" Src="~/Admin/Skins/Login.ascx" %>
<%@ Register TagPrefix="dnn" TagName="COPYRIGHT"
   Src="~/Admin/Skins/Copyright.ascx" %>
<%@ Register TagPrefix="dnn" TagName="TERMS" Src="~/Admin/Skins/Terms.ascx" %>
<%@ Register TagPrefix="dnn" TagName="PRIVACY" Src="~/Admin/Skins/Privacy.ascx" %>
<%@ Register TagPrefix="dnn" TagName="DOTNETNUKE"
   Src="~/Admin/Skins/DotNetNuke.ascx" %>
<div id="ControlPanel" runat="server"></div>
<div id="blogSkinContainer" class="skinContainer">
    <div id="headerContainer">
        <p>Montavilla Neighborhood Association</p>
    </div>
    <div id="contentContainer">
        <div id="LeftPane" runat="server" class="leftPane"></div>
        <div id="RightPane" runat="server" class="rightPane"></div>
        <div id="ContentPane" runat="server" class="contentPane"></div>
    </div>
    <div id="footerContainer">
```

```
        <dnn:COPYRIGHT runat="server" id="dnnCOPYRIGHT" />
        <dnn:TERMS runat="server" id="dnnTERMS" />
        <dnn:PRIVACY runat="server" id="dnnPRIVACY" /><br />
        <dnn:DOTNETNUKE runat="server" id="dnnDOTNETNUKE" />
    </div>
    <div id="userContainer">
        <dnn:USER runat="server" id="dnnUSER" />
        <dnn:LOGIN runat="server" id="dnnLOGIN" />
    </div>
    <div id="menuContainer">
        <div id="theMenu">
            <dnn:MENU runat="server" id="dnnMENU" />
        </div>
    </div>
</div>
```

Try It Out   **Create the Blog Skin**

For the blog skin, you know that three panes will be in play. The home page skin included a third pane simply to provide a more balanced look for the login form. The blog skin also uses the content pane as the centering pane, but it is adjacent to the left pane and the right pane. Literally, the only items that make this skin different from the home page skin are the filename and the id attribute value of the HTML `<div>` tag that envelops the skin. This id attribute is the essential hook that lets you target the content with CSS rules.

1. Use the files available online for this chapter, and copy the following files into the skin folder you just created:

    a. `blog.ascx`

    b. `blog.jpg`

    c. `skin-blog.css`

    d. `thumbnail_blog.jpg`

    e. `hdr-room.jpg`

2. You need a page to test this new skin on your local development server. The page named Blog is the only page currently planned to use this skin; create that page in DotNetNuke if you haven't already done so. This page exists under the Sharing Ideas page and is viewable by all users.

3. While logged in as the Host account, navigate to the Blog page in DotNetNuke and click on the Settings icon in the Control Panel. This will take you to the Settings page.

4. Set the Page Skin field to the item named Autumn – Blog.

5. Set the Page Container field to the item named Autumn – Standard.

6. Click the Update hyperlink to save your changes. The browser navigates back to the Blog page and displays the new skin.

7. Make sure the page contains one instance of the Blog module. Create the module instance if it doesn't already exist. Create the blog, and enter some sample content.

8. Move the Blog_List module into the left pane. Move the Search_Blog and Blog_Archive modules into the right pane. The other two modules can remain in the content pane.

How It Works

The blog skin uses the special id attribute value in the HTML <div> tag to show a custom background image at the top of the page as well as to position the panes. Examine the CSS file for the blog, and you'll find a custom rule for an HTML table in the right pane that sets the width. This rule fixes a minor width issue with the calendar control in the Blog_Archive module.

Deploying and Testing the Custom Skin

Now that all of the skin files have been constructed, it's time to package them up into a single zip file and install them on the remote server. You've tested them on the local development server, so you can be fairly confident that the skins will work well on the actual site.

Try It Out   Deploy the Custom Skin

In this section, you will bundle the code that you created and tested on the local development server and deploy it to the remote server. These steps are covered in detail in Chapter 5. You should review that section now if you're not yet familiar with the skin upload process.

1.   Navigate to the new skin folder you created in the first Try It Out section of this chapter, located in this folder:

```
<install folder> \Portals\_default\Skins\Autumn
```

2.   Copy all of the files in this skin folder into a single zip file named `skins.zip`. Make sure the zip file doesn't contain the `Thumbs.db` file that Windows creates automatically when previewing images. DotNetNuke will throw its hands up if it encounters this file while processing the skin package.

3.   Navigate to the custom container folder that you populated earlier:

```
<install folder>\Portals\_default\Containers\Autumn
```

4.   Copy all of the files in this container folder into a single zip file named `containers.zip`.

5.   On the desktop of your computer, create a third zip file named `Autumn.zip`. The name of this zip file is the group name for this set of skins.

6.   Drag the files named `skins.zip` and `containers.zip` into the file named `Autumn.zip`. Now the skin package has been created.

7.   Launch a new web browser and navigate to the remote server.

8.   Log in as the Host account and click Host, Skins in the menu.

9.   Click the Upload Skin hyperlink at the bottom of the page and install the Autumn skin package located on your desktop.

10.   Apply the skins to the various pages on the site using the same techniques as on the local development server.

How It Works

This process created the skin package in the same manner presented in previous chapters. This process puts the first release of the skin in place, and all of the Board Members (stakeholders) with access to the remote server can begin to see it take shape, now that the custom skin has been applied.

You can now save this skin zip file as a permanent version of this release. You can access every line of CSS and HTML you authored in this skin by accessing the zip file. It's a decent form of versioning if you don't have a more effective file versioning tool in place, like Subversion.

Testing the Blog Module

You looked at the Blog module on the local development server with the skin applied, but there are a couple of additional views that you can check out. The Blog module on the remote server should be configured to allow users to leave comments. Visitors should have to log in to the site to leave comments. The stakeholders don't want comments from anonymous visitors.

The Blog Settings page configures the comment policy for the blog. When you're logged in as the Host account, the New_Blog module is visible. This module contains the Blog Settings hyperlink. When you click this hyperlink, the browser takes you to a page with a litany of options for the blog. One of them is a checkbox labeled Allow users to post comments. This checkbox should be selected. The checkbox labeled Allow anonymous users to post comments should be cleared. This configures the blog to require the visitor to authenticate before being given the opportunity to leave a comment on a given blog post.

The Blog module on the remote server should have at least one sample blog post. If it doesn't already, go ahead and add one; you're about to test the comment feature. After you've confirmed the blog has at least one post, log in as a normal registered user; don't use the Host or Admin account. If you don't already have a regular account, you can create one by clicking on the Register hyperlink next to the Login hyperlink on any page.

After logging in as a registered user, navigate to the Blog page, and click the hyperlink labeled More located below the blog post. This will show the full blog post on the page, including the form fields to leave a comment about the blog post. When you navigate to the full blog post, you might be shocked to discover the skin goes a little awry. The center pane that contains the blog post is so bloated that it can no longer fit between the left and right panes. The skin applies float rules in CSS to position these side panes. Don't worry too much about float positioning just yet; you'll get to that in a subsequent chapter. The important thing to understand is that the module that used to fit in the center pane is now too wide. What happened?

These are the types of things that challenge the DotNetNuke skin developer. The skin is generic enough to permit any module to be dropped inside its panes, but there's no way of telling how big the module might grow until the damage is already done. In some cases, you can review the module and see what's going on. Sometimes, you can even fix the problem that's breaking your skin — examine that bloated Blog module now and see if your forensic investigation turns up anything.

Viewing the HTML source in the browser can give you a target to search for in the source code of the module. Just by looking at the page in the browser, you can observe the three text boxes that constitute the comment form — two single-line `textbox` controls and one multiline `textarea` control, to be exact. These controls appear as wide as the bloated center pane, so that's your first clue. Just searching for the `textarea` control in the HTML source yields a gem:

```
<TR>
    <TD colSpan="2">
        <textarea name="dnn:ctr373:MainView:ViewEntry:txtComment" rows="5"
            id="dnn_ctr373_MainView_ViewEntry_txtComment" class="NormalTextBox"
            style="width:430px;"></textarea>
    </TD>
</TR>
```

The previous HTML source code shows the text area has an inline style attribute that sets the width of the control to 430 pixels. This is an excellent place to start digging. Based on your basic understanding of DotNetNuke modules, you know at least some of the source code exists in the following folder:

```
<Install Folder>\DesktopModules
```

You can open this folder on your local development server and find the folder named Blog that contains the web user controls used by the Blog module. From this starting point you can use any number of search tools to scan the files in this folder for the line that contains your alleged culprit, or just open the files up one by one and look at all of them if you have some time to kill. Either way, your search should reveal that the file named `ViewEntry.ascx` contains your `textarea` control.

In fact, three controls in this file have a hard coded width. The following code block highlights the `ASP.Net` controls that contain a width that is too wide for your skin:

```
<TR>
    <TD>
        <asp:Label id="lblAuthor" CssClass="NormalBold" Runat="server"
            ResourceKey="lblAuthor" Width="80px">Your name:</asp:Label>
    </TD>
    <TD>
        <asp:TextBox id="txtAuthor" Runat="server"
            Width="350px"></asp:TextBox>
    </TD>
    </TD>
</TR>
<TR>
    <TD>
        <asp:Label id="lblCommentTitle" CssClass="NormalBold"
            Runat="server" ResourceKey="lblCommentTitle">Title:</asp:Label>
    </TD>
    <TD align="right">
        <asp:TextBox id="txtCommentTitle" Runat="server"
            Width="350px"></asp:TextBox>
    </TD>
</TR>
<TR>
    <TD colSpan="2">
        <asp:label id="lblComment" ResourceKey="lblComment"
```

```
            cssclass="NormalBold" runat="server">Comment:</asp:label>
      </TD>
   </TR>
   <TR>
      <TD colSpan="2">
         <asp:textbox id="txtComment" cssclass="NormalTextBox"
            runat="server" width="430" textmode="MultiLine"
            rows="5"></asp:textbox>
      </TD>
   </TR>
```

This is a good example of how hard coded widths in modules can be harmful. It limits the flexibility of the skins, and the problem is difficult to discover before the damage is done. On the other hand, this is the best thing you could have hoped for, given the fact that the module is breaking your skin. You can easily customize this DotNetNuke Blog module to be compatible with your skin by slimming it up a bit.

Take a look at the next code block. In here, the three ASP.Net controls have been modified by removing the hard coded width attribute and changing the CssClass attribute. The surrounding HTML table elements can remain unchanged.

```
<asp:TextBox id="txtAuthor" Runat="server"
   CssClass="txtAuthorCustomBlogClass"></asp:TextBox>

. . .

<asp:TextBox id="txtCommentTitle" Runat="server"
   CssClass="txtCommentTitleCustomBlogClass"></asp:TextBox>

. . .


<asp:textbox id="txtComment" cssclass="txtCommentCustomBlogClass"
   runat="server" textmode="MultiLine" rows="5"></asp:textbox>
```

Here are the CSS rules that you can add to the blog skin that will give the text box controls a good width, but not so wide that they break the skin:

```
.txtAuthorCustomBlogClass
{
   width:300px;
}

.txtCommentTitleCustomBlogClass
{
   width:300px;
}

.txtCommentCustomBlogClass
{
   width:100%;
}
```

You can fix this issue with the Blog module now by customizing the width attributes.

Customize the Blog Module

This section will customize the DotNetNuke Blog module on your local development server. Once you get an acceptable fix in place, the modified files can be copied over to the remote server.

1.   Launch Windows Explorer and navigate to the DotNetNuke Blog module folder that was identified earlier:

```
<Install Folder>\DesktopModules\Blog
```

2.   Open the file named `ViewEntry.ascx` in your favorite text editor.

3.   Delete the hard coded widths of the three `ASP.Net` text box controls as shown in the previous code blocks.

4.   For each of the three `ASP.Net` text box controls, assign the custom `CssClass` attribute value, as shown in the previous code blocks. Make sure that each text box control has only one `CssClass` attribute value. The website will complain if a single text box control has two `CssClass` attribute values.

5.   In the same folder, open the file named `module.css`. This is where CSS rules specific to the Blog module are defined. Append the CSS rules shown in the previous code block to this CSS file.

6.   Launch a web browser and navigate to the Blog page. Sign in as a regular user and click the More hyperlink to see the full blog and the comment form. The skin should now be fixed, and the text box fields should be wide enough to use, but not so wide that they break the skin.

How It Works

Technically, you had solved the problem at Step #4. The text box fields were too narrow to use, however, and made the page look incomplete. You had a choice of where to place the CSS rules for the custom classes on the text box controls. They could have gone inside your CSS file for the Autumn-Blog skin, but the CSS file used by the module was easily available. This is a good example of the set of challenges you'll come across as you skin a DotNetNuke website.

This fix edited just two files. Both of them happened to exist inside the Blog module folder, but they should seem similar to what you've already seen inside skin files. DotNetNuke has a good quality in that once you learn one part, you can reuse what you know in a new area of the system.

Testing the Forum Module

The Forum module presents another good challenge for skinning the site and integrating DotNetNuke modules. The Forum module is dropped into a page that uses the Autumn-Wide skin. When you configure this page on the remote server, you'll discover a problem immediately. The skin uses absolute positioning to move the menu to the top of the page.

On the Forum page, you'll see the menu is stuck inside the Forum module a few inches below where it ought to be. This type of problem suggests the HTML `<div>` tags contain an error, because you know these

You can always find someone
who "supports" DNN...

POWER DNN
DotNetNuke Done Right!

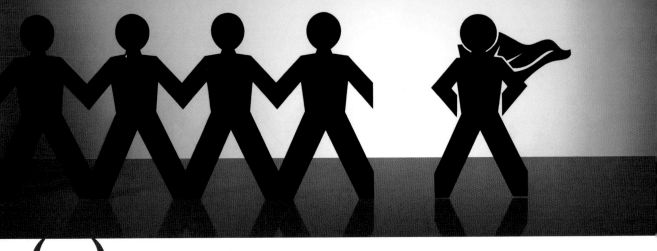

are the tags that anchor the menu through relative positioning. Remember that a single HTML `<div>` tag envelops the entire skin. This `<div>` tag is configured to use relative positioning in the CSS file.

You can investigate this problem by using the same technique you used in the Blog module — investing the HTML source in the browser. To eliminate the tag soup in this HTML source, you can manually delete all of the tags, except for the HTML `<div>` tags. This yields the following code block:

```
<div id="dnn_ControlPanel"></div>
<div id="wideSkinContainer" class="skinContainer">
    <div id="headerContainer"></div>
    <div id="contentContainer">
        <div id="dnn_ContentPane" class="contentPane">
            <div class="containerWrapper">
                <div id="dnn_ctr386_ContentPane" class="ContainerContentPane">
                    <div id="dnn_ctr386_ModuleContent">
                </div>
            </div>
        </div>
    </div>
    <div id="footerContainer"></div>
    <div id="userContainer"></div>
    <div id="menuContainer">
        <div id="theMenu"></div>
    </div>
</div>
```

The previous code block clearly shows the innermost HTML tag is missing the closing `</div>` tag. This is the cause of the problem that's breaking the menu. The same skin file and container file work well with the other pages. Why is the Forum module eating the closing `</div>` tag?

You'd be surprised by the actual number of mysteries in software development. If you had the skills and the time, you could debug the issue and potentially discover what is consuming the closing HTML `</div>` tag. You've got a site to build, however, and the forum is a big module. If you just create another container file that is identical to the standard container file, except for one tiny additional closing `</div>` tag, then you can be on your way.

The following code block shows the fix applied to a new container file named `standard-forum.ascx`. This extra HTML `</div>` tag is all that's needed to resolve this problem, so you don't have to get your hands too dirty.

```
<div id="ContentPane" runat="server" class="ContainerContentPane"></div>
<!--this orphaned html tag below fixes a problem in the forum component -->

</div>
```

Just patch the problem with the Forum module and get on with business.

Try It Out   Implement a Forum Module Workaround

This section will implement a workaround on your local development server. Once you get the Forum module working on your local machine, you can recreate the skin package using the same techniques as before and reload them onto the remote server to fix this issue.

Launch Windows Explorer and navigate to the custom container folder on your local development server located in the following directory:

```
<Install Folder>\Portals\_default\Containers\Autumn
```

1. Copy the file named `standard.ascx`, and name the new file `standard-forum.ascx`.

2. Open the file and add the extra closing HTML `</div>` tag, as shown in the previous code block.

3. Change the container for the Forum page at the page level. Configure the page to use the new container named Standard-forum.

4. Test the Forum page on the local development server to confirm that the menu is now appearing in the proper location.

5. Repackage all of the skin files using the same technique described earlier in this chapter. This time the skin package will include the additional container you just created.

6. Deploy this skin package to the remote server using the same technique. The remote server will happily overwrite the existing skin package with the new set of files.

7. Configure the Forum page on the remote server to use the new container, and confirm that page is now displaying the menu in the appropriate location, too.

How It Works

The forensic techniques you used on this problem quickly identified the solution, but the true problem remained a mystery. Such is life. This problem isn't hurting the application very much, and you have a simple workaround to curtail the issue. In this case, you're choosing to accept the problem and just add a simple closing HTML `</div>` tag to a custom container. You've labeled the container in such a way that you know it's targeted for the Forum module. Perhaps you can track down the true cause of this issue on a rainy Saturday afternoon.

Summary

This chapter ran the gamut for planning, designing, implementing, and debugging a set of custom skins for a DotNetNuke installation. Wire frames are a good place to start considering the requirements for a collection of web pages. They're easy to explain and modify during a casual conversation with a stakeholder.

The collection of skin files for this site included a custom home page, a general all-purpose skin, and a specialized skin for the Blog page and all of its modules. Sometimes a skin can get too special and break under certain conditions. In your case, one module grew in width just enough to push the floating pane over the top of another pane. In another case, a module consumed one of your closing `</div>` tags. As with most software development adventures, experience will be your best tool for learning techniques in how to debug and resolve the various issues you're bound to run into.

In this chapter, you were content with using the traditional horizontal menu in each of your skins. The next chapter takes your skins a step further and customizes the navigation components on the page. You get a little exposure to the vast set of opportunities available to you for customizing the menu.

Exercises

1. What is the name of the folder that contains the DotNetNuke module components?

2. What are the three common types of CSS positioning?

3. In CSS, what is the rule an absolutely positioned element uses to identify its 0,0 coordinate?

4. In a CSS file, what is the difference between the # character and the . character in a selector?

5. If you opened a custom skin file named MyCustomSkin.zip, what two files would you expect to see inside?

8

Designing the Navigation

The skinning project for the Montavilla Neighborhood Association website happily used the default menu skin object in DotNetNuke, until now. In this chapter, you take a closer look at the menu skin object and explore the options available to you.

A web page is rarely without a menu navigation system so visitors are subjected to many types of menus. Menus in DotNetNuke are usually implemented as skin objects. Skin objects are well suited for this specialized task. The following list describes the common traits of a skin object:

❑   Provides a small, contained feature for a DotNetNuke site.

❑   Exists inside of a DotNetNuke skin file.

❑   Can be customized through properties it makes available to the skin developer.

❑   Can be customized by editing the .ascx file in a text editor, if available.

❑   Can be customized by editing the VB.Net or C# code, if available.

❑   A similar skin object probably already exists.

❑   Easy to swap for a best-fit comparison.

Skin objects are nothing new, and you've dealt with them on a regular basis in the previous chapters. This chapter focuses on a particular type of skin object — those providing menu navigation services. A menu skin object has the ability to request the pages from DotNetNuke. The menu skin object formats the pages into a navigable list for a web page and emits the necessary HTML.

You'll see how to install a third-party skin object as well as configure alternative menu controls that are already available in a default installation. You'll leverage one of the alternative menus and apply it to the Neighborhood Association website.

Examining the Menu Provider Pattern

With the menu-centric focus of this chapter in mind, you're interested in comparing various aspects of different menus to find one that's best suited to your needs. This section examines the menu skin objects that come along with the default DotNetNuke installation and explores the concepts of the menu provider pattern.

Chapter 2 introduced the notion of provider patterns. As a quick refresher, the SQL Server database provider is a specific implementation of the provider pattern. You can search online for vendors today who sell DotNetNuke database providers for MySQL, an open source database, to use in place of SQL Server. A database provider is essentially code that knows how to communicate between DotNetNuke and a specific database. The database provider pattern architecture allows any database to be wired up to DotNetNuke with minimal fuss, as long as the given database provider is available.

A provider is just a wrapper around the component doing the actual work. Providers adhere to the specifications of the given system, DotNetNuke in this case, for the benefit of being easily exchanged for another provider. A provider knows how to communicate with the component it envelops, which might be in a very specialized or difficult process. On the outside, the provider has to implement the features specified by the given system. When the provider is snapped into place, the system calls the provider using these system specific methods. The provider converts a given external request into the equivalent internal request for the enveloped component, and voila! You have abstracted away the complicated details of the underlying component, and created an easy way to swap out service providers.

Moving from the conceptual to the practical — menu skin objects are another example of the provider pattern in DotNetNuke. The NavigationProvider control is the generic menu provider that defines all of the tasks menus must be capable of performing. A menu skin object that wants to participate in the menu provider pattern must implement the features defined by the NavigationProvider control. DotNetNuke 4.5.0 has five types of menus that implement this provider pattern, so you have a bunch to choose from, depending on the needs of the task at hand. As a skin developer, you don't really care about the details of the provider pattern. You just need to know how to configure them for your skin. If you were writing your own custom menu skin object in VB.Net or C#, it would be a different story. You can be content to treat these programmatic details like your refrigerator; you need only care about them when they stop working.

You can examine all of the DotNetNuke provider services by opening the file named `web.config` in a text editor and scrolling down to the `<dotnetnuke>` element. That element lists all of the service provider sections in the default `web.config` file:

❑   htmlEditor

❑   navigationControl

❑   searchIndex

❑   searchDataStore

❑   data

❑   logging

❑   scheduling

- ❑ friendlyUrl

- ❑ caching

- ❑ authentication

- ❑ members

- ❑ roles

- ❑ profiles

The name of each item gives a pretty good hint to the kind of service it provides to DotNetNuke. The provider pattern really gets its strength from its ability to swap out instances of providers with very little effort.

The truth is that you will probably never swap out the data provider. SQL Server is an excellent data repository and tough to beat by any metric. Nevertheless, a few providers do get swapped out frequently. In this chapter, you swap navigationControl providers, and later on in the book, you swap out instances of the htmlEditor provider. It might be hard to grasp fully the possibilities here until you actually do it, so let's get moving!

A Closer Look at the Default Menu

This book has been using the default menu. Until DotNetNuke version 4.5.0, this standard skin object was referred to directly inside the DNN-Blue skin file named `Horizontal Menu - Fixed Width.ascx`. The following control directive existed at the top of the skin file in DotNetNuke version 4.4.1:

```
<%@ Register TagPrefix="dnn" TagName="MENU"
    Src="~/Admin/Skins/SolPartMenu.ascx" %>
```

The web user control named `SolPartMenu.ascx` was contributed by Jon Henning of Solution Partners, Inc. It's a versatile and widely used menu for DotNetNuke sites that has its roots as far back as version 2.00.04, should you care enough to look for it in the DotNetNuke earliest ancestor version available in the `SourceForge.net` archives. The skinning chapter in *Professional DotNetNuke 4* contains a description of this particular skin object and a listing of SolPartMenu properties. It's a good reference for a highly customized implementation of this menu skin object.

The SolPartMenu control implements the menu by injecting a series of HTML tables into the page. It utilizes a collection of JavaScript functions to display the fly-out menus for the child pages on a site, too. The blogs and forums on `www.dotnetnuke.com` also provide a historical context for this widely used component.

DotNetNuke version 4.5.0 modified the default DNN-Blue skin to use the provider model for the menu navigation. This wasn't a completely new change. Recent versions of DotNetNuke included the `<navigationControl>` provider section in the `web.config` file, but the default skin had continued to refer to the SolPartMenu directly. Version 4.5.0 made a change to the default skin by referring to the web user control named Nav.ascx in the register directive shown in the following code:

```
<%@ Register TagPrefix="dnn" TagName="NAV" Src="~/Admin/Skins/Nav.ascx" %>
```

This alternative web user control implements a similar type of skin object to that implemented by the `solpartmenu.ascx` web user control that still exists in the same directory of DotNetNuke version 4.5.0. The Nav.ascx control provides an additional layer of abstraction over the actual menu skin object used by the page.

The `ProviderName` property in the following code block identifies which menu provider will be used in the skin. Changing the `ProviderName` property of the Nav.ascx control is the only edit required to swap menu providers. The following code block shows the default configuration of the DNN-Blue skin for the Nav.ascx web user control:

```
<dnn:NAV runat="server" id="dnnNAV"
    ProviderName="DNNMenuNavigationProvider"
    CSSControl="main_dnnmenu_bar"
    CSSContainerRoot="main_dnnmenu_container"
    CSSNode="main_dnnmenu_item"
    CSSNodeRoot="main_dnnmenu_rootitem"
    CSSIcon="main_dnnmenu_icon"
    CSSContainerSub="main_dnnmenu_submenu"
    CSSBreak="main_dnnmenu_break"
    CSSNodeHover="main_dnnmenu_itemhover"
    NodeLeftHTMLBreadCrumbRoot="<img alt=&quot;*&quot; BORDER=&quot;0&quot;
    src=&quot;breadcrumb.gif&quot;/>"
/>
```

As you can see in the previous code block, the Nav.ascx control implements a slightly different set of properties from its predecessor, the SolPartMenu. The well-named properties help to make the skin object easier to customize. The last property in the previous code block is interesting because the value is an HTML `<img>` tag. The quotes around the attributes of the `<img>` tag have been avoided by using their entity reference equivalent. When the control is rendered, the `&quot;` entity reference is converted into quotes that surround the attribute values of the `<img>` tag — clever!

Try It Out   Customize the DNNMenu Skin Object

As of DotNetNuke version 4.5.0, the DNN-Blue skin uses the Nav.ascx web user control to display the menu. By default, this control is configured to use the DNNMenu. The menu provider can be easily switched by editing the `ProviderName` property of the Nav.ascx web user control to another provider that's available in the system.

Switching providers is cool enough, and you'll try changing menu providers soon. In this section, you'll take advantage of some custom properties specific to the DNNMenu skin object. While the DNNMenu skin object has a provider that implements the generic menu provider interface, it also has some custom properties of its own. As a special custom feature, the DNNMenu skin object is capable of rendering the menu without HTML tables in the markup. You'll configure that property now. This section assumes you are using DotNetNuke version 4.5.0 or later.

1. Use Windows Explorer to navigate to the following folder inside your DotNetNuke installation:

```
<install folder>\Portals\_default\Skins\DNN-Blue
```

2. Copy the file named `Horizontal Menu - Fixed Width.ascx`. Name the new file `MyCustomSkin.ascx`. The new file should be in the same directory as the original file.

3. Log in as the Host account and create two test pages named Test1 and Test2. Test1 should use the default skin named Horizontal Menu - Fixed Width and Test2 should use the new skin named MyCustomSkin. Both files should be visible to all users. Configure Test1 as the parent of Test2 so that the environment has two levels of pages to display.

4. Log out of DotNetNuke and load Test2 in your browser. It should be identical to Test1.

5. Open the skin named MyCustomSkin.ascx in your favorite text editor.

6. Add the following register directive to this web user control file under the existing control directive:

```
<%@ Register TagPrefix="dnn" Namespace="DotNetNuke.UI.Skins"
    Assembly="DotNetNuke" %>
```

7. Edit the instance of the Nav.ascx user control. Change it to have a closing tag instead of a self-closing tag and add in the <CustomAttributes> section as shown in the following code block:

```
<dnn:NAV runat="server" id="dnnNAV" ProviderName="DNNMenuNavigationProvider">
    <CustomAttributes>
        <dnn:CustomAttribute Name="UseTables" Value="False"/>
    </CustomAttributes>
</dnn:NAV>
```

8. Save the changes to the skin file and reload Test2 in your browser.

9. Toggle between Test1 and Test2. Compare the HTML source code rendered in your browser and observe the changes caused by this custom property setting. You should see that Test2 does not include any HTML tables in the markup emitted by the Nav.ascx control.

How It Works

The additional register directive in the skin file allows DotNetNuke to get a handle on the custom properties available in the configured menu provider, DNNMenuNavigationProvider in this case. The developer of this menu skin object, Jon Henning, provided a custom attribute named UseTables. By default, this property is set to true and you see the result in the page named Test1.

You have the ability to flip this UseTables attribute to false and affect the output of the menu skin object as you see in the page named Test2.

The Firefox add-on named View Source Chart described in Chapter 5 provides excellent visibility into how the DNNMenu skin object has changed its output based on the value of the UseTables property. The skin object injects a JavaScript file named dnn.controls.dnnmenu.js into the web page to manipulate the browser's document object model. This JavaScript library is doing the heavy lifting on the client side to render the menu. With the UseTables property set to false, the HTML source in Internet Explorer looks like the following block of HTML code midway down the page:

```
<span><span width="100%" class="" name="dnn$dnnNAV$ctldnnNAV"
id="dnn_dnnNAV_ctldnnNAV" orient="0" sysimgpath="/dnn450/images/" rarrowimg="/
dnn450/images/menu_down.gif" carrowimg="/dnn450/images/breadcrumb.gif"
usetables="0" postback="__doPostBack('dnn$dnnNAV$ctldnnNAV','[NODEID]Click')"
callback="dnn.xmlhttp.doCallBack('ctldnnNAV dnn_dnnNAV_ctldnnNAV','[NODEXML]',
this.callBackSuccess,oMNode,this.callBackFail,this.callBackStatus,null,null,0);
"></span></span>
```

The previous block of HTML code isn't too exciting; it doesn't tell us much about the actual menu HTML. This markup made the initial journey across the wire with the rest of the page. After the page loaded, the JavaScript file took over and made some changes to the page before you actually began to read it in your browser. The JavaScript library injected the following HTML code that View Source Chart lets you see:

```
<span>
    <span tabindex="0" width="100%" class="" name="dnn$dnnNAV$ctldnnNAV"
        id="dnn_dnnNAV_ctldnnNAV" orient="0" sysimgpath="/dnn450/images/"
        rarrowimg="/dnn450/images/menu_down.gif"
        carrowimg="/dnn450/images/breadcrumb.gif" usetables="0"
        postback="__doPostBack('dnn$dnnNAV$ctldnnNAV','[NODEID]Click')"
        callback="dnn.xmlhttp.doCallBack('ctldnnNAV

        dnn_dnnNAV_ctldnnNAV','[NODEXML]',this.callBackSuccess,oMNode,
        this.callBackFail,this.callBackStatus,null,null,0);">
        <span class="" id="dnn_dnnNAV_ctldnnNAVctr37">
            <span class=""></span>
            <span style="cursor: pointer;" id="dnn_dnnNAV_ctldnnNAVt37">
                Home
            </span>
        </span>
        <span class="" style="background-image: url(/dnn450/images/menu_down.gif);
            background-repeat: no-repeat; background-position: right center;"
            id="dnn_dnnNAV_ctldnnNAVctr54">
            <span class=""></span>
            <span style="cursor: pointer;" id="dnn_dnnNAV_ctldnnNAVt54">
                Test1
            </span>
        </span>

        <table class=""
            style="position: absolute; top: 76px; left: 159px; display: none;"
            id="dnn_dnnNAV_ctldnnNAVsub54" border="0" cellpadding="0" cellspacing="0">
            <tbody>
            </tbody>
            <div class="" id="dnn_dnnNAV_ctldnnNAVctr55">
                <span class=""></span>
                <span style="cursor: pointer;" id="dnn_dnnNAV_ctldnnNAVt55">
                    Test2
                </span>
            </div>
        </table>

    </span>
</span>
```

The previous block of HTML code was made visible to you by the View Source Chart Add-on for Firefox. In there, you can see the Test1 item and the Test2 item. A combination of JavaScript and CSS make this into a fly-out menu in your browser. Without any additional CSS customizations on your part, it renders in varying degrees of success in the different browsers.

The View Source Chart Add-on also lets you become aware of some curious markup emitted by the DNNMenu skin object. It turns out that the child menu items, like Test2, are still surrounded by an HTML table tag. Technically, the Test2 item is outside of the <tbody> tag, so it's not actually inside a table cell, but it does shed some light on what's going on under the hood in the HTML that you're designing. Just to do a more complete comparison, flip the UseTables property setting back to true and look at the markup in Firefox with the View Source Chart Add-on. You'll see the Test2 item surrounded by HTML table cell tags. This isn't a horrible thing, but it's something to be aware of as you're creating skins inside DotNetNuke. After all, you should know what it is you're aiming at.

If you were to truly use this (very capable) menu skin object in your Neighborhood Association website, you would need to make a couple of CSS tweaks to the menu. This isn't a ton of work, but you are interested in comparing a couple of menu skin objects, so let's keep moving.

Changing Menu Providers

Now that you've customized the existing menu provider object, try going the other direction and swap it out completely. DotNetNuke version 4.5.0 started using the DNNMenu provider by default, but the SolPartMenu is still tucked away in the system and ready for use. There are some subtle differences in how it behaves, but if you know how to customize one, the other isn't much more difficult. You won't get into too much detail here because your first and foremost interest is in just swapping menu providers.

Try It Out   Exchange Menu Providers

In this section, you'll swap out the DNNMenu skin object in favor of the original SolPartMenu and observe any differences in the resulting HTML code.

1. You can reuse the same Test1 and Test2 pages you created in the previous section that customized the DNNMenu skin object. Make sure they're in place.

2. Open the skin file used for testing in the previous section in a text editor. Its filename is MyCustomSkin.ascx.

3. Edit the instance of the Nav.ascx web user control so it looks like the following code block. The control should be self-closing; it doesn't need an open tag and a closing tag. The ProviderName property is configured to use the SolpartMenuNavigationProvider.

```
<dnn:NAV runat="server" id="dnnNAV"
    ProviderName="SolpartMenuNavigationProvider" />
```

4. Load the Test2 page in your browser and look at the resulting HTML source code. Toggle between the Test1 page and the Test2 page and look for differences.

How It Works

A careful look at the HTML source code sent to the browser will reveal that the system is now injecting the JavaScript file named spmenu.js into the markup. The change in the menu provider sends the following text down the wire to the browser:

```
<span id="dnn_dnnNAV_ctldnnNAV" name="dnn$dnnNAV$ctldnnNAV" HlColor="White"
ShColor="Gray" SelForeColor="White" SelColor="Navy" FontStyle="font-family: ;
font-size: ; font-weight: normal; font-style: normal; text-decoration: "
```

```
SysImgPath="/dnn450/images/" Display="horizontal" IconWidth="15" MODisplay="Outset"
MenuTransition="None" IconImgPath="/dnn450/images/" ArrowImage="breadcrumb.gif"
RootArrowImage="menu_down.gif" RootArrow="-1" SupportsTrans="1"><xml
id="SolpartMenuDI" onreadystatechange="if (this.readyState == 'complete')
spm_initMyMenu(this, spm_getById('dnn_dnnNAV_ctldnnNAV'))"><root><menuitem id="37"
title="Home" url="http://andrew-m/dnn450/Home/tabid/37/Default.aspx" /><menuitem
id="54" title="Test1" url="http://andrew-m/dnn450/Test1/tabid/54/Default.aspx"
css=" "><menuitem id="55" title=" Test2" url="http://andrew-m/dnn450/
Test1/Test2/tabid/55/Default.aspx" /></menuitem></root></xml></span>
```

Again, it's tough to discern what's actually happening by just looking at this glob of HTML code before the JavaScript library has had a chance to modify it and build a usable menu in the browser. The following block of HTML shows an example of what the View Source Chart in Firefox tells us about the finished state of the browser's document object model. The SolPartMenu control implements the menu as a series of HTML tables. It's a bit more verbose than its more agile sibling, the DNNMenu. The markup is formatted as well as the page width would allow. Some of the HTML attributes are quite lengthy.

```
<table id="tbldnn_dnnNAV_ctldnnNAVMenuBar" class="dnn_dnnnav_ctldnnnav_spmbctr"
    style="vertical-align: middle;" border="0" cellpadding="0" cellspacing="0"
    width="100%">
<tbody>
    <tr>
        <td>
<table border="0" cellpadding="0" cellspacing="0" width="100%"><tbody>
<tr id="tddnn_dnnNAV_ctldnnNAV37"
    onmouseover="m_oSolpartMenu['dnn_dnnNAV_ctldnnNAV'].onMBMO(this);"
    onmouseout="m_oSolpartMenu['dnn_dnnNAV_ctldnnNAV'].onMBMOUT(this);"
    onclick="m_oSolpartMenu['dnn_dnnNAV_ctldnnNAV'].onMBC(this, event);"
    onmousedown="m_oSolpartMenu['dnn_dnnNAV_ctldnnNAV'].onMBMD(this);"
    onmouseup="m_oSolpartMenu['dnn_dnnNAV_ctldnnNAV'].onMBMU(this);"
    class="dnn_dnnnav_ctldnnnav_spmbar dnn_dnnnav_ctldnnnav_spmitm" savecss=""
    saveselcss=""
    menuclick="document.location.href='http://dnn/Home/tabid/37/Default.aspx';"
    style="">
    <td unselectable="on" title="" nowrap="NOWRAP">
      <img src="/dnn450/images/spacer.gif"> Home 
    </td>
</tr></tbody></table>
</td>
<td>
<table border="0" cellpadding="0" cellspacing="0" width="100%"><tbody>
<tr id="tddnn_dnnNAV_ctldnnNAV54"
    onmouseover="m_oSolpartMenu['dnn_dnnNAV_ctldnnNAV'].onMBMO(this);"
    onmouseout="m_oSolpartMenu['dnn_dnnNAV_ctldnnNAV'].onMBMOUT(this);"
    onclick="m_oSolpartMenu['dnn_dnnNAV_ctldnnNAV'].onMBC(this, event);"
    onmousedown="m_oSolpartMenu['dnn_dnnNAV_ctldnnNAV'].onMBMD(this);"
    onmouseup="m_oSolpartMenu['dnn_dnnNAV_ctldnnNAV'].onMBMU(this);"
    class="dnn_dnnnav_ctldnnnav_spmbar dnn_dnnnav_ctldnnnav_spmitm" savecss=" "
    saveselcss=""
    menuclick="document.location.href='http://dnn/Test1/tabid/54/Default.aspx';"
    style="top: 57px; left: 172px;">
```

```
    <td unselectable="on" title="" nowrap="NOWRAP">
        <img src="/dnn450/images/spacer.gif"> Test1
    </td>
    <td class="dnn_dnnnav_ctldnnnav_spmrarw" align="right">
        <img src="/dnn450/images/menu_down.gif" alt="&gt;">
    </td>
</tr></tbody></table>
</td>
<td width="100%">
  <img src="/dnn450/images/spacer.gif">
</td>
</tr></tbody></table>
```

Now that you've customized the DNNMenu skin object and switched to the SolPartMenu skin object, you have a deeper understanding of the different types of markup that affect the skinning process. If you've spent time on the DotNetNuke blogs and forum, you might have learned that the SolPartMenu has been superseded by the DNNMenu. Most of the time you'll pass on the SolPartMenu for new sites; however, this older skin object is still quite capable, and you'll run into it frequently if your DotNetNuke adventures bring you to established sites for maintenance and enhancements.

Using the ASP2 Menu Skin Object

Let's try one more menu skin object that's available in the default installation. This skin object starts to leverage components that exist in the core ASP.Net 2.0 Framework as opposed to the previous two custom built menu skin objects. ASP.Net 2.0 shipped with several new server controls; one of them was the menu control. This new control bundled up a lot of the work that was necessary to create a menu for a website. Prior to this, most folks used a third-party commercial component for complex web-based menus. Some savvy developers took on the task of writing menu controls on their own. When ASP.Net 2.0 shipped, anyone could drag the menu server control onto a web page and enlist the help of a powerful tool for their navigation needs.

DotNetNuke contains a provider for this alternative menu to enable the generic ASP.Net 2.0 menu control to interact with your system. Try using this type of menu skin object, and see what type of changes it makes to the system.

Try It Out   Use the ASP.Net 2.0 Menu Provider

This section will modify your test skin to use the menu component that comes with the ASP.Net 2.0 Framework. Because a DotNetNuke provider for this menu component exists, you know it supports the fundamental features that DotNetNuke demands of all menus in the provider model. You've also seen how menus are still free to implement these features in many ways with a variety of HTML markup. See how the ASP.Net 2.0 menu component stacks up.

1. Continue to reuse the same Test1 and Test2 pages from the prior sections of this chapter.

2. Open the test skin file in your favorite text editor. The filename is `MyCustomSkin.ascx`.

177

3. Edit the instance of the Nav.ascx web user control so that it looks like the following code block. The control should be self-closing; it doesn't need an open tag and a closing tag. The `ProviderName` property is configured to use the ASP2MenuNavigationProvider.

```
<dnn:NAV runat="server" id="dnnNAV"
    ProviderName="ASP2MenuNavigationProvider" />
```

4. Load Test2 in your browser and look at the resulting HTML source code. Toggle between Test1 and Test2 and look for differences.

How It Works

Among the several differences you'll see between Test1 and Test2, the alternative method of injecting JavaScript files into the page is worth noting. The following code block shows how the ASP.Net 2.0 Menu server control adds a JavaScript library to a page so its functions are available on the client side:

```
<script src="/WebResource.axd?d=tZCZzdnIkNHdPJf3P-2e6g2&amp;t=632963260127968750"
    type="text/javascript"></script>
```

Instead of the familiar file ending with the extension of `.js`, this JavaScript file reference looks more like a web page URL. It even has a query string that passes a couple of parameters to something that looks like a web page named `webresource.axd`. This isn't an actual file on the web server. It's a technique that ASP.Net 2.0 employs to extract embedded resources from components like the menu server control and send them down the wire to your browser.

You don't need to get too deep into the technical explanation for this alternative form of JavaScript file reference; it's sufficient to know that it operates just like any other type of JavaScript file. You can even load the URL for this JavaScript file directly in your address bar if you want to see the file the browser downloaded and prove to yourself that no voodoo is taking place.

By default, this menu component baked into the ASP.Net 2.0 Framework is much more verbose than either the DNNMenu or the SolPartMenu. Jon Henning lists some interesting size comparisons in his blog on the DotNetNuke website. The ASP.Net 2.0 menu was the largest in the list.

If your DotNetNuke site has several pages available in the navigation, this can be a large burden on the bandwidth of the website. Your visitors will download many more bits than they absolutely need. You might be tempted to shrug and discount that problem because many visitors have high-speed Internet access today. The problem lies in bandwidth cost. Larger operations are keenly aware of the costs of bandwidth. After labor costs, network bandwidth is usually the next highest cost on the minds of CTOs, CIOs, and CFOs. You'll take some good steps toward friendship if you can keep this costly issue under control.

Using the TreeViewMenu Skin Object

So far, you've customized a menu and swapped out the menu by taking advantage of the provider pattern in DotNetNuke. In addition to the horizontal menus you've been using so far, the default installation of DotNetNuke also includes a TreeViewMenu component. A version of the DNN-Blue skin named `Vertical Menu - Fixed Width.ascx` implements this alternative menu.

This menu acts much like Windows Explorer. You can expand and collapse sections of the navigation before selecting a menu item and navigating to the given page. Because of its height, width and expandable surface area, this type of control is usually placed on the left side of the page so that it has plenty of room to operate.

When you customize the menu system used by a skin in DotNetNuke, the provider model isn't the only technique. It's there if it provides value, but you can always go back down to the bare metal if necessary. This time, let's forgo the menu provider pattern and just implement the TreeViewMenu skin object directly in the skin.

Try It Out   Convert the Menu to a Horizontal Display

In this section, you'll bypass the menu provider pattern in DotNetNuke and just implement this menu skin object as you would any other custom skin object — by referring to it in the skin with the familiar ASP.Net syntax.

1. Open the test skin named `MyCustomSkin.ascx` again in your favorite text editor. This time, add a register directive to the top of the file, just under the control directive. Add the following code block that refers to the TreeViewMenu skin object so it can be instantiated in the skin:

```
<%@ Register TagPrefix="dnn" TagName="TREEVIEW"
      Src="~/Admin/Skins/TreeViewMenu.ascx" %>
```

2. Delete the instance of the Nav.ascx web user control in the skin file. You don't need this skin object in this version of the test skin.

3. Find the LeftPane in the test skin and delete the two attributes named `id` and `runat`. You want to reclaim this table cell for your TreeView and you don't want visitors dropping DotNetNuke modules into the pane.

4. Now that you've cleared out a spot in the skin, add an instance of the TreeView to the LeftPane so that it will show the menu skin object. The following code contains both the TreeView skin object and the table cell tags that envelop it:

```
<TD class="leftpane" valign="top" align="center">

    <dnn:TREEVIEW runat="server" id="dnnTREEVIEW" bodyCssClass="Normal"
        CssClass="TreeViewMenu" headerCssClass="TreeViewMenu_Header"
        headerTextCssClass="Head" level="root" nowrap="true"
        treeIndentWidth="5" />

</TD>
```

5. Load Test2 in your browser and take a look at the TreeView control.

How It Works

In this case, you didn't take advantage of the Nav.ascx web user control and its hook into the menu provider pattern. You wired up the menu directly, just as it was done by default in DotNetNuke version 4.4.1 and earlier versions.

These types of menus are good for sites that have a large number of pages at the top level. It's difficult to fit more than five or six pages side by side as top-level pages in a horizontal menu. Vertically positioned, the site can grow indefinitely, and more important to your concerns, the page design should be capable of supporting a variable number of pages. The left column should be designed in such a way that the page is able to flow vertically. On the other side, TreeViewMenu controls give the site the look of a business application or web utility. That might be completely contrary to the purpose of the site and therefore be an unacceptable choice. All of these factors need consideration when you're selecting a menu control to use on a custom skinned DotNetNuke website.

Implementing a Third-Party Menu Control

In addition to the choice of menu components inside a default instance of DotNetNuke, many third-party components are available. These developers saw a need for a component that emitted the HTML code in a slightly different way or provided a better way of configuring the menu for their particular needs.

Because exchanging components is a painless process, the evaluation of a given third-party menu is focused on the features. No component vendor claims "easier installation" because all DotNetNuke components are easy to install. Skin designers are interested in the type of markup emitted and the configuration effort required. You understand that a component is capable of emitting a large blob of HTML that completely trashes your page. Sometimes this is caused by lack of proficiency with the component. Problems can also happen when a specialized component is used outside of its niche market. Of course there's always another kind of problem — the component just plain stinks. These are the types of things to keep in mind while evaluating third-party components.

Sometimes component vendors will license a component for free as a way of attracting customers to evaluate additional commercial products. It's a good model that shows the vendor's support for the industry and their willingness to contribute to this open source platform as well as competing in the DotNetNuke vendor market space.

In the exploration of third-party menu components, you'll examine one that is available at www.houseofnuke.com from Tim Rolands. You'll examine the markup emitted by the component and what techniques are available to you for customizing the look and feel for your custom skin.

Using the HouseMenu Skin Object

The HouseMenu skin object is available for download at www.houseofnuke.com. The skin object can also be found in the code download for this book. The website indicates this menu component lends itself well to CSS, which means it's probably lightweight and doesn't add much in-line styles or presentation information to the markup.

Try It Out   House of Nuke Menu

To put this menu component through its paces, you need to install it into your DotNetNuke system and add it to a page. This section will install version 1.02.01 of the HouseMenu skin object. This component is under active development. At the time of this writing, a new version was in beta using the same major version number, so these instructions should continue to work well.

1. Obtain the skin object installation from the code download for this chapter. The name of the installation file is `HouseMenuSkinObjectPA_01.02.01.zip`.

2. Log in as the Host account on your local development installation of DotNetNuke.

3. The installation process for a third-party skin object is similar to installing a module or skin file. Click Host, Module Definitions in the menu to navigate to the Module Definitions page.

4. Scroll to the bottom of the page and click the hyperlink named Install New Module. The browser navigates to the install new module page. Modules and skin objects are installed using the same set of web pages.

5. Click the browse button on the form and locate the HouseMenu installation file named `HouseMenuSkinObjectPA_01.02.01.zip`. Then click the Install New Module hyperlink to start the upload process.

6. The system will process the installation file and show messages along the way. After it successfully uploads, log out of DotNetNuke and navigate to Test2. This is where you'll see the third-party menu skin object shortly.

7. Now that the skin object is installed in the DotNetNuke system, it's time to use it on a skin. Open the test skin file used all along this chapter in a text editor. Its filename is `MyCustomSkin.ascx`.

8. The first edit to make to the skin file is to delete the instance of the TreeView menu skin object that might be lurking in the left pane. If you like, you can also delete the control directive at the top of the page, although it's not altogether necessary. The unused control directives will chew up some additional processing cycles, but you're not likely to notice it in this menu skin object exploration.

9. Now add the control reference for the new HouseMenu skin object to the top of the skin file. The following code blocks indicate how this web user control should be referenced. Like the TreeView skin object, you're referring to the HouseMenu skin object directly instead of plugging in a provider control. All you have is the control to use directly; you don't have the luxury of a provider that wraps around the actual control.

```
<%@ Register TagPrefix="uc1" TagName="HouseMenu"
    Src="~/DesktopModules/HouseMenuSkinObject/HouseMenuSkinObject.ascx" %>
```

10. Add an instance of the HouseMenu skin object to the skin file. The following code block shows a basic example of the control with minimal properties:

```
<uc1:HouseMenu runat="server" id="HouseMenu1"
    Scope="-1"
    ShowAdmin="True"
    IsRecursive="True"
/>
```

11. The control has been installed in DotNetNuke; a control directive now refers to it, and an instance of the control has been added to the skin. It's time to see it in action. Refresh the Test2 page in your web browser, and take a look at the resulting HTML source code.

How It Works

The skin object uses a small number of configuration properties in its current form. The `Scope` property determines the level of the pages to show; in this case you want to see all of them. If you were logged in as the host account, the menu would include the admin pages because the `ShowAdmin` property is set to true. The control emits child pages, in this case the page Test2, because the `IsRecursive` property is also set to true.

Here's a look at the HTML emitted by the control. I formatted it a little to highlight the types of HTML elements it used to express the menu.

```
<div id='HouseMenuNav'>
    <ul id="HouseMenuNav0">

        <li id="HouseMenuNavItem37">
            <a id="HouseMenuNavLink37"
                href="http://localhost/dnn/Home/tabid/37/Default.aspx"
                tabindex="1">Home</a></li>

        <li id="HouseMenuNavItem54">
            <a id="HouseMenuNavLink54"
                href="http://localhost/dnn/Test1/tabid/54/Default.aspx"
                tabindex="1">Test1</a>

            <ul id="HouseMenuNavList54">
                <li id="HouseMenuNavCurrentItem">
                    <a id="HouseMenuNavCurrentLink"
                        href="http://localhost/dnn/Test1/Test2/tabid/55/Default.aspx"
                        tabindex="1">Test2</a></li>
            </ul>

        </li>

    </ul>
</div>
```

Based on its output, you can assume the code for this menu skin object traverses the list of pages in DotNetNuke and writes them out as anchor tags embedded in an unordered list.

Skin designers who embrace the use of CSS will be delighted to see the markup that comes out of this skin object. It's not burdened by any presentation markup that affects font size, colors, background, or anything else that can be easily contained in a CSS file. Each item is contained in a regular list item element of an unordered list.

This type of markup is preferred by designer specialists because it grants them the most amount of flexibility in a web page design. Plus, the markup is semantically accurate. This HTML content is actually a list. The use of HTML tables to produce a menu might solve some problems for someone less experienced in CSS, but at the same time, it burdens the page with more HTML code.

If your specific goal is to establish a decent menu and move on with your business of configuring DotNetNuke, you might choose to pass on a minimalist approach such as this. This skin object requires some CSS skills on your part to make the menu both functional and presentable. You probably noticed that the second-level menu doesn't appear in the browser, even though the second-level unordered list is present in the HTML source. This requires some CSS edits to fix. So, there's no clear winner here. The merits of each type of menu skin object need to be weighed against the need of the specific installation.

Because the focus of this book is creating a custom skin for DotNetNuke, you'll take on the challenge to get a more flexible menu and explore some CSS and other technologies to provide a custom experience for the visitors.

Building an Interactive Menu

This section will take some steps toward implementing the HouseMenu in the Neighborhood Association website. The design is already laid out, and all you want to do is use the HouseMenu and its clean, semantic HTML markup in place of the existing menu skin object.

The HouseMenu skin object emits the menu as an unordered list. Lower-level pages are nested inside the given list item tag and wrapped inside their own unordered list. The HTML tags used to represent this semantic structure help clarify the relationships between the pages.

To view the child pages in a pop-up or fly-out menu structure, you need a technique to show the nested unordered list when the mouse is over the parent page and another technique to hide the child pages when the mouse moves away from the list.

An HTML tag can have a CSS class attribute that enables a CSS rule to modify the look of the given tag. For example, the following code block shows a CSS class attribute on a paragraph tag:

```
<p class="IntroText">Lorem Ipsum</p>
```

The CSS file can include a selector and rule for the IntroText class like the following snippet:

```
p.IntroText
{
    font-size:16pt;
    color:#FF0000;
}
```

The previous selector is only targeting paragraph tags that have the IntroText class. It's a common and useful technique in CSS. When the page loads in the browser, the class is applied to the paragraph tag and that's about it. The given paragraph tag remains styled with this set of rules for the duration of the visit.

CSS includes some techniques for making a web page more interactive, too. The CSS *pseudo class* named hover is a special type of CSS class. It's used to express a CSS rule that only applies when the visitor is hovering over the given element. For example, the following HTML code is a good target for the hover pseudo class:

```
<div class="MenuContainer">
    <a href="default.aspx">Home</a>
    <a href="products.aspx">Products</a>
    <a href="about.aspx">About Us</a>
</div>
```

CSS can be used to make the previous menu more interactive by changing the color of the hyperlinks when the visitor is hovering over the given anchor tag. CSS can target the `<div>` tag that has the CSS class name of `MenuContainer` and apply a hover pseudo class on the anchor tags using the following rules:

```
div.MenuContainer a
{
    font-size:12pt;
    color:blue;
}

div.MenuContainer a:hover
{
    color:red;
}
```

The first CSS rule set in the previous block defines how the menu appears when the page first loads. The second CSS rule set uses the `hover` pseudo class to modify the look of the anchor tag when the mouse is hovering over it. In this case the font color of the given anchor tag text is changed to red when the visitor is hovering over the hyperlink and it returns to blue when the visitor moves away from the hyperlink. This `hover` pseudo class only applies to one anchor tag at a time because the visitor cannot hover over multiple hyperlinks simultaneously.

You can use this technique to help solve the challenge of hiding nested unordered lists when the visitor is not hovering over the hyperlink of the parent page. When the page first loads, all of the unordered lists of the child pages will be hidden through CSS rules. You'll apply the `hover` pseudo class to the `<li>` tag and specify CSS rules on the nested unordered list tags that make it visible so that it dynamically appears on the page. When the visitor moves away from the hyperlink, the unordered list of child pages will disappear and give the page a more interactive look — just by using CSS!

Try It Out   Apply a CSS Pseudo Class

Before getting too fired up about this interactivity, let's try it out in a controlled environment first. This section will create a simple HTML page with just enough code to prove it works.

1. Create the HTML file. You just need enough HTML to create a basic web page. Create a file named `test.html` on your desktop with the following content. Don't forget the doctype at the top of the file. That's a key factor to make this technique work across multiple browsers.

```
<!DOCTYPE html PUBLIC "-//W3C//DTD HTML 4.01 Transitional//EN"
    "http://www.w3.org/TR/html4/loose.dtd">
<html>
    <head>
        <link rel="stylesheet" type="text/css" href="style.css">
    </head>
    <body>
        <div>
            <ul>
                <li>One</li>
                <li>Two</li>
                <li>Three</li>
            </ul>
        </div>
```

```
        </body>
    </html>
```

2. Create another file named `style.css` on your desktop. This is the actual proving ground. You want to create a normal style for the unordered list and a `hover` pseudo class style that makes the page a little more interactive. Add the following styles to the CSS file:

```
li
{
    color:blue;
    font-size:30pt;
}

li:hover
{
    color:white;
    background-color:blue;
}
```

3. Now that the two files are in place, you're ready to run the test. Launch the HTML file in your browser and hover over the three items in the list. When the page loads, each item should be in blue in a vertical list. When you hover over each item, the text color becomes white and the background color becomes blue. Now the page has a much more interactive feel than it did without the CSS pseudo class.

How It Works

The mouse hovering over an item in the list activated the CSS pseudo class. At that moment, the CSS pseudo class took over and applied styles of color and background color to the item. When the mouse left the item, the CSS pseudo class disengaged and the original style was reapplied to the item. This lightweight technique was efficient at changing a large part of the page.

Here's a case where Standards Compliance mode and Quirks mode really stand out. If you remove the doctype from the top of the HTML file, the page will return to Quirks mode. This will cause the CSS pseudo classes to stop working in Internet Explorer 7 and change the look slightly in Firefox. Quirks mode can easily trash the advanced features available in CSS.

This same type of CSS class switching can be accomplished through JavaScript, too. The browser's Document Object Model (DOM) fires events when the mouse hovers over an item, specifically the `OnMouseOver` and `OnMouseOut` events. You could have attached some JavaScript functions to these events. When the events fired, the JavaScript would swap the CSS class of the given item and you would see the same effect. The JavaScript technique is more heavy-handed than just using the simple CSS pseudo class. Browsers that disable JavaScript (ack!) will still be able to see the interactive design of a site that uses CSS pseudo classes. Because there's more going on, there's also more that can go wrong in JavaScript — another reason why CSS pseudo classes are such a great technique to solve this challenge.

This small controlled environment is a great technique to employ when you think of a new feature. It's much safer than trying to hit a homerun and integrate a new idea into the larger project. When learning a new feature, try it out in the simplest possible environment that's free from any other distractions. Then, after some success you'll be more confident with integrating the new feature into the larger system.

Try It Out   **Create an Interactive Menu**

Now that you've established the basic CSS pseudo class feature and made it work in a small sample, it's time to take it to the next level. It's one thing to change the color of an HTML tag and it's quite another to get the top-level unordered list going horizontally and make the second-level unordered list pop up vertically. This section will get your sample code doing exactly that!

1. You're still working in your controlled environment. This time, you need to add a little more complexity to the unordered list. Add a couple of nested unordered lists to the HTML, as shown in the following code block:

```
<!DOCTYPE html PUBLIC "-//W3C//DTD HTML 4.01 Transitional//EN"
    "http://www.w3.org/TR/html4/loose.dtd">
<html>
    <head>
        <link rel="stylesheet" type="text/css" href="style.css">
    </head>
    <body>

        <div>
            <ul>
                <li>One
                    <ul>
                        <li>Page4</li>
                        <li>Page5</li>
                    </ul>
                </li>
                <li>Two
                    <ul>
                        <li>Page6</li>
                        <li>Page7</li>
                    </ul>
                </li>
                <li>Three</li>
            </ul>
        </div>

    </body>
</html>
```

2. Now that HTML is in place it's time to modify the existing CSS file so it can handle the nested unordered lists. Modify the existing CSS file so it matches the following block of CSS:

```
*
{
    margin:0;
    padding:0;
}

li
{
```

```
      color:blue;
      font-size:30pt;
      font-family:Verdana;
      padding:6px;
}

li:hover
{
      color:white;
      background-color:blue;
}

ul li
{

      display:inline;
      position:relative;
      top:0;
      left:0;
}

ul li ul
{

      visibility:hidden;
      position:absolute;
      top:50px;
      left:0;
      background-color:#EEE;
}

ul li:hover ul
{
      visibility:visible;
}

ul li ul li
{
      display:block;
}
```

3. You've created the HTML menu hierarchy and applied the necessary CSS to style the menu in a way that makes the second-level unordered lists pop up, so refresh the sample HTML page in your browser and test it out. Each second-level menu should only appear when you hover over its parent item. When the browser leaves the area, the second-level menu disappears.

    Figure 8-1 shows the interactive menu at work.

How It Works

Adding the menu hierarchy to the page was the easy part. The real work happens in the CSS file. Starting at the top of the CSS file, the * equalizes all margin and padding across all browsers. If left to their own devices, browsers will use slightly different margins and padding around a given HTML tag. This technique ensures that they're all playing by the same rules.

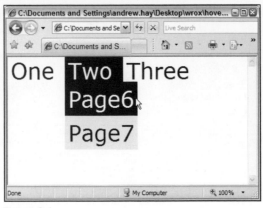

Figure 8-1

The next rule selector of `li` sets the style for all `<li>` tags in the page. The text is blue and in a large font with some uniform padding. The following `li:hover` rule uses a `hover` pseudo class to change the foreground and background color of any `<li>` tag on the page. This is just for aesthetics; it doesn't have anything to do with the pop-up menu. It does help the page appear more interactive.

The following rule of `ul li` starts some goodness. This rule is responsible for laying out the top-level `<li>` tags in a horizontal fashion. By default, `<li>` tags render vertically in the browser. Setting the CSS display property to inline causes this HTML tag to be rendered inline, like a `<span>` tag is normally rendered. This rule also prepares the `<li>` tag to serve as the 0,0 coordinate for positioning the second-level unordered list tags.

The next rule of `ul li ul` declares that any `<ul>` tag that is contained by an `<li>` tag is invisible. This is the way the second-level lists are made invisible when the page first loads. Furthermore, it is positioned absolutely 50 pixels from the top of its 0,0 coordinate, the parent `<li>` tag. The following rule of `ul li:hover ul` makes use of the `hover` pseudo class on the parent `<li>` tag to configure CSS properties of the second-level `<ul>` tag. In this case, its job is easy; it changes the `visibility` CSS property to make the unordered list visible.

The final rule in the CSS file, `ul li ul li`, reverses the display property for the second-level list items so they are displayed vertically. Reading the four-part selector from right to left, this rule affects `<li>` tags that are contained by `<ul>` tags, which are themselves contained by `<li>` tags that are also contained by other `<ul>` tags. That's quite a bit of selection packed into 11 characters! This selector targets the `<li>` tags of the second-level lists, but doesn't apply to the top-level `<li>` tags. Without this rule, the `<li>` tags in the second-level unordered list would be displayed horizontally, just as the top-level menu items are displayed; hence the cascading effect of CSS. Just for fun, you can delete this rule and refresh the page to see the menu items render horizontally.

This small sample has proved that you can create an interactive menu from a collection of unordered list tags and a few lines of CSS. The task requires some knowledge of how CSS can be leveraged, but you were able to achieve all of the goals with a liberally formatted CSS file that didn't exceed 50 lines of text. If you wanted, you could easily compress the CSS file to seven lines of text, one for each rule.

Skinning the HouseMenu

So far, the HouseMenu skin object has been installed in the DotNetNuke system. This component is emitting HTML for the navigation feature in the website as a collection of unordered list tags. The prior section explained the concepts behind the CSS rules used to build an interactive menu from `<ul>` and `<li>` tags. The next feat of strength is to consolidate this knowledge and construct a skinned menu system for the Neighborhood Association website.

The CSS for the menu is fairly specific. There's not much opportunity to reuse the CSS rules targeting the menu in other places on the website, which is a good reason to create a separate CSS file and place all of the menu styles in it. The CSS file named `skin.css` can refer to the menu-specific CSS file by including the following line at the top of the file:

```
@import url('customNavigation.css');
```

This instructs the CSS file to import the given CSS file named `customNavigation.css` and treat the rules in that external file as if they were inside the `skin.css` file. The HTML page that refers to the `skin.css` doesn't have to do anything special. The HTML file doesn't know, or care for that matter, that the menu CSS rules are actually inside a separate physical file. This is just a technique to help skin developers organize their CSS rules.

Try It Out   Apply and Style the HouseMenu

In this section, the CSS for the Neighborhood Association website will be modified to style the unordered list tags in a manner that's consistent with the design.

Because the concepts of the CSS pseudo class have been covered and the two formatted CSS files take up about 200 lines combined, you can download the files and take a look at them on your own. The vast majority of the new CSS is contained in the new file named `customNavigation.css`, and it follows the CSS rules described in the previous sample web page.

These steps will modify the DotNetNuke installation on the local development machine. You'll apply the HouseMenu to the three skins on the Neighborhood Association website and modify the CSS files on the development machine to make sure that all of the concepts are coming together well before deploying the skin package to the remote server.

1. Download the two CSS files for this chapter named `skin.css` and `customNavigation.css` so that they're available on your computer.

2. The HouseMenu skin object should be applied to the three skins. Use Windows Explorer to navigate to the skin folder on the local development machine.

3. Apply the HouseMenu to the three skin files. Use the same method described earlier in the chapter to add both the control directive and the instance of the control to each skin. The HouseMenu skin object should replace the existing menu skin object in each file. The HouseMenu instance should be configured with the same properties as earlier on the Test2 page.

4. Copy the new `skin.css` file and the `customNavigation.css` file obtained in step 1 into the folder for these skins.

5. Launch your web browser and navigate to the home page. The page should look similar, if not identical, to the previous version of the page. When you hover over the top-level pages, the

second-level pages should appear. They should disappear as you move the mouse away from the menu item.

Figure 8-2 shows the HouseMenu with a style that matches the prior menu skin object.

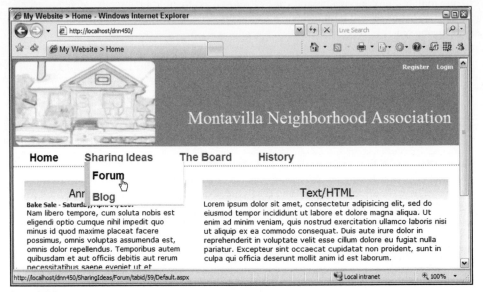

Figure 8-2

How It Works

The `skin.css` file was modified to include an external CSS file. This external CSS file could have existed anywhere, but you chose to put it in the same folder as the `skin.css` file. Designers sometimes use several CSS files and it helps to organize them into a collection of folders in that case.

The interactive menu for the Neighborhood Association website works the same as it did for the small sample HTML page. The CSS takes advantage of the pseudo classes and changes the visibility of the nested unordered lists when the visitor hovers over a menu item.

Summary

The provider model applies to a good deal more than just the database used by the DotNetNuke installation. It's a great technique for swapping out services with little effort and little understanding in how the service provider actually works. Of course, the provider model isn't the only game in town. If necessary, you can always refer to controls directly instead of using that additional layer of abstraction.

A surprising number of menu choices are right out of the box, and you might not have ever noticed them if you hadn't gone digging around. I really like the fact that DotNetNuke "just works" right out of the box while also providing a few gems under the hood if you're willing to poke around a little bit.

This chapter exposed quite a bit of freedom and flexibility with the menu. In exchange, you're obligated to have a reasonable understanding of CSS. If it's any consolation, this is probably the plateau for CSS complexity. You've covered fonts, margins, padding, background images, positioning, and now pseudo classes. There's certainly more to know, but it shouldn't be more complex than what you've already learned — just new combinations and crafty solutions to challenges. If you're becoming comfortable with this level of CSS, then you should be able to take on more sophisticated designs now and be able to ask insightful questions to more experienced CSS folks.

Exercises

1. Name three menus that exist in the default installation of DotNetNuke.

2. Write a CSS selector that will target the anchor tag inside a paragraph tag on a page only when the visitor is hovering over the hyperlink.

3. How can one style sheet be embedded into another style sheet?

4. If the web page looks different in Internet Explorer 7 and Firefox and the page is rendered in Quirks mode, what is the most likely cause of the problem?

Leveraging
Web User Controls

This chapter takes a good look at web user controls and their roles inside a DotNetNuke skin. Previous chapters explained their basic principles, such as how HTML skins are converted into web user controls, or how to create skins as `.ascx` files directly. Now you'll go just a little deeper and leverage custom web user controls in your skins.

In an effort to give you a well-rounded familiarity with the DotNetNuke skinning technology, this chapter introduces some ASP.Net coding concepts. You might find that you have a particular fondness for ASP.Net code and have some great ideas for new modules or skin objects. If that's the case, I highly recommend *Professional DotNetNuke 4* by Shaun Walker et al. (Wiley Publishing, Inc., 2006) for more information on writing custom code that targets the DotNetNuke API.

With that in mind, this chapter takes on the following topics:

❑ How to reduce the amount of redundant code

❑ How to create a more interactive skin

❑ How to develop a specialized skin object

Consolidating Code

Unless your job is to develop redundant systems in the case of a catastrophic event, it's generally a good idea to consolidate in technology. It doesn't matter if you're dealing with HTML, C# code, or databases. Technology tends to improve when it's placed in a singular location that can be modified, thoroughly tested, and reused as much as possible. Just such an opportunity exists inside the skins files for the Neighborhood Association website.

Currently three Neighborhood Association files are used for the home page skin, the blog page skin, and a generic wide skin. Individually, each file is well designed and easy to read. However, aside from key locations in the files, the three files have a good deal of code in common. When the files are viewed as pieces of a collection, a couple of refactoring opportunities jump out.

If the Neighborhood Association asked for changes to the header or footer of the skins, three separate skin files would need to be edited. With a little bit of refactoring, the overall skin design can be improved so that changes to common areas of the skin are made in just one file. The contents of this shared file cascade across all of the skins. This improves the efficiency of changes and ensures that related skin files are consistent.

The following code block displays the contents of the home page skin file:

```
<%@ Control language="vb" AutoEventWireup="false" Explicit="True"
    Inherits="DotNetNuke.UI.Skins.Skin" %>
<%@ Register TagPrefix="dnn" TagName="USER" Src="~/Admin/Skins/User.ascx" %>
<%@ Register TagPrefix="dnn" TagName="LOGIN" Src="~/Admin/Skins/Login.ascx" %>
<%@ Register TagPrefix="dnn" TagName="COPYRIGHT"
    Src="~/Admin/Skins/Copyright.ascx" %>
<%@ Register TagPrefix="dnn" TagName="TERMS" Src="~/Admin/Skins/Terms.ascx" %>
<%@ Register TagPrefix="dnn" TagName="PRIVACY" Src="~/Admin/Skins/Privacy.ascx" %>
<%@ Register TagPrefix="dnn" TagName="DOTNETNUKE"
    Src="~/Admin/Skins/DotNetNuke.ascx" %>
<%@ Register TagPrefix="uc1" TagName="HouseMenu"
    Src="~/DesktopModules/HouseMenuSkinObject/HouseMenuSkinObject.ascx" %>
<div id="ControlPanel" runat="server"></div>

<div id="homePageSkinContainer" class="skinContainer">

    <div id="headerContainer">
        <p>Montavilla Neighborhood Association</p>
    </div>

    <div id="contentContainer">
        <div id="LeftPane" runat="server" class="leftPane"></div>
        <div id="RightPane" runat="server" class="rightPane"></div>
        <div id="ContentPane" runat="server" class="contentPane"></div>
    </div>

    <div id="footerContainer">
        <dnn:COPYRIGHT runat="server" id="dnnCOPYRIGHT" />
        <dnn:TERMS runat="server" id="dnnTERMS" />
        <dnn:PRIVACY runat="server" id="dnnPRIVACY" /><br />
        <dnn:DOTNETNUKE runat="server" id="dnnDOTNETNUKE" />
    </div>
    <div id="userContainer">
        <dnn:USER runat="server" id="dnnUSER" />
        <dnn:LOGIN runat="server" id="dnnLOGIN" />
    </div>
    <div id="menuContainer">
        <div id="theMenu">
            <uc1:HouseMenu runat="server" id="HouseMenu1"
                Scope="-1"
                ShowAdmin="True"
                IsRecursive="True"
            />
        </div>
    </div>
</div>
```

If you examine the other skin files, you'll see that they are nearly identical. The second <div> tag in the home page skin file has a unique id attribute. Both of the other skin files also have unique id attributes. The module panes are also specific to the skin file. Everything below the module panes is identical in every skin file. Based on this information, you have some good opportunities for refactoring the skins.

If you have any experience with Classic ASP or PHP web pages, then you're probably familiar with the concept of including one file in another file. Every page in a twenty-page Classic ASP website can refer to a single file that contains the menu. Then, when the twenty-first page is added to the site, only the menu include file needs to change in order to see the menu link on every other page in the site — this is the power of the include file. You'll use a similar concept with web user controls in ASP.Net.

Try It Out   Refactor the Neighborhood Association Skins

The goal of this section is to reduce the amount of redundant code in the three Neighborhood Association skin files. To achieve this goal, you'll create two additional web user controls that are shared by all three skin files. When a change is made to a shared web user control, the modification is applied to every skin file that refers to the shared web user control.

At the end of this section, the web page in the browser will remain unchanged, but the amount of redundant code in the skin files will be dramatically reduced.

1. Navigate to the folder containing the Neighborhood Association skin files on your local development server.

```
<install folder>\Portals\_default\Skins\Spring
```

2. Create a new text file named sharedHeader.ascx in this folder.

3. Create another new text file named sharedFooter.ascx in this folder.

4. Use your favorite text editor to enter the following code for the sharedHeader.ascx file. Most of it can be copied from the upper portion of any existing skin files. It's OK if you don't understand every line now; all of it will be explained soon.

```
<%@ Control language="vb" AutoEventWireup="false" Explicit="True"
    Inherits="System.Web.UI.UserControl" %>

<script runat="server">
   Public CssTagId As String
</script>

<div id="<%= CssTagId %>" class="skinContainer">

   <div id="headerContainer">
      <p>Montavilla Neighborhood Association</p>
   </div>
   <div id="contentContainer">
```

5. Use your favorite text editor to enter the following code for the sharedFooter.ascx file. Most of it can be copied from the lower portion of any existing skin file.

```
<%@ Control language="vb" AutoEventWireup="false" Explicit="True"
```

```
            Inherits="System.Web.UI.UserControl" %>
<%@ Register TagPrefix="dnn" TagName="USER" Src="~/Admin/Skins/User.ascx" %>
<%@ Register TagPrefix="dnn" TagName="LOGIN" Src="~/Admin/Skins/Login.ascx" %>
<%@ Register TagPrefix="dnn" TagName="COPYRIGHT"
        Src="~/Admin/Skins/Copyright.ascx" %>
<%@ Register TagPrefix="dnn" TagName="TERMS" Src="~/Admin/Skins/Terms.ascx" %>
<%@ Register TagPrefix="dnn" TagName="PRIVACY" Src="~/Admin/Skins/Privacy.ascx" %>
<%@ Register TagPrefix="dnn" TagName="DOTNETNUKE"
        Src="~/Admin/Skins/DotNetNuke.ascx" %>
<%@ Register TagPrefix="uc1" TagName="HouseMenu"
        Src="~/DesktopModules/HouseMenuSkinObject/HouseMenuSkinObject.ascx" %>

    </div>

    <div id="footerContainer">
        <dnn:COPYRIGHT runat="server" id="dnnCOPYRIGHT" />
        <dnn:TERMS runat="server" id="dnnTERMS" />
        <dnn:PRIVACY runat="server" id="dnnPRIVACY" /><br />
        <dnn:DOTNETNUKE runat="server" id="dnnDOTNETNUKE" />
    </div>
    <div id="userContainer">
        <dnn:USER runat="server" id="dnnUSER" />
        <dnn:LOGIN runat="server" id="dnnLOGIN" />
    </div>
    <div id="menuContainer">
        <div id="theMenu">
            <uc1:HouseMenu runat="server" id="HouseMenu1"
                Scope="-1"
                ShowAdmin="True"
                IsRecursive="True"
            />
        </div>
    </div>
</div>
```

6. Use your favorite text editor to modify the home page skin file. First, add two new register
    directives to refer to the new web user controls, and then delete all of the other register direc-
    tives in the skin file. Add an instance of the `SharedHeader.ascx` web user control above the
    panes and an instance of the `SharedFooter.ascx` web user control below the panes. Delete all
    of the other code so the home page skin file looks like the following code:

```
<%@ Control language="vb" AutoEventWireup="false" Explicit="True"
Inherits="DotNetNuke.UI.Skins.Skin" %>
<%@ Register TagPrefix="uc" TagName="SharedHeader" Src="SharedHeader.ascx" %>
<%@ Register TagPrefix="uc" TagName="SharedFooter" Src="SharedFooter.ascx" %>

<div id="ControlPanel" runat="server"></div>

<uc:SharedHeader ID="SharedHeader1" runat="server"
        CssTagId="homePageSkinContainer" />

<div id="LeftPane" runat="server" class="leftPane"></div>
<div id="RightPane" runat="server" class="rightPane"></div>
```

```
<div id="ContentPane" runat="server" class="contentPane"></div>

<uc:SharedFooter id="SharedFooter1" runat="server" />
```

7. Apply this same technique to the blog skin and the wide skin. Each skin should have a ControlPanel, the SharedHeader instance, the panes, and the SharedFooter instance. Make sure to change SharedHeader attribute named `CssTagId` in the blog skin and the wide skin. This attribute contains the unique id for the first `<div>` tag in the `SharedHeader.ascx` file.

8. Launch the site in your browser. Confirm all of the pages are still working with the refactored code in place.

How It Works

It's worth mentioning that the two web user controls created in this exercise are highly dependent on each other. As a general rule, web user controls should be independent. When a control is present, it works, and nothing breaks when it's gone. However, if we didn't have any exceptions, it wouldn't be a rule.

The technique in this exercise relies on the bottom web user control to close any HTML tags that were opened in the top web user control. Sometimes goals come into conflict with each other and decisions are required. In this case, you're balancing the following needs:

❑ Guarantee that targetable HTML tags exist inside a skin for CSS

❑ Keep web user controls independent

❑ Minimize redundant code

This refactoring effort was fairly aggressive. The skin files only contain the control panel, the panes, and the two new web user controls. The first `<div>` tag in the `SharedHeader.ascx` file contains an important id attribute value. The CSS file targets this HTML tag and applies some fundamental styles to the page.

A less aggressive refactoring approach would have kept this HTML tag inside each of the three skin files. That redundant code isn't necessary. The top section of the `ShareHeader.ascx` file includes a server side script tag.

```
<script runat="server">
    Public CssTagId As String
</script>
```

This section of the page contains VB.Net code that is executed on the web server. The code simply declares a field that you can use to exchange data inside and outside of the web user control. In this case, the field is used to pass a value into the web user control. The data are used for the `<div>` tag's id attribute. Each skin using the `SharedHeader.ascx` file includes a value for this field named `CssTagId`.

Inside the `SharedHeader.ascx` file, the value passed in for the id of the `<div>` tag is written out to the browser using the following code:

```
<div id="<%= CssTagId %>" class="skinContainer">
```

The code between the bracket and percent characters is server-side code. The equals sign just tells ASP.Net to write out the value of the following expression. In this case, the following expression is the field you passed into the `SharedHeader.ascx` control from your skin file. The home page skin passed in a value of `homePageSkinContainer`, so that's what will be written out to the browser when the visitor requests the home page.

The `SharedFooter.ascx` file didn't need any extra data. Everything works fine as a hardcoded block of HTML. Now you can be much more confident that all of the skins are implementing a consistent look and feel for the header and footer sections of the page. Plus, if there's a change to make in the future, it will be much easier to make once, instead of duplicating the change in three places.

Developing Interactive Skins

This section constructs two types of interactive features for the Neighborhood Association skins. You already have a structured design implemented in the custom skins and a collection of pages that are configured to use them. You've selected the modules to use in the panes of each page, too. This section is about taking it up a notch in terms of custom interactive features.

The characteristics of each website will help inform what type of interactive behavior is appropriate. In this case, the site contains a set of pages that are only available to board members. The first interactive feature you'll add is a small visual clue on board member pages. This icon automatically appears on any private page that uses your skins. Only a few pages in the Neighborhood Association site will exhibit this behavior. Because skins can be applied to any type of page, the decision to inject the icon is based on the page-level security at run time.

The next interactive feature uses the color palette in your design and the personalization features available in DotNetNuke. After visitors are logged into the system, a small color block appears above their name in the header. The visitor can click any one of the colors in the block. When a color is selected, the background color of the header changes to match the selected item. These small interactive features help the administrator maintain a consistent site, but provide the visitor with a small bit of personalization.

Before you dive headlong into development, take a brief look at other sources of interactive features in DotNetNuke. Modules focus on large pieces of functionality. Modules are normally responsible for storing their own content in a database along with the chores of retrieving and updating it. DotNetNuke skin objects specialize in providing tiny bits of interactive content for a skin file. Generally speaking, skin objects leverage other data repositories and APIs instead of providing their own like DotNetNuke modules.

Skin objects and modules are skin agnostic. They provide varying levels of customization hooks for skins and CSS files, but deep down, they just don't care about their ambient environment. They use C#, VB.Net, JavaScript, and other means of expressing developer intent to provide a service. From a technical perspective, DotNetNuke modules utilize one set of classes built on the .Net Framework, and skin objects use another set of classes.

DotNetNuke modules and skin objects take a fair amount of programming experience to develop from the ground up (so, it's not my intent to go too far down this path); however, as a well-rounded developer, you should have a reasonable understanding of the programmatic features that lay just under the skin. It might lead to an interest in developing your own modules or skin objects, another great reason to pick up a copy of *Professional DotNetNuke 4*.

The default skin objects in DotNetNuke exist in the following folder:

```
<install folder>\admin\Skins
```

The skin objects created in the following sections aren't nearly as skin agnostic as those mentioned earlier. In fact, they're tightly coupled to the skin files that you've been creating throughout the course of the book. For that reason, and because DotNetNuke is so flexible, not to mention this book is focused on skin development instead of module or skin object development, the interactive elements you develop in this chapter will happily exist in the same folder as the skins themselves. You won't need to discover any ancillary packaging techniques for installation on other portals. Just include all of the files in the skin as you normally would when you bundle up the contents of this skin folder.

Inserting a Token on Private Pages

This section constructs a feature in your skin that injects a small visual token on password-protected pages that use your skin. Every page in the Neighborhood Association should be using one of the three skins you've created. So, as long as that's the case, you can be confident that any private page created in the future will also display the token.

Conceptually, you want the skin to append a special CSS class to a `<div>` tag when a private page is requested. Because page-level security can change at any time, this inspection has to occur at run time. The special CSS class will be targeted by your CSS file that contains a rule to display a background image or token on the page. When the CSS class is present, the token appears, and when the CSS class is not present, the token goes away. This solves your consistency requirement. You could have created an alternative skin for private pages that contained a hardcoded token, but this would have required future site managers to remember to use the right skin. The job of showing the token is best left automated.

The following code block shows how the `SharedHeader.ascx` file can be modified to inject a special class to a `<div>` tag when the given page is not available to all users:

```vb
<%@ Control language="vb" AutoEventWireup="true" Explicit="True"
        Inherits="System.Web.UI.UserControl" %>

<script runat="server">

    Public CssTagId As String
    Protected PrivatePageCssClass As String

    Protected Function IsPrivatePage() As Boolean

        Dim parentSkin As DotNetNuke.UI.Skins.Skin
        Dim roles As String

        parentSkin = CType(Me.Parent, DotNetNuke.UI.Skins.Skin)
        roles = parentSkin.PortalSettings.ActiveTab.AuthorizedRoles

        If roles.Contains("All Users") Then
            Return False
        Else
            Return True
        End If
```

```
        End Function

    Private Sub Page_Load(ByVal sender As Object, ByVal e As EventArgs)

        If IsPrivatePage() Then
            PrivatePageCssClass = " PrivatePage"
        Else
            PrivatePageCssClass = String.Empty
        End If

    End Sub

</script>

<div id="<%= CssTagId %>" class="skinContainer<%= PrivatePageCssClass %>">

    <div id="headerContainer">
        <p>Montavilla Neighborhood Association</p>
    </div>

    <div id="contentContainer">
```

The previous code block shows how the SharedHeader.ascx file has been expanded to include logic that automatically injects a special CSS class to a <div> tag when the given page is not available to everyone. Just like Classic ASP, the predecessor of ASP.Net, the server-side code is included in the same file as the HTML code.

Comparing it to the prior version, you can see that another field has been added to the VB.Net code inside the <script> tag, where the server-side code exists. Two members have been added to the script block, too. One is a function named IsPrivatePage(). Its job is to inspect the given page and return the value of True when the page is not available to all users. Otherwise, the function returns False. Well-named functions are critical to writing maintainable code.

This Boolean function reveals the use of the DotNetNuke API. First, the function defines the dimensions of the parentSkin variables and roles. The parentSkin variable is set to the parent of this web user control, which is known to be a DotNetNuke skin. The CType function is used to cast the parent as the skin data type. Once you have a hold on the skin object, you can use its inherent properties to reach into the DotNetNuke API and pull out the roles that have permission to view this page. If the list of roles with access to this page contains the special value of All Users, then you know the page is not private. Otherwise, the page has to be available to only a select group of users.

The other member in the server code section of this web user control is the Page_Load() event handler. This member executes every time a web page with this skin is requested. Inside this member, you'll find a simple If/Then structure that calls the IsPrivatePage() function. If the given page is not available to all users, then the field named PrivatePageCssClass is set to a special value. Otherwise, the field is empty.

Below the <script> tag, this web user control uses the familiar bracket and percent characters to emit the value of the PrivatePageCssClass field into the class attribute of the <div> tag.

HTML tags can have multiple class attribute values. Each value is separated from the prior value by a space character. When the page is not available to all users, the class attribute on this HTML <div> tag will have two values separated by a space. When the page is available to all users, the HTML <div> tag will have just one class attribute value because the PrivatePageCssClass field is empty.

This is the code added to the skin.css file that will show the image token if the class exists in the HTML <div> tag of the page.

```
div.PrivatePage
{
    background:transparent url(images/privatepage.png) no-repeat 0 200px;
}
```

Try It Out   Apply Token Injection

Now that the principles of this technique have been explained, try implementing it on the Neighborhood Association skins.

1. Use your favorite text editor to open the SharedHeader.ascx file inside the Neighborhood Association skin folder located here:

```
<install folder> \Portals\_default\Skins\Spring
```

2. Add the new field named PrivatePageCssClass, as shown in the prior web user control code block.

3. Add the new function named IsPrivatePage(), as shown in the prior web user control code block.

4. Add the new event handler named Page_Load(), as shown in the prior web user control code block.

5. Include the value of the new field named PrivatePageCssClass in the CSS class attribute of the HTML <div> tag, as shown in the previous web user control code block.

6. Add the new CSS code to display the image token on pages having an HTML <div> tag with a class attribute of PrivatePage, as shown in the prior CSS code block.

7. Create your own image named privatepage.png and drop it in the folder named Images in the skin folder, or copy the image of the same name from the downloadable code available for this chapter. This is the token image that appears on the private pages.

8. Launch your browser and navigate to the home page. The image token should not appear.

9. Now log in as a member of the Board Member Role or the host account and navigate to the private Shared Documents page located under the Board page. This time, the image token should appear on the top left portion of the web page.

How It Works

Figure 9-1 shows the image token applied to a private page. The SharedHeader.ascx file was the only file that required editing to affect all of the skins in the set, because you know all three skins include an instance of this web user control.

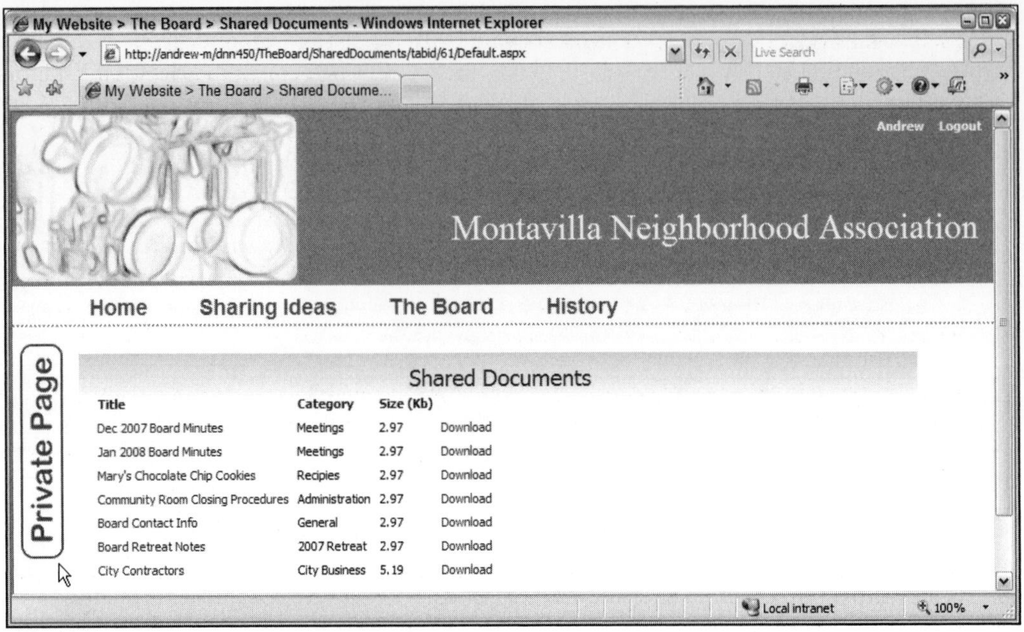

Figure 9-1

The following snippet shows a portion of the HTML rendered in the browser when an authorized user visits a private page. Notice the additional class attribute value in the HTML <div> tag. It's separated from the first class attribute value by a space character.

```
<div id="wideSkinContainer" class="skinContainer PrivatePage">

    <div id="headerContainer">
        <p>Montavilla Neighborhood Association</p>
    </div>

    <div id="contentContainer">
```

With just a few lines of code, the SharedHeader.ascx file now has the necessary logic to set a field to the proper value — either the name of the special CSS class or an empty value. This web user control has enough sense to include the image token on the appropriate pages in the system, and you don't have to think about it as you create new pages in the future.

Adding Personalization

This interactive feature is a simple concept, yet a powerful idea that can be expanded in numerous ways. Website personalization doesn't have to be complex or laborious. This feature simply gives the visitor a way to make a small visual alteration to the web pages. You're going to leverage the HTML structure in the skins, a few lines of CSS, and just two methods in the DotNetNuke API.

So far, you've created a set of skins with a common theme using a golden orange hue. As skin developers, you have the ability to modify the colors of skin, but a normal user cannot edit these CSS files. As DotNetNuke administrators, you have the ability to import a new set of skins and change the skin assigned to an installation, a portal, or a single page, but a normal user cannot change these DotNetNuke settings. The interactive feature you're about to add will empower the visitor to personalize the look of the web pages without giving away too much security.

This task aims to give the visitor a personalization tool for the website. After a visitor logs into the site, a collection of colorful blocks appears above his or her name in the top right corner of the page. By default, the background color of the website remains unchanged. The visitor can move the mouse over the color blocks and click one of them. As soon as the visitor clicks a color block, the page posts back to the server and returns to the browser with the selected background color.

If the visitor closes his or her browser, launches a new browser window and logs into the site again, the pages will immediately return to the color selected earlier. The same is true if the visitor accesses the website from a friend's computer. As soon as the system recognizes a user, it checks whether that user has configured a personalization setting. This color choice is only seen by one visitor. Another visitor can choose his or her own personalized color, and DotNetNuke will happily keep them organized.

Because this feature works across multiple computers, you can tell it's doing more than just setting a cookie on the browser. This personalization setting is stored in the database and associated with a visitor's account. ASP.Net 2.0 introduced some powerful new concepts in the .Net Framework, including personalization. The DotNetNuke team expanded on this concept and provided personalization tools in the DotNetNuke API.

By default, the personalization features are only available to authenticated users. It takes a few extra computing cycles to process the personalization features and handle the additional data storage, so it makes sense that the personalization code is only executed when dealing with a visitor who has committed a little bit to the website by creating an account.

This technique works by appending a CSS class to a specific HTML <div> tag based on the user's preferences. If the user has not expressed a preference, then the system uses a default preference on his or her behalf. The CSS file contains rules for all of the available choices.

This time you'll start with some changes to the SharedFooter.ascx web user control shown in the following code:

```
<%@ Control language="vb" AutoEventWireup="false" Explicit="True"
    Inherits="System.Web.UI.UserControl" %>
<%@ Register TagPrefix="dnn" TagName="USER" Src="~/Admin/Skins/User.ascx" %>
<%@ Register TagPrefix="dnn" TagName="LOGIN" Src="~/Admin/Skins/Login.ascx" %>
<%@ Register TagPrefix="dnn" TagName="COPYRIGHT"
    Src="~/Admin/Skins/Copyright.ascx" %>
<%@ Register TagPrefix="dnn" TagName="TERMS" Src="~/Admin/Skins/Terms.ascx" %>
<%@ Register TagPrefix="dnn" TagName="PRIVACY" Src="~/Admin/Skins/Privacy.ascx" %>
<%@ Register TagPrefix="dnn" TagName="DOTNETNUKE"
    Src="~/Admin/Skins/DotNetNuke.ascx" %>
<%@ Register TagPrefix="uc1" TagName="HouseMenu"
    Src="~/DesktopModules/HouseMenuSkinObject/HouseMenuSkinObject.ascx" %>
<script runat="server">
```

```
        Protected Sub ColorButtonCommand(ByVal sender As Object, ByVal e As CommandEventArgs)

            DotNetNuke.Services.Personalization.Personalization.SetProfile( _
                "VisitorSettings", "Color", e.CommandArgument)

        End Sub

    </script>

        </div>

        <div id="footerContainer">
            <dnn:COPYRIGHT runat="server" id="dnnCOPYRIGHT" />
            <dnn:TERMS runat="server" id="dnnTERMS" />
            <dnn:PRIVACY runat="server" id="dnnPRIVACY" /><br />
            <dnn:DOTNETNUKE runat="server" id="dnnDOTNETNUKE" />
        </div>

        <div id="userContainer">

            <% If Page.User.Identity.IsAuthenticated Then %>

            <div id="colorButtonContainer">
                <asp:ImageButton ID="btnAutumn" runat="server"
                    ImageUrl="images/colorButtonAutumn.png"
                    OnCommand="ColorButtonCommand"
                    CommandArgument="Autumn" />
                <asp:ImageButton ID="btnWinter" runat="server"
                    ImageUrl="images/colorButtonWinter.png"
                    OnCommand="ColorButtonCommand"
                    CommandArgument="Winter" />
                <asp:ImageButton ID="btnSpring" runat="server"
                    ImageUrl="images/colorButtonSpring.png"
                    OnCommand="ColorButtonCommand"
                    CommandArgument="Spring" />
                <asp:ImageButton ID="btnSummer" runat="server"
                    ImageUrl="images/colorButtonSummer.png"
                    OnCommand="ColorButtonCommand"
                    CommandArgument="Summer" />
            </div>

            <% End If %>

            <dnn:USER runat="server" id="dnnUSER" />
            <dnn:LOGIN runat="server" id="dnnLOGIN" />

        </div>

        <div id="menuContainer">
            <div id="theMenu">
                <uc1:HouseMenu runat="server" id="HouseMenu1"
                    Scope="-1"
                    ShowAdmin="True"
                    IsRecursive="True"
```

```
          />
      </div>
    </div>

  </div>
```

The first highlighted section in the previous code block shows the addition of a server-side script block. This is an event handler written in VB.Net. When the visitor clicks a color block, this code handles the event. The requested color enters the event handler as a parameter. There's just one line of code in this event handler; it calls the `SetProfile()` method of the DotNetNuke API. The method requires three parameters, and the code arbitrarily defines the first two as `VisitorSettings` and `Color`. These are just for your own classification purposes, so you can pull them out later. The third parameter is the value defined by the visitor when he or she clicked on a given color block. The DotNetNuke API handles all of the data storage and retrieval processes. All you need to do is ask the DotNetNuke API to store values under the classifications of `VisitorSettings` and `Color`. The system handles the rest.

The second highlighted section in the previous code block implements the color block. You already know that, by default, the personalization service is disabled for anonymous visitors. The `If` statement enveloping the button container only shows the color blocks to visitors who have logged into the system. The color blocks are implemented as four instances of the ASP.Net ImageButton control. Every ASP.Net server control has the attributes of `ID` and `runat`, so they should be familiar. The `ImageUrl` attribute identifies the location of the image that will appear as the button. The `OnCommand` attribute wires up the button to the event handler at the top of the page. The last attribute, `CommandArgument`, identifies the personalization value that is stored by the DotNetNuke API. Each ImageButton control has a different value. This section gives the visitor a way to indicate a personalization setting, and the event handler takes care of storing the setting through the call to the DotNetNuke API.

The following code block highlights the changes to the `SharedHeader.ascx` web user control:

```
<%@ Control language="vb" AutoEventWireup="true" Explicit="True"
     Inherits="System.Web.UI.UserControl" %>

<script runat="server">

    Public CssTagId As String
    Protected PrivatePageCssClass As String
    Protected ColorCssClass As String

    Protected Function IsPrivatePage() As Boolean

        Dim parentSkin As DotNetNuke.UI.Skins.Skin
        Dim roles As String

        parentSkin = CType(Me.Parent, DotNetNuke.UI.Skins.Skin)
        roles = parentSkin.PortalSettings.ActiveTab.AuthorizedRoles

        If roles.Contains("All Users") Then
            Return False
        Else
            Return True
        End If
```

```
    End Function

    Protected Sub Page_Load(ByVal sender As Object, ByVal e As EventArgs)

        If IsPrivatePage() Then
            PrivatePageCssClass = " PrivatePage"
        Else
            PrivatePageCssClass = String.Empty
        End If

    End Sub

    Protected Sub Page_PreRender(ByVal sender As Object, ByVal e As EventArgs)

        Dim colorObject As Object
        colorObject = _

            DotNetNuke.Services.Personalization.Personalization.GetProfile( _
                VisitorSettings", "Color")

        If colorObject Is Nothing Then
            ColorCssClass = String.Empty
        Else
            ColorCssClass = " " & CType(colorObject, String)
        End If

    End Sub

    </script>

<div id="<%= CssTagId %>"
    class="skinContainer<%= PrivatePageCssClass %><%= ColorCssClass %>">
    <div id="headerContainer">
        <p>Montavilla Neighborhood Association</p>
    </div>

    <div id="contentContainer">
```

The first highlighted section in the previous code block adds a new field to the `SharedHeader.ascx` web user control. As you can see, this field will either be set to the visitor's personalization choice, or to an empty field to indicate that no choice has been made.

The next highlighted section in the previous code block is an event handler that fires just before ASP.Net renders the page to the browser. This code is taking advantage of the specific order of operation in ASP.Net. First, the `Page_Load` event in every web user control fires. Then, any button click events fire, so the `OnCommand` event in the `SharedFooter.ascx` web user control will execute. Finally, the `Page_PreRender` event fires, just before the page is sent to the browser. As the page is being rendered to the browser, the values of the fields between the bracket and the percent characters are written out to the page.

When a visitor chooses a color, the page posts back to the server, and the `OnCommand` code handles the storage of the given personalization value. The `Page_PreRender` code in the `SharedHeader.ascx` web user control will retrieve this setting from the DotNetNuke API and inject it into the CSS class attribute of an HTML `<div>` tag. Because ASP.Net always fires these events in this order, you can place your code in the appropriate location and use the system to your advantage.

The following code block shows the necessary changes to the existing CSS file for the Neighborhood Association skins:

```
div#blogSkinContainer div#headerContainer
{
    background-image:url(images/hdr-room.jpg);
}

div#wideSkinContainer div#headerContainer
{
    background-image:url(images/hdr-pans.jpg);
}

div#colorButtonContainer
{
    background-color:#FFF;
    padding:4px 4px 0 4px;
}

div.Winter div#headerContainer
{
    background-color:#6083FF;
}

div.Spring div#headerContainer
{
    background-color:#87FF95;
}

div.Summer div#headerContainer
{
    background-color:#FFCE46;
}

div.Autumn div#headerContainer
{
    background-color:#D27E2F;
}
```

The first two rules in the previous CSS code block modify the existing header styles of the blog skin and the wide skin. They had contained a complete set of background rules, including color, image, repetition and offsets. Because this technique moves the color rules elsewhere, these existing rules need to be trimmed a bit. Just setting the background image rule is sufficient here.

The third rule in the previous CSS code block is a new rule using the `div#colorButtonContainer` selector. It styles the container of the color blocks in the top right corner of the page.

The last four rules in the previous CSS code block implement the personalization choice made by the visitor. Each color in the block is given the name of a season. When the visitor chooses a personalized color, the system injects a CSS class to the <div> tag surrounding the header. The web browser uses the rules defined here to present the header in the selected background color.

Try It Out   Add Skin Personalization

Now that the concepts and code changes have been explained, it's time to try it on your own. This section will apply the skin personalization feature on your local development server. You can also grab the files from the code download available for this chapter.

1.   Use your favorite text editor to open the `SharedFooter.ascx` file inside the Neighborhood Association skin folder located here:

```
<install folder>\Portals\_default\Skins\Spring
```

2.   Add the server-side script block that contains the `ColorButtonCommand()` code, as shown earlier in this section.

3.   Add the four ASP.Net ImageButton controls above the DotNetNuke User skin object, as shown earlier. Make sure these ImageButton controls are enveloped by an `If` statement that hides them from visitors that have not logged into the system. There's no use in showing this feature if the system is going to ignore personalization settings for anonymous visitors.

4.   Open the `SharedHeader.ascx` file located in the same folder.

5.   Append a new field named ColorCssClass, as shown in the previous code blocks. This stores the value of the visitor's personalization setting, if it exists.

6.   Add the `Page_PreRender` code, as shown earlier. This code uses the DotNetNuke API method named `GetProfile()` to retrieve the personalization setting. If it doesn't exist, the field named ColorCssClass is set to an empty value. Otherwise, it contains the visitor's selected value.

7.   Modify the existing HTML <div> tag to include the value of the field named ColorCssClass, similar to how the private page image token is displayed. This HTML tag can have up to three CSS class values now. Each one is separated by a space character.

8.   Open the `skin.css` file and make the edits described earlier that target the blog skin and the wide skin. Add the styles for the `colorButtonContainer` tag as well as the four styles for the personalized header sections.

9.   Now that the file edits are out of the way, copy the four image files from the downloadable code for this chapter into the Images folder. These are the images referred to by the ASP.Net ImageButton controls in the `SharedFooter.ascx` web user control.

10.   Launch your web browser and navigate to the home page. Nothing should have changed since the last time you accessed this page.

11.   Log in with any account and you should see the color blocks appear in the top right corner of the page.

12.   Click on any of the color blocks. The page should change its header to the selected item. If you close your browser and log in again, the browser should automatically remember the setting.

How It Works

Figure 9-2 shows the color block inserted above the User skin object in the top right section of the page. Each of the four image buttons is linked to a value that's stored in the database by the DotNetNuke API. The code makes use of just two methods, `SetProfile()` and `GetProfile()` to implement this feature. Everything else is just HTML and CSS.

Figure 9-2

This technique is using the same concept as the image token of the last section. Instead of requesting page-level security information in order to inject a CSS class into an HTML `<div>` tag, the code is requesting the personalization setting of the current user, if any. The code then goes about injecting the appropriate CSS class to the HTML `<div>` tag. The real visual change in the web page is rooted in the contents of the CSS file. Just a few lines of VB.Net code can modify the HTML content and change the visual aesthetics of the web page completely through CSS.

Summary

This chapter implemented some interactive features into your skins. Along the way, you took some steps to tidy up the redundant content in your skin collection. The broader sets of interactive features in DotNetNuke are classified as modules and skin objects. The items you created were tightly coupled to your skin files. They're not as transferrable as other skin objects, but they also require much less programming.

The DotNetNuke security APIs can be queried with just a few lines of code in order to take some action such as injecting a special CSS class into the page. Along the same lines, the personalization features in ASP.Net 2.0 and the enhancements provided by DotNetNuke enable you to deliver interesting tools that make web pages a little more playful and interactive.

As you implemented these interactive features in your own skins you got a good look at the programming interface of DotNetNuke without having to jump into the deep end of the pool. If you have some great ideas for modules and skin objects, then I encourage you to find a copy of *Professional DotNetNuke 4* and learn more about the tools that you can use to provide interactive features in your DotNetNuke installation.

Exercises

1. Why is personalization disabled by default for anonymous visitors?

2. Write an example of an HTML `<div>` tag that has three CSS class attributes.

3. What is the significance of an equals sign when placed inside bracket and percent characters on a web user control file?

   Example:

   ```
   <p> Name: <%= VisitorName %> </p>
   ```

4. Name three benefits of consolidating redundant code.

5. List some places web user controls are used in DotNetNuke.

Part III

Increasing the Property Value

10

Exploring Silverlight

Microsoft Silverlight is a new in-browser technology that adds rich interactive features to websites. HTML, CSS, and JavaScript are great tools, but they can only take a web page so far as a document. Silverlight provides a way to embed audio and video in a page that goes far beyond the capabilities of Windows Media Player. JavaScript can automate the functionality inside the Silverlight object model, too. Silverlight is an exciting way to learn more about rich interactive applications inside DotNetNuke. This chapter gives you a nickel tour of the technology.

The ubiquitous nature of video today makes it a compelling idea for your website. Video recorders are common in households, and many mobile phones even have video recording features. The source of video content is deep. This chapter takes advantage of the video resources available to you and applies it to the DotNetNuke site. In this chapter, you'll use Silverlight to perform the following tasks:

- ❑ Build the compulsory Hello World application in Silverlight
- ❑ Animate basic shapes on an HTML page
- ❑ Extend a DotNetNuke skin by adding an image rotation component through animation
- ❑ Build a custom video player with control buttons and video library

Getting Started with Silverlight

The Silverlight software development kit (SDK) is available online at the following URL:

```
www.microsoft.com/silverlight/tools.aspx
```

The SDK includes a lot of information such as samples, tutorials, help files, and tools for Visual Studio. Silverlight requires just a few files to get started. One file is copied from the SDK; you'll create the rest yourself throughout this chapter.

The SDK contains an important JavaScript file named Silverlight.js that abstracts some low-level details away from the Silverlight development experience. You will use it throughout this chapter. It can detect whether Silverlight is installed as well as create instances of the Silverlight object inside the browser.

Any version of the Silverlight SDK will work fine for your current purposes. The Silverlight 1.0 Beta was released at the same time as the Silverlight 1.1 Alpha in May of 2007. By the time you read this book, there are bound to be more Silverlight releases that continue to extend the feature set. As you'll soon see, the barrier to entry for this technology is low and the potential for sophisticated applications is high. The samples available online at `www.silverlight.net` are amazing. In this chapter, you'll use your favorite text editor to whip up a couple of short files to build your first set of Silverlight components.

Silverlight works by rendering the contents of a XAML (*pronounced "zamel"*) file in the browser. Writing XAML files for Silverlight is similar to developing applications for Windows Presentation Foundation (WPF). Silverlight applications run exclusively inside browsers like Internet Explorer, Firefox, and Safari whereas WPF applications run exclusively on the Windows operating system and require the .Net 3.0 Framework. The browser needs the Silverlight component, some JavaScript, and a XAML file to do its work. This chapter introduces you to all three parts as you build some Silverlight applications.

The excitement around Silverlight is also spawning a new library of books, a version 1.0 collection of developer tools such as the Microsoft Expression suite, and special XAML export utilities for existing tools like Photoshop. Learning the XAML syntax and tools such as Microsoft Expression Blend is well outside the scope of what you'll cover here. These topics are just too enormous to cover in a chapter, but you can learn some Silverlight fundamentals in a brief period. It's a good idea to have some deep roots in the fundamentals before starting down the more elaborate paths, so get started with everybody's favorite, the Hello World application

Try It Out   Build "Hello World" in Silverlight

In this section, you build the traditional Hello World application using Silverlight with just four files — one of them is copied from the SDK. This activity excludes IIS and ASP.Net to simplify the concepts. To get started, you need to download the 20MB Silverlight 1.0 SDK from the following URL to your computer:

```
www.microsoft.com/silverlight/tools.aspx
```

The rest of the files you need are available in the code for this chapter.

1. Create a new folder named `Silverlight` on your desktop.

2. This example leverages the JavaScript library available inside `Silverlight.js` found in the SDK. Copy that file from the Silverlight SDK to this new folder. If you install the Silverlight 1.0 SDK in the default location, you'll find the JavaScript file in the following folder.

```
C:\program files\Microsoft Silverlight 1.0 SDK\Resources
```

3. Use your favorite text editor to create a file named `Silverlight.xaml`. The `.xaml` file extension is for an eXtensible Application Markup Language file. This is just an XML file that conforms to a particular schema. XAML files describe how a user interface behaves through XML syntax.

4. Add the following XML to the file named `Silverlight.xaml`. This XML file has a root node of `<Canvas>` and one `<TextBlock>` child node. Aside from learning the XAML syntax, it's easy to see what's going on here at a broad level. Inside a canvas area, there's a block of text at a given position with a given font.

```
<Canvas xmlns="http://schemas.microsoft.com/client/2007">
    <TextBlock Canvas.Left="100" Canvas.Top="80"
```

```
          FontFamily="Arial" FontSize="20" Text="Hello World!" />
</Canvas>
```

5. Create a file named `CreateSilverlight.js` with your text editor. This is where your own unique JavaScript code will exist.

6. Add the following JavaScript code to the `CreateSilverlight.js` file. This code snippet is nearly identical to the examples found in the Silverlight SDK. This JavaScript function calls into the library made available by the `Silverlight.js` file you downloaded from the SDK. Each parameter is accompanied by a JavaScript comment to explain its purpose.

```
function createMySilverlightControl()
{
    Silverlight.createObject(
        "Silverlight.xaml",                    // Source property value.
        document.getElementById("mySilverlightControlHost"),
                                               // DOM reference to hosting DIV tag.
        "mySilverlightControl",                // Unique control ID value.
        {                                      // Control properties.
            width:'300',                       // Width of rectangular region of
                                               // control in pixels.
            height:'225',                      // Height of rectangular region of
                                               // control in pixels.
            inplaceInstallPrompt:true,         // Determines whether to display
                                               // in-place install prompt if
                                               // invalid version detected.
            background:'#CCC',                 // Background color of control.
            isWindowless:'false',              // Display control
                                               // in Windowless mode.
            framerate:'24',                    // MaxFrameRate property value.
            version:'0.9'                      // Control version to use.
        },
        {
            onError:null,                      // OnError property value --
                                               // event handler function name.
            onLoad:null                        // OnLoad property value --
                                               // event handler function name.
        },
        null);                                 // Context value -- event handler
}
```

7. Create the last file named `default.html` with your text editor. This HTML file stitches all of the previous work together to present "Hello World!" in your browser using Silverlight.

8. Add the following code to the new HTML file:

```
<!DOCTYPE html PUBLIC "-//W3C//DTD XHTML 1.0 Transitional//EN"
    "http://www.w3.org/TR/xhtml1/DTD/xhtml1-transitional.dtd">
<html xmlns="http://www.w3.org/1999/xhtml" xml:lang="en">
<head>
    <title>Hello World in Silverlight</title>
    <script src="Silverlight.js" type="text/javascript"></script>
    <script src="CreateSilverlight.js" type="text/javascript"></script>
</head>
```

```
<body>

    <div id="mySilverlightControlHost">
    </div>

    <script type="text/javascript">
        createMySilverlightControl();
    </script>

</body>
</html>
```

9. Double-click the `default.html` file to launch it in your browser. If you haven't installed the actual Silverlight component in your browser yet, you'll see a hyperlinked image to install it, as shown in Figure 10-1.

    Your browser might warn you about running ActiveX controls that could harm your computer. This is a good thing. The warning is caused by your browser security settings. Because you wrote the page and expect to get Microsoft Silverlight, click past the warning and allow the blocked content.

10. Click on the image to download and install Silverlight. As you would with any other executable downloaded from the Internet, closely examine the security warning shown in Figure 10-2 before clicking the Run button.

11. After Silverlight is installed, refresh the page and you'll see the famous "Hello World!" in your browser, as shown in Figure 10-3. Congratulations!

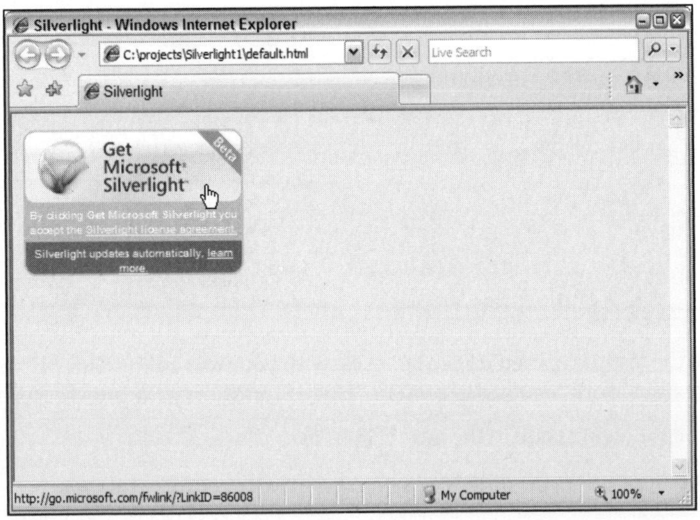

Figure 10-1

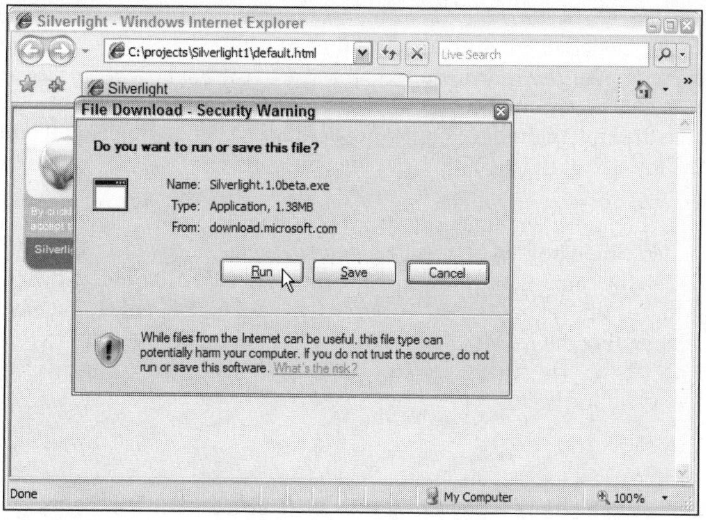

Figure 10-2

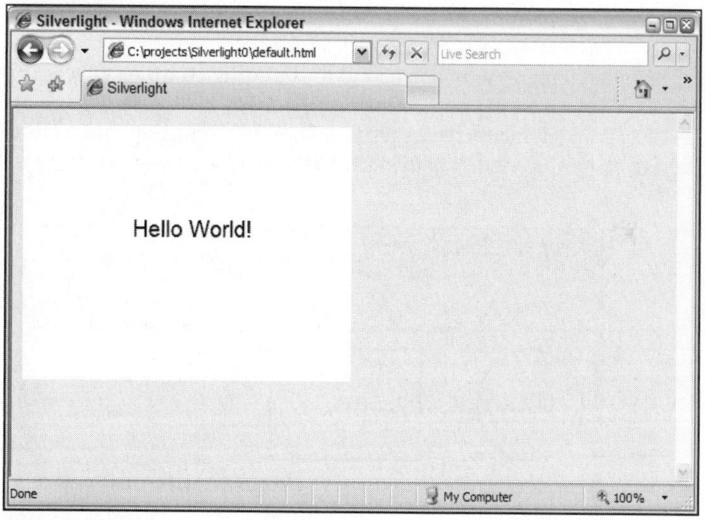

Figure 10-3

How It Works

The Silverlight.js file is a library that you don't ever need to open. The XAML and HTML files are fairly simple, so the most interesting part of this example is the custom JavaScript file named CreateSilverlight.js. This file is used repeatedly throughout this chapter, so you're bound to get familiar with it, if not memorize it.

Just as in the Silverlight SDK, the function inside `CreateSilverlight.js` is verbose, filled with all of the in-line parameter documentation. Take some time to read through the comments to understand the purpose of each parameter. The function affects the size of the Silverlight surface area, the XAML file loaded into Silverlight, background colors, and several other high-level features. Verbose comments are helpful early on in the Silverlight development experience. After a while you'll omit the JavaScript comments and shrink the size of the function by quite a bit.

XAML represents a big movement in declarative programming, where developers describe their general intent instead of describing how to perform a given task specifically. Later on, you'll see how just a few elements in a XAML file can describe how a shape ought to fade out of view over time. You won't have to write a single line of VB.Net or C# code to perform the animation, either; the Silverlight engine handles all of it for you by reading the XAML file.

Applying Animation in XAML

XAML has syntax for constructing basic shapes. Using XAML, you can build an ellipse, a rectangle, a line, and a polygon. Of course if you do your math right, you can create a circle from an ellipse or a square from a rectangle.

XAML also has a `<Path>` element, which is useful for building complex curves if you're into that whole Bezier curve thing or if you like to approach infinity. A `<Polyline>` element creates a shape that might not be closed. A `<Polygon>` element creates a shape that, by definition, must close. Figure 10-4 contains shapes constructed from simple elements using XAML.

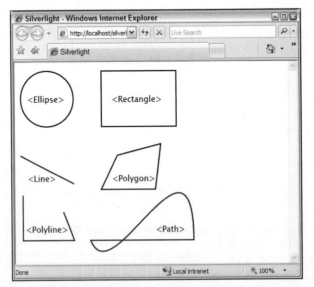

Figure 10-4

These types of shapes are good targets for animation. Next, you need some aspect of them to animate, such as their position on the canvas or their fill color. Each of these elements has basic properties in common, as well as properties that are specific to the given shape. For example, all shape elements have an opacity property. An opacity value of zero makes the shape invisible. If the value is less than one but greater than zero, the shape is partially transparent. Changing this value on the fly is a common animation technique.

Using Basic Animation

XAML uses Storyboards to organize animations. Animation commands can be placed in a Storyboard and the Storyboard can be wired up to execute at a particular time. The following code block shows an example of the <DoubleAnimation> element in XAML. This Storyboard will execute as soon as the canvas is loaded up because of the RoutedEvent property in the <EventTrigger> element shown in the following code:

```
<Canvas
    xmlns="http://schemas.microsoft.com/client/2007"
    xmlns:x="http://schemas.microsoft.com/winfx/2006/xaml">

    <Canvas.Triggers>
        <EventTrigger RoutedEvent="Canvas.Loaded">
            <EventTrigger.Actions>
                <BeginStoryboard>
                    <Storyboard>
                        <DoubleAnimation
                            Storyboard.TargetName="e1"
                            Storyboard.TargetProperty="Opacity"
                            From="1" To="0" Duration="0:0:5"  />
                    </Storyboard>
                </BeginStoryboard>
            </EventTrigger.Actions>
        </EventTrigger>
    </Canvas.Triggers>

    <Ellipse x:Name="e1" Fill="#000" Opacity="1"
        Height="100" Width="100"
        Canvas.Left="100" Canvas.Top="30"/>

</Canvas>
```

The <Ellipse> shape has been given a Name property of e1. Because it has a Name property, it can be targeted by other XAML elements or externally from JavaScript. The <DoubleAnimation> element shown above handles the task of changing the opacity value of the targeted shape from "1" to "0" in the specified duration of 5 seconds. This is how the animation occurs and makes the ellipse gradually disappear in five seconds. There's no need to write loop in VB.Net code to change the opacity because the XAML animation element handles it for you.

<DoubleAnimation> is just one kind of animation element in XAML. It's good at dealing with values that have a decimal format. Silverlight shapes can also be animated by <ColorAnimation> and <PointAnimation>. This is how shapes can gradually change from red to blue over time or move across the page at a specified pace. Because of your time constraints, you'll stick with <DoubleAnimation>.

Try It Out   **Animate a Hello World Application**

This section takes the previous Hello World application a step farther and animates some shapes around the Hello World text. This will give you a good taste of where animation can take your web applications in DotNetNuke.

1. Copy the folder on your desktop you created in the last section named Silverlight to a new folder named Silverlight2. You'll reuse nearly all of the same files here.

2. Open the file named `Silverlight.xaml` in your favorite text editor and replace the existing XAML with the following:

```xml
<Canvas
    xmlns="http://schemas.microsoft.com/client/2007"
    xmlns:x="http://schemas.microsoft.com/winfx/2006/xaml">

    <Canvas.Triggers>
        <EventTrigger RoutedEvent="Canvas.Loaded">
            <EventTrigger.Actions>
                <BeginStoryboard>
                    <Storyboard>
                        <DoubleAnimation
                            Storyboard.TargetName="r1"
                            Storyboard.TargetProperty="Opacity"
                            From="1" To="0" Duration="0:0:5" />
                        <DoubleAnimation
                            Storyboard.TargetName="e1"
                            Storyboard.TargetProperty="Opacity"
                            From="0" To="1" Duration="0:0:5" />
                    </Storyboard>
                </BeginStoryboard>
            </EventTrigger.Actions>
        </EventTrigger>
    </Canvas.Triggers>

    <Rectangle x:Name="r1"
        Fill="#FF0000" Opacity="1"
        Canvas.Left="50" Canvas.Top="50"
        Height="100" Width="100" />

    <Ellipse x:Name="e1"
        Fill="#0000FF" Opacity="0"
        Height="100" Width="100"
        Canvas.Left="30" Canvas.Top="30" />

    <TextBlock
        Canvas.Left="100" Canvas.Top="80"
        FontFamily="Arial" FontSize="20"
        Text="Hello World!" />

</Canvas>
```

3. Double-click the file named `default.html` to launch it in your browser. As before, you might have to click through an ActiveX control warning message. Because Silverlight is already installed on your browser, it automatically displays the page with the animation. The text is always visible while the red rectangle fades out and the blue circle fades in using the animation instructions contained in the XAML file. Figure 10-5 shows a snapshot of the transition where both shapes are visible and each is partially opaque.

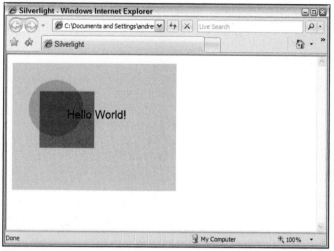

Figure 10-5

How It Works

This Silverlight animation uses the rectangle and the ellipse shape that have an opacity animation in opposite directions. The text is always visible and because it is lower in the XAML file, it is painted on top of anything that is above it in the XAML file. You can play with this by moving the `<TextBlock>` element higher in the XAML file and watching how it changes the Silverlight component.

The ellipse initially has an opacity of zero, so it's invisible. Gradually, the `<DoubleAnimation>` changes its opacity property so the shape becomes visible and finally, opaque. The opposite happens to the `<Rectangle>` element.

You didn't need to edit any of the JavaScript for this example because the Silverlight run time and the XAML file contain all of the activity. You'll integrate JavaScript code with Silverlight objects later on in this chapter.

Applying Animation to a DotNetNuke Skin

Now that you have a decent idea of how animation works in Silverlight, you'll apply this knowledge to the home page skin in the DotNetNuke site. Currently, the image in the top left corner of the page is static. It's placed there as a background image by a rule in the CSS file.

The goal of this next section is to make the home page skin appear a little more playful by rotating the image that appears in the top left corner of this page.

Animate the Skin Header

In this section, the header for the home page will receive some animation treatment from Silverlight. The home page skin will be edited to show an image rotation of all the header images in the site, and then stop on the last image. You'll apply the same principles as the last Try It Out section — this time you'll apply an animation on a set of images to modify their opacity.

1. Open the skin folder for the Neighborhood Association website on your local development machine.

```
<install folder>\Portals\_default\Skins\Spring
```

2. Create a new folder named Silverlight inside the skin folder

```
<install folder>\Portals\_default\Skins\Spring\Silverlight
```

3. Copy the Silverlight.js file from the SDK to this new folder.

4. Use your favorite text editor to create a new file named XamlContent.aspx in this new folder. Then paste in the following XAML content from the file available for download for this chapter. This is the source XAML content that enables the images to fade in and out. This XAML content is downloaded by Silverlight to the browser at run time. Because the file can't assume the URL for the images, it has to discover the path at run time using a few lines of VB.Net code. This ASP.Net "pretends" to be a XAML file by specifying the appropriate content type in the page declaration. When the browser receives this file, it won't know the difference and the image paths will be correct.

```vb
<%@ Page Language="vb" ContentType="text/xaml" %>

<script runat="server">
    Private ReadOnly Property BaseFolder() As String
        Get
            Dim file1 As String = Request.Path
            Dim dir1 = file1.Substring(0, file1.LastIndexOf("/"))
            Return dir1.Substring(0, dir1.LastIndexOf("/"))
        End Get
    End Property
</script>

<Canvas
    xmlns="http://schemas.microsoft.com/client/2007"
    xmlns:x="http://schemas.microsoft.com/winfx/2006/xaml">

    <Image x:Name="e1" Source="<%= BaseFolder %>/images/hdr-house.jpg"
            Canvas.Left="0" Canvas.Top="0" Opacity="0">

        <Image.Triggers>
            <EventTrigger RoutedEvent="Image.Loaded">
```

```
                    <BeginStoryboard>
                        <Storyboard BeginTime="0:0:0">
                            <DoubleAnimation
                                Storyboard.TargetName="e1"
                                Storyboard.TargetProperty="Opacity"
                                From="0.0" To="1.0" Duration="0:0:1" />
                        </Storyboard>
                    </BeginStoryboard>

                    <BeginStoryboard>
                        <Storyboard BeginTime="0:0:6">
                            <DoubleAnimation
                                Storyboard.TargetName="e1"
                                Storyboard.TargetProperty="Opacity"
                                From="1.0" To="0.0" Duration="0:0:4" />
                        </Storyboard>
                    </BeginStoryboard>

                </EventTrigger>
            </Image.Triggers>
    </Image>

<Image x:Name="e2"
    Source="<%= BaseFolder %>/images/hdr-pans.jpg"
    Canvas.Left="0" Canvas.Top="0" Opacity="0">
    <Image.Triggers>
        <EventTrigger RoutedEvent="Image.Loaded">

                    <BeginStoryboard>
                        <Storyboard BeginTime="0:0:9">
                            <DoubleAnimation
                                Storyboard.TargetName="e2"
                                Storyboard.TargetProperty="Opacity"
                                From="0.0" To="1.0" Duration="0:0:3" />
                        </Storyboard>
                    </BeginStoryboard>

                    <BeginStoryboard>
                        <Storyboard BeginTime="0:0:15">
                            <DoubleAnimation
                                Storyboard.TargetName="e2"
                                Storyboard.TargetProperty="Opacity"
                                From="1.0" To="0.0" Duration="0:0:4" />
                        </Storyboard>
                    </BeginStoryboard>

                </EventTrigger>
            </Image.Triggers>
    </Image>

<Image x:Name="e3" Source="<%= BaseFolder %>/images/hdr-room.jpg"
        Canvas.Left="0" Canvas.Top="0" Opacity="0">
    <Image.Triggers>
        <EventTrigger RoutedEvent="Image.Loaded">
```

```
        <BeginStoryboard>
          <Storyboard BeginTime="0:0:18">
            <DoubleAnimation
              Storyboard.TargetName="e3"
              Storyboard.TargetProperty="Opacity"
              From="0.0" To="1.0" Duration="0:0:4" />
          </Storyboard>
        </BeginStoryboard>


      </EventTrigger>
    </Image.Triggers>
  </Image>


</Canvas>
```

5. Create a new text file in the same folder named `CreateSilverlight.js`. This file is nearly identical to the previous versions, except for a few parameter changes highlighted in the following code. Notice that the XAML source parameter refers to a parameter named `xamlContentPath` instead of a hardcoded filename. You'll pass this filename parameter to the function. Copy the contents of the file available for download into this new file.

```
function createMySilverlightControl( xamlContentPath )
{
    Silverlight.createObject(
        xamlContentPath,                    // Source property value.
        document.getElementById("mySilverlightControlHost"),
                                            // DOM reference to hosting DIV tag.
        "mySilverlightControl",             // Unique control ID value.
        {                                   // Control properties.
            width:'262',                    // Width of rectangular region of
                                            // control in pixels.
            height:'146',                   // Height of rectangular region of
                                            // control in pixels.
            inplaceInstallPrompt:true,      // Determines whether to display
                                            // in-place install prompt if
                                            // invalid version detected.
            background:'#D78839',           // Background color of control.
            isWindowless:'false',           // Display control
                                            // in Windowless mode.
            framerate:'24',                 // MaxFrameRate property value.
            version:'0.9'                   // Control version to use.
        },
        {
            onError:null,                   // OnError property value --
                                            // event handler function name.
            onLoad:null                     // OnLoad property value --
                                            // event handler function name.
        },
        null);                              // Context value -- event handler
}
```

6. Now it's time to create the web user control to which the home page skin file will refer. Create a new file named `SilverlightHeader.ascx` in the Silverlight folder.

7. By now the web user control code will look familiar from the work in prior chapters with web user controls as well as from the Silverlight examples earlier in this chapter. Because the file paths in the browser are relative to the host page and not the web user control, a few lines of VB.Net code are needed to discover the path to the Silverlight folder at run time. Notice that just before the function `createMySilverlightControl()` is called, the global string variable `gsXamlContentPath` is defined with the help of some VB.Net injection. Copy the contents of the file available for download for this chapter into the new web user control file you just created.

```
<%@ Control language="vb" Inherits="System.Web.UI.UserControl" %>
<script runat="server">

    Protected ReadOnly Property SkinPath() As String
        Get
            Dim parentSkin As DotNetNuke.UI.Skins.Skin
            parentSkin = CType(Me.Parent, DotNetNuke.UI.Skins.Skin)
            Return parentSkin.SkinPath
        End Get
    End Property

    Protected ReadOnly Property XamlContentPath() As String
        Get
            Return SkinPath & "Silverlight/XAMLContent.aspx"
        End Get
    End Property

</script>

<script type="text/javascript"
    src="<%= SkinPath %>Silverlight/Silverlight.js"></script>
<script type="text/javascript"
    src="<%= SkinPath %>Silverlight/CreateSilverlight.js"></script>

<div id="mySilverlightControlHost"></div>

<script type="text/javascript">
    createMySilverlightControl('<%= XamlContentPath %>' );
</script>
```

8. Create an instance of this Silverlight web user control inside the home page skin file. Open the skin file named `homepage.ascx` in the skin folder and add the following highlighted sections to the existing skin.

```
<%@ Control language="vb" AutoEventWireup="false" Explicit="True"
    Inherits="DotNetNuke.UI.Skins.Skin" %>
<%@ Register TagPrefix="uc" TagName="SharedHeader" Src="SharedHeader.ascx" %>
<%@ Register TagPrefix="uc" TagName="SharedFooter" Src="SharedFooter.ascx" %>
<%@ Register TagPrefix="uc" TagName="Silverlight"
    Src="Silverlight/SilverlightHeader.ascx" %>

<div id="ControlPanel" runat="server"></div>
<uc:SharedHeader ID="SharedHeader1" runat="server"
    CssTagId="homePageSkinContainer" />
```

```
<uc:Silverlight ID="Silverlight1" runat="server" />

<div id="LeftPane" runat="server" class="leftPane"></div>
<div id="RightPane" runat="server" class="rightPane"></div>
<div id="ContentPane" runat="server" class="contentPane"></div>

<uc:SharedFooter id="SharedFooter1" runat="server" />
```

9. The final steps make some slight adjustments to the CSS file. By default, the skin shows a background image in the header. Two other skins have custom images that override this default setting. You need to modify the skin to disable the default image, but continue to implement the other useful settings. Open the file skin.css in your favorite text editor and modify the div#headerContainer rule with the following CSS instructions.

```
div#headerContainer
{
    height:154px;
    background:#D78839 no-repeat 2px 2px;
    /* background:#D78839 url(images/hdr-house.jpg) no-repeat 2px 2px; */
    position:relative;
    top:0;
    left:0;
}
```

10. The final CSS edit adds a new rule to the bottom of the file that targets the Silverlight container. It moves the component into position using absolute positioning. Add the following CSS to the bottom of the skin.css file.

```
div#mySilverlightControlHost
{
    position:absolute;
    top:-210px;
    left:-104px;
    z-index:200;
}
```

11. Now that the edits are in place, launch the home page of the site in your browser. The banner image in the top left corner should fade out and another image should fade in. You can play with the timing specified in the XAML file to adjust it to your taste.

How It Works

This example was just a different play on the animation you did for the Hello World Silverlight application. You created a web user control to envelop the Silverlight activity and placed it in a dedicated file. Because the DotNetNuke site can be installed under a web application domain name or at the actual root on a web server, a few lines of code are needed to discover the current path at run time. If the code were only run from a remote web server off the root directory, then you could bypass the VB.Net code and hardcode the image locations in the XAML file.

Each <Image> element contained its own Storyboard. The BeginTime property organized the start times for each Storyboard. You can play with these values to modify the timing of the Silverlight component.

Investigating Interactive Media

Interactive media is a sleek way to make a website current and compelling for repeat visits. By the same token, it obligates the administrators of the website to update the videos periodically before the site is stale and loses its appeal.

The Neighborhood Association website can benefit from video by advertising its recent events in a more active manner than just images and copy. While other external video channels exist, a strong argument can be made for controlling all aspects of video experience as well as customizing the video features over time with new ideas.

Silverlight provides a great media control named `<MediaElement>`. In its simplest form, the element only requires a value for its `Source` attribute to play a movie. The best way to learn it is to see it in action for yourself.

Try It Out   Add a Video Skin Object

This example adds a Silverlight component through the standard Text/HTML module provided in DotNetNuke. Because it relies on the content inside a system, you can afford to take some liberties with the file paths instead of discovering them at run time with VB.Net code.

1. Create a new folder named Silverlight in the root directory of DotNetNuke on your development machine. Most of the Silverlight assets exist in this folder.

2. Copy the `Silverlight.js` file from the SDK into this new folder.

3. The files available for download for this chapter include thumbnail images, sample Windows Media files, and the familiar files `CreateSilverlight.js` and `XamlContent.xaml`. Copy only the three image files and the three `.wmv` files into the new folder.

4. Create a new file named `XamlContent.xaml` in the new folder. Add the following XAML to the file using your favorite text editor. This version of the XAML file will be small, but you'll extend it to match the version in the downloaded code over time.

```
<Canvas
    xmlns=http://schemas.microsoft.com/client/2007
    xmlns:x="http://schemas.microsoft.com/winfx/2006/xaml">

    <!-- the movie player -->
    <MediaElement x:Name="media"
        Source="/dnn450/silverlight/burger.wmv"
        Width="320" Height="240"
        Canvas.Left="160" Canvas.Top="0"
        AutoPlay="True" Opacity="0" />

    <!-- the rounded corner skin for the player -->
    <Rectangle Width="320" Height="240"
        Canvas.Left="160" Canvas.Top="0" Stroke="#EEE" StrokeThickness="6"
        RadiusX="20" RadiusY="20">
        <Rectangle.Fill>
            <VideoBrush SourceName="media" />
        </Rectangle.Fill>
```

```
      </Rectangle>

</Canvas>
```

5. Create a new file named `CreateSilverlight.js` in the folder. Use your text editor to enter the following JavaScript, or copy it from the downloaded file. My web application on my local development machine is `/dnn450`. Notice the JavaScript function is hardcoded to a path of `/dnn450/Silverlight/XamlContent.xaml`. Change this XAML source parameter to point to your web application name and path.

```javascript
function createMySilverlightControl()
{
    Silverlight.createObject(
        '/dnn450/Silverlight/XamlContent.xaml', // Source property value.
        document.getElementById("SilverlightVideoContainer"),
                                        // DOM reference to hosting DIV tag.
        "SilverlightVideoContainer",    // Unique control ID value.
        {                               // Control properties.
            width:'700',                // Width of rectangular region of
                                        // control in pixels.
            height:'400',               // Height of rectangular region of
                                        // control in pixels.
            inplaceInstallPrompt:true,  // Determines whether to display
                                        // in-place install prompt if
                                        // invalid version detected.
            background:'#FFF',          // Background color of control.
            isWindowless:'false',       // Display control
                                        // in Windowless mode.
            framerate:'24',             // MaxFrameRate property value.
            version:'0.9'               // Control version to use.
        },
        {
            onError:null,               // OnError property value --
                                        // event handler function name.
            onLoad:null                 // OnLoad property value --
                                        // event handler function name.
        },
        null);                          // Context value -- event handler
}
```

6. Now that all of the supporting files are in place, it's time to enter the content into DotNetNuke. Log in to DotNetNuke on your local development machine as the host account.

7. Create a new page named Video and make it available for viewing by all users. The page named Sharing Ideas should be its parent page. Specify it to use the wide skin and the standard container.

8. Navigate to the Edit Text page for the default Text/HTML module that was inserted into the Video page by default. Because you're going a little deeper than simple HTML, switch to the source view of the content by clicking the Basic Text Box radio button or the Source button in the HTML Editor — you just need a way to see the angle brackets in the HTML tags.

9. In the source view of the default Text/HTML module enter the following content, and then click the Update hyperlink to save your changes.

```
<p>Lorem ipsum dolor sit amet, consectetur adipisicing elit, sed do eiusmod tempor
incididunt ut labore et dolore magna aliqua. Ut enim ad minim veniam, quis nostrud
exercitation ullamco laboris nisi</p>
<script type="text/javascript"
   src="/dnn450/Silverlight/Silverlight.js"></script>

<script type="text/javascript"
   src="/dnn450/Silverlight/CreateSilverlight.js"></script>

<div id="SilverlightVideoContainer"></div>

<script type="text/javascript">
   createMySilverlightControl();
</script>
```

10. You're done using the host account, so log out and refresh the Video page. It should automatically start playing the `burger.wmv` file. Figure 10-6 shows the Video page in action.

Figure 10-6

How It Works

This component uses the same familiar Silverlight elements of the previous exercises including the `Silverlight.js` file, the custom `CreateSilverlight.js` file, a XAML file, and some assets to show.

The container for the Silverlight component was added using the standard Text/HTML module inside DotNetNuke. Because this content is specific to a given DotNetNuke installation, you took some liberties with hard coding the file path to the images. When this is moved to the remote server, the content in the page will be entered again so the XAML file can be updated at the same time.

The video could have been played in the normal rectangular box of the `<MediaElement>`, but you overlaid a `<Rectangle>` to give the player some rounded corners for a nice modern feel. This targeting is possible because the XAML elements were given names.

Try It Out   Add Video Player Controls

Most video players have play and pause buttons as standard features. This section adds some buttons in XAML and wires them up to JavaScript code that will issue play and pause commands to the Silverlight media player.

1. Open the `XamlContent.xaml` file in your text editor and add highlighted code to the existing file. This is also a good opportunity to turn off the auto-play feature by changing the value of `AutoPlay` in the `MediaElement`.

```
<Canvas
    xmlns="http://schemas.microsoft.com/client/2007"
    xmlns:x="http://schemas.microsoft.com/winfx/2006/xaml">

    <!-- the movie player -->
    <MediaElement x:Name="media"
        Source="/dnn450/silverlight/burger.wmv"
        Width="320" Height="240"
        Canvas.Left="160" Canvas.Top="0"
        AutoPlay="False" Opacity="0" />

    <!-- the rounded corner skin for the player -->
    <Rectangle Width="320" Height="240"
        Canvas.Left="160" Canvas.Top="0" Stroke="#EEE" StrokeThickness="6"
        RadiusX="20" RadiusY="20">
        <Rectangle.Fill>
            <VideoBrush SourceName="media" />
        </Rectangle.Fill>
    </Rectangle>
    <!-- background for play button -->
    <Rectangle Canvas.Left="250" Canvas.Top="250"
        Height="30" Width="50"
        Stroke="#EEE" RadiusX="6" RadiusY="6">
        <Rectangle.Fill>
            <LinearGradientBrush>
                <GradientStop Color="#EEE" Offset="0.0" />
```

```
                <GradientStop Color="#666" Offset="0.25" />
                <GradientStop Color="#666" Offset="0.75" />
                <GradientStop Color="#CCC" Offset="1.0" />
            </LinearGradientBrush>
        </Rectangle.Fill>
    </Rectangle>

    <!-- play button text -->
    <TextBlock
        Canvas.Left="260" Canvas.Top="254" x:Name="btnPlay"
        Height="30" Width="50" Text="Play"
        Foreground="#FFF"
        MouseLeftButtonDown="btnPlay_Click" />

    <!-- background for pause button -->
    <Rectangle Canvas.Left="320" Canvas.Top="250"
        Height="30" Width="50"
        Stroke="#EEE" RadiusX="6" RadiusY="6">
        <Rectangle.Fill>
            <LinearGradientBrush>
                <GradientStop Color="#EEE" Offset="0.0" />
                <GradientStop Color="#666" Offset="0.25" />
                <GradientStop Color="#666" Offset="0.75" />
                <GradientStop Color="#CCC" Offset="1.0" />
            </LinearGradientBrush>
        </Rectangle.Fill>
    </Rectangle>

    <!-- pause button text -->
    <TextBlock Canvas.Left="326" Canvas.Top="254" x:Name="btnPause"
        Height="30" Width="50" Text="Pause" Foreground="#FFF"
        MouseLeftButtonDown="btnPause_Click" />
</Canvas>
```

2. Extend the existing `CreateSilverlight.js` file by appending two small JavaScript functions at the bottom of the file.

```
function btnPlay_Click(sender, args)
{
    var media = sender.findName('media');
    media.play();
}

function btnPause_Click(sender, args)
{
    var media = sender.findName('media');
    media.pause();
}
```

3. Refresh the web page, and the buttons should appear below the video. Click the play button to start the movie and click the pause button to stop it. Figure 10-7 shows the video player with the expanded functionality.

Figure 10-7

How It Works

XAML is wired up to JavaScript in a manner that is similar to HTML controls. The value of the `MouseLeftButtonDown` attribute is a JavaScript function. When the function is called, it receives two parameters from Silverlight. The JavaScript function uses the first argument to find the named `<MediaElement>` object in Silverlight. Once JavaScript has a handle on a given Silverlight object, it can issue commands to it and make it dance, or in this case, play and pause.

Try It Out   Create a Video Library

You could keep extending the video player for a while. In the interest of bringing this segment to a close, you'll implement one more feature — a clickable library of videos. You'll use the thumbnail images to create hyperlinks to the other two videos. When the thumbnail is clicked, the given video is loaded into the player and begins to play.

1. Open the `XamlContent.xaml` file in your text editor and add the following code to the top of the existing file, just under the `<Canvas>` element. These rectangles are filled with image files, and they have rounded corners via the `RadiusX` and `RadiusY` attributes. Again, some elements contain dependent references to an image. The three instances of the `<ImageBrush>` element include the web application domain name of `/dnn450`. Change this value to the name of your web application domain.

```xml
<!-- movie button #1 -->
<Rectangle Canvas.Left="0" Canvas.Top="0"
    Height="90" Width="120" MouseLeftButtonDown="Movie1_Click"
    Stroke="#EEE" StrokeThickness="4" RadiusX="10" RadiusY="10">
    <Rectangle.Fill>
        <ImageBrush ImageSource="/dnn450/silverlight/burger.png" />
    </Rectangle.Fill>
</Rectangle>

<!-- movie button #2 -->
<Rectangle Canvas.Left="0" Canvas.Top="100"
    Height="90" Width="120" MouseLeftButtonDown="Movie2_Click"
    Stroke="#EEE" StrokeThickness="4" RadiusX="10" RadiusY="10">
    <Rectangle.Fill>
        <ImageBrush ImageSource="/dnn450/silverlight/redbush.png" />
    </Rectangle.Fill>
</Rectangle>

<!-- movie button #3 -->
<Rectangle Canvas.Left="0" Canvas.Top="200"
    Height="90" Width="120" MouseLeftButtonDown="Movie3_Click"
    Stroke="#EEE" StrokeThickness="4" RadiusX="10" RadiusY="10">
    <Rectangle.Fill>
        <ImageBrush ImageSource="/dnn450/silverlight/whitebush.png" />
    </Rectangle.Fill>
</Rectangle>
```

2. While you're at it, add a place for some text to appear next to the movie to give it some context. JavaScript will be wired up to this `TextBlock` element to populate it at run time.

```xml
<!-- comment area for current movie -->
<TextBlock x:Name="mediaText"  Canvas.Left="500" Canvas.Top="0"
    Width="180" Height="300" Text="" TextWrapping="Wrap"
    Foreground="#666" FontFamily="Verdana" FontSize="18" />
```

3. The XAML is all in place, so it's time to wire it up to the JavaScript files and add some more interactive features to the page. Add the following JavaScript functions to the existing `CreateSilverlight.js` file. These functions swap movies in the video player, so it also has the web application domain name of `/dnn450` embedded in the JavaScript. Make sure to adjust this setting to your web application name in all three locations.

```javascript
function Movie1_Click(sender, args)
{
```

```
    var media = sender.findName('media');
    media.source = '/dnn450/silverlight/burger-1.wmv';

    var mediaText = sender.findName('mediaText');
    mediaText.Text = 'Grilling is great any time of year.  Bigger the better...
sometimes its just better for the dog.';
    media.play();
}

function Movie2_Click(sender, args)
{
    var media = sender.findName('media');
    media.source = '/dnn450/silverlight/redbush-1.wmv';

    var mediaText = sender.findName('mediaText');
    mediaText.Text = 'Gorgeous red blossums from Mrs. Bevelaqua';

    media.play();
}

function Movie3_Click(sender, args)
{
    var media = sender.findName('media');
    media.source = '/dnn450/silverlight/pinkbush-1.wmv';

    var mediaText = sender.findName('mediaText');
    mediaText.Text = 'A custom variety of white rhododendron given by Mr. Schlump';

    media.play();
}
```

4. Launch the Video page in your browser and take a look at what you've built. The three videos in the library on the left side of the player should appear. When you click on the thumbnail, the given video should load in the player and begin playing. The pause and play buttons should control whatever movie you're watching. Figure 10-8 shows the complete video page.

How It Works

This example extends the work of the previous example by adding three buttons to the Silverlight component. Each of these buttons is wired up to JavaScript functions using the same technique as the last exercise. In this case, each button changes the source attribute of the media player, and then instructs the media player to start playing the new video.

After this is all in place, it's just a small leap to dynamically populating the <TextBlock> element inside the Silverlight component with some context about the movie that is currently playing. If you have some .wmv files laying around, add them to the player and see how it works. Now the work has shifted from building good media players to finding good content and writing good copy — as it should be.

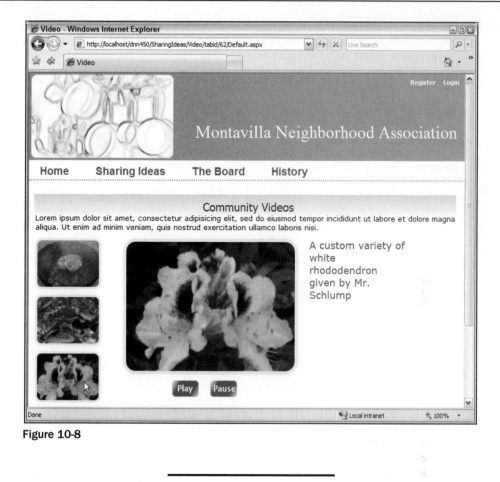

Figure 10-8

Summary

This chapter took an exploratory look at Microsoft Silverlight. This topic is too huge to cover at any exhaustive level in this book, but this quick tour has hopefully whet your appetite for more rich interactive applications.

Silverlight can render video content, custom shapes and images, and can enable animation with a level of interactivity that blurs the line between client application and web applications. One of the best features of Silverlight is that it's approachable by anyone, as you've just seen in this chapter.

Silverlight has the sophistication to go well beyond what's possible with HTML, CSS, and JavaScript with just a few lines of XAML. XAML is great with a text editor and in small samples but it can easily grow to an unwieldy size. Fortunately, you never have to look at the raw XAML file if you don't want to. Tools such as Microsoft Expression Blend help you build complex XAML files, and XAML export utilities help you create XAML files from tools you already use today.

Exercises

1. What type of animation is used on the Opacity property of a `<Rectangle>` shape?

2. What is the name of the file included in the Silverlight SDK that manages installation and injection into a web page?

3. What is the minimum syntax necessary to play a video in a Silverlight media player?

4. How can a Storyboard animation be configured to start five seconds after it has been instructed to execute?

Using Cascading Style Sheets

The previous chapters have given minimal explanation to CSS in lieu of other topics. DotNetNuke is so large that your focus at any given time on a project is limited to a small subset of the features. Hooray for checklists!

This chapter aims to make you proficient at reading and authoring a few CSS rules. You review some common CSS properties and how they can be used to build a custom design. Most sites make use of these rules in their style sheets; they always seem to throw in some uncommon CSS properties, too. If this is your starting point with CSS, you really ought to take a look at *Beginning CSS: Cascading Style Sheets for Web Design*, 2nd Edition by Richard York (Wiley Publishing, Inc., 2007), for a more detailed study of CSS.

In this chapter, you learn the following details about CSS:

- ❏ The structure of a CSS rule in a style sheet
- ❏ How to target a block of HTML with a selector
- ❏ How to use margins and padding
- ❏ How to apply font treatment
- ❏ How to use background images
- ❏ How to use positioning for a custom layout
- ❏ How to edit default styles in DotNetNuke

Although there are many CSS properties, mastering fewer than ten will get you well on your way to understanding nearly any style sheet. This chapter starts with a focus on common CSS rules used on modern, standards-compliant sites. After the fundamentals are covered, you'll apply these skills inside the DotNetNuke framework.

Exploring CSS Fundamentals

This section takes a look at some common CSS rules used on modern web pages. There is an enormous combination of rules that can be applied to a page, but a little CSS knowledge goes a long way. This chapter assumes the web pages are operating under Standards Compliance mode with a specified doctype at the top of the file. Things have a tendency to act weird under Quirks mode — hence, the name.

This section will focus on the fundamental concepts used on modern, standards-compliant websites. By leveraging the use of semantic HTML markup, most of the design can be left to the CSS file. Using clean HTML markup and leveraging CSS provides some powerful capabilities for updating the site down the road and helps to minimize unnecessary coupling of the content to the design.

The best kind of markup to style with CSS already has a semantic flow of HTML elements; headers have an `<h1>` tag, paragraphs of text have `<p>` tags, and so on. Good HTML code is not littered with presentation details. When you turn off style sheets in your browser, the page should continue to present the information to the reader clearly. The text will be a uniform font and obey the basic style inherent in the given browser.

If the web page content contains embedded images using the `<img/>` tag, they should augment the text and provide real value. Background gradients or rounded corner images shouldn't exist in the best HTML markup. These ancillary items are presentation elements and better off defined in the CSS. Of course, sometimes a balance must be struck between competing interests of pure semantic HTML and going home to your family on time.

Targeting HTML

There are a couple of ways to target a specific block of HTML inside a page with CSS, and you'll explore them shortly. Figure 11-1 maps out the basic structure for CSS rules in a style sheet.

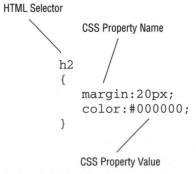

HTML Selector

CSS Property Name

```
h2
{
    margin:20px;
    color:#000000;
}
```

CSS Property Value

Figure 11-1

Each rule in a style sheet starts with a *selector*, a specification of which HTML element(s) will receive the given style. The selector can target all tags that share a class attribute, as well as individual tags through their ID attributes. For example, a selector can apply a set of rules to all paragraph tags in the page, every paragraph tag having a class attribute of `ItemDetail`, or to just the one paragraph tag on the page that has the unique ID attribute of `LeadText`. The HTML specification tells you that no two tags on a given page should have the same ID attribute value, but they can have the same class attribute value.

Bracket characters envelop the set of CSS properties following a selector. A single CSS property contains two parts: the name and the value. For example, the CSS property color can be set to the value of blue. A colon separates this name/value pair. Multiple CSS properties in a single CSS rule are separated by a semicolon. You can drop as many CSS properties into a rule as you like.

There are many conventions for writing a CSS rule. A CSS rule can be all on one line, but using multiple lines helps make them more readable. Some folks like conserving space by placing the opening bracket on the same line as the selector. I prefer to maximize readability by using one line for the selector, one line per bracket, and one line per CSS rule. I encourage you to use whatever technique makes you the most comfortable. If you don't have a convention, just pick one and stick with it for a while. It is important to be consistent; especially when dealing with multiple developers.

You'll probably want to comment out a CSS property from time to time during development. You should document complex or important CSS rules, too. It's surprising to see how much is forgotten in six months. The CSS comment syntax begins with a forward slash and an asterisk. The comment terminates with the reverse pattern, and everything between the open and closing comment characters is ignored by the browser. The first property in the following code block shows an example of a CSS comment. The last property is commented out so it will not apply to this CSS rule that targets all paragraph elements.

```
P
{
    color:#006699;  /* client requested this shade of blue!! */
    font-weight:bold;
    /* font-family:verdana; */
}
```

Modern text editors can provide great assistance when they recognize the CSS schema and show CSS rules and comments in special colors. Windows Notepad isn't the easiest tool to help you track down a missing semi-colon or a comment that never terminates. In addition to color coding, Visual Studio.Net will also provide Intellisense so the CSS properties will pop up in the window as you type the first few characters.

Using Class Attributes

Multiple HTML elements in a given page can share the same class attribute. The CSS selector can target all of these elements through a simple syntax. The period character in a selector indicates the following text is a class attribute. The following code block shows a CSS rule that applies to all elements having a class attribute value of LeadText. It doesn't matter what element(s) have the class; it could be <div> tags, <p> tags, and <td> tags, and this selector will find them if they have the given class attribute.

```
.LeadText
{
    color:#006699;  /* client requested this shade of blue!! */
    font-weight:bold;
    /* font-family:verdana; */
}
```

CSS is case sensitive, so make sure that your capitalization is correct for the class attribute value. A camel case standard in your HTML file coupled with a Pascal case standard in your CSS file won't get you very far. They have to match!

Using ID Attributes

If your HTML document is playing by the rules, the ID attribute of any element on a given page will be unique. With this knowledge, the CSS selector can target a specific element by using the hash character followed by the ID attribute value. The following code block shows a CSS rule that applies to the single element on the page having the ID attribute of `SideBar`:

```
#SideBar
{
    background-color:#CCC;
    padding:20px;
}
```

Using the Document Object Model Hierarchy

So far, the CSS rules have been very broad in their reach. Any element that used the class attribute of `LeadText` or any element that had an ID attribute value of `SideBar` would pick up on the respective rules. The CSS syntax includes some ways to be a little more discriminating while allowing multiple elements on a page to be selected.

Sometimes you need a CSS rule that only affects particular HTML tags that have a given class. The following code block limits the style to `<p>` tags that also have the class attribute of `LeadText`:

```
p.LeadText
{
    color:#006699;
}
```

All other `<p>` tags in the page will not be affected by this CSS rule. An `<h2>` tag that has a class attribute of `LeadText` will also be unaffected because of the prefix on this CSS selector.

Suppose that a website contains several pages. Some pages contain a `<p>` tag with a CSS attribute of `LeadText`. Other pages contain a `<p>` tag with an ID attribute of `SideBar`. The following code block shows how to target the paragraph tag when it has a class attribute value of `LeadText` and an ID attribute value of `SideBar` at the same time:

```
p.LeadText#SideBar
{
    font-size:14pt;
    color:#0000FF;
}
```

The previous code block will only be applied to a very special type of tag. It requires the tag to be a paragraph, have a specific class attribute, and a specific ID attribute. Many of the rules in a style sheet will take the class attribute or the ID attribute approach to selecting elements. As explained next, another common technique for selectors is to leverage the hierarchy of tags in the Document Object Model.

CSS selectors can specify a hierarchical pattern. Suppose you are working with a web page that contains a `<div>` tag with the ID attribute of `SideBar`. A series of `<p>` tags exists inside this `<div>` tag as shown in the following HTML snippet:

```
<div id="SideBar">
    <p>lorem ipsum</p>
```

```
    <p>lorem ipsum</p>
    <p>lorem ipsum</p>
</div>
```

If you wanted to target just these <p> tags without affecting any <p> tags located elsewhere in the HTML document, you *could* edit the HTML and configure a class attribute on every <p> tag or give each of them a unique ID attribute. Then, you could define a custom CSS rule in the style sheet using the techniques described earlier.

It's often the case that adding attributes is either unnecessary or impossible, because the HTML is built at run time by a component you cannot edit. However, CSS provides a way to target elements by their position in the Document Object Model. Using the prior HTML snippet as an example, the following CSS block leverages the relative position of the <div> tag and the <p> tags in the selector. A selector can target all <p> tags that are contained by a <div> tag having the ID attribute value of SideBar.

```
div#SideBar p
{
    font-size:16pt;
    color:#00FFFF;
}
```

The selector in the previous CSS block contains a space character before the p. This selector will target all <p> tags within the matching <div> tag. In fact, the previous CSS rule would also target the <p> tags in the following HTML snippet:

```
<div id="SideBar">
    <div>
        <p>lorem ipsum</p>
        <div>
            <p>lorem ipsum</p>
            <p>lorem ipsum</p>
            <p>lorem ipsum</p>
        </div>
        <p>lorem ipsum</p>
    </div>
</div>
```

The previous HTML snippet shows how the <p> tags are still a descendent of the SideBar <div> tag; therefore all of the <p> tags will continue to receive the contents of the given CSS rule.

Selectors can have as many levels as you like and use any type of class or ID attribute constraint. Most of the time, you'll see hierarchical selectors that go two or three levels deep. They're very useful for adding CSS rules to <ul> tags where you want to apply styles on the <ul> tag, the <li> tag inside it, or the contents of the <li> tag. The following HTML snippet shows a clear hierarchy that can be targeted by CSS, which is why professional CSS developers love ordered and unordered lists so much.

```
<ul id="menu">
    <li>
        <a href="home.aspx">Home</a>
    </li>
    <li>
        <a href="products.aspx">Products</a>
    </li>
```

```
    <li>
        <a href="about.aspx">About Us</a>
    </li>
</ul>
```

The following CSS block can use the hierarchy of the HTML to target the anchor tags embedded inside the unordered list with a three-part selector:

```
ul#menu li a
{
    text-decoration:none;      /* turn off the underlines on these hyperlinks */
    font:normal normal bold 12pt Arial;
    color:#006699;
}
```

Sharing Rules with Targets

Reducing redundant code is a good thing in software development. There are many cases where it makes sense to construct a single block of CSS properties and apply them to multiple HTML elements. A comma can serve as a delimiter between multiple selectors.

For example, imagine two <div> tags that have unique ID attribute values. Both of them can receive the same CSS properties, reducing the opportunity for one of them to get out of sync if the design calls for both of them to line up and share the same background color. The following CSS block shows how this is achieved:

```
div#LeftColumn, div#RightColumn
{
    height:400px;
    width:300px;
    background-color:#CCC;
}
```

In the previous CSS block, both <div> tags will receive the same treatment through the three CSS properties. You can string as many selectors together with a comma delimiter as you like.

Working with CSS is sometimes like solving a crossword puzzle. You might get close to the end and realize a word that fit really well before is now obviously wrong and prevents you from finishing the puzzle. You'll unwind your answers and find a better word to complete the crossword. In CSS, you might be able to get almost everything styled by leveraging the hierarchy of the HTML elements as described earlier, yet sometimes you will need to make slight adjustments to your plan or edit the HTML to achieve your goal. You combine features and try different approaches until you figure out the puzzle of your design through CSS.

Applying a Custom Font Treatment

CSS has several properties related to specifying the font characteristics of text on a web page. For the most part, they're easy to understand and use. First, you'll cover some basic font styles, and then follow up with some shorthand techniques that help speed up development.

The `font-family` property specifies the desired font to use when rendering a given block of HTML text.

```
p.LeadText
{
    font-family:Verdana;
}
```

If you select a nonstandard font, there's a reasonable chance that a visitor's browser will not have it. Therefore, you have the option of specifying several fonts using a comma delimiter, as shown in the following CSS block. The browser traverses the list of fonts from left to right and applies the first font it understands. If a browser doesn't have your first choice of font, you can supply a backup font. You can have as many backup fonts as desired, although I seldom see more than three fonts in a list.

```
p.LeadText
{
    font-family:Georgia, Arial, Verdana;
}
```

The `font-size` property specifies how large to render a given block of HTML text.

```
p.LeadText
{
    font-family:Georgia, Arial, Verdana;
    font-size:12pt;
}
```

The `font-size` property accepts a wide variety of units, including absolute measurements such as pixel and point units, as well as relative sizes such as `larger` and `smaller` or percentage units. If you're just starting out in your CSS studies, then I recommend sticking to the absolute measurements to simplify the process. Use the `pt` measurement until you feel as though you're being limited by the technology. Then you can branch into other units such as `%` and `em` units.

The `font-weight` property specifies how bold the font is rendered in the browser. Sometimes the HTML content will contain `<b>` tags or `<strong>` tags that provide a similar behavior. If you're authoring the HTML, you should limit the use of these tags to their semantic definition and use CSS to present all other content as bold.

```
p.LeadText
{
    font-family:Georgia, Arial, Verdana;
    font-size:12pt;
    font-weight:bold;
}
```

The `font-weight` property normally has the value of `bold` in a style sheet. You can also turn off a bold font-weight by setting the value to `normal`.

The `font-style` property can convert the given HTML text into italics. This is similar to using the `<i>` tag in the content.

```
p.LeadText
{
```

```
    font-family:Georgia, Arial, Verdana;
    font-size:12pt;
    font-weight:bold;
    font-style:italic;
}
```

Similar to the `font-weight` property, you can turn off italics by setting the value to `normal`.

The `font-variant` property can perform an interesting typography effect by converting the selected HTML content into small capital letters. This technique is a nice design element for the opening phrase or sentence in a series of paragraphs.

```
p.LeadText
{
    font-family:Georgia, Arial, Verdana;
    font-size:12pt;
    font-weight:bold;
    font-style:italic;
    font-variant:small-caps;
}
```

As you might expect now, this property can be turned off by specifying a value of `normal` in the CSS rule.

You've only covered a few font-related properties, and already the CSS rule has grown to several lines. CSS has several techniques for writing rules using a shorthand technique. This is a good practice to help keep your style sheets manageable while giving you the flexibility to make subtle adjustments. The `font` property is one that accepts several parameters delimited by a space character. The following CSS block demonstrates how to set the same values in a single line. The CSS comment below the CSS rule documents the five parameters used in the `font` property.

```
p.LeadText
{
    font:italic small-caps bold 12pt Georgia, Arial, Verdana;
}

/*
    font parameters: 1: font-style:italic;
                     2: font-variant:small-caps;
                     3: font-weight:bold;
                     4: font-size:12pt;
                     5: font-family:Georgia, Arial, Verdana;
*/
```

The previous CSS property uses a specific order to specify the values for the `font` property. Notice the last parameter is the `font-family` and the value is a comma delimited set of fonts to apply to the selected HTML text. The previous code block shows how the `font` property can be used to configure five properties in a single line and retain its readability — a good technique to learn and use.

The last item you'll cover related to fonts is the `color` property. This setting controls the color of the text in the browser. The following code block shows how to set the color using a hexadecimal value.

Although you are able to use words such as red and green to configure colors, it's more common to appeal to a particular variant of a color.

```
p.LeadText
{
    color:#006699; /* this is blueish color */
}
```

In the previous CSS block, the value of the color property begins with the hash character to indicate a hexadecimal number. The value consists of three groups of two numbers. Each pair can range in value from 00 to FF, which gives a range of 256 different values for red, green, and blue. That's over 16 million colors! You can experiment by cranking up one color to the maximum of FF and leaving the other two set to 00 to see this for yourself.

```
p.red    { color:#FF0000; }
p.green  { color:#00FF00; }
p.blue   { color:#0000FF; }
```

You'll want to choose good colors when you use them for informational purposes in your web page. Approximately 10 percent of all males in the United States have some form of color blindness.

Colors are used in several properties such as backgrounds and borders that you'll get into shortly. When you specify a hexadecimal color, you have the option of using a shorthand notation for some colors. For example, the following CSS block shows two ways to specify the same color:

```
div.black  { color:#000000; }  /* this is the long way, using all six digits */
div.black2 { color:#000;     }  /* this is the shorthand way */
```

The previous code block shows how six repeating digits can be expressed in just three digits. With this technique, you can specify a grey color such as #CCCCCC with a few less keystrokes. You'll see this technique employed often when reviewing hand-crafted style sheets written by professionals.

Try It Out   Apply Custom Fonts

In this exercise, you'll pull away from DotNetNuke and just work with a single HTML file on your desktop. For brevity and clarity, you'll drop the CSS rules inside the <style> tag on the page. The following HTML content will serve as the starting point. If you don't want to create a new file from scratch, you can find default.htm in the files available online for this chapter.

```
<!DOCTYPE html PUBLIC "-//W3C//DTD XHTML 1.1//EN"
                 "http://www.w3.org/TR/xhtml11/DTD/xhtml11.dtd">
<html>
   <head>
      <title>CSS</title>
      <style type="text/css">
      </style>
   </head>
   <body>
      <div>

         <h1>Lorem Ipsum</h1>
```

```
        <p>Nisi laboris ullamco exercitation  nostrud quis.</p>

        <h2>Dolor Sit Amet</h2>
        <p>Sed do eiusmod tempor incididunt ut labore et
            dolore magna aliqua.</p>

        <div id="callout">
            <h2>Consectetur Adipisicing Elit</h2>
            <p>Ut enim ad minim veniam, quis nostrud
                exercitation ullamco.</p>
        </div>

      </div>
    </body>
</html>
```

Once you have this file saved on your desktop, you should be able to open it in Internet Explorer or Firefox using Standards Compliance mode. Your browser will render its default styles for the <h1>, <h2>, and <p> tags because no other styles are defined.

1. Open the default.htm file with your browser and your favorite text editor.

2. After the opening <style> tag, insert the following CSS rule to target the <h1> tag:

```
h1
{
    font:normal normal bold 30pt Georgia, Arial, Verdana;
}
```

3. Refresh the browser and observe the changes in the first header.

4. Add the following CSS rule below the first rule to target the <h2> tags:

```
h2
{
    font:normal normal normal 20pt Arial;
}
```

5. Refresh the browser and observe the changes in the second-level headers.

6. Add the following CSS rule below the second rule to target the <p> tags:

```
p
{
    font:normal normal normal 12pt Verdana;
    color:#FF0000;
}
```

7. Refresh the browser and observe the changes in the paragraphs.

8. Add the following CSS rule below the third rule to target the <p> tag located inside a special <div> tag.

```
div#callout p
{
    font-weight:bold;
```

```
        color:#CCC;
    }
```

9. Refresh the browser and observe the changes in the paragraphs. You should see something similar to Figure 11-2.

Figure 11-2

How It Works

The CSS rules you created began by overriding some default styles applied by the browser to the elements. These defaults can vary from browser to browser, so it's important to specify everything you care about.

The fourth CSS rule used an override to specify a bold font and a grey color on the paragraph located under the `<div>` tag having the ID attribute of `callout`. This `<p>` tag continued to inherit the other properties of `font-size` and `font-family` specified in the third CSS rule. This is an example of how CSS rules can cascade across several elements. The thoughtful use of selectors can help reduce the amount of redundant properties you configure to achieve the desired result.

Working with Rectangles

Creating an intentional rectangular shaped object with a given height and width might be a little puzzling at first. You'll cover the major parts now, one at a time. First, a simple `<div>` tag will serve as the starting point.

```
<div>
    Lorem Ipsum
</div>
```

The previous HTML tag, consuming just three lines, can be customized through CSS by editing its margin, padding, and border properties, as shown in Figure 11-3.

In Figure 11-3, the area between the text and the black border is styled through the padding property. The border property controls the 10-pixel-wide rectangle around the edge of the <div> tag. The area between the black rectangle and the edge of the browser window is styled by the margin property. All three of these properties are configured on the <div> tag to produce the previous design.

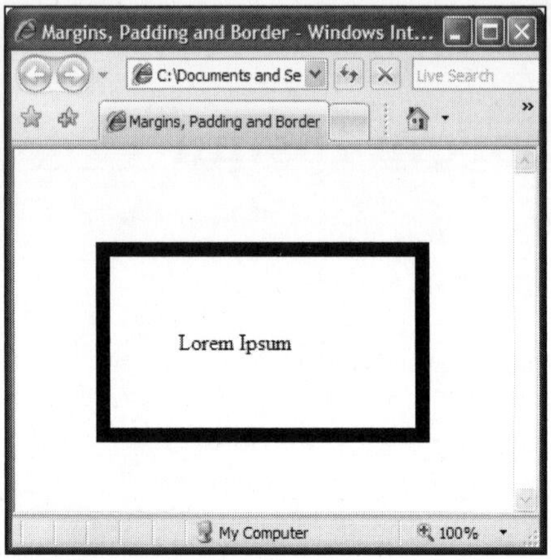

Figure 11-3

Using Margins

The margin property of an element controls the distance between the exterior of an HTML tag and its adjacent elements. It affects the external area around the object. The CSS syntax has four intuitive properties to deal with each side individually, as shown in the following CSS block:

```
div
{
    margin-left:20px;
    margin-right:20px;
    margin-top:20px;
    margin-bottom:20px;
}
```

Applying this type of style syntax across several <div> tags can be quite verbose. Therefore, the previous CSS block can also be expressed with the following shorthand syntax:

```
div
{
    margin:20px;
}
```

The previous CSS block applies the same margin value of 20px to all four sides. This technique does a good job of reducing the complexity of the property assignments when all four sides have the same value. Sometimes the top and bottom sides will have one value and the left and right sides will have another value. The following CSS block shows this technique:

```
div
{
    margin:20px 40px;
}
```

The first value of 20px in the previous CSS block controls both the top and bottom margins. By definition, the top and bottom margins are the same value. The second value of 40px controls the left and right margins. Alternatively, the margin property can also accept a unique value for all four sides in a single line, as shown in the following CSS block:

```
div
{
    margin:10px 20px 30px 40px;
}
```

The previous CSS block operates in a specific order: top, right, bottom, and left. The first value of 10px applies to the top margin and the values continue around the rectangle clockwise. The final value of 40px applies to the left side of the rectangle created by the <div> tag.

The margin property applies to *block* elements. HTML tags such as <div> and <p> are block elements because they occupy the entire line of content in a browser window by default. HTML elements such as <span> and <strong> are *inline* elements because they flow with the HTML content. Of course, CSS has a property named display that can modify these default behaviors, but that's beyond the scope of this chapter.

Margins are normally specified in pixel units, but zero is zero in any unit. Sometimes you'll spot margin specifications like the following CSS block:

```
div
{
    margin:20px 0;
}
```

The previous CSS block applies a value of zero pixels to the left and right margins, essentially none, and a value of 20px to the top and bottom margins. The zero value does not require a unit suffix, such as px because it's unnecessary. This technique is often used for any CSS property that has a zero unit value.

Left to their own accord, <div> tags will consume the entire row in a browser, providing they have child content to display. When a specific pixel width value is provided, the <div> tag will be constrained to a fixed size. The total width calculation for a <div> tag with a specified dimension includes the horizontal margin properties, both the margin-left and the margin-right values. Therefore, if a <div> tag has a specified width of 100 pixels, and a margin-left and margin-right property of 50 pixels each, then the total width consumed by the <div> tag is 200 pixels.

Figure 11-4 depicts how the total width is calculated. The grey rectangle represents the fixed width <div> tag and the dashed line represents the overall width, including the horizontal margins configured on the <div> tag.

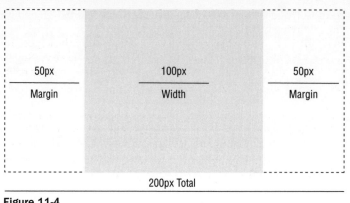

Figure 11-4

Vertical margins are another story. The `margin-top` and the `margin-bottom` properties extend the object above and below its default edge. Unlike horizontal margins, which are additive, *vertical margins collapse.*

The following HTML snippet shows a basic example with three `<div>` tags:

```
<div class="box1">
    Lorem
</div>
<div class="box2">
    Ipsum
</div>
<div class="box3">
    Dolar
</div>
```

The following CSS block can apply different vertical margins to the `<div>` tags. The top `<div>` tag has a vertical margin of `40px`, the middle `<div>` tag has a vertical margin of `10px`, and the bottom element has a margin of zero pixels. All elements have a background color to show their internal shape, yet will not affect their surface area.

```
div.box1
{
    margin:50px 0;
    background:#FF0000;
}
div.box2
{
    margin:25px 0;
    background:#0000FF;
}
div.box3
{
    margin:0;
    background:#FFFF00;
}
```

Figure 11-5 shows how the vertical margins are rendered in the browser.

As you can see in Figure 11-5, the vertical margins have collapsed to the largest adjacent value. While horizontal margins on an individual element are additive, the middle <div> tag has collapsed upward and defers to the 50px value of the top <div> tag. The bottom <div> tag has no margin. Therefore it defers to the 25px value of the middle element.

If vertical margins were additive, which they are not, you would expect to see a larger margin between the first and second element. It turns out that the margin above and below the top <div> tag is roughly the same on each side in the browser. The margin below the second <div> tag doesn't seem to be reflected above it. So you can be confident that vertical margins do collapse to the larger of the two values. This might take a while to settle in, so read this over and take a good look at the code and the previous figure.

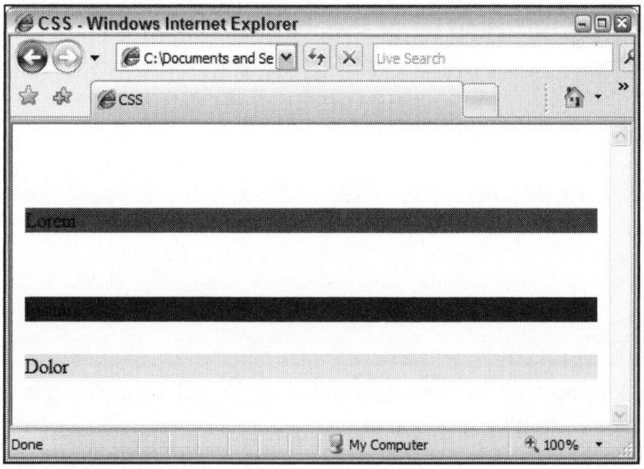

Figure 11-5

Using Padding

The CSS padding property controls the space between the border of the object and its internal content. Like margins, padding can also be specified individually or all at once. The following CSS block shows how to specify padding through a variety of techniques similar to margins. Because padding is within an individual element, vertical padding does not collapse.

```
div#Class1   /* verbose technique */
{
    padding-top:10px;
    padding-right:20px;
    padding-bottom:10px;
    padding-left:20px;
}

div#Class2   /* top & bottom share value, left & right share value */
{
    padding:10px 20px;
}

div#Class3   /* every side has same value */
```

```
{
    padding:20px;
}

div#Class4   /* every side has unique value */
{
    padding:10px 20px 30px 0;
}
```

A small amount of space created through margins or padding can do wonders for readability on a block of text. HTML block elements will also include background colors or images. So for aesthetic reasons, the exact alignment of borders becomes significant across various browsers. CSS has a good technique for leveling the playing field through the universal selector.

Applying the Universal Selector

The *universal selector* will apply the given CSS properties to all HTML tags inside its scope. It's a good time to review this feature because it's often used in combination with margins and padding as shown in the following CSS block:

```
*         /* zero out margin and padding in all tags */
{
   margin:0;
   padding:0;
}
```

The previous CSS block shows an asterisk character in the selector portion of the rule. This is the universal selector. The asterisk in the previous rule has no ancestors in the selector to limit its scope. Therefore, the browser will apply the styles to all HTML tags on the page. This rule is setting the margin and padding values to zero, a common way of leveling the field in all browsers.

As a thought experiment, imagine what would happen if Internet Explorer's default margin on a <p> tag were 4 pixels and the default margin in Firefox on the same HTML element were 6 pixels. Highly customized websites would look broken across various browsers because images would not line up, and adjacent borders would be misaligned. This is exactly the problem solved by the previous CSS rule. Because you cannot trust the default values to be identical across all popular browsers, developers are interested in leveling out the playing field.

Many professional CSS developers will include the previous rule at the top of a CSS file to zero out all margin and padding values that the browsers will apply by default. It's better for highly customized websites to start at the same place, zero, across all browsers. If the developer wishes to apply a nonzero value to the margin or padding of an HTML tag, a subsequent rule is created to override the initialization rule.

Using Borders

The CSS border property is a great technique to highlight an edge with a solid color because it's much more lightweight than using an image for the same result. There are several variations of the CSS border property, but you'll just focus on a few for now.

The following CSS block uses the longhand method of specifying the same type of border on every side of a <div> tag:

```
div#sidebar    /* verbose technique */
{
    border-top:10px solid #FF0000;
    border-right:10px solid #FF0000;
    border-bottom:10px solid #FF0000;
    border-left:10px solid #FF0000;
}
```

The previous CSS block shows three values configured for each property. Each value is delimited by a space character. The first value is the width of the border in pixels. The second property is the style of the border. This property touts ten different styles, such as dotted, dashed, double, and groove. The last value is the color of the border. As you might expect, the previous CSS block can be consolidated into the following CSS rule:

```
div#sidebar    /* shorthand technique */
{
    border:10px solid #FF0000;
}
```

So far, you've taken a look at margins, padding and borders for rectangular objects like the HTML <div> tag. It's a good time to take these properties out for a spin and get a feel for how they operate in your own browser.

Try It Out   Customize a Collection of Blocks

In this section, you'll continue on with the same HTML file from the last section. At this point, the file contains CSS rules that customize the fonts. Now you'll modify the structure of the page by adding more CSS rules. Refresh your browser to show the results after each step in the following list.

1. Using your favorite text editor, open the default.htm file used in the previous Try It Out section.

2. Add a universal selector just under the opening <style> tag in the file and add the following CSS rule to zero out the margins and padding for all elements. This shrinks the content on the browser by eliminating the default (nonzero) values.

```
*
{
    margin:0;
    padding:0;
}
```

3. Add the following CSS rule that will modify the margins for all <div> tags on the page. After you refresh the page, notice how the nested <div> tag also receives the margin property value so it's pulled in twice as much from the browser's edge as the outer <div> tag.

```
div
{
    margin:10px 30px;
}
```

4. Add the following CSS rule to give the paragraph tags some custom padding. Remember, the values apply in a special order of top, right, bottom, and left.

```
p
{
    padding:0 0 10px 2px;
}
```

5. Add a custom border to the nested `<div>` tag through the following CSS rule:

```
div#callout
{
    border-left:10px solid #CCC;
}
```

How It Works

The page in your browser should resemble Figure 11-6.

First, the default margins and padding were cleared out with some help from the universal selector. Next, you applied some custom margins and padding as well as a border to a specific HTML tag inside the page. Most of the CSS properties took advantage of the shorthand technique to reduce the lines of code and increase readability.

Figure 11-6

Working in the Background

The background related properties in CSS have quite a bit to them, but nearly every page makes use of background colors and images. Background colors can apply a consistent shade across the entire page, or part of a page, while remaining lightweight and easy to change. Background images provide an excellent opportunity to give a page the appropriate mood without resorting to `<img/>` tags inside the markup. The following CSS block shows how to apply a color background to a given `<div>` tag:

```
div#sidebar
{
    background-color:#CCC;
}
```

As a general guideline, you should limit the use of `<img/>` tags only to those images that provide real content to the page, such as diagrams, logos, and some photos. Rounded corner images and giant photos that don't provide any real support to the content are better left to background images. The text content as well as informational diagrams and logos are very much at the heart of the web page. These are things you would expect to see on paper if you received a hard copy of the page.

You'll have a much easier time refreshing the design of a page or an entire site if you spend most of your time editing CSS files instead of figuring out how to modify the HTML content to achieve a pleasing aesthetic. CSS includes a shorthand method for specifying several values in a single line as shown in the following CSS block:

```
div#sidebar
{
    background:transparent url(grandient.png) repeat-y;
}
```

The previous CSS block specifies three values. The first is the background color property; in this case it is set to a transparent value so the content behind the HTML block shows through, but it could also be a hexadecimal value. The second value is an image reference. The selected `<div>` tag will show the given image as part of the background. If the website visitor views the HTML source, they will not see a file reference to `gradient.png` because it only exists in the CSS file. The last property value affects how the background is rendered. In this case, the background image is repeated along the Y-axis so it covers the element from top to bottom. A value of `no-repeat` would only show one instance of the image. A value of `repeat-x` would cover the element along the X-axis. Omitting the repeat value entirely would repeat the image in both directions by default.

If the image is of a small animal, perhaps your pet, you can instantly apply the pinnacle of the late 90's design aesthetic by repeating a small rectangular image across the `<body>` tag in both directions with the `repeat-x` and `repeat-y` settings. Please don't do this.

CSS also makes it possible to position images in the background. This works especially well when the background image is smaller than its container, and you want it to be left-aligned to the container or positioned a given number of pixels away from the edge. The following code block shows an example of a positioned background image:

```
div#sidebar
{
    background:transparent url(sailboat.png) no-repeat 100px 10px;
}
```

Keep in mind that background images will not affect the height and width of the containing element. If the given element only contains one line of text, a large background image will go largely unseen, as it will not extend beyond the border of the container.

Apply a Background

This section will continue the development of the sample HTML file used in the previous Try It Out sections for this chapter. In this exercise, you'll add a gradient background image to the web page. Before starting this section, locate the file named `gradient.png` available in the download section for this chapter.

1. Copy the file named `gradient.png` to the same folder as your `default.htm` file used in the previous Try It Out section.

2. Open the `default.htm` file using your favorite text editor.

3. Append the following CSS rule to the growing list inside the `<style>` tag of the `.htm` file:

```
body
{
    background:#FFF url(gradient.png) repeat-x 0 57px;
}
```

4. Refresh the browser and observe the effect of the background color, image, and position.

5. Try changing the background color to a different hexadecimal value or moving the position of the background image, and observe the results in the browser.

How It Works

Your browser should resemble Figure 11-7. The color gradient is implemented as background image in CSS. It starts 57 pixels from the top of the browser and repeats horizontally across the page. Where the body element does not display the background image, the given color of white is shown. All of these settings are provided in the single line of CSS properties you created.

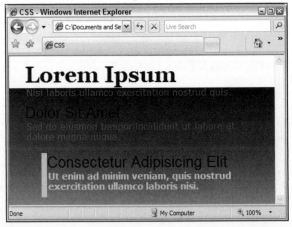

Figure 11-7

Defining Position

The final CSS topic you'll cover in your temporary vacuum of the single static HTML page is positioning. At first, it might seem like an overly complicated process of specifying locations for various HTML elements. With just a few quick tips, you'll be able to unravel how relative and absolute positioning work inside CSS.

Through positioning, the developer has the ability to move an HTML element anywhere on the page, sometimes even off the page, out of view. Left untouched, most elements will consume space as expected in the browser and either flow character by character like a `<span>` tag, or flow line by line like a `<div>` tag.

Using Relative Positioning

The position of a `<div>` tag in a web page can be modified by configuring the CSS `position` property to a value of `relative`. Once this `position` property is set, the HTML element can be moved incrementally in any direction through the `top` and `left` properties. For example, the following CSS block adjusts the normal layout of a `<div>` tag by a few pixels to the right and a few pixels lower than it would normally display.

```
div#callout
{
    position:relative;
    top:10px;
    left:10px;
}
```

The selected `<div>` tag in the previous CSS block could have been moved in the opposite direction by specifying negative values instead of positive values for the `top` and `left` CSS properties.

If the top and left CSS properties were set to zero or omitted entirely, the HTML element would behave as if the position property was not set. This is because the 0,0 coordinate of a relatively positioned element is wherever the top left corner of the element would normally appear in the document flow.

The use of the relative position setting has some interesting effects on the web page. First, the flow of the adjacent elements in the web page is not changed; those elements act as if the selected element is still in the original spot on the page, and flow accordingly. Second, the positioned element has the potential to overlap adjacent elements. This can be a good thing as well as a bad thing. Figure 11-8 shows an example of a relative positioned element that is overlapping the adjacent text and causing problems.

Using Absolute Positioning

The other kind of positioning you'll cover in this chapter is absolute positioning. Recall that the 0,0 coordinate of a relative positioned element is the top left corner of its normal flow in the document. The 0,0 coordinate of an absolute positioned element is the same as its *positioning context*. This is the first parent element that is relatively positioned.

Imagine a `<div>` tag that contains another nested `<div>` tag on a regular HTML page. If the nested `<div>` tag is configured with absolute positioning and the outer `<div>` tag is configured with relative positioning, then the 0,0 coordinate of inner and outer `<div>` tags is the same point.

Figure 11-8

Now suppose the outer `<div>` tag no longer has relative positioning configured in the CSS. When the browser prepares to render the page, it will calculate the positioning context of the nested `<div>` tag. It will observe that the outer `<div>` tag is not using relative positioning, so it moves up the DOM hierarchy in its search for a parent element with relative positioning. In this case, the browser runs into the `<body>` tag of the web page. By default, the `<body>` tag has the relative positioning so the 0,0 coordinate of the inner `<div>` tag in this scenario is the top left corner of the web browser. The positioning context is always the nearest parent having relative positioning. If no HTML element claims this CSS property value in the hierarchy, the `<body>` tag is the catchall.

When an element is relatively positioned, the ambient document flow is unchanged. When an element is absolutely positioned, the element pops out of the normal document flow, and the adjacent elements behave as if the absolutely positioned element does not exist. Elements lower in the document will flow up and become adjacent to the element above the absolutely positioned item.

Consider the following HTML snippet that contains some nested HTML elements:

```
<div id="outside">
   <div id="inside">
      <p>Dolor Sit</p>
   </div>
   <p>Lorem Ipsum</p>
</div>
```

The following CSS block can configure the outer `<div>` tag with relative positioning so it will serve as the positioning context for the nested `<div>` tag that is absolutely positioned.

```
div#outside
{
   position:relative;
   top:0;
   left:0;
```

```
        height:400px;
        width:500px;
    }
    div#inside
    {
        position:absolute;
        top:200px;
        left:100px;
        height:100px;
        width:200px;
    }
```

Try It Out   **Apply Absolute Positioning**

In this section, you'll finish off the sample .htm file with some CSS positioning. You'll move the background image to the nested element and apply some positioning rules through CSS to customize the look without modifying any of the HTML content inside the <body> tag. Remember to refresh the browser after each step to keep up with the changes that are occurring in the CSS.

1.   Using your favorite text editor, open the default.htm file used in the previous Try It Out section.

2.   Delete or comment out the CSS rule for the <body> tag.

3.   Modify the rule with the selector of div#callout as follows:

```
div#callout
{
    border-left:10px solid #CCC;
    position:absolute;
    top:10px;
    left:300px;
    background:#FFF url(gradient.png) repeat-x 0 -300px;
    width:250px;
}
```

4.   Now that the callout box is positioned, it's overlapping the normal content. Modify the outer <div> tag by changing the following CSS rule as shown in the following code. This will constrain the outer element so it is not under the positioned element.

```
div
{
    margin:10px 30px;
    width:300px;
}
```

Your browser should resemble Figure 11-9.

How It Works

The CSS background property of the callout box uses negative positioning to move the background image up in the containing element. Because the background image is a gradient that is taller than the container, you can control the contrast of the text and the image by sliding the image higher through negative values.

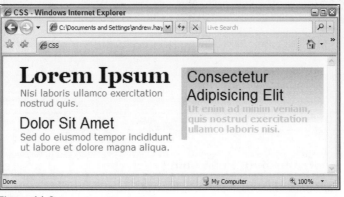

Figure 11-9

Both `<div>` tags display the margin property specified in Step 4, but the callout box has its own width value of `250px` that overrides the value of `300px` specified in the more general CSS rule. You can try changing both of them to see the effects on the two `<div>` tags.

There's a lot more to CSS properties, and I encourage you to dive deeper into the capabilities of positioning, colors, margins, padding, fonts, and other settings. It's certainly enough to keep you busy for a while.

Clearing Default DNN Styles

Now that you've taken a step back from DotNetNuke and explored some CSS rules in detail during the previous sections in this chapter, you are prepared to return to DotNetNuke to apply these skills. This mindset is similar to experts who already come to DotNetNuke with a wealth of CSS knowledge.

DotNetNuke includes several CSS rules by default to help the entry-level user. These help get folks up and running fast; after a while, experienced DotNetNuke designers will want to discard these styles and construct their own custom skins.

It's not uncommon to find a few roadblocks in your custom skinning pursuits, whether you're working with a new DotNetNuke installation or an existing site that's inherited from previous developers. Even with a new site, DotNetNuke remains a web application framework and delivers a load of features out of the box. From time to time, you'll want to find ways to turn off some default switches that get in the way of your custom design.

Customizing the Portal Style Sheet

A file named `portal.css` exists at the root of every portal of a DotNetNuke installation. For example, you can find the style sheet for the default instance at the following location on your computer:

```
<DotNetNuke Install Folder>\Portals\0\portal.css
```

When DotNetNuke builds a page and renders it to a browser, the `portal.css` file is the last style sheet in the list. Therefore, this file carries special significance because it gives the CSS author the ability to override any previous CSS rule. Because CSS works in a hierarchical fashion, rules at the top can be overridden by rules at the bottom. This fact holds true across multiple CSS files, too. Files referred to at the top of the HTML source can be overridden by CSS files referred to subsequently.

By default, this file is empty, even though it contains some CSS selectors to help you override common elements in the system. This file can be edited manually through your favorite text editor, or it can be edited by the online tools inside DotNetNuke.

The Site Settings page for a portal contains a section labeled Style Sheet Editor. Figure 11-10 shows the browser-based editor in action, along with the empty CSS rules.

There are two hyperlinks below the CSS editor: One link saves your changes and the other link restores the style sheet to its original condition. That's a handy feature if you make an error and can't quite figure out what's gone wrong; sometimes just purging your edits can be very satisfying. Of course, clicking this hyperlink on a customized file that's working properly might cause some grief.

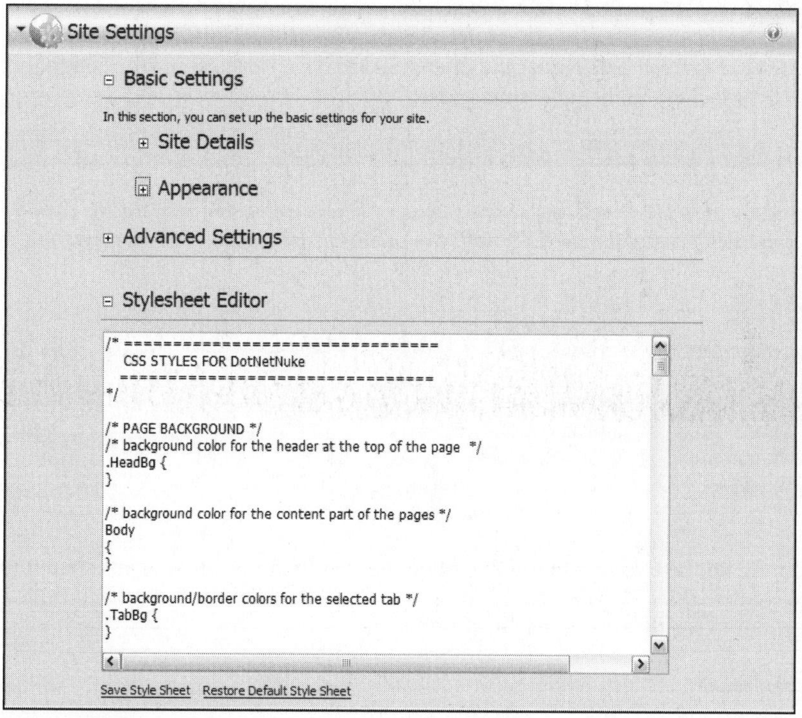

Figure 11-10

Customizing the Global Style Sheet

Developers who are a little more experienced in CSS than DotNetNuke might be interested in making some changes to the global style sheet in DotNetNuke. The global file affects all portals in an installation.

Therefore, the HTML file lists the CSS file reference above the skin style sheet, the container style sheet, and the portal style sheet you just reviewed in the previous section.

The global style sheet named `default.css` is located in the following folder:

```
<DotNetNuke Install Folder>\Portals\_default\default.css
```

This file is chock full of CSS rules. From classes named `Head` and `SubHead` to `MainMenu_MenuBar` and `MainMenu_MenuItemSel`, if you didn't write it, it's probably here. The standard menu lists its styles here as well as in the control panel. If you want a complete custom look to your DotNetNuke installation, this is the file to edit.

Because this file applies to all portals for a DotNetNuke installation, make sure that changes are applied carefully and thoroughly tested in all places.

Try It Out   Edit the Default Styles

In this section, you will apply the CSS skills of the prior sections of this chapter and tidy up some rules in the style sheet. Launch the Neighborhood Association site that you've been building all along throughout the chapters and make sure it's working well before making any changes.

1. Use your favorite text editor and open the default style sheet for the Neighborhood Association website located in the following folder:

```
<DotNetNuke Install Folder>\Portals\_default\default.css
```

2. Find the rule for the classes named `ControlPanel` and `PagingTable`. They share the same CSS properties. Currently, the CSS rules are using the long format for configuring the values:

```css
.ControlPanel, .PagingTable
{
    width: 100%;
    background-color: #FFFFFF;
    BORDER-RIGHT: #003366 1px solid;
    BORDER-TOP: #003366 1px solid;
    BORDER-LEFT: #003366 1px solid;
    BORDER-BOTTOM: #003366 1px solid;
}
```

Configure the CSS rule to use the following shorthand technique, and then refresh the browser to confirm the new rule is still equivalent to the old rule. You need to be logged in as an administrator to see the control panel.

```css
.ControlPanel, .PagingTable
{
    width: 100%;
    background-color: #FFF8DC;
    border: #003366 1px solid;
}
```

3. Now that it's equivalent, you can spice it up a bit. Copy the `gradient.png` file used earlier in this chapter to the same folder as the CSS file you're editing right now.

4. Modify the rule for the `ControlPanel` and `PagingTable` CSS classes by applying a slight edit to the background property, as shown in the following code:

```
.ControlPanel, .PagingTable
{
    width: 100%;
    background: #FFF url(gradient.png) repeat-x 0 -300px;
    border: #003366 1px solid;
}
```

How It Works

When you're logged into the website as the Host account, the browser should render the control panel with the customizations, as shown in Figure 11-11.

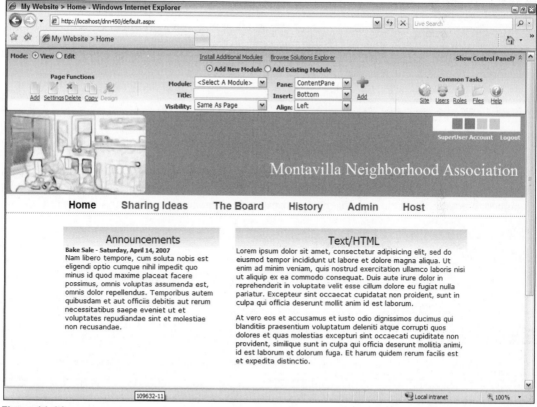

Figure 11-11

This edit improved the default style sheet by removing redundant rules and gave the control panel a slight gradient background. Without the negative value to push the background higher, the text would not be easy to read. The value of -300px moves the gradient to a better position.

Remember that images referred to through CSS rules are relative to the style sheet file location and not the path of the given web page that uses the style sheet. That's why the gradient image was added to the same directory as the style sheet. If you refer to a lot of images in your style sheet, you would do well to create a directory for them and just use that relative path in the CSS rule.

You could perform quite a few edits to the default style sheet to improve its efficiency and bend it toward your specific goals for your own custom skin. Make sure that you have a good backup of your edits so that subsequent changes can be made safely.

Summary

This chapter covered some fundamentals of CSS and how they apply to custom skins in DotNetNuke. There are a few core principles in CSS that transcend several CSS properties. With a little knowledge from this chapter and a good CSS reference book, you'll have the tools necessary to decipher the most complex style sheet. There's certainly a lot more that can be done with the CSS properties you've used in this chapter, let alone the rest of the CSS realm. Hopefully, this whetted your appetite for more.

Margins and padding have a few oddities in their behavior, but after a few weeks of applying your own styles they'll start to feel normal. You'll be able to calculate easily the required dimensions of an element to get the background image aligned properly.

Absolute positioning is all about finding the positioning context, the nearest parent element that has relative positioning enabled. The HTML body tag is the catchall if no parent elements are relatively positioned. A good understanding of the hierarchy in an HTML page can really help simplify this topic.

Applying these skills to a DotNetNuke site starts with finding the CSS files to edit. If you're seeing a style applied in the browser and it's not inside the skin or container files, then it could be in the portal level style sheet or the default style sheet for the entire DotNetNuke installation. Evaluate edits to these style sheets often to ensure that you don't get too far down the road with a broken CSS rule.

Exercises

1. What is the name of the CSS selector that will select all elements? Provide an example of its use.

2. Calculate the total width occupied by a `<div>` tag with the following CSS rule:

```
div
{
    padding:20px;
    margin:30px;
    width:40px;
}
```

3.   If the following two <div> tags were above and below each other, evaluate the margin
     between them:

```
div#top
{
    margin:30px;
}
div#bottom
{
    margin:60px;
}
```

4.   Write a shorthand CSS rule for all paragraphs following a <div> tag having an ID attribute of
     sidebar that will make the text appear in the Georgia font, 12pt, and bold. Instruct the browser
     to apply Verdana if the Georgia font is not available.

Web Standards
and Compliance

The HTML and CSS syntax have been around for long enough that several standards have evolved. The HTML 4.01 specification available on the World Wide Web Consortium's site reached recommendation status on December 24, 1999. More recent specifications, such as XHTML 1.0, bring additional values to the party, like a predictable document object model. It's far more important to use a specification consistently on a site than to debate which one to employ.

DotNetNuke has made strides toward compliance in their default installation. Earlier versions contained more issues than later versions. I anticipate DotNetNuke will make a shift to full web standards compliance over time. As you'll see later on in this chapter, DotNetNuke can be customized to achieve a web standards-based architecture today.

The popularity of DotNetNuke and the vast market for third-party components can also work against a developer and make it difficult to maintain a standards-based system. Envision a graph where the X axis represents the number of unique modules on a DotNetNuke site and the Y axis represents the work exerted to maintain a standards-compliant site. My hypothesis is the line is not flat and probably not even linear. Web standards are not critical to every software vendor — if you don't intend to have guests over, why bother cleaning the house?

This chapter aims to describe standards-based architectures in greater detail. Chapter 5 introduced related topics including Quirks mode and employing a doctype in a web page. This chapter expands upon that web standards discussion and applies its merits to DotNetNuke. This chapter covers the following topics:

❑ Testing for standards compliance

❑ Constructing a standards-based DotNetNuke site

❑ Applying a standards-based menu skin object

❑ Swapping the HTML editor provider

Web Standards

Web standards can be a hot topic for some folks. In my experience, most web developers either are benignly ignorant of them, or approach web standards with a near zealot fervor. I have yet to meet someone who genuinely works to build a non-compliant site to mock the standards bodies. Compliance to web standards is a feature that often finds itself on the chopping block when solutions become too expensive. It's understandable when time and money grow tight.

I knew a little about web standards several years ago, but they never represented a reasonable value proposition to me. My code worked well enough back then and I had enough issues on my plate without worrying about a <p> tag that wasn't closed properly or building a page with semantic markup. When I began working with CSS enthusiasts, I saw the real promise of compliance come alive. Page sizes became dramatically smaller and easier to understand. Elaborate designs that were a full afternoon headache using a table-based layout became a 30-minute cinch using a couple of <div> tags and some CSS. More important, it became easier to walk back into code six or twelve months later for a refresh when the content and presentation were separated and bloat-free. Over time, I've developed a sincere appreciation for CSS. I genuinely work to implement CSS-friendly web pages because I've seen what they can do for a solution.

Let's start with the prima façie argument that automated tests are good. Tests are repeatable things that anyone can perform the same way every time and do not require implicit knowledge from a person. The ability to execute a number of tests with the click of a button or on a scheduled basis is a good thing.

Given this fact, automated tests can be developed to prove the system is either in or out of compliance. When a result from an automated test indicates a failure, I know a problem exists. This helps me manage a project, a team, or an external contractor. It's not a silver bullet, but it is one more useful metric that my computer will happily produce to help manage my time. If I don't concern myself with a standards-based system, then I can't create an automated test for it, and I've lost some insight into the health of my system.

Web standards-based development is merely about following a prescribed set of rules for HTML and CSS. Most developers have rules for checking code into a source code repository, writing a sufficient amount of comments in the code, or even placing curly braces in a consistent location. Web standards-based development is just another set of rules that help get a job done right.

Understanding validation utilities is a prerequisite for using automated tests. This chapter focuses on understanding HTML validation and hopefully piques your interest in exploring automated testing in the future.

HTML Standards Validation

The W3C maintains a good HTML validation service that is freely available at http://validator.w3.org. This page can validate HTML in three ways. First, you can enter a URL into the Address text box. The page will retrieve the HTML at the given URL and display the validation results. This works great for public websites, but doesn't help much for internal sites, or those still under development on your local machine.

The second and third options on the W3C validation page help you validate markup when the page isn't open to the public. If you've saved the HTML source to a file, you can upload it with the Browse button and click the Check button. When I'm developing a site, I normally copy the HTML source to my clipboard, paste it into the text area control at the bottom of the page, and click the Check button. Figure 12-1 shows the W3C HTML Validation page.

The Internet Explorer Developer Toolbar available for free from Microsoft contains a utility that leverages the W3C validation website. Figure 12-2 shows the Validate menu options in the IE developer toolbar. Either of these components will get you started with HTML validation.

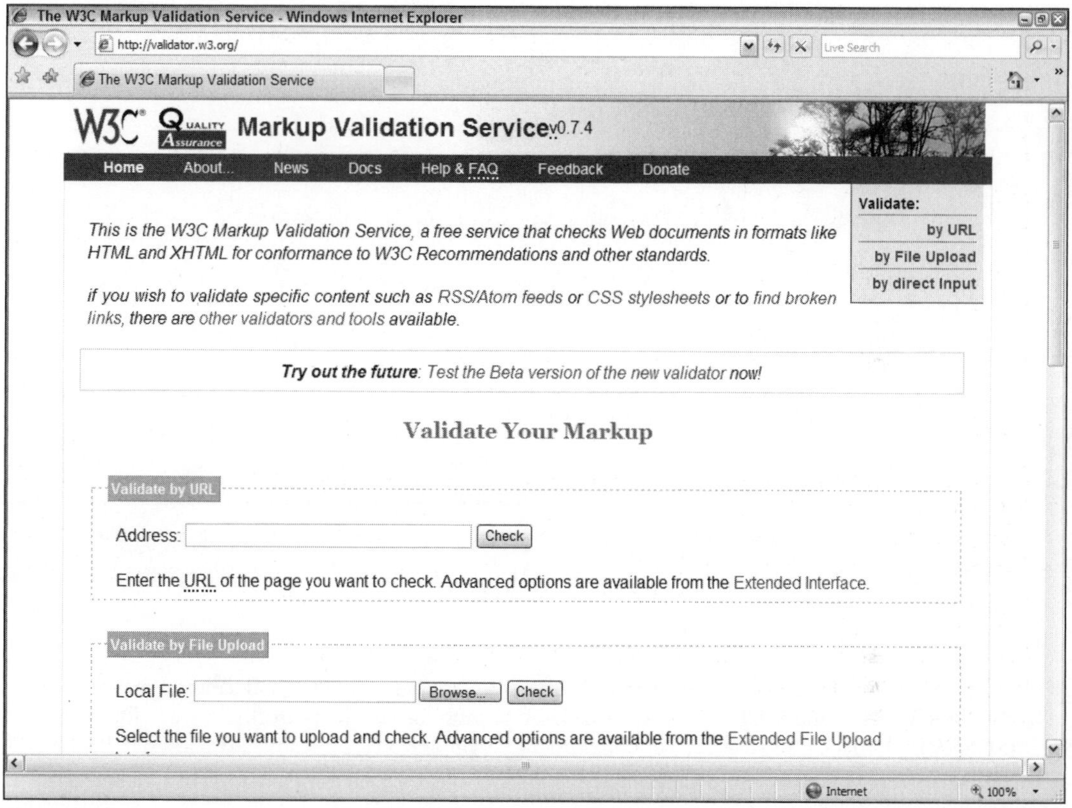

Figure 12-1

CSS Standards Validation

Similar to HTML validation, your Cascading Style Sheet files can be validated through a utility on the W3C site at `http://jigsaw.w3.org/css-validator`.

The process of developing standards-based CSS is a little less tense than building compliant HTML. It's probably because of the smaller number of people involved in producing the CSS files. All types of developers and managers can influence a component that emits HTML on a web page. The CSS file is cleanly separated from the rest of the project. This small margin of distance gives you the ability to be agile and responsive to change.

Figure 12-2

Figure 12-3 shows the CSS validation utility on the W3C site. As with its HTML counterpart, you can validate files through a public URL, a file upload, or by pasting the CSS text directly into a field. After you click the Check button, the CSS rules are validated by the server and the test results are shown in the browser.

Moving Toward Compliance

Building a web standards-based system is certainly easier at the start of a project than modifying an existing system. In prior versions of DotNetNuke, the core framework required edits to make it emit compliant HTML.

Although DotNetNuke is an open source platform, editing the core framework is not a task to take lightly. The moment you change code in the core framework, you make it exponentially more difficult to upgrade your installation, one of the best features of DotNetNuke. The developers who work on improving the core on a regular basis are some of your best assets; so don't get left behind!

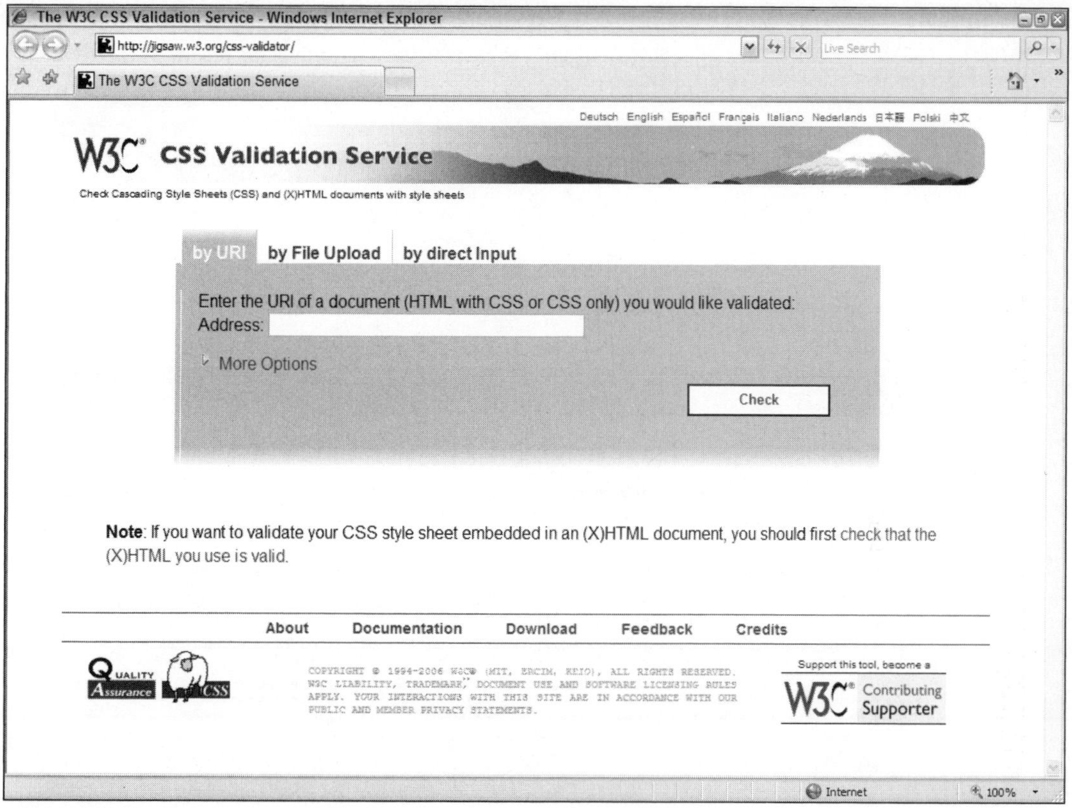

Figure 12-3

In recent versions of DotNetNuke, you can achieve compliance by editing the skins and the skin objects they contain. You're still at the mercy of any modules you employ on a web page, but you can (and should) be selective in which third-party components you buy, if any at all. This section will show you how to bring the core DotNetNuke system into standards compliance.

Implementing Standards Compliance in DotNetNuke

Through a couple of modifications, DotNetNuke can become XHTML compliant. The following exercises cover the steps necessary to convert a standard DotNetNuke installation to a standards-compliant site. This is a longer process than other exercises in this book, so I've tried to split up the work into manageable chunks and provide a description of what's going on along the way as you execute this multipart process to bring DotNetNuke into standards compliance.

You'll start with a default installation of DotNetNuke. Figure 12-4 shows 136 errors present on the home page.

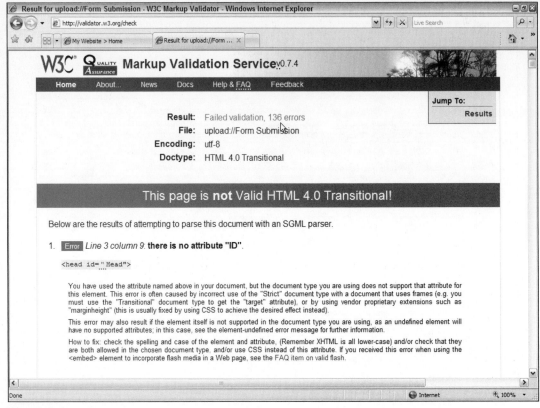

Figure 12-4

Configure a Test Page

In this section, you'll strip out all of the default modules and add a simple snippet of HTML content to the page. This will reduce the total number of issues flagged by the HTML validation utility.

1. Install a default instance of DotNetNuke version 4.5.3 or higher on your computer.

2. Log in as the Host account and create a new page named Products. The page should be viewable by the public and not have a parent page.

3. Edit the default Text/Html module so it contains the following HTML code:

```
<p>Hello World!</p>
```

4. Log out of the Host account.

5. Navigate to the Products page and validate the HTML source. You should see several HTML standards compliance errors in the validation summary.

How It Works

The standard modules cause some of the issues. Removing all of the modules on a page will reduce it to 89 errors. Figure 12-5 shows the DNN-Blue skin with just one module containing simple HTML content.

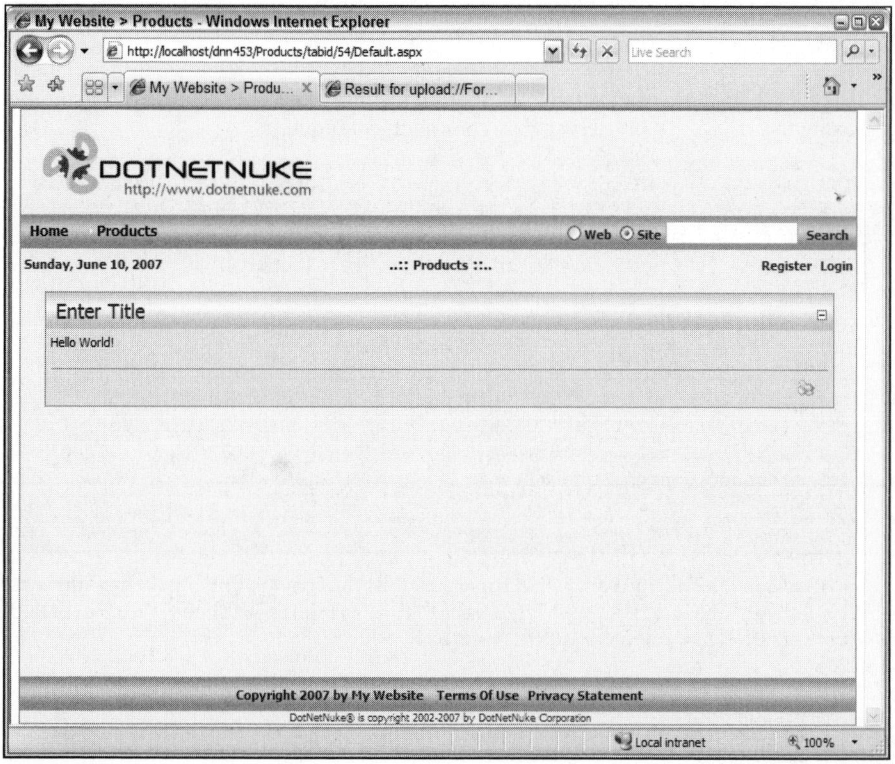

Figure 12-5

Try It Out   Remove the Menu

The first step of creating a test page with just one module has eliminated a large number of variables at work here. The overall goal is to build a page that contains valid HTML content with DotNetNuke. The number of issues flagged by the validation tool can be reduced even further by removing the menu component.

At this point, your only goal is finding a configuration that provides you with a valid base to build upon. Chapter 8 introduced you to several types of menu providers in the default installation of

DotNetNuke — for now you should place all of them on a suspect list. Later on you can add back menu components that are proven to be valid or provide so much value that you discount the negative impact they bring with non-compliant markup.

1. Use your favorite text editor to open the file named `Horizontal Menu - Fixed Width.ascx` located in the following directory:

```
<install folder>\Portals\_default\Skins\DNN-Blue\
```

2. Locate the instance of the DNN Navigation web user control in the file and comment it out using the `<%--    --%>` server-side comment technique.

```
<TABLE class="skingradient" cellSpacing="0" cellPadding="3" width="100%"
border="0">
  <TR>
    <TD width="100%" vAlign="middle" align="left" nowrap>
<%--
<dnn:NAV runat="server" id="dnnNAV" ProviderName="DNNMenuNavigationProvider"
CSSControl="main_dnnmenu_bar" CSSContainerRoot="main_dnnmenu_container"
CSSNode="main_dnnmenu_item" CSSNodeRoot="main_dnnmenu_rootitem"
CSSIcon="main_dnnmenu_icon" CSSContainerSub="main_dnnmenu_submenu"
CSSBreak="main_dnnmenu_break" CSSNodeHover="main_dnnmenu_itemhover"
NodeLeftHTMLBreadCrumbRoot="<img alt=&quot;*&quot; BORDER=&quot;0&quot;
src=&quot;breadcrumb.gif&quot;/>" />
--%>

    </TD>
    <TD class="skingradient" vAlign="middle" align="right" nowrap><dnn:SEARCH
runat="server" id="dnnSEARCH" showWeb="True" showSite="True" /><dnn:LANGUAGE
runat="server" id="dnnLANGUAGE" /></TD>
  </TR>
</TABLE>
```

3. Refresh the page in the browser and confirm that the menu no longer appears.

4. Validate the HTML source.

How It Works

These simple, albeit draconian, steps reduced the number of errors in the HTML validation tool to a total of 32, as shown in Figure 12-6. That's a reduction of over 50 issues just by eliminating one control! This one is really important though, so you'll find a newer version of it or a replacement for it shortly. For now, you can get by and just feel good about getting really close.

Figure 12-6

Try It Out   Simplify the Skin

So far, you've removed over 100 issues raised by the HTML validation tool. While you are going backward in terms of features and content, you are making solid progress on construction of a clean, standards-based website. There's still a little more trimming to do.

The DNN-Blue skin is a little too verbose for your specific needs here. The following steps build a mini-malist skin for your test environment that only contains the necessary elements to achieve standards compliance. These are similar to the skins created for the Neighborhood Association website, but you don't need to spend any time on the CSS because the focus is on the HTML this time.

Although you've been concerned about standards compliance throughout this exercise, the page hasn't made a commitment to a particular published standard. This section will also apply the doctype to the page and indicate that the page is following the XHTML 1.0 Transitional standard.

1. Use Windows Explorer to create a new skin folder named `Simple`, as shown in the following path:

```
<install folder>\Portals\_default\Skins\Simple\
```

2. Use your favorite text editor to create a skin file named `simple.ascx` in the new folder with the following content. You can download this from the files available online for this chapter, too.

```
<%@ Control language="vb" Inherits="DotNetNuke.UI.Skins.Skin" %>
<%@ Register TagPrefix="dnn" TagName="NAV" Src="~/Admin/Skins/Nav.ascx" %>
<%@ Register TagPrefix="dnn" TagName="USER" Src="~/Admin/Skins/User.ascx" %>
<%@ Register TagPrefix="dnn" TagName="LOGIN"
    Src="~/Admin/Skins/Login.ascx" %>
<%@ Register TagPrefix="dnn" TagName="COPYRIGHT"
    Src="~/Admin/Skins/Copyright.ascx" %>
<%@ Register TagPrefix="dnn" TagName="TERMS"
    Src="~/Admin/Skins/Terms.ascx" %>
<%@ Register TagPrefix="dnn" TagName="PRIVACY"
    Src="~/Admin/Skins/Privacy.ascx" %>
<%@ Register TagPrefix="dnn" TagName="DOTNETNUKE"
    Src="~/Admin/Skins/DotNetNuke.ascx" %>

<div id="ControlPanel" runat="server"></div>

<div>

    <div id="contentContainer">
        <div id="ContentPane" runat="server" class="contentPane"></div>
    </div>

    <div id="footerContainer">
        <dnn:COPYRIGHT runat="server" id="dnnCOPYRIGHT" />
        <dnn:TERMS runat="server" id="dnnTERMS" />
        <dnn:PRIVACY runat="server" id="dnnPRIVACY" /><br />
        <dnn:DOTNETNUKE runat="server" id="dnnDOTNETNUKE" />
    </div>

    <div id="userContainer">
        <dnn:USER runat="server" id="dnnUSER" />
        <dnn:LOGIN runat="server" id="dnnLOGIN" />
    </div>

    <div id="navContainer">
        <dnn:NAV runat="server" id="dnnNAV"
            ProviderName="DNNDropDownNavigationProvider" />
    </div>

</div>
```

3. Use your favorite text editor to create a file named `simple.doctype.xml` in the new folder with the following content:

```
<SkinDocType><![CDATA[<!DOCTYPE html PUBLIC
  "-//W3C//DTD XHTML 1.0 Transitional//EN"
  "http://www.w3.org/TR/xhtml1/DTD/xhtml1transitional.dtd">]]></SkinDocType>
```

4. Use Windows Explorer to create a new container folder named `Simple`, as shown in the following path:

```
<install folder>\Portals\_default\Containers\Simple
```

5. Use your favorite text editor to create a container file named `simple.ascx` in the new folder with the following content:

```
<%@ Control Language="vb" Inherits="DotNetNuke.UI.Containers.Container" %>
<%@ Register TagPrefix="dnn" TagName="ACTIONS"
    Src="~/Admin/Containers/Actions.ascx" %>
<%@ Register TagPrefix="dnn" TagName="TITLE"
    Src="~/Admin/Containers/Title.ascx" %>
<%@ Register TagPrefix="dnn" TagName="ACTIONBUTTON"
    Src="~/Admin/Containers/ActionButton.ascx" %>

<div>
    <dnn:ACTIONS runat="server" ID="dnnACTIONS"
        ProviderName="DNNMenuNavigationProvider"
        ExpandDepth="1" PopulateNodesFromClient="True" />
    <dnn:TITLE runat="server" ID="dnnTITLE" />
    <dnn:ACTIONBUTTON runat="server" ID="dnnACTIONBUTTON1"
        CommandName="ModuleHelp.Action"
        DisplayIcon="True" DisplayLink="False" />
</div>

<div id="ContentPane" runat="server">
</div>

<div>
    <dnn:ACTIONBUTTON runat="server" ID="dnnACTIONBUTTON2"
        CommandName="AddContent.Action"
        DisplayIcon="True" DisplayLink="True" />
    <dnn:ACTIONBUTTON runat="server" ID="dnnACTIONBUTTON3"
        CommandName="ModuleSettings.Action"
        DisplayIcon="True" DisplayLink="False" />
</div>
```

6. Log in as the Host account and assign the new skin and container to the page using the online administration tools.

7. Log out of the Host account and validate the HTML source of the new page as a public visitor would see it.

How It Works

Your simplification efforts are really paying off. By using a bare bones skin, you're able to reduce the total number of standards compliance issues to just six! The temporary menu navigation is implemented as a drop-down list box for now. That control will be swapped out later on in the chapter. Figure 12-7 shows the current validation results.

Figure 12-7

Try It Out   Achieve Standards Compliance

The final step that will enable 100 percent standards compliance involves a quick edit to the file named `default.aspx` located in the web root folder. After this final change, you'll be able to add components back into the website as you see fit, test them individually, and maintain standards compliance.

1. Use your favorite text editor to open the `default.aspx` file located in the web root folder.

2. Edit the `<body>` tag in the file by removing the non-compliant attributes, as shown in the following code block:

```
<%@ Page Language="vb" AutoEventWireup="false" Explicit="True"
    Inherits="DotNetNuke.Framework.DefaultPage"
    CodeFile="Default.aspx.vb" %>
<%@ Register TagPrefix="dnn" Namespace="DotNetNuke.Common.Controls"
    Assembly="DotNetNuke" %>
<asp:literal id="skinDocType" runat="server"></asp:literal>
<html>
<head id="Head" runat="server">
    <meta id="MetaRefresh" runat="Server" name="Refresh" />
    <meta id="MetaDescription" runat="Server" name="DESCRIPTION" />
    <meta id="MetaKeywords" runat="Server" name="KEYWORDS" />
    <meta id="MetaCopyright" runat="Server" name="COPYRIGHT" />
    <meta id="MetaGenerator" runat="Server" name="GENERATOR" />
    <meta id="MetaAuthor" runat="Server" name="AUTHOR" />
    <meta name="RESOURCE-TYPE" content="DOCUMENT">
    <meta name="DISTRIBUTION" content="GLOBAL">
    <meta name="ROBOTS" content="INDEX, FOLLOW">
    <meta name="REVISIT-AFTER" content="1 DAYS">
    <meta name="RATING" content="GENERAL">
    <meta http-equiv="PAGE-ENTER" content="RevealTrans(Duration=0,Transition=1)">
    <style type="text/css" id="StylePlaceholder" runat="server"></style>
    <asp:placeholder id="CSS" runat="server"></asp:placeholder>
</head>
<body id="Body" runat="server">
    <noscript></noscript>
    <dnn:Form id="Form" runat="server" ENCTYPE="multipart/form-data"
style=""height: 100%;">
        <asp:Label ID="SkinError" runat="server" CssClass="NormalRed"
Visible="False"></asp:Label>
        <asp:PlaceHolder ID="SkinPlaceHolder" runat="server" />
        <input id="ScrollTop" runat="server" name="ScrollTop" type="hidden">
        <input id="__dnnVariable" runat="server" name="__dnnVariable"
type="hidden">
    </dnn:Form>
</body>
</html>
```

3. Refresh the page in your browser and validate the HTML source.

How It Works

The validation tool should indicate that the HTML source is now standards compliant. Figure 12-8 shows the result you've been working for.

Now that the goal has been achieved, you inherit the task of maintaining standards compliance. You can now apply your skin development abilities and extend this skin into a beautiful, custom design that continues to follow the XHTML 1.0 Transitional standards. Each time you make a change to the skin, or add an untested DotNetNuke module, you can check for compliance on the W3C website.

Figure 12-8

Changing Menu Providers

The previous section constructed a standards-based web page using a minimalist skin. While a drop-down list box for a menu is standards compliant, it's none too attractive. Many software developers and vendors work diligently to provide components for DotNetNuke. In this section, you'll take one out for a spin and apply it to the simple skin you just created.

Telerik has been a long-time sponsor of DotNetNuke, and they offer a wide variety of controls to the DotNetNuke developer. You can download these controls for free and try them out before deciding to invest in a control for your site.

Try It Out   **Implement Telerik's RadMenu Control**

Telerik offers a free trial download of their RadMenu control for ASP.Net on their website. Like most third-party components that have been outfitted for DotNetNuke, it uses a provider model to link the component to the DotNetNuke framework. Telerik has a large line of products for the .Net platform, including WinForms and ASP.Net. They also have a targeted offering for DotNetNuke enthusiasts at the following URL:

```
http://dnn.telerik.com/
```

In this section, you'll download and install the Telerik RadMenu component to replace the default menu navigation component. After it's installed, you can test the page to evaluate whether it meets the same standards compliance rules it passed before the component was installed. Telerik offers an entire suite of tools labeled as RadControls. RadMenu is just one of the components inside the RadControls suite.

1. Obtain the trial version of the RadMenu component from the Telerik website. Visit the following URL and download the DNN Sample Site components. Several files are available for download on this page. You're interested in the hyperlink labeled DNN Sample Site.

    ```
    www.telerik.com/products/dnn/download-trial.aspx
    ```

2. Unzip the file you downloaded from Telerik to a temporary folder on your computer. Inside the unzipped file, you should find a file named `Telerik.DNN.SkinObjects.Menu.zip` in the following path:

    ```
    <unzip folder>\net2\Website\Install\Module\Telerik.DNN.SkinObjects.Menu.zip
    ```

3. Log in to your local DotNetNuke installation as the Host account.

4. The file `Telerik.DNN.SkinObjects.Menu.zip` is a DotNetNuke skin object installation file. Install it like any other skin object by navigating to Host, Module Definitions in the menu. Click the Install New Module hyperlink, click the Browse button to point to the file named `Telerik.DNN.SkinObjects.Menu.zip`, and click the Install New Module hyperlink. DotNetNuke processes the zip file and installs the new skin object.

5. The components are in place, so it's time to apply them to the minimalist skin. Use your favorite text editor to open the skin file named `simple.ascx` that you built while constructing the standards-compliant web page in the previous section.

6. Append the following register directive under the existing directives in the skin file:

    ```
    <%@ Register TagPrefix="dnn" TagName="RADMENU"
        Src="~/DesktopModules/RadMenu/RadMenu.ascx" %>
    ```

7. Overwrite the existing navigation web user control with the following web user control instance that applies the Telerik RadMenu trial software component:

    ```
    <dnn:RADMENU runat="server" id= "dnnMENU" />
    ```

8. The moment of truth has arrived. Log out of the Host account, and then launch the test page in your browser and validate the HTML source for standards compliance!

How It Works

If everything worked out as it should, the page should render a fancy new navigation structure, as shown in Figure 12-9. You can add a couple of child pages as shown in the figure to confirm that it will continue to render standards-compliant markup in more complex scenarios.

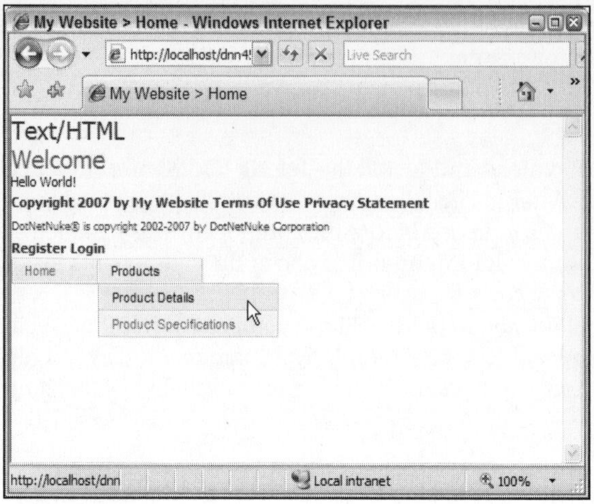

Figure 12-9

Your tests should prove that the page is indeed standards compliant after adding the new menu component. If you examine the HTML emitted by the control, you'll also see a lovely unordered list, which is a delight to any CSS enthusiast! This vendor provides plenty of opportunities for customization through CSS and property settings. If this interests you, then download the documentation and take it for another spin in your test environment.

Changing HTML Editor Providers

The FCKeditor is the standard HTML editor component in the current version of DotNetNuke. This free utility simplifies the task of authoring HTML code. It's a great component, but it's not the only HTML editor. Telerik also offers a commercial HTML editor with a provider plug-in for DotNetNuke.

The FCKeditor and the Telerik editor offer the same features to DotNetNuke because they support the provider pattern in the system. As you'll see, each component implements these features in a slightly different way.

Try It Out   Change HTML Provider

In this section, you'll swap out the default FCKeditor provider in exchange for a free trial version of Telerik's commercial product, RadEditor. You'll gain experience in using an alternative HTML editor component, as well as swapping out components that implement the provider pattern. This exercise will use the same unzipped file you downloaded from the Telerik website in the previous exercise.

1. Locate the following folder named RadControls in the file you unzipped from the Telerik website. It contains all the bits for using this component inside any ASP.Net website.

```
<unzip folder>\net2\Website\controls\RadControls
```

2. Copy the entire RadControls folder into the Controls folder located in your DotNetNuke installation at the following path. The Controls folder should contain a few existing files and folders, and the RadControls folder you just copied.

```
<install folder>\Controls
```

3. The next step is to copy some assembly files that RadEditor uses to perform its job inside DotNetNuke. Locate the following three assembly files inside the unzipped file from Telerik:

```
<unzip folder>\net2\Website\bin\RadEditor.Net2.dll
<unzip folder>\net2\Website\bin\RadSpell.NET2.dll
<unzip folder>\net2\Website\bin\Telerik.DNN.Providers.RadHtmlEditorProvider.dll
```

4. Copy the three assembly files to the \bin folder of your DotNetNuke installation.

```
<install folder>\bin
```

5. Now it's time to edit the web.config file of your DotNetNuke installation. Use your favorite text editor to open the web.config file located in the root folder and find the <htmlEditor> element in the file. This element should contain one element named <providers>. Under this element, you'll see two child elements: <clear/> and <add>.

6. Once you've located this position in the web.config file, you need to configure another HTML editor provider for DotNetNuke. You accomplish this by inserting another <add> element under the existing element. Append the following XML as the last element inside the <providers> element:

```
<htmlEditor defaultProvider="FckHtmlEditorProvider ">
    <providers>
        <clear />
        <add name="FckHtmlEditorProvider"  ...omitted long xml attributes here... />
        <add name="RadHtmlEditorProvider"
            type="Telerik.DNN.Providers.RadHtmlEditorProvider,
Telerik.DNN.Providers.RadHtmlEditorProvider"
            providerPath="~\Providers\HtmlEditorProviders\RadHtmlEditorProvider\"
            AutoCreatePaths="true" />
    </providers>
</htmlEditor>
```

The previous code block omits several attributes from the existing <add> element of the FckEditor for clarity. Make sure you don't actually remove any existing configuration values.

7. Now that you've added an alternative HTML editor, configure it as the default provider. Change the defaultProvider attribute value in the <htmlEditor> element as shown in the following code:

```
<htmlEditor defaultProvider="RadHtmlEditorProvider">
```

8. Everything should be in place. Log in as the Host account and edit the Text/HTML module on the test page. When you click the edit text hyperlink, the RadEditor component should appear in place of the FCKeditor component.

Figure 12-10 shows the Telerik RadEditor component loaded into a DotNetNuke page.

Figure 12-10

How It Works

The provider model makes it really easy to swap components. The provider model in DotNetNuke expects participating software to exist in specific locations. With a little practice, you could write a simple Windows batch file that executed a series of XCOPY statements that would drop the necessary files into any new DotNetNuke installation. The only other task is to edit the `web.config` file; not a bad challenge for a savvy .Net developer.

Once you copied the files into the proper location and performed the necessary configuration in the `web.config` file, the system had all the information it needed to launch the alternative HTML editor software. In fact, the system would have happily continued to load the FCKeditor until the `defaultProvider` attribute of the `<htmlEditor/>` element was changed to the component from Telerik. That's the switch that made DotNetNuke show the Telerik editor instead of the default editor.

While Telerik offers a commercial version of the product for use in DotNetNuke, the FCKeditor is also a very compelling utility. Both will do a good job of providing an HTML editor for your users. Historically, some editors have been better than others in the metric of producing valid HTML markup. These tools have come a long way in the past 18 months toward standards compliance.

Maintaining Compliance

It's one thing to craft a set of standards-compliant DotNetNuke skins and unveil them to a client. It's quite another thing to come back six months later and expect to see a standards-compliant site. The Telerik component takes a step in this direction with a Validation button at the bottom of the browser.

The author of the HTML can click this button to validate his or her content against the same W3C validation tool described earlier in this chapter. Figure 12-11 shows the results of a compliance test in the RadEditor window. These types of extended services that help authors maintain standards compliance are a great help to the overall health of the system.

It's a good idea to implement a process that periodically reviews your websites for standards compliance. If the site makes use of a number of modules, there's a good chance that some of them are emitting non-compliant HTML. Depending on your circumstances, this might be a harmless issue.

If you have the developer skills available, you can develop an automated validation process that runs on a weekly or nightly basis.

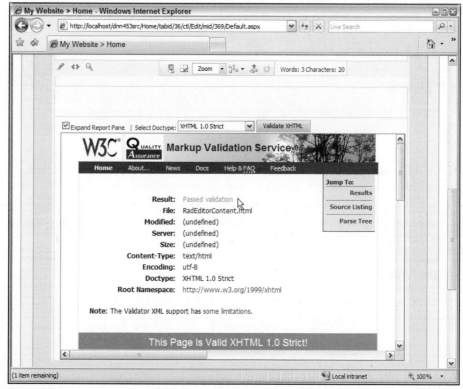

Figure 12-11

Summary

This chapter focused on developing solutions with a standards-compliant mindset. The W3C offers a couple of valuable tools online that can help you test and validate HTML and CSS as you're building the site and after it deploys.

Moving toward standards compliance with DotNetNuke can be an arduous task with a large number of modules emitting various flavors of HTML. By moving methodically through the site, you can detect and isolate features that are emitting invalid markup. Then, you'll be in a position to make a decision based on balancing the needs of the given website with the value of the component and the agility of a standards-based solution.

The last section of this chapter swapped menu and HTML editor providers for a trial edition from a third-party vendor. Most third-party components should be this easy to pop in and out of your DotNetNuke system.

When you're evaluating third-party components for your DotNetNuke site, it's important to make decisions based on real data. Block out an hour for installing and configuring a third-party component. Then you can make a written evaluation of the documentation, ease of use, and content that it emits in the browser. After you evaluate the component and how well it suits your needs, you can choose to keep looking or purchase a license.

Exercises

1. HTML can be commented out on the client side using the following syntax:

    ```
    <!--        -->
    ```

    The browser ignores everything inside HTML comments, but they still exist on the page. How can you comment out something on the server side so it is not even sent down to the browser?

2. Consider a scenario where Page1 on a DotNetNuke site is standards compliant but Page2 is not. List some possible reasons that would cause the issues in the non-compliant page and how each potential issue can be addressed.

3. Explain how DotNetNuke determines which HTML editor component to use inside the Text/HTML module.

Targeting Modules with CSS

When a developer builds his or her own module or a designer works in tandem with a developer, they have a large impact on the HTML emitted by the component. When a developer customizes an existing component using CSS and other techniques, he or she continues to have a need to research and evaluate the HTML emitted by the component. Developers and designers target blocks of HTML with CSS. This chapter focuses on honing these targeting skills.

You'll dissect an assortment of DotNetNuke modules, including one available for free as a separate download from the DotNetNuke website. The goal is to learn some techniques for skinning existing modules by examining their structures, classes, IDs, and hierarchies. You'll see how some modules are more customizable with CSS than others, based on how much presentation layer code exists in the actual HTML emitted by the components.

Each module presented in this chapter includes an evaluation of the default content it presented to you. Then you'll experiment with a technique in building a custom design with one of the opportunities presented.

This chapter develops custom designs with CSS using the following modules:

❑   UsersOnline
❑   Contacts
❑   Wiki
❑   News Feeds

Getting Started with Module Styling

Most of the modules you'll dissect in this chapter are available in the default installation of DotNetNuke, and one is available for free on the DotNetNuke website. The top of the Downloads page contains hyperlinks to the latest DotNetNuke bits. The bottom of the page contains hyperlinks to additional modules.

When downloading the latest DotNetNuke build, you might notice a separate set of projects available on www.dotnetnuke.com/tabid/125/default.aspx. Each hyperlink in the bottom section navigates to the given project's home page. Each project home page contains a hyperlink to download the latest module installation files. Later on in this chapter, you'll work with one of these external projects and build a custom design.

This chapter starts with simple techniques for styling modules and advances into more complex designs with each new component. These skills will help you tackle styling the plethora of third-party modules that exist in the DotNetNuke marketplace.

CSS provides several ways to target specific sections of HTML. Targeting HTML tags is a very broad stroke, such as specifying a particular font for all <p> tags on a page. The id and class attributes of an HTML tag are used for more specific targeting. CSS can also make use of the hierarchy inside the HTML page with a CSS selector like div#headline p.normal. This only applies to the <p> tags that have a class of normal and are contained by a <div> tag with an id attribute of headline. The same CSS principles apply to a DotNetNuke web page as to a web page created by a room full of monkeys. In other words, these are a great set of cross-platform skills to add to your repertoire.

The previous chapters explained conventional places for customized CSS files in DotNetNuke. Without knowing any details about a given DotNetNuke website, you can probably guess all of the locations where CSS files exist. The folder path /Portals/default/ contains the default.css file. The folder /Portals/0/ contains the portal.css file for the first portal in a DotNetNuke solution. Skin and container files can exist in either of the previous two folders, too. Finally, the folder /DesktopModules/ contains all of the modules installed in the solution, and you can expect to find some CSS files there.

The content can get a little messy, as you will see later in this chapter; modules can introduce new locations for style sheets, too. When you customize the style of a new module, you need to know the standard places to begin looking for existing classes and to discover how the existing design is accomplished. When you have these places comfortably memorized, you'll be on solid footing to begin evaluating the presentation architecture and the extensibility of various third-party modules.

UsersOnline Module

The UsersOnline module is a fun component to add to a website. It's one of the core modules that comes along with the DotNetNuke bits. There's just something very appealing about viewing a summary of visitors actively browsing the website, whether it's just a few people on a niche website or many more on a popular community website.

The team lead for this project is Scott McCulloch, and version 3.1 was released on June 21, 2006. Figure 13-1 shows a sample instance of the module.

Evaluation

This module shows its long history with DotNetNuke through its deep integration. The Host Settings page contains a special setting to enable or disable the UsersOnline module. This setting is located under Host Settings, Advanced Settings, and Other Settings where a checkbox is labeled Disable Users Online.

Figure 13-1

The following code snippet shows the HTML that is rendered in Figure 13-1:

```html
<table cellspacing="0" cellpadding="4" width="100%">
    <tr class="Normal">
        <td>
            <div id="dnn_ctr391_UsersOnline_pnlMembership">
                <TABLE cellSpacing="0" cellPadding="0" border="0">
                    <TR>
                        <TD align="center" width="25">
                            <img src="/dnn453/DesktopModules/UsersOnline/uoGroup1.gif"
                                id="dnn_ctr391_UsersOnline_imgMembership"
                                height="14" alt="Membership" width="17"
                                align="absMiddle" /></TD>
                        <TD class="NormalBold">
                            <span id="dnn_ctr391_UsersOnline_MembershipLabel">
                                <u>Membership:</u></span></TD>
                    </TR>
                    <TR>
                        <TD align="center" width="25">
                            <img src="/dnn453/DesktopModules/UsersOnline/uoLatest.gif"
                                id="dnn_ctr391_UsersOnline_imgLatest"
                                height="14" alt="Latest New User"
                                width="17" align="absMiddle" /></TD>
                        <TD class="Normal">
                            <span id="dnn_ctr391_UsersOnline_LatestUserLabel">
                                <u>Latest:</u></span>
                            <span id="dnn_ctr391_UsersOnline_lblLatestUserName"
                                    class="NormalBold">admin</span></TD>
                    </TR>
                    <TR>
                        <TD align="center" width="25">
                            <img src="/dnn453/DesktopModules/UsersOnline/uoNewToday.gif"
                                id="dnn_ctr391_UsersOnline_imgNewToday"
                                height="14" alt="New Today" width="17"
                                align="absMiddle" /></TD>
                        <TD class="Normal">
                            <span id="dnn_ctr391_UsersOnline_NewTodayLabel">
                                New Today:</span>
```

```
                        <span id="dnn_ctr391_UsersOnline_lblNewToday"
                              class="NormalBold">0</span></TD>
                </TR>
                <TR>
                    <TD align="center" width="25">
                        <img src="/dnn453/DesktopModules/UsersOnline/
uoNewYesterday.gif"
                              id="dnn_ctr391_UsersOnline_imgNewYesterday"
                              height="14" alt="New Yesterday"
                              width="17" align="absMiddle" /></TD>
                    <TD class="Normal">
                        <span id="dnn_ctr391_UsersOnline_NewYesterdayLabel">
                           New Yesterday:</span>
                        <span id="dnn_ctr391_UsersOnline_lblNewYesterday"
                              class="NormalBold">0</span></TD>
                </TR>
                <TR>
                    <TD align="center" width="25">
                        <img src="/dnn453/DesktopModules/UsersOnline/uoOverall.gif"
                              id="dnn_ctr391_UsersOnline_imgUserCount"
                              height="14" alt="User Count"
                              width="17" align="absMiddle" /></TD>
                    <TD class="Normal">
                        <span id="dnn_ctr391_UsersOnline_OverallLabel">
                           Overall:</span>
                        <span id="dnn_ctr391_UsersOnline_lblUserCount"
                              class="NormalBold">1</span></TD>
                </TR>
            </TABLE>
            <HR>
        </div>
        <div id="dnn_ctr391_UsersOnline_pnlUsersOnline">
            <TABLE cellSpacing="0" cellPadding="0" border="0">
                <TR>
                    <TD align="center" width="25">
                        <img src="/dnn453/DesktopModules/UsersOnline/uoGroup2.gif"
                              id="dnn_ctr391_UsersOnline_imgPeopleOnline"
                              height="14" alt="People Online"
                              width="17" align="absMiddle" /></TD>
                    <TD class="NormalBold">
                        <span id="dnn_ctr391_UsersOnline_PeopleOnlineLabel"><u>People
Online:</u></span></TD>
                </TR>
                <TR>
                    <TD align="center" width="25"><img src="/dnn453/DesktopModules/
UsersOnline/uoVisitors.gif" id="dnn_ctr391_UsersOnline_imgVisitors" height="14"
alt="Visitors" width="17" align="absMiddle" /></TD>
                    <TD class="Normal">
                        <span id="dnn_ctr391_UsersOnline_VisitorsLabel">
Visitors:</span>
                        <span id="dnn_ctr391_UsersOnline_lblGuestCount"
class="NormalBold">0</span></TD>
                </TR>
                <TR>
```

```
                <TD align="center" width="25"><img src="/dnn453/DesktopModules/
UsersOnline/uoMembers.gif" id="dnn_ctr391_UsersOnline_imgMemberCount" height="14"
alt="Members" width="17" align="absMiddle" /></TD>
                <TD class="Normal">
                    <span id="dnn_ctr391_UsersOnline_MembersLabel">Members:</span>
                    <span id="dnn_ctr391_UsersOnline_lblMemberCount"
class="NormalBold">0</span></TD>
            </TR>
            <TR>
                <TD align="center" width="25"><img src="/dnn453/DesktopModules/
UsersOnline/uoTotal.gif" id="dnn_ctr391_UsersOnline_imgTotalCount" height="14"
alt="Total" width="17" align="absMiddle" /></TD>
                <TD class="Normal">
                    <span id="dnn_ctr391_UsersOnline_TotalLabel">Total:</span>
                    <span id="dnn_ctr391_UsersOnline_lblTotalCount"
class="NormalBold">0</span></TD>
            </TR>
        </TABLE>
        <HR>
    </div>
    <div id="dnn_ctr391_UsersOnline_pnlOnlineNow">
        <img src="/dnn453/DesktopModules/UsersOnline/uoGroup3.gif"
            id="dnn_ctr391_UsersOnline_rptOnlineNow_ctl00_imgOnlineNow"
            height="14" width="17" align="absMiddle"
            alt="Online Now" />
        <span id="dnn_ctr391_UsersOnline_rptOnlineNow_ctl00_OnlineNowLabel"
            class="NormalBold">Online Now:</span><br>
    </div>
  </td>
 </tr>
</table>
```

The previous code snippet shows how the UsersOnline module makes use of <table> tags, <div> tags, <span> tags, and <img> tags to express the three segments of information. A single row, single column table wraps the entire component. Inside this table, a set of <div> tags envelops each section. Last, a multirow, two-column table holds the information in each section except the last.

The UsersOnline module does not use a module level style sheet. As you can see, most of the presentation exists in the HTML. The code does refer to some common CSS classes such as Normal and NormalBold.

Customization

On paper, this module feels a little more verbose than it needs to be. Using the information displayed in Figure 13-1, a developer could also express the same content using the following HTML code snippet:

```
<ul>
    <li id="membership">Membership:
        <ul>
            <li id="latest">Latest: <strong>admin</strong></li>
            <li id="newToday">New Today: <strong>0</strong></li>
            <li id="newYesterday">New Yesterday: <strong>0</strong></li>
            <li id="overall">Overall: <strong>0</strong></li>
```

```
        </ul>
    </li>
    <li id="peopleOnline">People Online:
        <ul>
            <li id="visitors">Visitors: <strong>0</strong></li>
            <li id="members">Members: <strong>0</strong></li>
            <li id="total">Total: <strong>0</strong></li>
        </ul>
    </li>
    <li id="onlineNow">Online Now:</li>
</ul>
```

This "wishful thinking version" of the UsersOnline module output represents the same information and defers most of the presentation layer code to a CSS file. Everything in Figure 13-1 can be reproduced with CSS rules. For example, the icon next to each unordered list item can be configured as a custom image instead of the default bullet mark.

This shows just how small the HTML footprint can be on a page when it's reworked to leverage CSS. When the time comes to customize how the component looks in a browser, it's a simple matter of editing a CSS file instead of reaching into the code base. It's much safer to swap CSS files than to modify how a component actually works.

Your goal is to remove the text underlines in the component because they are not clickable. As a general rule, only hyperlinked text should be underlined on a web page. You're limited by the structural changes available.

At first blush, one might choose to make short work of this task by targeting the ID attributes of the tags surrounding the underline text; however, that would be an unwise move. These ID attribute values are dependent upon several factors. Don't target ID attribute values generated dynamically by ASP.Net because they can change over time for several reasons. When the ID attribute value does change, the CSS selectors will no longer be valid and the style will revert to its default flavor.

In my installation, the ID attribute value of the first item is dnn_ctr391_UsersOnline_pnlMembership, and I'm confident that many of you will have a different numeric from my 391. This is an aspect of ASP.Net that you should be aware of. It guarantees that ID attributes of server controls are unique by concatenating the names of the parent controls into the name prefix. Therefore, the control named pnlMembership grows considerably as it is rendered on the page via the prefix of all the parent controls that envelop it. You should only target ID attribute values that you know to be static and intentionally available for CSS usage. If you need to target an HTML tag that is an ASP.Net server control, use its class attribute instead.

Try It Out   Remove Underlines in the UsersOnline Module

In this section, you'll remove the underlines from three locations in the HTML content using the hooks provided to us by the developers of the UsersOnline module. There are several places you could add CSS rules — in this section you'll just add them to the portal style sheet.

1. If you haven't already, install the UsersOnline module into your DotNetNuke installation. You can do this by logging in as the Host account and navigating to the Module Definitions page in the Host menu. Select the UsersOnline checkbox in the Available Modules section, and click

the hyperlink to install the selected module. Finally, drop an instance of the component onto an empty test page.

2. Take a look at the HTML source code of the page. To achieve the goal of removing the underlines, you'll need to see what's available in the HTML to be able to build the appropriate CSS selectors and manipulate how the browser displays them. Find the `<u>Membership:</u>` tag in the module. Notice the `<td>` tag that envelops the `<u>` tag and the class on the `<td>` tag. This looks like a good place for a CSS selector to latch onto.

3. In this section you'll edit the portal style sheet. Navigate to the Admin, Site Settings page and expand the Stylesheet Editor section.

4. Enter the following CSS rule into the editor to target the `<u>` tag enclosed in the `<td>` tag you saw earlier in the HTML source:

```
td.NormalBold u
{
    text-decoration:none;
    font:normal normal normal 12pt Arial;
}
```

5. Click the Save Style Sheet hyperlink and return to the test page.

6. The text Membership and People Online should be larger and without an underline now. You might have to do a hard refresh by pressing Ctrl+F5 to bypass any cached versions of the files in your browser.

7. Now, you need to target the HTML content `<u>Latest:</u>` in the module. Return to the Stylesheet Editor and enter the following CSS rule below your first rule. Notice this selector targets a `<td>` tag with a different class.

```
td.Normal u
{
    text-decoration:none;
    font:normal normal normal 11px Tahoma;
}
```

8. Click the Save Style Sheet hyperlink and return to the test page. This time, all the underlines should be removed from the module, and only the horizontal rules separate the sections.

How It Works

This technique leveraged the existing class attributes in the module. It also played off the hierarchy of the `<u>` tags embedded inside the `<td>` tags. By analyzing the HTML emitted from the module you saw it might one day be optimized for a more CSS friendly approach but opportunities still exist for moderate customization.

Although you were selective as to which HTML content would receive this custom text-decoration property, it can also affect other pages unintentionally because the rules exist in the portal style sheet. You might be better off by further reducing the risk of unintended changes by isolating these rules in a module-specific style sheet that is only included when the page utilizes the module.

Contacts Module

This module is a practical component for an intranet application where one or more phone numbers always seem to change every month and outdated paper sheets cause problems. Other companies might create a custom portal for each customer and include a specialized contact list for their clients. Either one of these scenarios can call for a customization of the Contacts module.

This module is available for download on the DotNetNuke Downloads page at the following URL. Go ahead and download the install package for the Contacts module now.

```
www.dotnetnuke.com/tabid/125/default.aspx
```

The team lead for this project is Tony Valenti, and version 3.1 was released on June 20, 2006. Figure 13-2 shows a sample instance of the module.

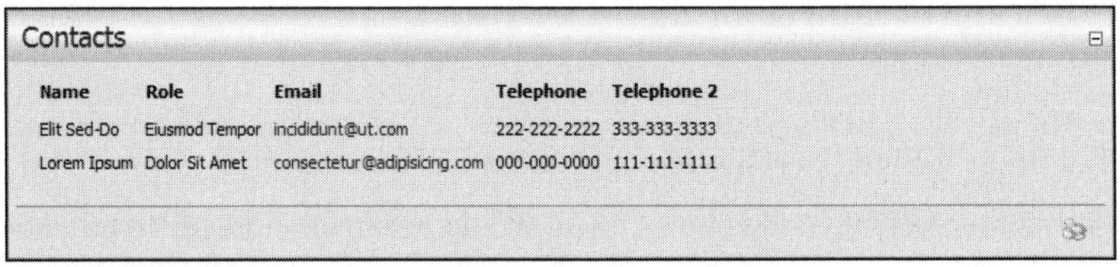

Figure 13-2

Evaluation

The following code snippet shows the HTML that is rendered in Figure 13-2:

```
<table cellspacing="0"
       cellpadding="4"
       rules="all"
       Summary="This table shows various contacts with information like name,
email, and phone number."
       border="0"
       id="dnn_ctr381_Contacts_grdContacts"
       style="border-width:0px;border-collapse:collapse;">
    <tr>
       <td> </td>
       <td class="NormalBold" Scope="col">Name</td>
       <td class="NormalBold" Scope="col">Role</td>
       <td class="NormalBold" Scope="col">Email</td>
       <td class="NormalBold" Scope="col">Telephone</td>
       <td class="NormalBold" Scope="col">Telephone 2</td>
    </tr>
    <tr>
       <td></td>
       <td class="Normal">Elit Sed-Do </td>
       <td class="Normal">Eiusmod Tempor </td>
       <td class="Normal">
```

```
                    <span id="dnn_ctr381_Contacts_grdContacts_ct102_lblEmail">
                        <script language="javascript">
                        <!--
                            document.write(String.fromCharCode(60,97,32,104,114,101,102,61,34,
109,97,105,108,116,111,58,105,110,99,105,100,105,100,117,110,116,64,117,116,46,99,
111,109,34,62,105,110,99,105,100,105,100,117,110,
116,64,117,116,46,99,111,109,60,47,97,62))
                        // -->
                        </script>
                    </span>
                </td>
                <td class="Normal">222-222-2222</td>
                <td class="Normal">333-333-3333</td>
            </tr>
            <tr>
                <td></td>
                <td class="Normal">Lorem Ipsum </td>
                <td class="Normal">Dolor Sit Amet</td>
                <td class="Normal">
                    <span id="dnn_ctr381_Contacts_grdContacts_ct103_lblEmail">
                        <script language="javascript">
                        <!--
                            document.write(String.fromCharCode(60,97,32,104,114,101,102,61,34,
109,97,105,108,116,111,58,99,111,110,115,101,99,116,101,116,117,114,64,97,100,105,
112,105,115,105,99,105,110,103,46,99,111,109,34,62,99,111,110,115,101,99,116,101,
116,117,114,64,97,100,105,112,105,115,105,99,105,110,103,46,99,111,109,60,47,97,62))
                        // -->
                        </script>
                    </span>
                </td>
                <td class="Normal">000-000-0000</td>
                <td class="Normal">111-111-1111</td>
            </tr>
        </table>
```

This component makes a good case for using an HTML table because the information is tabular. Each data cell in the table has a class of Normal and the table header cells use NormalBold.

The other interesting aspect of this module is the obfuscation technique employed on the e-mail address column. Each e-mail address is rendered with client-side JavaScript that converts a series of character codes into the actual character so they can be viewed in the browser. Figure 13-2 shows both e-mail addresses ending with .com and you can see the last four numbers in both sequences end with 60,47,97,62, which indicate 60 is the period, 47 is the letter "c," and so on.

An enormous number of programs are scanning the public Internet for e-mail addresses. Some of these robots will then send e-mail messages to the addresses gleaned from the public website and offer all types of products and services — also known as spam. Some nefarious types will send messages with malware attachments meant to track your behavior or steal your secret information. I trust that all of you are firmly aware of this and know that you should never open an e-mail attachment from someone you do not either know or trust.

The obfuscation technique works by tricking robots into thinking that a JavaScript function has been embedded into the HTML content. JavaScript functions typically don't hold anything of value for the robots as normal HTML text might. Therefore, many robots will be fooled and completely overlook the hidden e-mail address simply because they are not expecting to see it in this format. It's one thing to search for a standard e-mail address format of `name@domain.com` using pattern matching programs, but it's quite another to decipher JavaScript that converts a series of numbers into letters on the fly, hence a trick that works well enough to be worth the effort.

Customization

In this case, the module developers chose to use the well-known CSS class instead of targeting the table with a unique class or id attribute. Therefore, you only have access to the `NormalBold` and `Normal` class attribute values. As a consequence, the repeated text of Normal is all over the HTML source code.

The last section uses a technique for overriding the behavior of a `<u>` tag based in part on targeting the Normal class. This time, you'll do something a little different. Lists, especially long lists, are difficult to read when each row has the same background color. Your goal is to customize the tabular data by varying the background color of alternating rows.

Try It Out   Alternate the Row Color in the Contacts Module

In this section, you'll apply CSS rules to alternate the row color of the Contacts module. The previous evaluation showed how the HTML content is structured with an HTML table. By applying a set of sibling CSS selectors, you can make a long list easier to read.

1. Install the Contacts module into your DotNetNuke installation, and drop an instance of the component onto an empty test page.

2. Log in as the Admin account and add at least four entries into the Contacts module for testing.

3. The CSS rules you're about to use rely on Standards Compliance mode and are ignored under Quirks mode. My test page uses the default DNN-Blue skin, which is currently in Quirks mode. As you learned in previous chapters, add an XML file to the DNN-Blue skin folder to bring the page into Standards Compliance mode. Create a text file named `Horizontal Menu - Fixed Width.doctype.xml` and place it in the folder `<install folder>\Portals\_default\Skins\DNN-Blue` with the following content:

```
<SkinDocType><![CDATA[<!DOCTYPE html PUBLIC "-//W3C//DTD HTML 4.01
Transitional//EN" "http://www.w3.org/TR/html4/loose.dtd">]]></SkinDocType>
```

4. Browse the page with Firefox, and click Tools, Page Info and confirm the page is rendering in Standards Compliance mode.

5. You need to create a good target for the CSS. Navigate to the module settings page for the Contacts module by clicking the Settings button in the lower right corner.

6. Expand the Advanced Settings section and enter the following HTML content in the Header field:

```
<div id="MyContacts">
```

7. Enter the following HTML content in the Footer field:

```
</div>
```

8. Click the Update hyperlink at the bottom of the page to save this custom `<div>` tag that will envelop the list.

9. Now that all the pieces are in place, it's time to apply the CSS. Create a text file named `module.css` and drop it into the folder named `\DesktopModules\Contacts`.

10. The first CSS rule will target the header row with a dark background color. Add the following rule to the CSS file:

```
div#MyContacts tr
{
    background:#CCC;
}
```

11. The next rule will target the even numbered rules below the header and apply a white background color. Add the following rule to the CSS file:

```
div#MyContacts tr + tr,
div#MyContacts tr + tr + tr + tr,
div#MyContacts tr + tr + tr + tr + tr + tr
{
    background-color:#FFF;
}
```

12. The last rule will target odd numbered rows below the header and apply the alternating row color. Add the following rule to the CSS file:

```
div#MyContacts tr + tr + tr,
div#MyContacts tr + tr + tr + tr + tr,
div#MyContacts tr + tr + tr + tr + tr + tr + tr
{
    background-color:#EEE;
}
```

13. Save your changes to the CSS file, and refresh your browser to see the new look for the HTML table. Each row should have alternating colors, and the HTML source code should include a reference to the `module.css` file as well as the `<div>` tag that you added to wrap the HTML table.

How It Works

Figure 13-3 shows the Contacts module with alternating row colors.

Figure 13-3

This example started with moving into Standards Compliance mode. Occasionally, you'll run into CSS properties, such as the adjacent selector, that are overlooked in Internet Explorer unless the page is rendered in Standards Compliance mode. Next, you used a handy feature in DotNetNuke to inject a simple `<div>` tag into the page that envelops the module. This is a nice way to get around the problem of finding an adequate hook into the HTML content so your CSS rules are precise, and to minimize the chance of unintended consequences.

The CSS file made use of adjacent selectors in the CSS file. Multiple selectors are separated by a comma and stacked over the same CSS rule. The plus sign in each selector instructs the browser to find the next adjacent tag and apply the rule. You needed two sets of selectors, one for the even rows and one for the odd rows.

One downside to this CSS technique is that the number of selectors must be equal to or greater than the number of rows in the table. If the table contains hundreds of rows, this technique falls apart fast. You can try this out by adding more rows to the table to view the effect.

The current style sheet will handle up to seven data rows. It's OK to handle about 30 rows of data, but you're probably working too hard to handle more. The benefit of this approach is that you didn't have to modify the HTML content of the module to achieve the result. That's a handy little trick to have in your repertoire.

Wiki Module

A wiki is an excellent alternative to sending multiple versions of Word documents around the network. It thrives in a scenario where ideas abound and a tight-knit structure of documentation submission and approval clashes with the culture of the organization.

A wiki sets a tone of openness and trust among the authors. They can edit content on a page at any time using a simple text box or a more sophisticated WYSIWYG component such as the FCKeditor found in DotNetNuke.

Instead of using HTML anchor tags to create hyperlinks to other pages, a wiki uses the double bracket syntax to indicate hyperlink text. The wiki engine translates the text between the double brackets into hyperlinks and uses the text as a type of URL.

If the URL exists, a visitor can click the text and the wiki engine will navigate the visitor to the other page. If the page does not yet exist, it's the wiki technology that automatically creates the page on the fly and invites the user to author the first bit of content on this new page.

Of course two hyperlinks can intend to link to the same page, but have slight variations in the hyperlink text resulting in an unintended consequence of different pages. Therefore, a wiki needs to keep a constant eye on the recent changes to review and correct issues that come up. Most wiki engines include a hyperlink named Recent Changes that will list the URLs that have been recently updated just for this review purpose.

This is the spirit of the wiki, an organic network of related pages that have no need for a traditional top-down navigation hierarchy. A wiki site consists entirely of cross-linked pages using the wiki syntax of double brackets to create hyperlinks. In DotNetNuke, a wiki module is a sort of mini-site nested within the DotNetNuke portal.

The team lead for this project is Chris Hammond. The team members include Henry Kenuam, Laurence Neville, and Josh Handel. Version 4.00.01 of the Wiki module was released on May 7, 2007. Figure 13-4 shows a sample instance of the module.

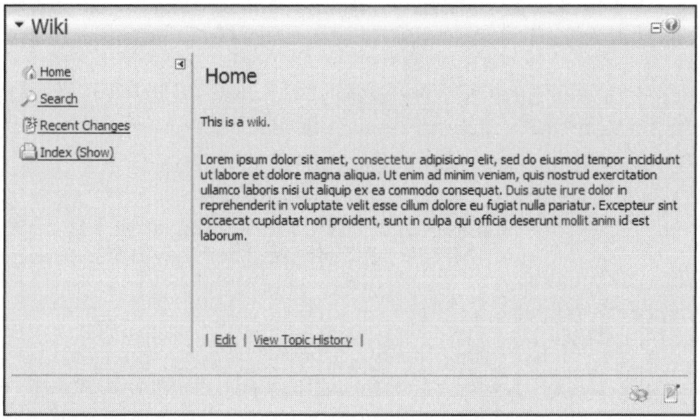

Figure 13-4

Evaluation

The following code snippet shows the HTML that is rendered in Figure 13-4:

```
<TABLE id="Table1" cellSpacing="2" width="100%" border="0" cellpadding="5">
  <TR>
    <TD nowrap valign="top">
      <div id="dnn_ctr392_Router_LinksPanel" style="width:125px;">
        <a id="dnn_ctr392_Router_HomeBtn"
          class="CommandButton"
          href="http://localhost/dnn453/Products/Wiki/tabid/62/Default.aspx">
            <img src="/dnn453/DesktopModules/Wiki/images/Home.gif"
                border="0"
                align="middle" > Home</a><BR>
        <a id="dnn_ctr392_Router_SearchBtn"
          class="CommandButton"
          href="http://localhost/dnn453/Products/Wiki/tabid/62/loc/search/
Default.aspx">
            <img src="/dnn453/DesktopModules/Wiki/images/Search.gif"
                border="0"
                align="middle" > Search</a><BR>
        <a id="dnn_ctr392_Router_RecChangeBtn"
          class="CommandButton"
```

```
                    href="http://localhost/dnn453/Products/Wiki/tabid/62/loc/
recentchanges/Default.aspx">
                    <img src="/dnn453/DesktopModules/Wiki/images/RecentChanges.gif"
                        border="0"
                        align="middle" > Recent Changes</a><BR>
            <a id="dnn_ctr392_Router_IndexBtn"
                class="CommandButton"
                href="javascript:__doPostBack('dnn$ctr392$Router$IndexBtn','')">
                <img src="/dnn453/DesktopModules/Wiki/images/Index.gif"
                    border="0"
                    align="middle" /> Index (Show)</a><BR>
        </div>
    </TD>
    <td style="BORDER-RIGHT: darkgray thin solid; WIDTH: 12px"
        valign="top" align="right">
        <input type="image"
                name="dnn$ctr392$Router$ImageButton1"
                id="dnn_ctr392_Router_ImageButton1"
                src="/dnn453/DesktopModules/Wiki/images/HideNav.gif"
                alt="Hide Navigation" style="border-width:0px;" /></td>
    <TD width="100%"
        style="MARGIN-LEFT: 5px"
        valign="top">
        <style>
            .inlineStyle
            {
                BORDER-RIGHT: darkgray 1px solid;
                BORDER-TOP: darkgray 1px solid;
                BORDER-LEFT: darkgray 1px solid;
                BORDER-BOTTOM: darkgray 1px solid;
                BACKGROUND-COLOR: gainsboro
            }
        </style>
        <table width="100%">
            <tr>
                <td vAlign="top"
                    noWrap align="left"
                    width="100%">
                    <span id="dnn_ctr392_Router_ctl00_lblPageTopic"
                        class="Head">Home</span></td>
                <td class="normal" vAlign="top" noWrap align="left"><br></td>
            </tr>
        </table>
        <div id="dnn_ctr392_Router_ctl00_ContentPanel">
            <SPAN class="Normal">
                <p>This is a <a href="/dnn453/Products/Wiki/tabid/62/topic/wiki/
Default.aspx">wiki</a>.</p>
                <p>Lorem ipsum dolor sit amet,
                    <a href="/dnn453/Products/Wiki/tabid/62/topic/consectetur/
Default.aspx">
                    consectetur</a> adipisicing elit, sed do eiusmod tempor
                    incididunt ut labore et dolore magna aliqua. Ut enim ad
                    minim veniam, quis nostrud exercitation ullamco laboris
                    nisi ut aliquip ex ea commodo consequat.
```

```
                    <a href="/dnn453/Products/Wiki/tabid/62/topic/
Duis+aute+irure+dolor/Default.aspx">
                    Duis aute irure dolor</a> in reprehenderit in voluptate
                    velit esse cillum dolore eu fugiat nulla pariatur.
                    Excepteur sint occaecat cupidatat non proident, sunt in
                    culpa qui officia deserunt
                    <a href="/dnn453/Products/Wiki/tabid/62/topic/mollit+anim/
Default.aspx">
                    mollit anim</a> id est laborum.</p>
            </SPAN>
            <BR><BR><BR>
            <SPAN class="CommandButton"> | 
                <a id="dnn_ctr392_Router_ct100_txtViewHistory"
                class="CommandButton"
                href="http://localhost/dnn453/Products/Wiki/tabid/62/loc/
TopicHistory/topic/WikiHomePage/Default.aspx">
                    View Topic History</a> |</SPAN>
        </div>
      </TD>
    </TR>
</TABLE>
```

The previous code snippet reveals a table structure used in conjunction with a few in-line styles and some presentation markup in the HTML. There's also a `<style>` element embedded in the content; according to the HTML specification, these belong in the `<head>` tag. Yet, both IE7 and Firefox 2 are forgiving enough to render the rules in the `<style>` tag. This is a good case for overlooking a little non-compliant code in lieu of the benefits of a great wiki engine inside DotNetNuke.

The style of the content depends a great deal on the markup produced by the authors, much like the content of a standard Text/HTML module on a DotNetNuke page. The wiki page content is surrounded by an HTML element with a class attribute of Normal as a baseline style.

Customization

Customizing the content of a wiki is mostly about understanding and effectively applying a set of rules for the content. Because the content is edited continuously by the members, it's tough to get a full understanding of the content; it's always changing.

A safe bet is to establish and enforce a semantic markup policy for the content. Section headers are marked up with `<h1>`, `<h2>`, or `<h3>` tags; regular content uses `<p>` tags; and lists are marked up with `<ul>` or `<ol>` tags.

A content policy that permits free usage of the font drop-down list box in the FCKeditor will quickly see an abundance of text using Comic Sans MS — akin to seeing a patch of weeds growing in an otherwise well-tended garden. The size and style drop-down list boxes share a similar peril. It's tempting to use these preconfigured features but it can quickly pollute an agile website.

My own policy starts with an acknowledgement that creating style and content are two separate tasks. A custom design reflects over the content and the audience to produce a design plan that balances flexibility, comprehension, and ease of use. In turn, the content creation policy utilizes the policy to add information value to the page. This is a symbiotic relationship for the optimists or a chicken-and-the-egg for the pessimists.

Your customization goal is to develop a unique design for the Wiki module. You have the FCKeditor available as an outstanding content editor. In design mode, you'll view the raw HTML source and work with a CSS style sheet to make your edits instead of injecting presentation markup into the semantic HTML.

Try It Out   Customize the Wiki Module

In this section, you'll create a custom design for the Wiki module using a set of semantic HTML tags.

1. Install the Wiki module into your DotNetNuke installation, and drop an instance of the component onto an empty test page.

2. Log in as the Admin account and add some test content to the Wiki module that uses the following HTML tags: `<p>`, `<h2>`, `<strong>`, `<ul>`, and `<li>`. Make sure to include a hyperlink to another wiki page using the double bracket syntax, too. The following code snippet is my sample content:

```
<p>A wiki is an alternative form of content management where everyone can edit the
page.</p>
<h2>More Information</h2>
<p>Most wiki sites include a fancy HTML editor where content can be
<strong>styled</strong>.</p>
<h2>Common Features</h2>
<ul>
    <li>a [[standard wiki hyperlink technique]].</li>
    <li>a [[WYSIWYG]] editor</li>
    <li>a recent changes hyperlink</li>
</ul>
```

3. Save your changes and browse the resulting page. Your double brackets should be converted into hyperlinks by the wiki engine, and the hyperlink text becomes part of the URL to the other page.

4. Now you need a method of targeting the content inside the Wiki module. Launch Windows Explorer and navigate to the DotNetNuke container folder for this module. The Wiki module on my test page is using the container named `Image Header - Color Background.ascx` located in the folder located in `<install folder>\Portals\_default\Containers\DNN-Blue`.

5. Make a copy of this file and name it `WikiContainer.ascx`. Then, open this file in your favorite text editor.

6. Locate the `<td>` tag with the id attribute of `ContentPane` and append a class attribute, as shown in the following code snippet:

```
<TD id="ContentPane" runat="server" align="center" class="wiki"></TD>
```

7. Now, return to DotNetNuke and configure the module to use the custom container named WikiContainer. To do this, click the pencil icon next to the module to navigate to the Settings page, and then expand the Page Settings section. The Module Container field is located in the Basic Settings section. Choose the item named WikiContainer inside this list box control.

8. Click the Update hyperlink on the Module Settings page and return to the wiki test page. View the HTML source and confirm that the container around the Wiki module shows the new custom class attribute.

9. Now that the HTML target is in place, you need a place to drop some HTML rules. Add a new text file named `module.css` to the `\wiki` folder under `\DesktopModules`, and then open it in your favorite text editor.

10. Add the following CSS to the `module.css` file and define the custom styles:

```css
td.wiki p
{
   font:normal normal normal 10pt Arial;
   color:#000;
   margin:0 10px;
}

td.wiki h2
{
   border-top:solid 1px #FFF;
   font:small-caps normal normal 10pt Georgia, Verdana;
   color:#999;
   margin:20px 0 0 0;
   padding:6px 0;
}

td.wiki strong
{
   color:#006699;
}

td.wiki ul
{
   margin:0 0 0 30px;
}

td.wiki li
{
   list-style-type:lower-alpha;
}

td.wiki a
{
   text-decoration:underline;
   color:#666;
}
```

If you don't see the reference to the `module.css` *file in the HTML source, you'll need to restart your web application. There are a couple of ways to do this. I'll usually "touch" the* `web.config` *file by opening it in a text editor, hit the enter button a few times, save the file, and then undo my changes and hit save again. You can also restart the application by navigating to the Host Settings page and clicking the Restart Application hyperlink.*

How It Works

Figure 13-5 shows the styled wiki content.

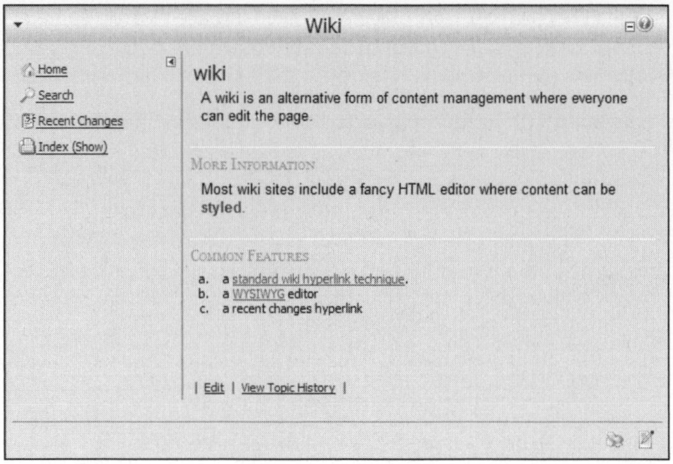

Figure 13-5

This is another method of injecting an HTML target near a module without actually modifying the component. It's a useful technique when multiple modules use the same HTML target and you can reuse the same custom container. Sometimes injecting HTML tags via the header/footer fields in the Module Settings page is insufficient for the skinning technique you want to apply. This is just one more technique to stash in your book.

You need to keep a keen eye on the Recent Changes page of this Wiki module and make sure that all users are entering content according to your policy as well as following the markup rules. You can well imagine the verbose HTML code that would be necessary to achieve the same design effect without CSS. In addition to the added baggage of the HTML code, it would be more difficult to change the design later on, because every page with the `<font>` tags and other markup would require edits.

If you have problems enforcing the semantic HTML policy, you can edit the tools available in the FCKeditor by editing the files in the following folder:

```
<install folder>\Providers\HtmlEditorProviders\Fck\
```

News Feeds Module

DotNetNuke can make every module available as an RSS feed using the standard features in the framework. A simple checkbox in the Module Settings page will inject the familiar RSS icon in the page near the module and expose the module content as an RSS feed. In this sense, the DotNetNuke modules are a source for an RSS feed.

DotNetNuke can also act as a client of an external RSS feed where visitors can view the news feeds from several external websites in a central location. This chapter uses an external news feed available on the Wrox website at the following URL to demonstrate the capabilities:

```
www.wrox.com/WileyCDA/feed/RSS_WROX_ALLNEW.xml
```

This feed returns information on new books from the publisher, such as the title, a brief description, and an image of the cover. If you're an avid fan, it's a good news feed to read and stay up to date on the latest books.

If you launch the previous URL in IE7 or Firefox 2, the browser will recognize the content as a news feed and render the XML as a formatted HTML page using the embedded style sheet reference. You can still see the raw XML if you view the HTML source as you would on any other web page. The first two lines in this feed are declarations about content and a default style sheet to apply to the feed, respectively.

A news feed is simply a URL that returns XML as a standard format. Several news feed formats are in existence today, including RSS version 0.9, RSS 1.0, RSS 2.0, and Atom. These are just XML schemas that describe the expectations of how the XML in the news feed will be formatted. The version isn't too much of a concern for most people as long as you know what XML elements to expect when formatting a given feed.

The News Feeds module is similar to the more complex XML/XSL module. Both of these modules can be configured to convert an XML file into HTML content. The News Feeds module has a targeted niche of RSS news feeds whereas the XML/XSL module has a broader scope and therefore has a huge number of configurable options.

The News Feed reader accepts two parameters: an XML feed and an XSL file. The XML feed contains the source data. The XSL file contains instructions on how to convert an XML file from one format to another. In your case, you're interested in output having customized HTML tags embedded with the module content.

The team lead for the News Feed project is Peter Donker, and the Core Team Sponsor is Stefan Cullmann. Version 3.1.1 of the News Feeds module was released on June 21, 2006. Figure 13-6 shows a sample instance of the module.

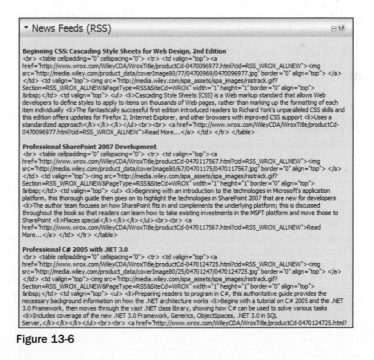

Figure 13-6

Evaluation

The following snippet shows the default output of the News Feeds module when the Wrox URL is configured with the Edit News Feed hyperlink. This truncated snippet shows just two items in the news feed.

```
<span class="Normal"><br>
  <strong>
    <a href="http://www.wrox.com/WileyCDA/WroxTitle/
productCd-0470096977.html?cid=RSS_WROX_ALLNEW"
       target="_main">Beginning CSS: Cascading Style Sheets for Web Design, 2nd
Edition</a>
  </strong>
  <br>&lt;br&gt; &lt;table cellpadding="0" cellspacing="0"&gt; &lt;tr&gt; &lt;td
valign="top"&gt;&lt;a href="http://www.wrox.com/WileyCDA/WroxTitle/
productCd-0470096977.html?cid=RSS_WROX_ALLNEW"&gt;&lt;img src="http://
media.wiley.com/product_data/coverImage80/77/04700969/0470096977.jpg" border="0"
align="top"&gt; &lt;/a&gt; &lt;/td&gt; &lt;td valign="top"&gt;&lt;img src="http://
media.wiley.com/spa_assets/spa_images/rsstrack.gif?Section=RSS_WROX_ALLNEW&amp;
PageType=RSS&amp;SiteCd=WROX" width="1" height="1" border="0" align="top"&gt;
 &lt;/td&gt; &lt;td valign="top"&gt; &lt;ul&gt; &lt;li&gt;Cascading Style
Sheets (CSS) is a Web markup standard that allows Web developers to define styles
to apply to items on thousands of Web pages, rather than marking up the formatting
of each item individually &lt;li&gt;The fantastically successful first edition
introduced readers to Richard York's unparalleled CSS skills and this edition
offers updates for Firefox 2, Internet Explorer, and other browsers with improved
CSS support &lt;li&gt;Uses a standardized approach&lt;/li&gt;&lt;/li&gt;&lt;/
li&gt;&lt;/ul&gt;&lt;br&gt;&lt;br&gt; &lt;a href="http://www.wrox.com/WileyCDA/
WroxTitle/productCd-0470096977.html?cid=RSS_WROX_ALLNEW"&gt;Read More...&lt;/a&gt;
&lt;/td&gt; &lt;/tr&gt; &lt;/table&gt;
<br>
<br>
  <strong>
    <a href="http://www.wrox.com/WileyCDA/WroxTitle/productCd-0470117567.html?cid=
RSS_WROX_ALLNEW"
       target="_main">Professional SharePoint 2007 Development</a>
  </strong>
  <br>&lt;br&gt; &lt;table cellpadding="0" cellspacing="0"&gt; &lt;tr&gt; &lt;td
valign="top"&gt;&lt;a href="http://www.wrox.com/WileyCDA/WroxTitle/
productCd-0470117567.html?cid=RSS_WROX_ALLNEW"&gt;&lt;img src="http://
media.wiley.com/product_data/coverImage80/67/04701175/0470117567.jpg" border="0"
align="top"&gt; &lt;/a&gt; &lt;/td&gt; &lt;td valign="top"&gt;&lt;img src="http://
media.wiley.com/spa_assets/spa_images/rsstrack.gif?Section=RSS_WROX_ALLNEW&amp;
PageType=RSS&amp;SiteCd=WROX" width="1" height="1" border="0" align="top"&gt;
 &lt;/td&gt; &lt;td valign="top"&gt; &lt;ul&gt; &lt;li&gt;Beginning with
an introduction to the technologies in Microsoft's application platform, this
thorough guide then goes on to highlight the technologies in SharePoint 2007 that
are new for developers &lt;li&gt;The author team focuses on how SharePoint fits in
and complements the underlying platform; this is discussed throughout the book so
that readers can learn how to take existing investments in the MSFT platform and
move those to SharePoint &lt;li&gt;Places special&lt;/li&gt;&lt;/li&gt;&lt;/
li&gt;&lt;/ul&gt;&lt;br&gt;&lt;br&gt; &lt;a href="http://www.wrox.com/
WileyCDA/WroxTitle/productCd-0470117567.html?cid=RSS_WROX_ALLNEW"&gt;Read
More...&lt;/a&gt; &lt;/td&gt; &lt;/tr&gt; &lt;/table&gt;
<br>
<br>
```

As you can see, the news feed output can be quite verbose. This output doesn't tell us too much except that a potential problem exists with the default XSL file and this RSS feed. It appears the HTML tags in the raw news feed are appearing as entity references instead of the actual characters. For example, the left angle bracket is appearing as <. You need to address this issue in your custom XSL file.

Unlike with the previous modules, you need to trace the path of the module output upstream and examine both the XML feed and the XSL file that converts the feed into HTML. The following code snippet is a truncated version of the raw XML feed from the Wrox URL. It shows the first few XML elements, including two <item> elements.

```
<?xml version="1.0" encoding="utf-8"?>
<?xml-stylesheet title="XSL_formatting" type="text/xsl"
href="/WileyCDA/feed/RSS_WROX_ALLNEW.xsl"?>

<rss xmlns:dc="http://purl.org/dc/elements/1.1/"
xmlns:rdf="http://www.w3.org/1999/02/22-rdf-syntax-ns#"
xmlns:taxo="http://purl.org/rss/1.0/modules/taxonomy/" version="2.0">
  <channel>
    <title>Wrox: All New Titles</title>
    <link>http://www.wrox.com/</link>
    <description>New titles on Wrox.com &lt;!-- ckey="1E5F1C44"
--&gt;</description>
    <copyright>Copyright &amp;copy; 2000-2006 by John Wiley &amp;amp; Sons, Inc. or
related companies. All rights reserved.</copyright>

    <pubDate>Mon, 02 Jul 2007 18:22:54 GMT</pubDate>
    <dc:date>2007-07-02T18:22:54Z</dc:date>
    <dc:rights>Copyright &amp;copy; 2000-2006 by John Wiley &amp;amp; Sons, Inc. or
related companies. All rights reserved.</dc:rights>
    <image>
      <title>Wrox: All New Titles</title>
      <url>http://media.wiley.com/assets/1103/76/wrox_logo_sm.gif</url>

      <link>http://www.wrox.com/</link>
    </image>
    <item>
      <title>Visual Basic 2005 Instant Results</title>
      <link>http://www.wrox.com/WileyCDA/WroxTitle/
productCd-0470118717.html?cid=RSS_WROX_ALLNEW</link>
      <description>&lt;br&gt; &lt;table cellpadding="0" cellspacing="0"&gt;
&lt;tr&gt; &lt;td valign="top"&gt;&lt;a href="http://www.wrox.com/WileyCDA/
WroxTitle/productCd-0470118717.html?cid=RSS_WROX_ALLNEW"&gt;&lt;img src="http://
media.wiley.com/product_data/coverImage80/17/04701187/0470118717.jpg" border="0"
align="top"&gt; &lt;/a&gt; &lt;/td&gt; &lt;td valign="top"&gt;&lt;img src="http://
media.wiley.com/spa_assets/spa_images/rsstrack.gif?Section=RSS_WROX_ALLNEW&amp;
PageType=RSS&amp;SiteCd=WROX" width="1" height="1" border="0" align="top"&gt;
 &lt;/td&gt; &lt;td valign="top"&gt; &lt;ul&gt; &lt;li&gt;Visual Basic,
one of the most popular programming languages today with more than 6 million
developers, has released the 2005 version, which continues to expand on the
functionality and flexibility of its framework-.NET 3.0 &lt;li&gt;Covering Visual
Basic .NET 2005 programming in a Windows environment as well as accessing SQL
Server Express 2005 and Web Services, this book allows intermediate-level
programmers to get up to speed quickly with complete sample&lt;/li&gt;&lt;/
```

```
li&gt;&lt;/ul&gt;&lt;br&gt;&lt;br&gt; &lt;a href="http://www.wrox.com/WileyCDA/
WroxTitle/productCd-0470118717.html?cid=RSS_WROX_ALLNEW"&gt;Read More...&lt;/a&gt;
&lt;/td&gt; &lt;/tr&gt; &lt;/table&gt;</description>

        <pubDate>Mon, 25 Jun 2007 04:00:00 GMT</pubDate>
        <guid>http://www.wrox.com/WileyCDA/WroxTitle/productCd-0470118717.html?cid=
RSS_WROX_ALLNEW</guid>
        <dc:creator>Thearon Willis</dc:creator>
        <dc:date>2007-06-25T04:00:00Z</dc:date>
    </item>
    <item>
        <title>Beginning CSS: Cascading Style Sheets for Web Design, 2nd
Edition</title>

        <link>http://www.wrox.com/WileyCDA/WroxTitle/productCd-0470096977.html?cid=
RSS_WROX_ALLNEW</link>
        <description>&lt;br&gt; &lt;table cellpadding="0" cellspacing="0"&gt;
&lt;tr&gt; &lt;td valign="top"&gt;&lt;a href="http://www.wrox.com/WileyCDA/
WroxTitle/productCd-0470096977.html?cid=RSS_WROX_ALLNEW"&gt;&lt;img src="http://
media.wiley.com/product_data/coverImage80/77/04700969/0470096977.jpg" border="0"
align="top"&gt; &lt;/a&gt; &lt;/td&gt; &lt;td valign="top"&gt;&lt;img src="http://
media.wiley.com/spa_assets/spa_images/rsstrack.gif?Section=RSS_WROX_ALLNEW&amp;Page
Type=RSS&amp;SiteCd=WROX" width="1" height="1" border="0" align="top"&gt;
 &lt;/td&gt; &lt;td valign="top"&gt; &lt;ul&gt; &lt;li&gt;Cascading Style
Sheets (CSS) is a Web markup standard that allows Web developers to define styles
to apply to items on thousands of Web pages, rather than marking up the formatting
of each item individually &lt;li&gt;The fantastically successful first edition
introduced readers to Richard York's unparalleled CSS skills and this edition
offers updates for Firefox 2, Internet Explorer, and other browsers with improved
CSS support &lt;li&gt;Uses a standardized approach&lt;/li&gt;&lt;/li&gt;&lt;/
li&gt;&lt;/ul&gt;&lt;br&gt;&lt;br&gt; &lt;a href="http://www.wrox.com/WileyCDA/
WroxTitle/productCd-0470096977.html?cid=RSS_WROX_ALLNEW"&gt;Read More...&lt;/a&gt;
&lt;/td&gt; &lt;/tr&gt; &lt;/table&gt;</description>

        <pubDate>Tue, 12 Jun 2007 04:00:00 GMT</pubDate>
        <guid>http://www.wrox.com/WileyCDA/WroxTitle/productCd-0470096977.html?cid=
RSS_WROX_ALLNEW</guid>
        <dc:creator>Richard York</dc:creator>
        <dc:date>2007-06-12T04:00:00Z</dc:date>
    </item>
```

Each `<item>` element in the previous feed shows a single book. Each `<item>` element contains the following child elements:

- ❑ `<title>`
- ❑ `<link>`
- ❑ `<description>`
- ❑ `<pubDate>`
- ❑ `<creator>`
- ❑ `<date>`

All of these child elements combine to describe a single book in the news feed. There's nothing particular about books in this RSS feed. The same XML elements can be used to describe items in a beer blog or in technology news.

> *Specialized newsreader clients such as Google Reader and SharpReader can use elements such as* <pubDate> *and* <date> *to create a mini-database and sort and remember which posts to the feed you've read and which are new or unread.*

The following code snippet is the default XSL file used by the News Feed module to transform the XML if a custom file isn't specified. It's a simple file that you can probably figure out without much XSL experience, if any at all. Just look at all the HTML tags in the file that you already know and then extrapolate what the XSL syntax is likely to inject around them.

```
<?xml version="1.0"?>
<xsl:stylesheet version="1.0"
    xmlns:xsl="http://www.w3.org/1999/XSL/Transform">

    <xsl:output method="html" indent="yes"/>
    <xsl:param name="TITLE"/>

    <xsl:template match="rss">

        <!-- Do not show channel image -->
        <xsl:for-each select="channel/item">

            <br>
            <strong><a href="{link}" target="_main">
                <xsl:value-of select="title"/></a>
            </strong>
            <br></br>

            <!-- only display markup for description if it's present -->
            <xsl:value-of select="description"/>
            </br><br></br>

        </xsl:for-each>

    </xsl:template>

    <xsl:template match="description">
        <br>
        <xsl:value-of select="."/>
        </br>
    </xsl:template>

</xsl:stylesheet>
```

XSL is a special language expressed as an XML file. The syntax follows the basic XML rules and includes the expected features of a programming language such as input, output, parameters, loops, and functions.

The root element of the previous XSL file indicates that the enclosed content is an XSL file. The next element named <output> configures some output parameters, and the <param> element is a way to pass variables into the XSL file during the transformation.

The real meat of the XSL file is inside the first `<template>` element shown in the following XSL snippet:

```
<xsl:template match="rss">
    <!-- Do not show channel image -->
    <xsl:for-each select="channel/item">

        <br>
        <strong><a href="{link}" target="_main">
            <xsl:value-of select="title"/></a>
        </strong>
        <br></br>

        <!-- only display markup for description if it's present -->
        <xsl:value-of select="description"/>
        </br><br></br>

    </xsl:for-each>
</xsl:template>
```

The previous XSL snippet includes a `<template>` element that finds the `<rss>` element in the source XML file during the transformation process. Once it finds this matching element, the XSL file starts a `for-each` loop over each `<item>` element under the `<channel>` element. Remember that each `<item>` element represents a different book in the feed.

So this XSL file emits a series of HTML tags (`<br>`, `<strong>`, and `<a>`) near the values of the `<title>` and `<description>` elements it plucks out of the XML file during each loop. Comments operate the same way in XSL as they do in HTML. It's a good idea to use them liberally so you can understand the code with less effort later on.

Now you ought to be able to go back to the first code snippet in this section and pick out the parts of the HTML text injected by the XSL file and the parts that were plucked from the XML file within the for-each loop.

> *If you're new to XML and XSL, then I recommend picking up a copy of* Beginning XML, 4th Edition *by David Hunter, Jeff Rafter, Joe Fawcett, Eric van der Vlist, Danny Ayers, Jon Duckett, Andrew Watt, Linda McKinnon (Wiley Publishing, Inc., 2007) to better understand the fundamentals of the technology.*

So far, you've examined the default HTML output of the News Feed module, the raw RSS input feed, and the default XSL file that transforms the RSS feed into HTML. These are all of the components of the News Feed module that you'll take into account as you develop a custom RSS client.

Customization

The goal of this customization effort is to author your own XSL file and to instruct the News Feed module to emit the HTML code of your own choosing around the data in the RSS feed. You won't need any deep XSL skills in this section. Although the syntax can be a bit tricky, remember that it's still just a programming language with input, output, variables, and loops.

Because you know the RSS feed contains a series of `<item>` elements that represent each book, let's build an XSL file that emits an unordered list, where each list item is a separate book. Then you can do away with the `<br>` tags in the default XSL file and move to a slightly more standards based approach.

Try It Out   Implement the News Feed Module

This exercise will build a custom XSL file and attach it to a News Feed module to display the upcoming books from Wrox as a custom news feed.

1. Install the News Feed module into your DotNetNuke installation and drop an instance of the component onto an empty test page.

2. While logged in as the Host account, click the Edit Newsfeed hyperlink at the bottom of the module to navigate the browser to the Edit News Feeds page.

3. The top field selects the News Feed source. Enter the following URL in the News Feed source field:

   ```
   www.wrox.com/WileyCDA/feed/RSS_WROX_ALLNEW.xml
   ```

4. The bottom field selects the News Feed Style Sheet. Leave it empty for now and click the Update hyperlink.

5. Review the default content emitted by the News Feed module, and then analyze the HTML source. It should resemble the code snippets earlier in this section. Because you didn't specify an XSL file, the module used a default file to transform the RSS feed into HTML.

6. Now it's time to create a custom XSL file. Create a new text file named `MyNewsFeed.xsl`, and save it to the portal root folder, as shown in the following path.

   ```
   <install folder>\Portals\0\MyNewsFeed.xsl
   ```

7. Use your favorite text editor to enter the following XSL into the file. If you like, you can simply copy the file from the code available online for this chapter.

```xml
<?xml version="1.0"?>
<xsl:stylesheet version="1.0" xmlns:xsl="http://www.w3.org/1999/XSL/Transform"
    xmlns:dc="http://purl.org/dc/elements/1.1/">

    <xsl:output method="html" indent="yes"/>
    <xsl:param name="TITLE"/>

    <xsl:template match="rss">

        <div class="feedContainer">

            <div class="feedHeader">
                <h2 class="feedTitle">
                    <xsl:value-of select="channel/title"/>
                </h2>
                <p><xsl:value-of select="channel/description"
disable-output-escaping="yes"/></p>
            </div>

            <div class="feedImage">
                <a>
                    <xsl:attribute name="href">
                        <xsl:value-of select="channel/image/link"/>
                    </xsl:attribute>
```

```
            <img>
                <xsl:attribute name="src">
                    <xsl:value-of select="channel/image/url"/>
                </xsl:attribute>
                <xsl:attribute name="alt">
                    <xsl:value-of select="channel/image/title"/>
                </xsl:attribute>
            </img>
        </a>
    </div>

    <ul class="feedList">
        <xsl:for-each select="channel/item">
            <li class="feedItem">
                <h3 class="feedItemTitle">
                    <a href="{link}" target="_main">
                        <xsl:value-of select="title"
disable-output-escaping="yes"/>
                    </a>
                </h3>
                <p class="feedAuthor">
                    By <xsl:value-of select="dc:creator"/>
                </p>
                <p class="feedPubDate">
                    <xsl:value-of select="pubDate"/>
                </p>
                <div class="feedDescription">
                    <xsl:value-of select="description"
disable-output-escaping="yes"/>
                </div>
            </li>
        </xsl:for-each>
    </ul>
    <p class="feedCopyright">
        <xsl:value-of select="channel/copyright"
disable-output-escaping="yes" />
    </p>

    </div>

  </xsl:template>

</xsl:stylesheet>
```

8. Now that the XSL file is saved to the portal root folder, it's time to configure it for use in the News Feed module. Click the Edit Newsfeed hyperlink at the bottom left side of the module.

9. On the Edit News Feeds page, select the File radio button in the field labeled News Feed Style Sheet.

10. Using the drop-down list box fields, select the path to your custom XSL file named MyNewsFeed.xsl located in the portal root folder.

11. Click the Update hyperlink to save your changes, and return to the test page with the News Feed module.

12. The custom XSL file injects some CSS classes into the HTML, so you need a CSS file to utilize these hooks. Create a new file named `module.css` in the News module folder, as shown in the following path:

```
<install folder>\DesktopModules\News\module.css
```

13. Enter the following CSS rules into the `module.css` file or copy and paste them from the code available online for this chapter:

```
div.feedContainer
{
    position:relative;
    top:0;
    left:0;
}
div.feedHeader
{
    padding:5px 0 5px 100px;
    background:#FFF;
    vertical-align:top;
}
h2.feedTitle
{
    font:normal normal normal 18pt Georgia, Verdana;
}
div.feedHeader p
{
    font:normal normal normal 12pt Verdana;
}
div.feedImage
{
    position:absolute;
    top:0;
    left:0;
    width:100px;
    height:100px;
}
div.feedImage img
{
    border:0;
    margin:10px;
}
ul.feedList
{
    margin:0;
    background:#EEE;
    padding:0;
```

```
}
li.feedItem
{
    margin:16px 4px 0 10px;
    list-style-type:none;
}
h3.feedItemTitle
{
    font:normal normal bold 12pt Arial;
    margin:0;
}
p.feedAuthor
{
    margin:0;
}
p.feedPubDate
{
    float:right;
    color:#666;
}
div.feedDescription
{
    background:#FFF;
    padding:4px 10px;
}
p.feedCopyright
{
    text-align:center;
}
```

14. The page should render the RSS feed using the custom XSL file to produce semantic HTML that is in turn styled by your custom CSS file. If you don't see the design expressed in the `module.css` file, you might need to restart your web application by *touching* the `web.config` file. Just open the `web.config` file in a text editor, add a few benign carriage returns to the very bottom of the file, and then save your changes. This causes ASP.Net to restart the application domain, and your CSS file will be picked up in the process.

How It Works

Your test page should resemble Figure 13-7.

The custom XSL file follows the same general pattern of the default file. It does add some class attributes to key locations so the CSS file can target the appropriate HTML content. As you might have gleaned from the context, the elements prefixed with `xsl:` in the XSL file represent commands in the XSL syntax. Most of them are intuitively named, such as the `<xsl:for-each>` and the `<xsl:value-of>` elements. The former element is a looping structure, and the latter simply plucks out the value of the selected XML node. You can spend quite a while in XSL, and it's a lot of fun. I recommend you pick up a book and take a look for yourself.

The custom CSS file dropped into the News Feed module folder continues to play off the same target opportunities used through the chapter. The key difference here is the News Feed module gives you full access to the ambient HTML surrounding the news feed. Although you are at the mercy of the RSS feed content, you can do a lot with well-defined sections around each one of the feed items.

Figure 13-7

Summary

This chapter explored four DotNetNuke modules and the channels they provide for custom designs. As you've seen, modules can have a wide variation in the HTML content that can be targeted by CSS.

In some instances, the module makes a class attribute available for selection in a CSS file. Even a basic HTML element such as a `<tr>` tag can be targeted, providing an enveloping element limits the influence of such a broad CSS selector. Adjacent selectors are a powerful technique for styling alternating rows in an HTML table.

This chapter demonstrated two techniques for generating a custom target by using the header/footer properties in the module settings or creating a custom container file that supplies the necessary class or id attributes. Both techniques are valid methods for augmenting a module without actually modifying the code.

Finally, the News Reader module supplied a brief introduction to the world of RSS feeds and XSL files. This component is as close to programming as you can get, without actually compiling something or remembering to include the semicolon character. This component enabled DotNetNuke developers to construct their own HTML content as it was emitted by the module while transforming the RSS feed — all while leaving the core module code in place and enabling a simple upgrade path for future versions.

Exercises

1. If you don't have the authority to customize a container, how else might you envelop a module with a `<div>` tag and a unique ID attribute?

2. What is the significance of the + characters in the following CSS selector?

   ```
   table#sales td+td+td { background-color:#CCC; }
   ```

3. What is the difference between RSS 0.9, RSS 1.0, RSS 2.0, and Atom?

4. What happens if two style sheets in the same web page contain rules for the same CSS selector?

5. What is the lowest style sheet on a page in a default instance of DotNetNuke, and how can you edit it?

Exploring AJAX in DotNetNuke

AJAX is the acronym for asynchronous JavaScript and XML. It's a slick technique for improving the experiences of website visitors in very specific scenarios. Most web pages won't have a case for implementing AJAX, but when the scenario is right, it can significantly elevate the visitor's perception of the website.

This chapter explores ways DotNetNuke websites can embrace features available through AJAX without becoming too bogged down in the details. The Microsoft ASP.Net 2.0 AJAX Extensions 1.0 offers a solid framework for DotNetNuke developers as well as designers. As you might have expected, the DotNetNuke team has also been working on a compelling set of AJAX features for the past few years.

To help ensure that you have a good experience with the exercises in this chapter, use DotNetNuke version 4.5.5 or later. Earlier versions might not work as well with the AJAX features you'll use in this chapter.

This chapter works through the following concepts:

- ❑ Understanding the components of Microsoft ASP.Net AJAX
- ❑ Understanding the context of the Client API inside the DotNetNuke framework
- ❑ Customizing DotNetNuke with minor enhancements
- ❑ Skinning a custom module with AJAX features

Examining Microsoft ASP.Net AJAX

The ASP.Net AJAX features are categorized into a handful of related components. All of them can be downloaded for free from the AJAX tab located at the top of the http://ajax.asp.net website. There's a ton of great video and community content available there along with recommended books for delving into the technology, like *Professional ASP.NET 2.0 AJAX* by Matt Gibbs and Dan Wahlin (Wiley Publishing, Inc., 2007).

The following sections dissect each of the components starting with the foundation and moving out into the future. There's a longer than normal setup in this chapter, but I promise the Try It Out sections later on will be totally worth it.

ASP.Net AJAX Extensions

This is the core of the ASP.Net AJAX technology. This free download on `http://ajax.asp.net` contains the assembly file named `System.Web.Extensions.dll` for server-side programming as well as embedded resources for working with AJAX inside the web browser. Most folks will start with this component in their adventures with ASP.Net AJAX technology.

The `System.Web.Extensions` assembly includes a couple of ASP.Net controls such as the ScriptManager, UpdatePanel, and Timer. These controls can be dropped onto an ASP.Net page just like a GridView or Button control and used to enhance a functional web page. You'll use the ScriptManager control in just a bit. It's an essential starting block for working with ASP.Net AJAX.

This component also adds special AJAX project templates into Visual Studio 2005. After installation, you can launch Visual Studio, click File, New Project, and select the ASP.Net AJAX-Enabled Web Application template to start building your custom solution right away. This project template refers to the `System.Web.Extensions.dll` file in your project, and includes the necessary `web.config` items. All of this works together to support out-of-band callbacks to the web server so your website visitors have a better experience using the system.

It's helpful to have an appreciation for the amount of work provided by the ASP.Net AJAX Extensions. The items in the `web.config` file lend some insight into the amount of plumbing code necessary for AJAX behaviors, or at least some insight into how the team at Microsoft constructed their offering in this space. For comparison, the following code block shows the small default `web.config` file from the ASP.Net Web Application template in Visual Studio 2005:

```
<?xml version="1.0"?>
<configuration>

    <appSettings/>
    <connectionStrings/>

    <system.web>
        <!--
            Set compilation debug="true" to insert debugging
            symbols into the compiled page. Because this
            affects performance, set this value to true only
            during development.
        -->
        <compilation debug="true" />
        <!--
            The <authentication> section enables configuration
            of the security authentication mode used by
            ASP.NET to identify an incoming user.
        -->
        <authentication mode="Windows" />
        <!--
            The <customErrors> section enables configuration
            of what to do if/when an unhandled error occurs
            during the execution of a request. Specifically,
```

```
                it enables developers to configure HTML error pages
                to be displayed in place of an error stack trace.

        <customErrors mode="RemoteOnly" defaultRedirect="GenericErrorPage.htm">
            <error statusCode="403" redirect="NoAccess.htm" />
            <error statusCode="404" redirect="FileNotFound.htm" />
        </customErrors>
        -->
    </system.web>
</configuration>
```

The previous code block is concise and has more comments than an actual configuration. ASP.Net doesn't need much to run a website. The file contains placeholders for standard application settings and database connection string values. By default, this file is configured for debug mode and uses Windows authentication.

Once the intent of ASP.Net AJAX is declared for a new website by selecting the ASP.Net AJAX-Enabled Web Application template, more specific assumptions can be made and the following web.config file can be constructed by Visual Studio 2005:

```
<?xml version="1.0"?>
<configuration>
  <configSections>
    <sectionGroup name="system.web.extensions"
type="System.Web.Configuration.SystemWebExtensionsSectionGroup,
System.Web.Extensions, Version=1.0.61025.0, Culture=neutral,
PublicKeyToken=31bf3856ad364e35">
      <sectionGroup name="scripting"
type="System.Web.Configuration.ScriptingSectionGroup, System.Web.Extensions,
Version=1.0.61025.0, Culture=neutral, PublicKeyToken=31bf3856ad364e35">
        <section name="scriptResourceHandler"
type="System.Web.Configuration.ScriptingScriptResourceHandlerSection,
System.Web.Extensions, Version=1.0.61025.0, Culture=neutral,
PublicKeyToken=31bf3856ad364e35" requirePermission="false"
allowDefinition="MachineToApplication"/>
        <sectionGroup name="webServices"
type="System.Web.Configuration.ScriptingWebServicesSectionGroup,
System.Web.Extensions, Version=1.0.61025.0, Culture=neutral,
PublicKeyToken=31bf3856ad364e35">
          <section name="jsonSerialization"
type="System.Web.Configuration.ScriptingJsonSerializationSection,
System.Web.Extensions, Version=1.0.61025.0, Culture=neutral,
PublicKeyToken=31bf3856ad364e35" requirePermission="false"
allowDefinition="Everywhere" />
          <section name="profileService"
type="System.Web.Configuration.ScriptingProfileServiceSection,
System.Web.Extensions, Version=1.0.61025.0, Culture=neutral,
PublicKeyToken=31bf3856ad364e35" requirePermission="false"
allowDefinition="MachineToApplication" />
          <section name="authenticationService"
type="System.Web.Configuration.ScriptingAuthenticationServiceSection,
System.Web.Extensions, Version=1.0.61025.0, Culture=neutral,
PublicKeyToken=31bf3856ad364e35" requirePermission="false"
allowDefinition="MachineToApplication" />
        </sectionGroup>
```

```
        </sectionGroup>
      </sectionGroup>
    </configSections>

    <system.web>
      <pages>
        <controls>
          <add tagPrefix="asp" namespace="System.Web.UI"
assembly="System.Web.Extensions, Version=1.0.61025.0, Culture=neutral,
PublicKeyToken=31bf3856ad364e35"/>
        </controls>
      </pages>
      <!--
          Set compilation debug="true" to insert debugging
          symbols into the compiled page. Because this
          affects performance, set this value to true only
          during development.
      -->
      <compilation debug="false">
        <assemblies>
          <add assembly="System.Web.Extensions, Version=1.0.61025.0, Culture=neutral,
PublicKeyToken=31bf3856ad364e35"/>
        </assemblies>
      </compilation>

      <httpHandlers>
        <remove verb="*" path="*.asmx"/>
        <add verb="*" path="*.asmx" validate="false"
type="System.Web.Script.Services.ScriptHandlerFactory, System.Web.Extensions,
Version=1.0.61025.0, Culture=neutral, PublicKeyToken=31bf3856ad364e35"/>
        <add verb="*" path="*_AppService.axd" validate="false"
type="System.Web.Script.Services.ScriptHandlerFactory, System.Web.Extensions,
Version=1.0.61025.0, Culture=neutral, PublicKeyToken=31bf3856ad364e35"/>
        <add verb="GET,HEAD" path="ScriptResource.axd"
type="System.Web.Handlers.ScriptResourceHandler, System.Web.Extensions,
Version=1.0.61025.0, Culture=neutral, PublicKeyToken=31bf3856ad364e35"
validate="false"/>
      </httpHandlers>

      <httpModules>
        <add name="ScriptModule" type="System.Web.Handlers.ScriptModule,
System.Web.Extensions, Version=1.0.61025.0, Culture=neutral,
PublicKeyToken=31bf3856ad364e35"/>
      </httpModules>
    </system.web>

    <system.web.extensions>
      <scripting>
        <webServices>
        <!-- Uncomment this line to customize maxJsonLength and add a custom
converter -->
        <!--
        <jsonSerialization maxJsonLength="500">
          <converters>
            <add name="ConvertMe" type="Acme.SubAcme.ConvertMeTypeConverter"/>
          </converters>
```

```
        </jsonSerialization>
        -->
        <!-- Uncomment this line to enable the authentication service. Include
requireSSL="true" if appropriate. -->
        <!--
          <authenticationService enabled="true" requireSSL = "true|false"/>
        -->

        <!-- Uncomment these lines to enable the profile service. To allow profile
properties to be retrieved
              and modified in ASP.NET AJAX applications, you need to add each property
name to the readAccessProperties and
              writeAccessProperties attributes. -->
        <!--
        <profileService enabled="true"
                        readAccessProperties="propertyname1,propertyname2"
                        writeAccessProperties="propertyname1,propertyname2" />
        -->
        </webServices>
        <!--
        <scriptResourceHandler enableCompression="true" enableCaching="true" />
        -->
    </scripting>
  </system.web.extensions>

  <system.webServer>
    <validation validateIntegratedModeConfiguration="false"/>
    <modules>
      <add name="ScriptModule" preCondition="integratedMode"
type="System.Web.Handlers.ScriptModule, System.Web.Extensions, Version=1.0.61025.0,
Culture=neutral, PublicKeyToken=31bf3856ad364e35"/>
    </modules>
    <handlers>
      <remove name="WebServiceHandlerFactory-Integrated" />
      <add name="ScriptHandlerFactory" verb="*" path="*.asmx"
preCondition="integratedMode"
          type="System.Web.Script.Services.ScriptHandlerFactory,
System.Web.Extensions, Version=1.0.61025.0, Culture=neutral,
PublicKeyToken=31bf3856ad364e35"/>
      <add name="ScriptHandlerFactoryAppServices" verb="*" path="*_AppService.axd"
preCondition="integratedMode"
          type="System.Web.Script.Services.ScriptHandlerFactory,
System.Web.Extensions, Version=1.0.61025.0, Culture=neutral,
PublicKeyToken=31bf3856ad364e35"/>
      <add name="ScriptResource" preCondition="integratedMode" verb="GET,HEAD"
path="ScriptResource.axd" type="System.Web.Handlers.ScriptResourceHandler,
System.Web.Extensions, Version=1.0.61025.0, Culture=neutral,
PublicKeyToken=31bf3856ad364e35" />
    </handlers>
  </system.webServer>
</configuration>
```

The previous code block handles a lot of tedious work by wiring up various asynchronous communication components. The heavy lifting happens inside the System.Web.Extensions assembly. Most of the items in web.config make references to data types located inside this assembly.

This is a great of example of where XML shines; this human readable file can help someone completely unfamiliar with ASP.Net AJAX glean just a little deeper understanding and introduce some interesting areas to follow up with deeper research. For example, you might be curious to learn more about HttpHandlers or HttpModules in ASP.Net by taking a look at *Professional ASP.NET 2.0 AJAX* by Matt Gibbs and Dan Wahlin (Wiley Publishing, Inc., 2007). The bigger picture here is to understand that a developer can literally launch Visual Studio 2005, click File, New Project, select the AJAX project template and start implementing features without worrying about the plumbing that makes it possible.

Although the previous default `web.config` file generated by the ASP.Net AJAX-Enabled Web Application template might seem verbose at first, it's only one-third as long as the default `web.config` file inside DotNetNuke. As you'll see in just a bit, the default `web.config` file in DotNetNuke has already integrated references to the `System.Web.Extensions` assembly. Because ASP.Net AJAX is integrating with an existing system in DotNetNuke, the configuration is a little different from the `web.config` file of a brand-new ASP.Net AJAX project.

If you don't use Visual Studio 2005, ASP.Net AJAX Extensions can be added to a new solution by adding a reference to `System.Web.Extensions.dll` and applying the changes to `web.config` by hand. Regardless of the IDE, the `web.config` file is manually edited to add AJAX configuration settings to existing solutions.

ASP.Net AJAX Control Toolkit

The Control Toolkit is a separate download listed on the `http://ajax.asp.net` website. Much like the AJAX Extensions component, the Control Toolkit contains an assembly named `AjaxControlToolkit.dll` that's just loaded with features. Inside you'll find over 30 controls that extend the capabilities of your web solution.

Although AJAX Extensions are a prerequisite, the only installation step for using the AJAX Control Toolkit is to drop the `AjaxControlToolkit.dll` assembly into the `\bin` folder of your website. The `web.config` items already in place for the AJAX Extensions will provide the plumbing for working with controls and .NET code on the server side, or working with JavaScript on the client side.

The AJAX Control Toolkit has an interesting open source story, too. It was originally developed inside Microsoft as a means to provide more features that used the framework of the core product, ASP.Net AJAX Extensions. This Control Toolkit project eventually moved to `www.codeplex.com` and became an open source project that Microsoft shares with the world.

The source control system on CodePlex is available through several different client programs. You can work with a command-line client program, install a Visual Studio 2005 add-in, or work with a stand-alone GUI client program. The CodePlex team is also working on a way for the TortoiseSVN client program to communicate with CodePlex, even though CodePlex doesn't use *Subversion*, which is perhaps the best open source platform in existence today for source control needs.

On the CodePlex site, anyone can download the latest builds or become involved with the project. The project grants various rights based on your role. Someone who merely signs up for a free account on CodePlex can do several tasks, including voting for work items and uploading patches into the system. People who become more involved with enhancing the code can be granted the role of Developer. This role can edit the wiki and check-in changes to the source control system. The Project Coordinator role is the highest role with all of the available permissions.

Later on in this chapter, you'll apply a couple of the controls available in the Control Toolkit to an existing DotNetNuke site. This component is a great way to gain more familiarity with AJAX without requiring too many JavaScript skills. At the same time, both the AJAX Extensions and Control Toolkit can offer some of the most intense challenges for JavaScript experts who want to dive deep into an interesting space. Each of these AJAX components can be extended and customized to create a unique feature of your own.

AJAX Library

The AJAX Library represents an interesting notion from Microsoft. To use the AJAX Extensions, you need to drop an assembly into the \bin folder and edit the web.config file of your ASP.Net solution. What happens if your web solution isn't running ASP.Net? What if your solution is using PHP, or running on an Apache web server?

Microsoft extended the AJAX offering from the normal Microsoft development group to include anyone using a web server to transmit HTML, CSS, and JavaScript. Although this component doesn't include any of the server-side controls that make AJAX programming incredibly easy to get started, it does include the client-side JavaScript libraries that are leveraged by the AJAX Extensions and Control Toolkit. People who use the AJAX library can drop the files onto any web server, including Apache, and utilize the JavaScript library inside their own scripts.

Because DotNetNuke is an ASP.Net solution, this will not invite too much use from the DNN developer community, but it does provide another skill base to learn. DNN developers often work in multiple environments when they're not spending time customizing their favorite DotNetNuke site. People who extend their knowledge of the Microsoft AJAX technology can also use their skills inside other environments as a type of cross-pollination. You won't spend any more time on it here other than a little encouragement from me to download the files for this component on the http://ajax.asp.net website; see what's in there and try out some samples. Perhaps you'll be struck by some inspiration on your next PHP solution!

ASP.Net Futures

Over the past several years, Microsoft has developed a culture of openness by providing several Community Technology Previews (CTPs). Before the advent of CTPs, a new product or component was developed behind closed doors and only a few prominent folks outside of Microsoft were given an opportunity to weigh in and give their thoughts. Microsoft recognized they could build a better product with more feedback from the developer community. CTPs provide a way to provide feedback before the next release is fully baked.

Today, it's almost too easy to become lost in a sea of CTPs and get bogged down with software that hasn't been released yet. It also has a strange affect on the release parties thrown by Microsoft each year, because most of the people in the conference halls have already seen the given product before getting out of bed, driving to the event, and listening to the keynote speech. I find it's best to know who you are and stick to the essential CTP offerings that you have a genuine interest in using. Then, find some great bloggers who comment about the CTPs of your second- and third-tier interests. The launch parties and conferences you attend will have a better level of communication enabled because you've either worked directly with a pre-release version or closely followed the blogs of those who do.

The ASP.Net Futures component contains exactly that, the future. These are the features that Microsoft is putting a great deal of thought and effort into, potentially launching as a fully supported product. In here, you'll be able to put the ideas of the next release through its paces and see how much better it solves the business problems you tackle today. Armed with this knowledge, you'll be well equipped to curb your learning curve dramatically with the released product as well as help your own clients use these features when they're actually released on day one — time to market is a big deal.

So, like the AJAX library component, you won't cover much more of this last component of the four parts of the Microsoft AJAX story in this chapter. It's an interesting place to watch if you plan to work deeply with the AJAX technologies in the future.

Merging the Client API and ASP.Net AJAX

The DotNetNuke Client API project is nestled inside the core components of the system. It's aligned closer to programmer oriented tasks than designer oriented tasks. The whole point of AJAX enabled websites is to provide an improved user experience, a concept with deep ties to web design principles. Therefore, this project provides a good crossroad opportunity where programmers and designers can work closely together and collaborate on a solution. Designers can benefit from a little technical knowledge and programmers can improve their aesthetic chops. So you'll just touch lightly on the Client API here and move swiftly into the more designer oriented aspects of AJAX shortly to stay aligned with the focus of this book.

Like RSS feeds, DotNetNuke has long had a vested interest in AJAX behaviors. Jon Henning is the DotNetNuke team lead for the Client API project. The project page on the DotNetNuke website contains Jon's sample modules, patches, and documentation from as early as September, 2005.

As a core part of DotNetNuke, this project is charged with delivering a common set of techniques to shuttle information between the client and the server in an asynchronous manner. This is no small challenge considering the broad array of browsers to support and the multiple technology disciplines required to work in this space.

The features related to the DotNetNuke Client API project exist in a couple of places. The root folder of a DotNetNuke installation contains a folder named `js`. Inside this folder, you'll see several JavaScript files used for Client API features while visiting a DotNetNuke website. The filenames are descriptive and provide a good idea of what each of them do. Some are generic utilities for passing messages to a web server with the HTTP protocol and others are specific to a given control, such as the DotNetNuke Menu control.

While JavaScript files handle the work on the client side, the main assembly handling the Client API work on the server side is `DotNetNuke.WebUtility.dll`, located in the `bin` folder just off the web application root folder. Module developers can utilize the functions available inside this assembly to make server-side resources such as complex business calculations and database information available to the browser through asynchronous callbacks.

The DotNetNuke Client API, like many other AJAX libraries, works to provide a set of use methods for its community. The major goal of any AJAX library is to help move data between the web server and the client browser outside of the normal means. Over time, the asynchronous experience in DotNetNuke has become quite sophisticated. From drag-and-drop support for moving modules to click-and-edit updating of labels and Text/HTML modules, this team has done a lot of good work.

Recent versions of DotNetNuke have made inroads to integrate the ASP.Net AJAX Extensions. You can see evidence of this by finding the assembly file from Microsoft named `System.Web.Extensions.dll` in the `bin` folder along with several references to it in the `web.config` file in the web application root folder. Coupled with this new Microsoft assembly, the main DotNetNuke assembly named `DotNetNuke.dll` also includes a class named `AJAX` that provides some helper features for using ASP.Net AJAX inside DotNetNuke.

Because integration with ASP.Net AJAX appears to be the direction of the DotNetNuke platform and the future of ASP.Net in general, you'll dive directly into this approach for integrating AJAX behavior in DotNetNuke.

Using ASP.Net AJAX in DotNetNuke

OK, it's time to bring some of these concepts into reality and see them do something inside of DotNetNuke. Because the focus of this book is designing DotNetNuke sites more than writing programs for them, you won't venture too far down the path of complex server-side coding or JavaScript, but there's still plenty of exploration available within the AJAX Control Toolkit.

The following sections will introduce you to several visual aspects of ASP.Net AJAX by adding a few selected controls to your DotNetNuke installation. Once you have a good grasp of these features, you'll be able to have deeper and more meaningful conversations with your programming team or explore it on your own!

Adding a Watermark to the Search Text Box

The TextBoxWatermark is one type of extender control inside the AJAX Control Toolkit. Extender controls provide additional features to other controls on the page, but they're not very useful in isolation. The ASP.Net validation controls have a similar relationship; the RequiredFieldValidator control can work with a TextBox control to make sure a value exists, but it doesn't do much all by itself.

A TextBoxWatermark control injects a small message inside a given TextBox control when the page first loads. A helpful message can give a little more context for the purpose of the TextBox control and augments the label to the left or above the field, if one exists. When the visitor moves the cursor inside the textbox, the watermark disappears and the visitor can enter the field value as normal.

Applying this feature to DotNetNuke will tell you whether the ASP.Net AJAX Extensions are enabled on your system, and you'll be ready to tackle more complicated customizations in future Try It Out sections of this chapter.

Try It Out   Add a TextBoxWatermark Control

This section will add the TextBoxWatermark control to DotNetNuke by injecting a helpful message inside the keyword search text box. Because the neighborhood association skin doesn't currently make use of the search features inside DotNetNuke, you'll just create a test page that uses the default DNN-Blue skin and see it in action there.

Because this section moves straight into the AJAX Control Toolkit, you need to download this component from the Downloads section on http://ajax.asp.net before getting started. Make sure that you're using DotNetNuke version 4.5.5 or later, too.

1. Open the zip file from the AJAX Control Toolkit. Inside the \SampleWebsite\bin folder you'll see two files: AjaxControlToolkit.dll and AjaxControlToolkit.pdb. Copy both of them to the \bin folder inside your own local DotNetNuke installation.

2. Just for a quick sanity check, confirm that the \bin folder of your local DotNetNuke installation also includes an assembly file named System.Web.Extensions.dll; this is the ASP.Net AJAX Extensions component. It's already installed and configured inside your DotNetNuke website.

3. Log in to your local DotNetNuke installation as the Admin or Host account, and create a test page that uses the default DNN-Blue skin. It doesn't matter where you place the page; you're only interested in trying out the TextBoxWatermark control. Make sure the file is visible to all users.

4. Using your favorite text editor, open the default DNN-Blue skin located in the following file path:

```
\Portals\_default\Skins\DNN-Blue\Horizontal Menu - Fixed Width.ascx
```

5. Locate the instance of the web user control that provides the DotNetNuke search features for this skin. You should see the following control declaration in the skin file:

```
<dnn:SEARCH runat="server" id="dnnSEARCH" showWeb="True" showSite="True" />
```

6. Trace the location of the source code for the search web user control by finding the register directive at the top of the file having a TagPrefix of dnn and a TagName of SEARCH. This register directive identifies the source code for the web user control in the attribute named Src. The ~ character tells ASP.Net to start at the root folder for the website and follow the given path to the .ascx file. You should see the following register directive that tells you which file to edit in order to apply the TextBoxWatermark control.

```
<%@ Register TagPrefix="dnn" TagName="SEARCH"
    Src="~/Admin/Skins/Search.ascx" %>
```

7. Open the web user control file located at \admin\skins\search.ascx. This is the file you traced down through the default DNN-Blue skin file. Inside this file, you'll see the four ASP.Net controls that provide the search features: two radio buttons, a text box, and a button control. You need to target the TextBox control named txtSearch with the TextBoxWatermark control.

8. The first file edit you'll perform is the addition of a register directive just under the control directive at the top of the file. Add the following register directive to refer to the components inside the AJAX Control Toolkit:

```
<%@ Register Assembly="AjaxControlToolkit" Namespace="AjaxControlToolkit"
    TagPrefix="ajax" %>
```

9. Add an instance of the TextBoxWatermark control by adding the following control declaration at the bottom of the file:

```
<ajax:TextBoxWatermarkExtender ID="TextBoxWatermarkExtender1" runat="server"
```

```
TargetControlID="txtSearch"
WatermarkText="Enter Keyword Here"
WatermarkCssClass="Watermark" />
```

10. Configure the `CssClass` property of the TextBox control so that it has a value of `NoWatermark`, like the following Textbox declaration:

```
<asp:TextBox id="txtSearch" runat="server" CssClass="NoWatermark" maxlength="255"
enableviewstate="False"></asp:TextBox>
```

11. You've used two CSS classes in the web user control, `NoWatermark` and `Watermark`. Now, it's time to specify the corresponding rules. Use your favorite text editor to open the `Portal.css` file located in the following file path:

```
\Portals\0\portal.css
```

12. Append the following CSS rules to the `portal.css` file so the watermark will appear with your custom styles:

```
.NoWatermark,
.Watermark
{
    font-style:normal;
    color:#000;
    width:120px;
    font:normal normal normal 8pt Arial;
}

.Watermark
{
    font-style:italic;
    color:#CCC;
}
```

13. You're nearly complete. You've added the TextBoxWatermark control to the appropriate web user control and edited some CSS values. If you view the web page now, it will render fine, but the watermark will not be present. Although the ASP.Net AJAX Extensions are integrated with DotNetNuke by default, they are also disabled! In order to use them, you must tell DotNetNuke that this page is using an AJAX feature. To do that you need to add just a few lines of code. Use your favorite text editor to open the following code-behind file:

```
<install folder>\admin\Skins\Search.ascx.vb
```

14. Inside this web user control, locate the `Page_Load()` procedure. Add the highlighted three-line `If` statement at the very top of the `Page_Load` procedure, and then save your changes.

```
Private Sub Page_Load(ByVal sender As System.Object, ByVal e As System.EventArgs)
Handles MyBase.Load

    If DotNetNuke.Framework.AJAX.IsInstalled Then
        DotNetNuke.Framework.AJAX.RegisterScriptManager()
    End If

    If Not Page.IsPostBack Then
```

15. Now, you have completed all of the necessary edits. Reload the test page and see the message inside the keyword search text box injected by the TextBoxWatermark control. Then, move the cursor inside the text box and watch the message disappear! Because this was just a temporary test page, you can delete it now, if you like.

If you get an "object not found" error when you refresh the page, *touch* your `web.config` file by making a benign change to it such as adding a few carriage returns at the bottom and saving your changes. This will cause the ASP.Net application domain to restart and ought to resolve the problem.

How It Works

Because you added this feature to the skin object file, any skin that uses this search text box will gain the watermark feature. Figure 14-1 shows a close up of the watermark in the default DNN-Blue skin.

Adding the `AjaxControlToolkit.dll` assembly to the `\bin` folder of your DotNetNuke instantly enabled the use of over 30 prebuilt AJAX controls. There is quite a bit inside that assembly. The register directive you added to the `search.ascx` file makes a direct reference to the assembly you added in the `\bin` folder.

This particular control works well for fields that are empty by default. Using a watermark for an updatable text box would be the wrong approach because the field already contains a value when the page first loads.

The TextBoxWatermark control takes care of attaching the appropriate JavaScript to the page so the message appears and disappears at the right moment. The CSS class you added to customize the default style makes the watermark just barely visible with an italic font. When the actual value is entered by the visitor, the other CSS class makes the value appear in a dark font that's more readable.

Enabling AJAX behaviors does take some bandwidth and processing cycles; therefore it's disabled by default. Skin objects and modules that make use of ASP.Net AJAX components also need to signal to DotNetNuke that it should be flipped on. Just a three-line `If` statement is all that's needed to make the dynamic application of AJAX technology appear on your page.

Although this particular control doesn't make extensive use of out-of-band calls back to the web server, all of the principles apply. You needed to confirm that the necessary AJAX assemblies existed in the `\bin` folder and include register directives in order to use them. Once the desired controls were added to the skin object, you just flipped a switch with some simple VB.Net code in order to inform DotNetNuke that you want to use some AJAX technology on this page.

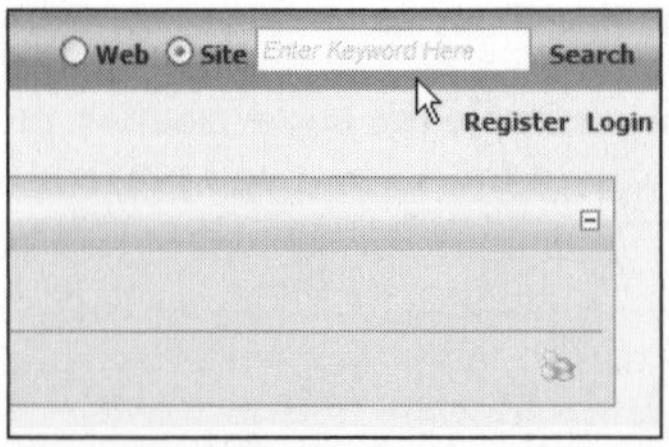

Figure 14-1

Checking DotNetNuke Password Strength

Now that you've gotten your first custom DotNetNuke AJAX feature working, it's time to make some adjustments to the Neighborhood Association website. This time you'll add a more interactive feature from the AJAX Control Toolkit.

Because you hope a lot of visitors from the neighborhood and beyond will visit the website and create accounts, it would be helpful to encourage the use of strong passwords. You're planning to make this website publicly available on the Internet, so you know it will be exposed to all types of users, including robot programs that continuously scan the Internet. You're interested in protecting your accounts from malicious or fraudulent people.

The PasswordStrength control inside the AJAX Control Toolkit provides a visual indication of the calculated strength of a visitor's password as they are entering it into the form field of the browser. Instant feedback is one of the best methods of improving the actual metrics of an intended outcome. In your case, you want your users to choose strong passwords. If visitors can immediately see how strong their passwords are, you stand a better chance of everyone applying a more critical eye to website security.

Try It Out   **Check Password Strength During Login**

In this section, you'll add the PasswordStrength control to the User Log In form on the Neighborhood Association website. This section builds off the prior exercise by using the `AjaxControlToolkit.dll` assembly that you installed in the `\bin` folder of the website.

1.   Confirm that the `\bin` folder of your local DotNetNuke installation contains the following two ASP.Net AJAX assemblies. Without these, you'll be dead in the water. If you don't have both, go back and run through the steps to add the TextBoxWatermark control to a test page as discussed in the previous section.

```
\bin\System.Web.Extensions.dll
\bin\AjaxControlToolkit.dll
```

2.   Edit the web user control that contains the Log In form. Use your favorite text editor to open the following file inside your local DotNetNuke installation:

```
<install folder>\admin\Security\signin.ascx
```

3.   Just like embedding any other control inside another web user control, you need to add a register directive to the top of this file, directly under the existing register directives. Add the following register directive to this file so you can refer to the `AjaxControlToolkit.dll` assembly in this Log In form.

```
<%@ Register Assembly="AjaxControlToolkit" Namespace="AjaxControlToolkit"
       TagPrefix="ajax" %>
```

4.   Locate the TextBox server control that you want to target. Add the PasswordStrength control immediately after the password text box, as represented in the following highlighted section of the code, and then save your changes:

```
<tr>
    <td colspan="2" align="center">
        <asp:textbox id="txtPassword" columns="9" width="130" textmode="password"
```

```
                 cssclass="NormalTextBox" runat="server" />
        <ajax:PasswordStrength ID="PasswordStrength1" runat="server"
           TargetControlID="txtPassword" />
    </td>
 </tr>
```

5. Just as in the previous section that used the TextBoxWatermark control, you need to inform DotNetNuke that this skin object uses ASP.Net AJAX features. Open the code-behind file named `Signin.ascx.vb` located in the same folder.

6. Find the `Page_Load()` procedure in this code-behind file. You need to add the following three lines of highlighted code to the top of this procedure in order to inform DotNetNuke of the AJAX intensions for this web user control. Then, save your changes to the file.

```
Private Sub Page_Load(ByVal sender As System.Object, ByVal e As System.EventArgs)
Handles MyBase.Load

            If DotNetNuke.Framework.AJAX.IsInstalled Then
                DotNetNuke.Framework.AJAX.RegisterScriptManager()
            End If

            ' Verify if portal has a customized login page
            If Not Null.IsNull(PortalSettings.LoginTabId) And IsAdminControl() Then
```

7. All of the essential changes are in place, so it's time to test it out. Launch your local installation of the neighborhood association website, and click the Login hyperlink in the top right corner of the page. Then, enter your User Name and Password. When you begin typing the password, a block of text should appear to the right side of the form that indicates your password strength. As you type additional characters, the password strength improves.

How It Works

Figure 14-2 shows the PasswordStrength control in action after a few characters are entered in the password field.

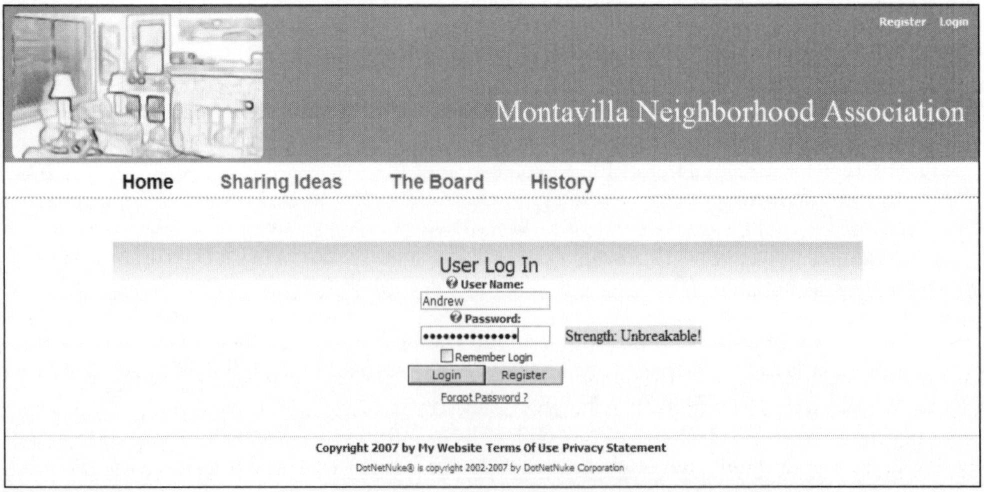

Figure 14-2

Without any customizations, the PasswordStrength control uses a fairly low bar for evaluating complexity. Like most controls in DotNetNuke and ASP.Net, this control is configurable. The following URL lists all of the properties for the PasswordStrength control so you can customize how the messages appear as well as how the evaluation is performed:

```
http://ajax.asp.net/ajaxtoolkit/PasswordStrength/PasswordStrength.aspx
```

For example, you can affect the evaluation by adding a property named `MinimumNumericCharacters` to the control. The default value is zero, which is why just typing in a long string of letters will achieve the top strength rating. If you set this property to a value above zero, the visitor must enter at least that many numeric characters in order to achieve the top rating.

Like the TextBoxWatermark control, the PasswordStrength controls manage all of the steps to wire up JavaScript functions to the events that fire when you enter information into the password text box. You certainly could write all of this functionality by hand, providing you were proficient with JavaScript and DHTML programming. The control inside the AJAX Control Toolkit makes adding this feature a snap.

Skinning a Custom Module with AJAX

So far, you've examined some core concepts of AJAX technology and how they apply to DotNetNuke. Then you implemented these concepts and customizations to the DotNetNuke system itself. While these minor edits to the DotNetNuke core system may seem like minor improvements, they do introduce a potential problem for future upgrades. One of the key features of DotNetNuke is the ease of upgrading your installation to the latest version of the framework. The DotNetNuke team spends a considerable amount of time ensuring that this path is available to you. Sometimes, upgrades are vitally important to the security of your software. This isn't something to cast aside lightly.

The previous techniques of modifying DotNetNuke were small steps and easily discarded. In this section, you'll take on a more formidable challenge and style a partially completed module. Modules are on separate upgrade paths from the DotNetNuke system, so they provide great opportunities to flex your wings and try out some great customizations.

The vision of this module is to provide an online game for the Neighborhood Association website. The idea came during a planning session for the upcoming neighborhood block party. Another member of the Neighborhood Association is programming the custom DotNetNuke module and you're on board to skin it.

The programmer is willing to provide a vendor tent, a table, and an LCD projector. You'll provide a laptop with wireless access to the Internet and place it in a protective box under the table. The laptop is connected to a USB keyboard and mouse on top of the table and the LCD projector displays a 6x8 image on the back of the vendor tent wall.

During the block party, guests will enter the vendor tent and play a virtual balloon pop game that will help highlight the presence of the new neighborhood association website. Your programmer friend and you will run the booth, collect the fee to play the game, and instruct guests on how to play. You can make up any number of different games to play, but the basic idea is that a web page shows a grid of balloons.

Players click on a balloon to pop it and see the prize ticket inside. The possible tickets are gold, silver, and bronze; some balloons don't have a prize ticket inside. This is where your programmer friend added the randomization code.

You have several tasks ahead of you. First, you'll grab the installation file of the game created by the programmer. Although it is "functionally" complete, the game experience itself could use a little work. That's where you come in. You'll apply your skill and knowledge of customizing DotNetNuke to make the game a fun experience for the folks visiting the Neighborhood Association block party!

Installing the Balloon Pop Game

The first milestone for you to achieve is installing the basic game written by the programmer. This custom DotNetNuke module is available as a zip file. You'll find it in the files available for download for this chapter. Go ahead and find the zip file named `BalloonPop_1.0_Install.zip` now.

You'll install the basic game into your local installation of DotNetNuke, add some custom designs, and then create an updated version of the zip file so it can be installed on any other DotNetNuke installation, like the public web server that hosts the Neighborhood Association website.

<table>
<tr><td>Try It Out</td><td>Install BalloonPop Version 1.0</td></tr>
</table>

This section will install the first version of the BalloonPop game created by your neighbor. Once the game is installed, you'll run through the basic functionality and explore the files given to you.

1. Locate the file `BalloonPop_1.0_Install.zip` available in the downloadable code for this chapter.

2. Log in as the Host account on your local DotNetNuke installation and navigate to the Host, Module Definitions page.

3. On the Module Definitions page, scroll down to the bottom of the page and click the hyperlink named Install New Module. This navigates the browser to the Install New Module form.

4. Click the browse button and select the zip file named `BalloonPop_1.0_Install.zip`. Then, click the hyperlink named Install New Module. The system will process the custom module installation file and add the BalloonPop game as a module in the drop-down box at the top of the page.

5. Create a new page in DotNetNuke named Balloon Pop and place it under the Sharing Ideas page. Configure the page to use the wide skin file for this neighborhood association theme and the standard container. Make sure the page is viewable by all users.

6. Drop an instance of the BalloonPop module into the ContentPane of this new page, and then log out so you can see the page as a normal visitor who will play the game.

How It Works

In its current format, the game consists of a welcome message, fifteen numbered hyperlinks, and a reset button. The game tracks the order in which you click the links as well as indicates the prize ticket behind the balloon. Each time you click the reset button, the prizes for the balloons are shuffled.

Several game variations can be derived by limiting the number of pops a player is allowed or holding a competition for the number of empty bronze and silver prizes found before finding a gold prize.

Figure 14-3 shows the game in action during this initial version. It's not much to look at, but the features are there.

Launch Windows Explorer and take a look at the `DesktopModules` folder inside DotNetNuke. When you installed the custom module, a new folder named `BalloonPop` was created here. This folder contains the essential files for playing the game. Open up each of the files and take a look inside.

Because this game doesn't make use of any database features, the module is fairly lightweight. It includes a JavaScript file and a CSS file to separate and simplify different parts of the game. The `settings.ascx` file exists just for completeness, because this module does not have any custom module settings. The `BalloonPop.ascx` file contains a mixture of HTML and server-side code to keep your design modifications simple. A more complex module will separate the server-side code into its own assembly; in your case, it's all right there in one file.

The heart of the server-side code is a small loop that generates 10 random winning numbers between 0 and 14, inclusive. Because you know there are 15 balloons, that means there are five balloons without a prize. The bottom of the web user control includes a JavaScript section with three array objects. The first array gets the first random number for the gold prize and the silver and bronze arrays follow suit. There are three silver prizes and six bronze prizes. Now the external JavaScript file named `BalloonPop.js` has three populated arrays to work with when the function named `popBalloon()` is called. Each time the page is posted back to the server, a new set of random numbers is generated. The person running the booth will have to make sure no savvy players view the HTML source code!

Your goal as a DotNetNuke designer is to improve the visual aspects of the game and make improvements that increase its appeal to the players. You'll use a component in the AJAX Control Toolkit that will help you in this endeavor, not to mention HTML and CSS skills that you have at your disposal.

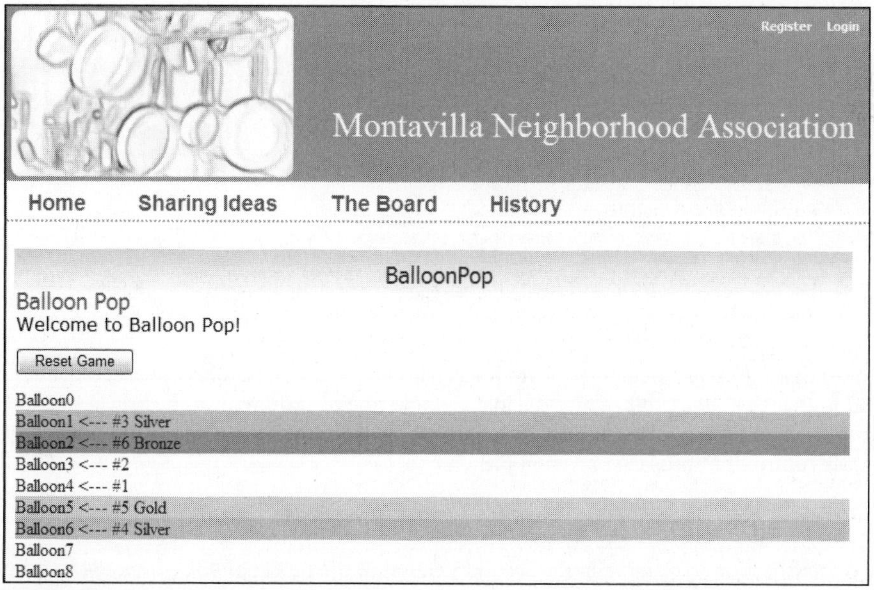

Figure 14-3

Enhancing the Existing Game with AJAX Controls

Because there are so many changes, sometimes in awkward places, it makes more sense for you to look at the two versions of the game from the code available online for this chapter and learn by comparing the differences with a good file comparison utility such as BeyondCompare. You can download a free 30-day trial of BeyondCompare at the following URL.

```
www.scootersoftware.com/download.php
```

Download both versions of the game to your computer from the code available online and follow along as the changes are described. Then, you can use your file comparison utility to see the actual changes on a line-by-line basis.

It is important to understand what changes are taking place in order to apply the AJAX controls, so the following descriptions examine the changes on a section-by-section basis rather than split them up into multiple Try It Out sections for you to execute. Follow the descriptions of the files below by opening version two of the module and examining its contents. At the end of this section, you'll install version two of the Balloon Pop module.

Register the AJAX ScriptManager in C#

Because several steps are required to chisel out a polished game from the existing code base, the modifications are broken up in to small steps. The first change adds the familiar register directive at the top of the `BalloonPop.ascx` file, so it can include some controls from the AJAX Control Toolkit. Take a look at the following register directive in the second version of the `BalloonPop.ascx` file available in the code online.

```
<%@ Register Assembly="AjaxControlToolkit" Namespace="AjaxControlToolkit"
        TagPrefix="ajax" %>
```

The next important change in the second version of the game informs DotNetNuke of the intent to use ASP.NET AJAX controls on this page. The code-behind file named `BalloonPop.ascx.cs` contains the AJAX configuration instructions. This time, the code is written in C# instead of Visual Basic.

```
void Page_Load(object sender, EventArgs e)
{
    if( DotNetNuke.Framework.AJAX.IsInstalled() )
    {
        DotNetNuke.Framework.AJAX.RegisterScriptManager();
    }
}
```

Remember that C# is case sensitive, as are JavaScript and CSS. The bracket characters aren't technically required in this `If` statement because it's just a single line of code within the brackets, but I like to keep them in place and on the same column for consistency. Note the register directive is exactly the same in a web user control that uses C# or Visual Basic.

Convert the Game into Targetable Server Controls

The next modification to observe in the second version of the `BalloonPop.ascx` file is a deceptively large change. The following code block shows the modifications that you need to make. The first version of this game contained anchor tags and text for each balloon. This modification will swap that static HTML text for a more targetable equivalent.

The first and second shaded blocks of the following code block add targetable tags around all of the content and the button control respectively. This enables an easy set of selectors in the CSS file. The third applies some descriptive content to the page so the visitors can glean some context for the purpose of the page.

The fourth shaded block in the following code block is where the subtle changes occur. Instead of anchor tags wired up to JavaScript functions, the `<li>` tags are wrapped around instances of the HtmlImage control, which is just a standard `<img>` tag with an `ID` and `Runat` attribute so that it can be modified by server-side code before being sent down to the browser.

```
<div class="BalloonPopContainer">

    <p class="resetButton">
        <asp:Button ID="btnResetGame" runat="server"
          Text="Reset Game" OnClick="btnResetGame_OnClick" /></p>

    <div class="BallonPopHeader">
        <h1>Welcome</h1>
        <p>This is Balloon Pop!</p>
        <p>Help support your neighborhood association website.</p>
        <p>Buy a game token and try to win a prize!</p>
    </div>

    <ul>
        <li id="b0"><img id="img0" runat="server" alt="" /></li>
        <li id="b1"><img id="img1" runat="server" alt="" /></li>
        <li id="b2"><img id="img2" runat="server" alt="" /></li>
        <li id="b3"><img id="img3" runat="server" alt="" /></li>
        <li id="b4"><img id="img4" runat="server" alt="" /></li>
    </ul>
    <ul>
        <li id="b5"><img id="img5" runat="server" alt="" /></li>
        <li id="b6"><img id="img6" runat="server" alt="" /></li>
        <li id="b7"><img id="img7" runat="server" alt="" /></li>
        <li id="b8"><img id="img8" runat="server" alt="" /></li>
        <li id="b9"><img id="img9" runat="server" alt="" /></li>
    </ul>
    <ul>
        <li id="b10"><img id="img10" runat="server" alt="" /></li>
        <li id="b11"><img id="img11" runat="server" alt="" /></li>
        <li id="b12"><img id="img12" runat="server" alt="" /></li>
        <li id="b13"><img id="img13" runat="server" alt="" /></li>
        <li id="b14"><img id="img14" runat="server" alt="" /></li>
    </ul>

</div>
```

Generally, it's not a good idea to hardcode ID attributes into HTML text inside a custom DotNetNuke module because multiple modules can be added to the same page. ID attribute values should be unique on a given web page. In this case, it's not very likely that two instances of the game will exist on the same page.

Add the Animation Controls

Below the collection of unordered lists, the `BalloonPop.ascx` web user control contains fifteen of the following `<ajax:AnimationExtender>` controls. There's one for each balloon. This component of the

AJAX Control Toolkit makes it insanely easy to add complex animations to a web page with just a few lines of XML.

```
<ajax:AnimationExtender id="animation0" runat="server"
    TargetControlID="img0">
    <Animations>
        <OnClick>
            <Sequence>
                <Pulse duration="0.25" fps="30" iterations="3" />
                <ScriptAction Script="popBalloon(0);" />
            </Sequence>
        </OnClick>
    </Animations>
</ajax:AnimationExtender>
```

Starting at the top of the previous code block, the attribute `TargetControlID` tells the AJAX component which object on the page is receiving the animation. This is why the `<img>` tags were converted into HtmlImage controls. The `<AnimationExtender>` control wants to hook up to these HtmlImage controls on the server side before the information is sent across the wire to the browser.

The next element down the hierarchy in the previous code block is the `<Animations>` element. Its job is to contain all of the possible animation elements that can occur on the targeted control. There are several types of animation triggers such as OnClick, OnHoverOut, OnHoverOver, OnLoad, OnMouseOut, and OnMouseOver. All of these self-describing events can trigger a variety of animated effects. Your simple code just makes use of the OnClick trigger.

Effects in an animation can occur in parallel or in sequence. Your game first issues a `<Pulse>` command that oscillates the opacity of the targeted control for three iterations at 30 frames per second. Each single oscillation takes 0.25 seconds. Following the completion of this effect, the JavaScript function named `popBalloon()` is called with the appropriate parameter. Each balloon has its own `<AnimationExtender>` control, so the arguments are 0 through 14 for your zero-based array.

There are a lot of ways to achieve this affect, so just let this one technique wash over you, and then feel free to modify and extend the game as you see fit.

Change the JavaScript Behavior

The main line section of the JavaScript at the very bottom of the static file named `BalloonPop.js` becomes just three lines. The JavaScript functions use a global Boolean variable named `gbIsWinner` to track whether a given balloon pop contains a winning ticket.

```
// MAIN LINE SECTION

var gaTrackingList = new Array();
var gbIsWinner = null;
var giPopCounter = 0;
```

The function `checkTag()` has been modified from the initial version to include an additional parameter that contains a reference to the `<img>` tag the player clicked. If this function locates a prize-winning balloon, the unselected image is replaced with the color of the hidden prize ticket. If the balloon is not a prize-winner, the image replacement occurs elsewhere.

```
// examine the given prize array for a matching balloon number
function checkTag( prizeName, prizeArray, balloonNumber, img )
{
    for( var x=0; x<prizeArray.length; x++ )
    {
        if( prizeArray[ x ] == balloonNumber )
        {
            img.src = img.src.replace( 'blue', prizeName );
            gbIsWinner = true;
            break;
        }
    }
}
```

The original version of the popBalloon() function injected the color and the order of selection into the anchor tag. This time, the color is injected visually by modifying an <img> tag. The second shaded area in the following block of code shows how the <img> tag embedded within the given <li> tag is targeted and passed as a reference to the checkTag() function.

The fourth shaded area shows how the case of no prize ticket affects the image displayed in the <img> tag. In version two of the files for the BalloonPop game, you'll find an images folder that contains the matching set of filenames used in the JavaScript code. With this information, you can more easily see how the replace() function in the fourth shaded area in the following code swaps the file blue.png for the file pop.png:

```
// call when visitor selects a balloon
function popBalloon( balloonNumber )
{
    // evaluate if this is a new balloon number
    if( IsNewBalloonNumber( balloonNumber ) == false )
    {
        return;  // no rethrows allowed
    }

    // init variables to default values
    giPopCounter++;
    gbIsWinner = false;

    var id = 'b' + balloonNumber;
    var e = window.document.getElementById( id );
    var img = e.childNodes[ 0 ];

    // check the prize lists
    checkTag( 'Gold', gaGold, balloonNumber, img );
    checkTag( 'Silver', gaSilver, balloonNumber, img );
    checkTag( 'Bronze', gaBronze, balloonNumber, img );

    // handle case of no prize ticket
    if( gbIsWinner == false )
    {
        img.src = img.src.replace( 'blue', 'pop' );
    }

    e.innerHTML += '<p>#' + giPopCounter + '</p>';
}
```

The final shaded area in the previous code block shows how a `<p>` tag containing the order of selection is injected into the selected `<li>` tag. Remember that the `<li>` tags each have an ID attribute of b0 through b14. The JavaScript variable e in the previous code block holds a reference to the selected `<li>` tag. The `<AnimationExtender>` element is responsible for calling the `popBalloon()` JavaScript function and passing the appropriate balloon number as an argument. This is why there are 15 `<AnimationExtender>` controls.

Update the Module Style Sheet

The following code block shows the updates to the CSS file for version 2 of the Balloon Pop game. The container is configured as a relatively positioned element so the reset button can be slid over to the far right through a negative absolute position.

```
/* changes for v2 */

.BalloonPopContainer
{
   position:relative;
   top:0;
   left:0;
}

.BalloonPopContainer .resetButton
{
   position:absolute;
   top:0px;
   right:-120px;
}

.BalloonPopContainer .BallonPopHeader
{
   position:absolute;
   top:0;
   right:0;
   width:160px;
   border:1px solid #000;
   padding:0 10px;
   height:320px;
}

.BalloonPopContainer .BallonPopHeader h1
{
   margin:10px 0;
   color:#000;
}

.BalloonPopContainer img
{
   border:0;
}

.BalloonPopContainer ul
{
```

```
        margin:20px 0;
    }

    .BalloonPopContainer ul li
    {
        display:inline;
        width:100px;
        height:100px;
        margin:6px;
        padding:6px;
        position:relative;
    }

    .BalloonPopContainer ul li p
    {
        position:absolute;
        top:0;
        left:0;
        font:normal normal normal 16pt Verdana;
    }
```

The other interesting aspect of the previous block of CSS rules is the section that makes the <li> tags appear in a single line instead of their default single file list structure. The display property for the <li> tags is configured with a value of inline which overrides the default block value. The rest should be fairly self-explanatory.

Upgrading the Module

One aspect that I've glossed over so far is the file named BalloonPop.dnn. This is the file that DotNetNuke uses to install the module into the system. DotNetNuke will open up the zip file and look for this specific file in order to start the installation process.

If you compare version one to version two of this file you see that version one merely includes the version numbers and names of all the files that constitute the module. The second version of the module added several image files but otherwise remained mostly unchanged. More complex modules will also refer to SQL script files that can be run automatically to install a module or upgrade it to a newer version.

Because you've examined all of the important changes, go ahead and install the second version of the module into your local DotNetNuke system now. Just repeat the same installation steps you performed with version 1 of the game. It should overlay version 1 and show an improved interface, complete with the animation controls from the AJAX Control Toolkit.

Figure 14-4 shows version 2 of the Balloon Pop module with a few balloons selected.

The new version of the game shows how components of the AJAX Control Toolkit can be combined to form some interesting features. When you click on a balloon, it flashes a couple of times, and then pops into the randomly selected color. The text containing the name of the color and the order it was selected overlay the selected balloon. As you've seen, the experience of this game is a lot like DotNetNuke. It's controlled by a wide range of technologies including CSS, JavaScript, AJAX components, and even some C# code. As you get more involved in DotNetNuke, you'll get to touch quite a few areas of website development.

Figure 14-4

Summary

This chapter highlighted some of the fantastic features available through AJAX and DotNetNuke. Although the Client API project has been steadily churning out great features with client-side JavaScript and web service callbacks, the recent merger of the ASP.Net AJAX Extensions has greatly expanded the number of possibilities.

Although it's helpful to have a good understanding of JavaScript and server-side coding to augment your ASP.Net AJAX skills, it's not essential to getting started. There are several controls in the AJAX Control Toolkit that can get you on your way to developing powerful and compelling sites. You learned that DotNetNuke disables the AJAX controls by default, but just a simple snippet of code in the right place can turn it on. Then, it's as easy as dropping an ASP.Net server control onto a page. Of course, there are plenty of opportunities to dig deeper and really get your hands dirty with some complex JavaScript and server-side programming, if that's your thing.

There are also plenty of opportunities to become involved in the AJAX community that is blossoming on www.codeplex.com. This open source project is continuing to improve the code base and eliminate inconsistencies. If you've a strong desire to participate in the community and you have a lot of interest in AJAX programming, it's not a bad place to hang out.

Exercises

1. What are the four AJAX components available on `http://ajax.asp.net`?

2. What is the name of the Microsoft AJAX Extensions assembly that comes with a default installation of DotNetNuke?

3. Suppose you added a register directive for the AJAX Control Toolkit inside a DotNetNuke module and dropped one of its components onto the page, but the component wasn't appearing in the browser. What might cause this behavior?

4. If you're reading JavaScript code written by another person, and you come across a variable named `gbIsValid`, what can you presume from the context of the variable name and common coding conventions?

15

Using sIFR with DotNetNuke

In a traditional website production process, selected headers of a web page are expressed as image files embedded in the HTML content, sometimes called *image-text* files. An image-text file enables the display of fonts that are not installed on the visitor's operating system. It's simply a picture of the formatted word or phrase. The font specifications inside a CSS file are at the mercy of the visitor's operating system, which make image-text files a good alternative for showing a specific font on all browsers. CSS files generally specify well-known and widely distributed fonts. Depending on the size of the site, a designer might have to create a hundred or more image-text files. As a negative side effect, the practice of using image-text files discourages the work of copy editors who swoop in later and request small changes to the words inside the image-text files.

Scalable Inman Flash Replacement, or sIFR (pronounced siff-er), is a great technology for adding interesting fonts to a web page that might not be installed on the visitor's computer. This chapter explains how to add unique and distinctive fonts to a web page without going through the hassle of managing a series of image-text files or distributing rare fonts to the visitors of the website before they browse it.

The technology inside sIFR replaces selected parts of a web page with Adobe Flash content on the fly using the client-side resources of JavaScript, Flash, and CSS. The standard HTML content inside the page is unchanged, so it's easily tweaked by copy editors. The down-level browser experience is as good as it gets, too! When a user without Flash visits a sIFR-enabled site, the browser simply skips the Flash replacement of the selected content and the page renders as standard HTML.

This chapter shows how to achieve the following tasks:

❑   Download and understand the basic sIFR components.

❑   Select and install a new font for a website.

❑   Generate Adobe `.swf` files with and without Adobe Flash CS3 Professional.

❑   Add sIFR to a custom DotNetNuke container.

Getting Started with sIFR

Mike Davidson hosts a site at www.mikeindustries.com/sifr/. It's a good place to get started with sIFR. He is just one of the folks working to improve the Flash Replacement concept. At the time of this writing, sIFR version 2.0.2 is the current release and version 3.0 is available as a beta release. The idea that culminated in what you know today as sIFR 2.0.2 originated with Shaun Inman, hence the name Scalable Inman Flash Replacement. The previous URL includes some additional context and the interesting history of sIFR. It's informative and well written; you should definitely give it a look.

The first goal is to download the sIFR components to your computer and get acquainted with the various parts. Go ahead and navigate to the previous URL now, and then download the current version of sIFR using the hyperlink at the bottom of the page. To see a quick example of sIFR in action now, click the example page link just below the download link. The example page displays several different large and distinctive font styles without a single <img> tag in the page content.

Unzip the sIFR version 2.0.2 package you downloaded and take a look inside. It contains several files, including a documentation folder with great information on general use. The most important file in this package is the file named sifr.js. This is the JavaScript file that contains the logic necessary to drop a dynamic Adobe Flash movie onto a page and overlay a selected bit of HTML text. Another important file is named sIFR-screen.css. When the sIFR JavaScript detects that a browser has Flash installed, it injects a special CSS class attribute to the <html> tag as the page is loading in the browser. The rules inside this CSS file take advantage of that special CSS class. You'll work with both of these files shortly.

Selecting and Embedding Fonts

Using sIFR on a web page is the culmination of a couple of talents including Typography, Flash, JavaScript, HTML, and CSS. The technology utilizes a font inside an Adobe .swf file. Before you can get started using the Flash file inside a page, you need to identify and prepare a font.

Selecting a Font

Fonts mean a lot to designers. The expressiveness inherent in an uncommon font is the reason why hordes of websites use image-text files instead of plain HTML text. CSS can do a lot with position, color and background images, but its power is constrained when it comes to fonts. The editor in the standard Text/HTML module will reveal the standard list of distributed fonts. In my experience, few websites have gone out of their way to express a rare font on a website through CSS or its predecessor, the <font> tag. Until sIFR came along, scarcely anything else was available.

> One alternative to sIFR is to create image-text media on the web server dynamically. The Microsoft .Net Framework enables the dynamic construction of an image file through the System.Drawing namespace.
>
> With this technique, an <img> tag is used on a web page as usual, but the src attribute is pointed to a special ASP.Net URL instead of a normal image file. The text to include in the image can be expressed in the query string of the special URL. When the web server processes the request, a dynamic image is

constructed on the fly and is sent down the wire as binary content to the web browser — as if the image file was just read off the hard drive like a normal .gif or .jpg file. If you're interested in this option, check out the System.Drawing namespace in the Microsoft .Net Framework; it might turn into a fun weekend project!

Although image-text files are great at showing a picture of the text in the desired font, it's hard for search engines to read the text inside a picture. Search engines like to catalog and index text, so it's important to know that a lot of image-text files on a page won't do much to support the search engine rank of a website.

In order to move any further, you need to select a font file to embed inside Flash. It's worth noting that fonts are the creation of other people; perhaps you have created a font in the past. Therefore, many of the fonts seen today are used with a specific license agreement. Some agreements will license the use of a font for a specific period of time, such as six months from the date of purchase. Other licenses are broader in scope; you can purchase a license for a collection of fonts that enable complete control over their use. Fortunately, in your case of learning how fonts can be injected through sIFR onto a DotNetNuke web page, plenty of free and personal use only fonts are available for playing around.

A simple search will yield plenty of free font websites. One of the favorite sites used by my font aficionado friend, Dave Selden, is www.dafont.com. This site has an enormous number of free and personal use fonts available for download. Click through this site, or use your own favorite site to find a couple of font files to download. Again, please check the licensing terms of the font you select to make sure it's compatible with your intentions.

Try It Out   Install a New Font on your Computer

In this section, you'll install the font you downloaded from a website. I selected a free font named Vanilla Whale by Larabie Fonts from www.dafont.com, and then downloaded the zip file to my computer. If you select another font, then just exchange the name of your font for the one in the instructions.

1. Unzip the font file to your computer and open the zip file.

2. The Vanilla Whale folder includes a read me file and the font file named vanilla.ttf. Examine the read me file and verify that the font is available for the intended use.

3. Double-click the vanilla.ttf file to see the typography in various font sizes. Figure 15-1 shows the font in different point sizes.

4. In Windows XP, click Start, Control Panel, and then open the Fonts folder in the Control Panel window. This folder shows all of the fonts installed on your operating system.

5. In the menu bar of the Font window, you can click File, Install New Font and follow the dialog to add a new font into the system. A much faster way is simply to drag and drop the vanilla.ttf font file into the Font window and watch it automatically install itself.

6. To verify that the font installation was successful, launch Windows Notepad.

7. In the menu bar of Windows Notepad, click Format, Font and select Vanilla Whale as the font, and then click OK.

8. The text inside Windows Notepad should be rendered as the new font.

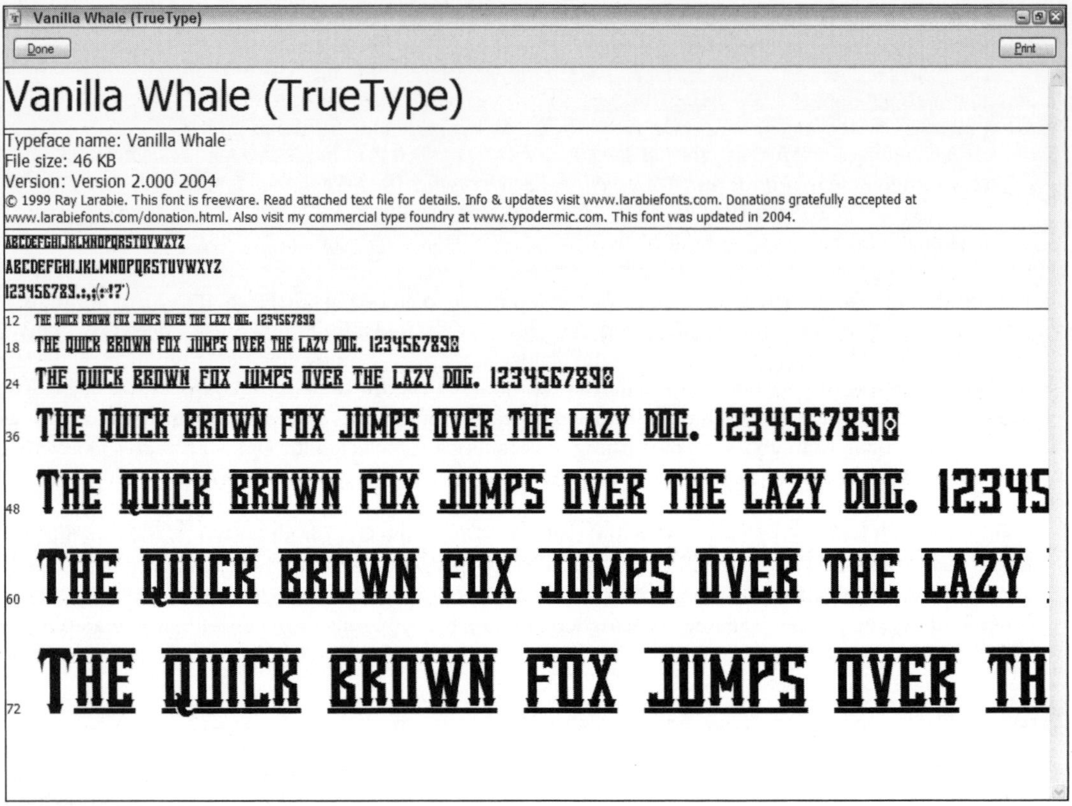

Figure 15-1

How It Works

A standard installation of Windows XP includes nearly 300 fonts. You can add many more custom fonts, but realize that each of these is another entry in the Windows Registry. If you're not actively using the additional fonts, they're causing more bloat than good in the Windows Registry.

The .ttf extension of the Vanilla Whale.ttf file indicates the file is a TrueType font. These font types were originally developed by Apple Computer and have spread in use to be normal Windows and Macintosh font collections. Another popular font technology is ClearType. This was developed by Microsoft and first used in 1999. ClearType is intended for better readability on LCD displays like laptop screens and PDAs.

Using Adobe Flash CS3 Professional

Now that you've selected a special font and installed it on your computer, the next step is to embed the font inside an Adobe Flash file. The sIFR JavaScript file uses this .swf file to display the image on the web page. This is a relatively simple task, on par with installing a font onto your computer, provided you have a licensed copy of Adobe Flash.

If you haven't purchased an Adobe Flash CS3 Professional license, you can demo Adobe Flash CS3 Professional free for 30 days. The demo download is available at the following URL:

```
www.adobe.com/products/flash/
```

You'll export a movie that's compatible with Flash 6, so you can use an earlier version of the IDE if you have it available.

Try It Out   Embed a Font with Adobe Flash

In this section, you'll embed your selected font inside an Adobe Flash movie file. At the end of these instructions, you'll have everything you need to get started with sIFR on your website.

1. Launch Windows Explorer and navigate to the unzipped `sIFR2.0.2` folder on your computer.

2. Use your favorite text editor to open the file named `customize_me.as`. This file contains a few settings you can use to protect your fonts from unintended uses when they go out into the wild.

3. If the font you're working with now or in the future has specific licensing terms, you can make some modifications to this file. The first configuration item stored a Boolean value that indicates whether the Flash movie will work on your local development machine. If you change the value to false, the Flash movie will only work on the specified domains.

```
// true unlocks .swf for usage on local networks (and testing locally)
// false locks .swf so it may only be served from a domain below

allowlocal = true;
```

4. The other configuration item is an array of domains that are permitted for the Flash movie. If you want to lock down the websites that can use this Flash movie, this is the place to do it. By default, this setting allows all domains with the asterisk character shown in the following code. Save any changes to this file, and close your text editor.

```
// fill in whatever domains you want this to work on...
// must be exact matches... asterisk means all

allowedDomains = new Array("*","www.yourdomain.com","yourdomain.com");
```

5. Launch Adobe Flash CS3 Professional (or any version that can compile a Flash 6 movie file).

6. Open the file named `sifr.fla` in the folder named `sIFR2.0.2` using Adobe Flash IDE. This file contains a single hidden text box on the canvas.

7. Double-click the center of the canvas to select the hidden text box. After you double-click the canvas, the text "Do not remove this text" should appear.

8. Click the canvas to bring up the properties window at the bottom of the IDE.

9. Locate the font drop-down list field in the properties window. Select the font you installed earlier in this control. After you make the selection, the text in the canvas should change to use the new font. Figure 15-2 shows the font field inside Adobe Flash CS3 Professional.

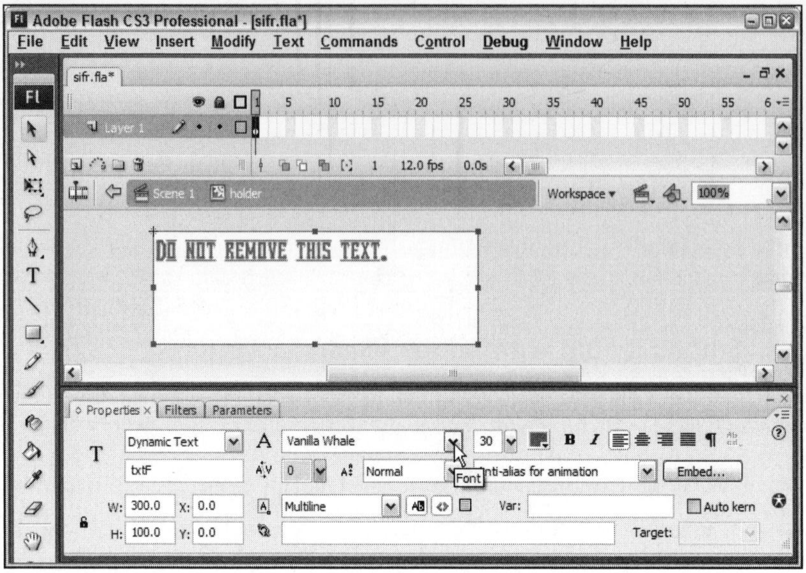

Figure 15-2

10. In the menu bar, click File, Export, Export Movie.

11. Enter the filename for the new `.swf` file. It's a good idea to match the font name with the Flash movie name to keep things organized. Save the Flash movie in the `sIFR2.0.2` folder. Then you can close Adobe Flash CS3 Professional. There's no need to save your changes to the `sifr.fla` file.

How It Works

Flash movies can show any font installed on the Flash designer's computer. As Flash movies are exported to `.swf` files, the font is embedded inside. This allows the font to travel along with the movie and render on another computer that may not have the font installed. The sIFR files you downloaded earlier contain a `sifr.fla` file that's ready for a simple font modification and export.

Flash is a good solution for distributing fonts to other computers that might not have them installed on the operating system. Most visitors have Flash 6 or better installed; this product has truly saturated the market. Most browsers will happily download a Flash movie and play it. In the case of sIFR, the JavaScript file runs immediately after being downloaded and manipulates the Flash movie to show the given text with the distinctive font.

Using sIFR Font Embedder

If the idea of loading up another beefy application doesn't sit well with you or your available hard disk space, then you must explore alternatives — one of which is a Windows client application named sIFR

Font Embedder. You can download the source code or the compiled Windows application at the following URL:

```
http://digitalretrograde.com/Projects/sifrFontEmbedder/
```

Before you can run the sIFR Font Embedder application, you need to make sure you have the prerequisite software installed. This Windows client application uses the Microsoft .Net 2.0 Framework. Because you're already building DotNetNuke sites with ASP.Net 2.0, you're covered there.

This lightweight application creates .swf files without the full Adobe Flash CS3 Professional application; hence the attraction to this alternative. Another prerequisite is the sIFR folder that you've already downloaded and worked with in the previous section, so you're covered there, too.

The final prerequisite is a program named swfmill.exe that does the actual work of generating the SWF movie file. The sIFR Font Embedder application is just a nice GUI wrapper around the command line program swfmill.exe, which does all the heavy lifting. You can download swfmill.exe from the following URL:

```
http://swfmill.org
```

If you have the curiosity, you can certainly organize your own input arguments and run swfmill.exe from the command line without using sIFR Font Embedder. You can get a good idea of how the sIFR Font Embedder application does this in the background by examining the source code available for download on the sIFR Font Embedder website.

It's worth noting that the sIFR Font Embedder author readily admits that the program is alpha quality and you might run into a few problems. So if you run into any issues, you can download the source code and debug the problem yourself or you can move down a layer and work with swfmill.exe directly on the command line, or you can acquire a licensed copy of Adobe Flash CS3 Professional and bypass the entire problem altogether.

Try It Out   Generate a Flash Movie with Free Tools

In this section, you'll use the lightweight alternative to Adobe Flash CS3 Professional to generate a .swf movie file with the embedded font for use on a sIFR enabled website. These steps assume you have already downloaded a font to use on the website, the swfmill.exe program, and the sIFR Font Embedder application.

1. Open Windows Explorer and navigate to the unzipped folder you downloaded that contains the sIFR Font Embedder application. Launch the application by double-clicking the sifrFontEmbedder.exe file.

2. Click the Browse button for the Font TTF File field and select the font file you downloaded earlier.

3. Click the Browse button for the swfmill.exe field and point to the executable file you downloaded.

4. Click the Browse button for the sIFR Location field and point to the sIFR folder that you downloaded. Figure 15-3 shows the sIFR Font Embedder application configured with the file paths for my computer.

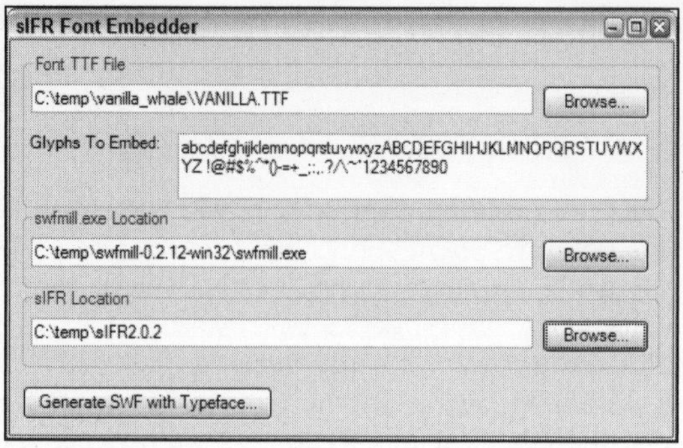

Figure 15-3

5. Click the Generate SWF with Typeface button and enter a filename for the `.swf` file. Store the `.swf` file inside the `sIFR2.0.2` folder, just as you did in the previous exercise. Append a number to the filename, such as `vanilla2.swf`, so you don't overwrite the Flash movie you created with Adobe Flash CS3 Professional.

How It Works

By default, the sIFR Font Embedder application loads the standard set of characters in the Glyphs To Embed field. This includes a-z, A-Z, 0-9, standard punctuation characters, the space, and a few other letters thrown in for good measure. If the glyph isn't included in the text box, it won't be embedded inside the Flash movie and will be unavailable for display on a web page. By contrast, the Flash movie exported from Adobe Flash CS3 Professional included 117 glyphs.

This Windows client application is just a graphical user interface for the `swfmill.exe` program. The GUI program takes care of formatting the command-line arguments and calling `swfmill.exe` for you. Hopefully, the result is the same as using the Adobe product, just with a smaller foot print.

Customizing a Page with sIFR

So far, you've gone about preparing the files necessary for using sIFR inside a web page. Now it's time to see the files in action. The folder named `sIFR2.0.2` that you downloaded earlier contains a simple HTML page that's fully integrated with sIFR. This demo version includes two Flash movie files for two unique fonts.

These demo files inside the sIFR folder provide a quick method of confirming that the Flash movie files generated in the previous sections will work. By eliminating several variables, you can see an existing page work with the default Flash movie files, and then inject your `.swf` objects and see if the page continues to work.

Try It Out   Test Your Generated Flash File

In this section, you'll test out the Flash movies you created in the earlier section. These instructions assume you have Flash installed inside your browser and you have two different Flash movies available for testing.

1. Launch Windows Explorer and navigate to the sIFR2.0.2 folder on your computer.

2. Double-click the file named index.html to launch it inside your browser. The page should display two fonts in various sizes and styles on the page.

3. Confirm that your two Flash movie files exist inside this folder. If not, copy them to this folder now.

4. Launch your favorite text editor and open the file named index.html. The bottom of this file determines which fonts are used for various parts of the web page.

5. Scroll to the bottom of this page and locate the following JavaScript code block. You'll modify a few arguments of the sIFR.replaceElement() method calls.

```
<script type="text/javascript">
//<![CDATA[
/* Replacement calls. Please see documentation for more information. */

if(typeof sIFR == "function"){

  // This is the preferred "named argument" syntax
     sIFR.replaceElement(named({sSelector:"body h1",
   sFlashSrc:"vandenkeere.swf", sColor:"#000000", sLinkColor:"#000000",
   sBgColor:"#FFFFFF", sHoverColor:"#CCCCCC", nPaddingTop:20,
   nPaddingBottom:20, sFlashVars:"textalign=center&offsetTop=6"}));

  // This is the older, ordered syntax
     sIFR.replaceElement("h5#pullquote", "vandenkeere.swf", "#000000",
   "#000000", "#FFFFFF", "#FFFFFF", 0, 0, 0, 0);

     sIFR.replaceElement("h2", "tradegothic.swf", "#000000", null, null,
   null, 0, 0, 0, 0);

     sIFR.replaceElement("h4.subhead", "tradegothic.swf", "#660000", null,
   null, null, 0, 0, 0, 0);

     sIFR.replaceElement("h3.sidebox","tradegothic.swf","#000000", "#000000",
   "#DCDCDC", "#DCDCDC", 0, 0, 0, 0, null);

  sIFR.replaceElement("h3", "tradegothic.swf", "#000000", null, null, null,
     0, 0, 0, 0, null);

};

//]]>
</script>
```

6. Inside the argument list for the `sIFR.replaceElement()` methods, change `tradegothic.swf` to one of the Flash movie files you created, as shown in the following code block. I inserted a reference to the `vanilla.swf` file that I created earlier.

```
sIFR.replaceElement("h5#pullquote", "vandenkeere.swf", "#000000",
   "#000000", "#FFFFFF", "#FFFFFF", 0, 0, 0, 0);
```

```
sIFR.replaceElement("h2", "vanilla.swf", "#000000", null, null,
   null, 0, 0, 0, 0);
```

7. Save your changes to the file and refresh your browser. The page should show the new font using the resources embedded inside the Flash movie you generated. Go ahead and swap the other `.swf` file parameters for your own files, and observe the result on the demo page.

How It Works

Figure 15-4 shows the result of swapping the Trade Gothic font in the `<h2>` element for the Vanilla Whale font embedded inside my Flash movie file. The font I selected has an upper and lower line that runs through from the second character to the end of each word to create a particular feel for the page.

The `index.html` file contains all of the essential items for a sIFR-enabled web page. It refers to an external JavaScript file that contains the core of the sIFR technology. Plus, it links in a CSS file that helps sIFR determine the appropriate size of the Flash Movie that will render the new font. The very bottom of this file contains the instructions in JavaScript that specify exactly which bit of HTML content will be replaced with a Flash movie. The first argument of the JavaScript method you edited contains the selector. This functions just like a selector in a CSS file.

You'll investigate the methods inside the JavaScript sIFR object shortly. You can probably deduce from the `replaceElement()` method that you have quite a few parameters available for applying slight adjustments to the font as it's rendered on the page.

Figure 15-4

Calling sIFR.replaceElement()

An important part of the sIFR customizations you'll make for a given implementation include the number of calls to `sIFR.replaceElement()` and the parameters used in each method call. This is the method that instructs sIFR how to find a specific piece of content inside your page and what to do with it after it's located on the page.

The following table lists the parameters available for this important method. The first letter of each parameter indicates the type of data it contains: "s" is used for string data types while "n" is used for numeric data types. Note the string values use quotes and the numeric values do not use quotes.

#	Parameter	Description	Example
1	sSelector	This is the same as a selector used inside a CSS file. It identifies the HTML content to target with Flash Replacement.	`"h2.LeadText"`
2	sFlashSrc	The name of the Flash movie file to inject into the page.	`"vanilla.swf"`
3	sColor	The hex color value of the text in the selected area.	`"#006699"`
4	sLinkColor	The color of the hyperlink text of the selected area.	`"#FF0000"`
5	sHoverColor	The color of the hyper-link text while hovering over the selected area.	`"#00FFFF"`
6	sBgColor	The background color of the selected area.	`"#0000FF"`
7	nPaddingTop	The padding above the text inside the selected area.	10
8	nPaddingRight	The padding on the right side of the selected area.	20
9	nPaddingBottom	The padding below the text inside the selected area.	30

Continued

#	Parameter	Description	Example
10	nPaddingLeft	The padding to the left side of the selected area.	`40`
11	sFlashVars	A delimited list of special Flash variables, similar to what can be passed to a standard Flash movie inside a web page.	`"textalign=right&offsetTop=20"`
12	sCase	Modifies the case of the selected text.	`"upper"` or `"lower"`
13	sWmode	This setting can apply a transparent or opaque background to the Flash movie.	`"transparent"` or `"opaque"`

There are two ways of calling the `sIFR.replaceElement()` method. One technique relies on the perfect positioning of parameters in the method call. If you want to configure the padding above the text in the Flash movie as 10 pixels, you must configure the number as the seventh argument in the list, as shown in the following code block:

```
sIFR.replaceElement("h2", "vanilla.swf", "#000000", null, null,
    null, 10, 0, 0, 0);
```

Although this works fine, it's a little harder to read than it has to be. There's another technique for calling `sIFR.relplaceElement()` that relies on parameter names instead of the position of the parameter. The following code block is the equivalent of the previous code block. Each parameter is called out by name. This technique can change the order of the parameters, as long as each one has the correct name.

```
sIFR.replaceElement(named({sSelector:"h2", sFlashSrc:"vanilla.swf",
    sColor:"#000000", nPaddingTop:10}));
```

The named argument syntax is easy to read. The argument name is on the left and the value is on the right. A colon character separates the pair. Comma characters separate the arguments. Because the position-based version of the method call set the right, bottom, and left padding to zero, it can be omitted in the name-based method call. The same is true for the null values passed into the string parameters.

This named argument syntax is just a simple feature nestled inside JavaScript. It has its roots in JavaScript Object Notation or JSON, which is heavily used in AJAX-enabled websites.

So with a sufficient understanding of how to call `sIFR.replaceElement()`, you're ready to make as many calls as necessary to select different parts of the web page. It's important to note that the word "scalable" in the sIFR acronym refers to height and width and not the number of Flash movies used on a web page. In fact, using more than just a few instances on a single web page can bring it to a crawl.

During a project back in 2006, my team applied sIFR to a page that displayed a list of events. The title of each event was nicely formatted in a special font using Flash replacement and it worked great in development with about ten events on the page. When the system was loaded up with the 100+ events, the long page slowed to a crawl when sIFR was enabled. With sIFR turned off, the page downloaded and displayed in a respectable time. The JavaScript library for sIFR does a lot of work under the hood, but it can easily become a burden instead of a blessing when abused. Make sure you test your websites with real data so you'll know what to expect when it's deployed.

Creating Decoy Styles in CSS

The sIFR engine uses *decoy* styles in CSS to help construct the intended Flash replacement on the web page. The JavaScript code inside `sifr.js` reads the CSS rules of the decoy styles and generates an equivalent Flash movie. You'll tweak the decoy styles to adjust the font you see on the page. JavaScript must be enabled on the browser in order for sIFR to work — if it's disabled because of corporate policy or any other reason, the show stops right there.

The decoy styles provide a good insight into how sIFR works. When a sIFR-enabled web page is downloaded to a browser, a couple of things happen. First, the code inside `sifr.js` checks to see if Flash is installed. Second, the code injects a class attribute into the `<html>` tag of the web page. The value of this class attribute is `sIFR-hasFlash`.

All decoy selectors found in the `sIFR-screen.css` file of the demo sIFR page use this attribute as a prefix. When this prefix is in place, the CSS file used for sIFR decoy styles can be downloaded along with any other style sheets but do not affect sites with JavaScript or Flash disabled.

The following code block shows one of the CSS rules inside the `sIFR-screen.css` file of the demo SIFR page. See how the visibility property is set to hidden so the decoy style doesn't actually appear on the page while it is loading.

```
.sIFR-hasFlash h2
{
    visibility:hidden;
    letter-spacing:-9px;
    font-size:55px;
}
```

The most common CSS properties you will see here affect the font size, line height, letter spacing, and visibility. This should give you a clear signal that the selector argument used for a call to `sIFR.replaceElement()` will correspond to a CSS decoy style, as shown in the previous CSS block. As you might have guessed, you can specify some values in either the JavaScript method call or in the style sheet. The background color is one such property in this shared space.

Applying sIFR to DotNetNuke

So far, you've traced the route sIFR travels on a standard HTML web page and explored some of the customizations that can be used inside this technology. In this section, you'll apply this knowledge to a custom DotNetNuke container and study any implications that come your way. Whenever you integrate two established, yet complimentary technologies, there are bound to be a few "gotchas" along the way.

Modifying a DotNetNuke Container

In your sIFR exploration, you'll choose to put sIFR into a special container. This will lend some flexibility to the decision of where to use it. You can choose to apply a sIFR-enabled container for a specific module on a page without affecting other modules on the same page.

This task is just a small expansion from what you've already accomplished. You'll need to import a few key components into the DotNetNuke solution including the `sifr.js` file, the default style sheet from the sIFR folder, and the Flash movie file that contains the font to use.

Try It Out   Add sIFR to a DotNetNuke Container

In this section, you'll apply a new font to the home page of the Neighborhood Association site using sIFR. The following instructions assume that you have downloaded the `sIFR2.0.2` folder and have generated a Flash movie file that contains the font to use on the web page.

1. You're about to make some changes to an existing container file. There's a good chance you'll want to use the existing container file as-is sometime in the future as well as not to affect any other modules that are currently using the container, so go ahead and make a copy of it. Launch Windows Explorer and navigate to the folder that contains the "Autumn" container files you constructed in Chapter 7. The container file named `standard.ascx` should be located in the following folder. Name the new file `sIFR.ascx`.

```
<install folder>\Portals\_default\Containers\Autumn
```

2. Log in as the Host account and navigate to the home page of the Neighborhood Association website. Change the Announcements module to use the new container named `sIFR.ascx`, and then log out. The rest of your changes will be accomplished through a text editor.

3. The first task specific to the sIFR integration is file migration. Use Windows Explorer to copy the `sifr.js` file from the folder named `sIFR2.0.2` to the Autumn container folder. Then, copy the Flash movie file you generated to the container folder and copy the file named `sIFR-screen.css` to the container folder. At this point, the container folder should have four new files, including the new `sIFR.ascx` web user control.

4. Launch your favorite text editor and open the new container file named `sIFR.ascx`.

5. The first edit will add a reference to `sifr.js` inside the container. The following code uses an ASP.Net feature to insert the path of the container dynamically at run time. The variable named `SkinPath` contains the path of the Spring container at run time. Add the following `<script>` tag to the container file, just below the last Register directive at the top of the file.

```
<script type="text/javascript" src="<%= SkinPath %>sifr.js"></script>
```

6. Add the following JavaScript at the very end of the container file. These are two calls to the `sIFR.replaceElement()` method as discussed earlier in the chapter. Just like the reference

to the JavaScript file, the in-line JavaScript below uses the ASP.Net technique to inject the value of a key variable with the `<%= SkinPath %>` syntax shown in the following code.

```
<script type="text/javascript">
if(typeof sIFR == "function")
{
    sIFR.replaceElement(named({sSelector:"td.sifrTitle",
        sFlashSrc:"<%= SkinPath %>vanilla.swf",
        sColor:"#000000",
        sWmode:"transparent"}));

    sIFR.replaceElement(named({sSelector:"div.sifrContent span.SubHead",
        sFlashSrc:"<%= SkinPath %>vanilla.swf",
        sColor:"#666666",
        sWmode:"transparent"}));
};
</script>
```

7. Now, you need some way to target specific elements inside this container without affecting elements of the original container. Plus, you want to leverage the existing CSS rules instead of creating a lot of work. Therefore, you need to add another CSS class beside `titleCell`, as shown in the following line of code:

```
<td
    class="titleCell sifrTitle">
    <dnn:TITLE runat="server" ID="dnnTITLE" /></td>
```

8. Add one more targetable class to this file for sIFR beside the class named `ContainerContentPane`, as shown in the following code block:

```
<div id="ContentPane" runat="server"
class="ContainerContentPane sifrContent">
</div>
```

9. You need to get DotNetNuke to use the new CSS file you added to the container folder. You could copy the contents of the new file into the file named `container.css`, but you'll use a little more sophisticated technique instead. Open the `container.css` file in your favorite text editor and add the following line of code at the top of the file. This imports the rules of the external CSS file into the `container.css` file at run time, when the visitor is browsing the site. Plus, it keeps your styles a little tidier.

```
@import url("sIFR-screen.css ");
```

10. Your final edit will modify the contents of `sIFR-screen.css`. Launch this file in your favorite text editor. Then, delete all of the decoy styles for h1 through h5. You don't need these styles because you'll be adding your own.

11. Add the following two CSS rules where the five original decoy styles were once defined. These styles will provide the necessary instructions for sIFR to build an equivalent font using Flash replacement.

```
.sIFR-hasFlash .sifrTitle
{
```

```
            visibility:hidden;
    line-height:70px;
}

.sIFR-hasFlash div.sifrContent span.SubHead
{
            visibility:hidden;
    font-size:20px;
}
```

12. Now that all the pieces are in place, refresh your home page and take a look at the new distinctive font!

How It Works

Figure 15-5 gives you an idea of how the Vanilla Whale font appears in the Announcements section of the home page for the Neighborhood Association website.

Figure 15-5

The largest variant you ran into while integrating sIFR with a DotNetNuke page was the reference to the `sifr.js` file and the Flash movie. Relative paths don't work because you can't be certain about the depth of the page in relation to the container folder. Fortunately, DotNetNuke provides a full path from the root folder all the way to the container folder. It's a little odd that the variable is called `SkinPath` instead of `ContainerPath`, but as long as it gives you an avenue for referring to the file, you're happy to have it around.

Working with JavaScript Timing

You can put a stop to a lot of needless suffering while debugging code if you pay attention to timing and placement of JavaScript in a file. The current code in the container file is OK; it could be better, but it's probably sufficient for your purposes. This section will explore a couple of "gotchas" with JavaScript and how to solve them. The sIFR technology you implemented creates a great test bed for a couple of scenarios.

Remember, your edits to the container file included two `<script>` tags, one above the content and one below the content. In a basic ASP.Net solution, you could even place the top `<script>` tag inside the HTML `<head>` tag. Although it's possible to modify the `default.aspx` file and add another tag to the `<head>` region, it's seldom a good idea.

Modifying the core DotNetNuke files can quickly turn future upgrades into a hassle. Making future upgrades harder is usually a failure of planning instead of an abundance of it. Plus, you have a perfectly reasonable solution available to you by inserting the `<script>` tag as part of the container file.

You'll explore what happens when the JavaScript you added to this container is moved around to different locations in the same file. First, you'll observe the most egregious error.

Try It Out   Move the Library to the Bottom

In this section, you'll explore what happens when a JavaScript library is added below the code that calls the library.

1. Open the container file named `sifr.ascx` that you constructed in the previous exercise.

2. Locate the `<script>` tag that refers to the `sifr.js` file. It should be at the top of the file, just below the register directives.

3. Move this entire `<script>` tag below the in-line JavaScript code at the bottom of the page. Then save your changes.

4. Modify the `if` statement surrounding the two calls to `sIFR.replaceElement()` as shown in the following code block by adding an `else` statement:

```
if(typeof sIFR == "function")
{
    sIFR.replaceElement(named({sSelector:"td.sifrTitle",
        sFlashSrc:"<%= SkinPath %>vanilla.swf",
        sColor:"#000000",
```

```
        sWmode:"transparent"}));

    sIFR.replaceElement(named({sSelector:"div.sifrContent span.SubHead",
        sFlashSrc:"<%= SkinPath %>vanilla.swf",
        sColor:"#666666",
        sWmode:"transparent"}));
}
else
{
    alert( 'What is sIFR?' );
}
```

5. Refresh the home page in your browser by pressing Ctrl+F5 to bypass any cached data in your browser.

6. The browser should show the alert box and render a large blank spot where the sIFR text was previously displayed. This modification has broken sIFR!

How It Works

The fact that this seemingly minor modification breaks the page gives a good clue into how the browser loads the page. When a browser submits a request to a given URL, the web server sends back a stream of characters using the HTTP protocol that the browser interprets as HTML text. As the browser receives the HTML text, it can make some evaluations about additional resources that it must request in order to show the entire page.

For example, the browser must make a follow-up request for each URL embedded in <img> tags on a page. The browser can cache images, so it doesn't have to make a second request when two <img> tags refer to the same image. JavaScript files are a lot like the source of an <img> tag. The browser must make a follow-up request for the JavaScript file after receiving response to the initial request.

Herein lies the rub. The previous exercise just made a change to the JavaScript timing. The browser couldn't possibly know about the existence of the external JavaScript file when the call was executed. The in-line JavaScript runs immediately. It's calling a method that exists in the external JavaScript file before that external file is downloaded — and that is the root cause of the blank spots on the page.

The if statement wrapping the two calls to sIFR.replaceElement() protects the page from throwing an error. The else addition that you made sheds some light on the problem. JavaScript was not aware of an object called sIFR when it executed those lines of code. This problem exists because of the location of the <script> tag that refers to the external JavaScript library.

Try It Out   Move the Library Above the In-Line Script

So now that it's abundantly clear that calling JavaScript functions before they're expressed in the HTML source is a bad idea, let's tweak the code a bit. In this section, you'll explore what happens when the JavaScript library moves above the in-line JavaScript section, but below the HTML content it targets.

1. Open the container file named sifr.ascx that you broke in the previous exercise.

2. Locate the <script> tag that refers to the sifr.js file. It should be at the very bottom of the file.

3. Move this entire `<script>` tag to just above the in-line JavaScript code. Save your changes.

4. Refresh the home page in your browser by pressing `Ctrl+F5` to bypass any cached data in your browser. You might have to do this a couple of times to see the intermittent problem.

5. Perhaps not every time, but occasionally, you'll see the HTML text for a brief moment in the browser, before it is replaced by the Flash font. My own browser showed the problem about one out of four requests with the site loaded on my laptop.

How It Works

Although the site seemingly fixes itself, the blink of the HTML Text gives an unprofessional feel to the quality of the website. The reason the blink occurs is again related to the position of the reference in the JavaScript library. This external JavaScript file has code that runs as soon as it is loaded in the browser. If this code doesn't get a chance to run before the HTML text is presented in the browser, the visitor will see a quick blink or the original text followed by the Flash replacement text. That's why placing the external JavaScript library above the text it is targeting, or in the `<head>` tag of the page is a better idea.

Try It Out   Move the JavaScript to the Onload Event

The final edit to your ailing JavaScript code will resolve your problems and guarantee that your calls to `sIFR.relpaceElement()` will only occur after all of the resources have been received by the browser.

You'll wrap the existing in-line JavaScript with a function named `replaceText()`. This method will be called as soon as the browser indicates it has loaded all of the resources; this is the `onload` event fired by the browser. You can attach code to the `onload` event through some savvy JavaScript calls.

1. Open the container file named `sifr.ascx` that is now partially broken from the previous exercises.

2. Locate the `<script>` tag that refers to the `sifr.js` file. You'll find it just above the in-line JavaScript near the bottom of the file. Move the `<script>` tag that refers to `sifr.js` back up to the top of the file where it was originally.

3. Modify the in-line JavaScript so the code that currently exists in the main line section is wrapped in a function named `replaceText()`, as shown in the following code block:

```
function replaceText()
{
    if(typeof sIFR == "function")
    {
        sIFR.replaceElement(named({sSelector:"td.sifrTitle",
            sFlashSrc:"<%= SkinPath %>vanilla.swf",
            sColor:"#000000",
            sWmode:"transparent"}));

        sIFR.replaceElement(named({sSelector:"div.sifrContent span.SubHead",
            sFlashSrc:"<%= SkinPath %>vanilla.swf",
            sColor:"#666666",
            sWmode:"transparent"}));
    }
    else
    {
```

```
        alert( 'What is sIFR?' );
    }
}
```

4. Now add a new JavaScript function named `addLoadEvent()` below the `replaceText()` function, as shown in the following code block:

```
function addLoadEvent(func)
{
    var oldonload = window.onload;

    if (typeof window.onload != 'function')
    {
        window.onload = func;
    }
    else
    {
        window.onload =
            function()
            {
                if (oldonload)
                {
                    oldonload();
                }

                func();
            }
    }
}
```

5. Add a single method call in the main line section of the JavaScript below the new method you just added to the file. You'll call the `addLoadEvent()` function and pass in a reference to the name of the function you want to call when the `onload` event is fired by the browser, as shown in the following code block:

```
addLoadEvent( replaceText );
```

6. Now, you're ready to test in the changes in the browser. Refresh the page and observe the results. The blink of the HTML text should be taken care of by moving the `sifr.js` file reference to a higher position in the file. You're also protected from making a call to a JavaScript library that hasn't loaded yet. The call to `replaceText()` is blocked until the browser fires the `onload` event.

How It Works

Moving the reference to the external JavaScript file named `sifr.js` fixes the blink problem. It's a little easier to understand if you open the file and see the single line of code at the bottom of this file. It's in the main line section of the JavaScript file, which means it executes as soon as the browser reads it. Code in the main line doesn't wait for function calls like all other lines of code.

The next bit of savvy code named addLoadEvent was gleaned from the public blog of Simon Willison at the following URL: http://simonwillison.net/2004/May/26/addLoadEvent/

In this blog post, Simon expresses some of the concern in the community about event-based programming. Then he provides a solution to a common problem in web development, the onload event.

The HTML <body> tag can have an attribute named onload. The value of this attribute is a bit of JavaScript that will be executed when the browser finishes loading all the resources on the page, so it's a good spot to inject a function call to start the JavaScript wheels turning on a web page and be guaranteed that all the JavaScript libraries are in place. It's a nice level setter.

When you're working on an existing site and tempted to add some code to the onload event, you might be chagrined to learn that someone already beat you to it with an unrelated JavaScript call, and you're not that excited about suffixing their code with calls to your functions. Under some conditions, you might not even be able to write code in the HTML <body> tag. These are the challenges that are solved by Simon Willison's handy function that stacks up code for the onload event and calls all of them in turn.

If you analyze the previous code block of the addLoadEvent() for a bit, you'll soon grasp its cleverness. First the function retrieves the existing functions to call during the onload event. It's possible that none exists and the current caller of the addLoadEvent() is the first to register a function for this important event. If the caller to addLoadEvent() is at least second in line for this event, the function simply wraps the existing code designated for the onload event inside another function wrapper.

This code block allows an infinite number of functions to be called when the browser fires the onload event; plus you don't have to juggle a long attribute in the HTML <body> tag. These can be added from any place in your JavaScript. C# 2.0 has a similar feature set with anonymous delegates. They're a bit of a challenge to get your head around the first few times, but once you do, you will have discovered valuable asset.

Summary

This chapter introduced you to sIFR and how to embed it inside a DotNetNuke website. Adding sIFR to a standard HTML page is a quick and painless procedure, but it does require a certain comfort level with a wide variety of technologies. There's certainly a lot more that you can do with sIFR, such as sifr-addons .js JavaScript library and print style sheets for starters. Hopefully, this chapter encouraged you to explore sIFR in greater detail.

SIFR is a good culmination of both the JavaScript and CSS skills that you've been developing throughout the entire book. Hopefully, this has given some insight and stirred some interest in the large collection of commercial and free fonts available online. If you apply a little discretion and don't replace every word on the page, you can literally design a web page with any font you find.

This technology is a great combination of style and aesthetic value without causing headaches for the production staff when phrases or entire sections are tweaked by the copy editor. The content remains in the source code and is just as search engine friendly as it was before the application of sIFR. Visitors can still use the mouse to highlight and select text just as they can with standard HTML content.

Exercises

1. Describe the two methods of calling `sIFR.replaceElement()`.

2. What is a decoy style in sIFR?

3. How does sIFR prevent a decoy style from affecting a page that does not have Flash or JavaScript enabled?

4. Suppose you want to use two distinctive fonts on a page with sIFR. How can this be accomplished?

Exercises and Solutions

Chapter 3

1. What types of files will you find in a skin package?

A skin package can contain folders for skins as well as containers. Both types of folders can include HTML files, web user controls, an XML file, CSS files as well as image file assets used by the skins and containers.

2. Which DotNetNuke accounts are permitted to upload skin packages?

The Host account can upload a skin package using the online tools. Anyone with write access to the DotNetNuke file system can upload a skin package and subsequently install it using a special DotNetNuke URL.

3. Which DotNetNuke accounts are permitted to browse and apply skin packages?

By default, the Host and the Admin accounts can browse and apply skin packages to pages or the entire portal.

4. If a page is not displaying a skin set at the portal level, what might be the reason?

It's possible that the Portal has a default skin that overrides the Host settings. It's also possible the page has a specific skin setting. Either of these would override a skin set at the Host level.

5. What is the difference between a parent portal and a child portal?

A parent portal has a unique domain name among all of the portals in the installation. A child portal exists under a parent portal and shares its domain name as a prefix.

6. How can a skin be installed in DotNetNuke without using the credentials for the host account?

The skin can be copied to the server via FTP or by drag-and-drop through Windows Explorer. Then, a special URL is accessed in DotNetNuke to install the skin.

Chapter 4

1. What's the difference between a control directive and a register directive?

A control directive informs ASP.Net that the file is a web user control and a register directive informs ASP.Net where it can reference an external web user control.

2. What tags are commonly used as panes in a skin?

The <div>, <p>, and <td> tags are commonly used as panes.

3. What changes are necessary to convert an ordinary HTML <div> tag into a server control?

The <div> tag must have both an "id" attribute and a "runat" attribute in order to become a server control: <div id="MyPane" runat="server"></div>

4. How could you insert all hyperlinks to sibling pages, which share the same parent page and never worry about broken links were the site map to change over time?

Use the links skin object inside a skin file to display all of the sibling links for a page.

5. What benefits are derived from standards compliant HTML markup?

Standards compliant HTML markup has the best chance of displaying the same way in all modern browsers. It also produces a less complex Document Object Model for search engines to crawl and developers to maintain over time. Because most of the presentation information is moved to CSS files, modifications to the structure as well as the design are easier due to the clean separation.

6. If the Module Settings object were omitted from a container, how might an administrator still access the module settings page?

The module settings page is also available from the Settings menu item in the pop-up window of the Actions menu located in the top left corner of a default container.

Chapter 5

1. If the name of a skin file is MyCustomSkin.ascx, what is the name of the XML file that will inject a skin specific doctype value at the top of the page and where should the file be placed?

    MyCustomSkin.doctype.xml

The XML file must be in the same folder as the skin file.

2. What types of files are you likely to find in a skin package?

    a. The skin/container file(s) in the form of an .HTML *file or* .ASCX *file*

    b. A CSS file used by the skin/container

    c. An XML file if the skin/container file is implemented as an .HTML *file*

    d. Image files referenced by the skin/container file or CSS file, plus a full-size and thumbnail sample version of the skin/container

3. What happens when a browser doesn't find a doctype at the top of a web page?

The browser goes into Quirks mode and attempts to render the page using its best guess at the version of HTML used in this page, which can cause the page to render differently in various browsers.

4. Write a few lines of HTML as semantic markup; then write the same content using a non-semantic markup.

Semantic Markup:

```
<h1>this is the header</h1>
<p>this is a detail</p>
<p>this is another detail</p>
```

Non-semantic Markup:

```
<table>
    <tr>
        <td>this is the header</td>
    </tr>
    <tr>
        <td>this is a detail</td>
    </tr>
    <tr>
        <td>this is another detail</td>
    </tr>
</table>
```

Chapter 6

1. What is the name of the Microsoft tool that helps migrate a database from one computer to another?

The Database Publishing Wizard, which is available at www.codeplex.com

2. What are the steps to securing a page so only members of a specific security role can see it?

Navigate to the page settings and change the permissions field to grant view authority to the given security role. Make sure that no other roles, aside from the administrator, are selected in the View and Edit columns.

3. How can you switch the order of the title and the Publish Date fields for all items in the Announcement module?

Navigate to the Module Settings page for the Announcements module. Edit the template field to switch the order of the tokens for the title and publish fields.

4. What are the steps necessary to regulate the posts on a forum so they can be reviewed for conformance to the website policy?

First, configure the forum to require moderated posts. This will prevent post from appearing in the list until they are accepted or rejected by a moderator. Next, configure a forum moderator so this role can review or accept posts in a given forum. The Host account does not have moderator authority by default, but the Host can grant the authority to themselves.

5. After a role has been given edit authority on a Documents module, what must be configured before they can upload documents into the module?

    The role must also be granted read/write authority on the Portal Root folder using the permission settings on the File Manager page.

Chapter 7

1. What is the name of the folder that contains the DotNetNuke module components?

    ```
    /DesktopModules
    ```

2. What are the three common types of CSS positioning?

    Static, relative, and absolute

3. In CSS, what is the rule an absolutely positioned element uses to identify its 0,0 coordinate?

    The nearest ancestor that is relatively positioned, or the HTML <body> tag is the 0,0 coordinate for an absolutely positioned element.

4. In a CSS file, what is the difference between the # character and the . character in a selector?

    The # character is a prefix for an ID attribute selector and the . character is a prefix for a class attribute selector. Therefore, a CSS selector can identify an HTML element by its ID attribute or its class attribute or a combination of the two.

5. If you opened a custom skin file named MyCustomSkin.zip, what two files would you expect to see inside?

    Skins.zip *and* Containers.zip

Chapter 8

1. Name three menus that exist in the default installation of DotNetNuke.

    The SolPartMenu, the DNNMenu, and the TreeViewMenu

2. Write a CSS selector that will target the anchor tag inside a paragraph tag on a page only when the visitor is hovering over the hyperlink.

    ```
    p a:hover { }
    ```

3. How can one stylesheet be embedded into another stylesheet?

    Use the "import" statement in one CSS file to refer to the other CSS file:

    ```
    @import url('externalStyleSheetFileName.css');
    ```

4. If the web page looks different in Internet Explorer 7 and Firefox and the page is rendered in Quirks mode, what is the most likely cause of the problem?

    The web page is missing the doctype at the top of the file.

Chapter 9

1. Why is personalization disabled by default for anonymous visitors?

Personalization processes add computer cycles to a page request. As a means of improving overall performance, extra features are disabled until a visitor commits to an account. Casual visitors do not bog down the system.

2. Write an example of an HTML `<div>` tag that has three CSS class attributes.

```
<div class="Class1 Class2 Class3"></div>
```

3. What is the significance of an equals sign when placed inside bracket and percent characters on a web user control file?

Example:

```
<p> Name: <%= VisitorName %> </p>
```

The equals sign instructs ASP.Net to write out the value of the following expression as it renders the page. If the value of VisitorName were Andrew, the resulting HTML source would look like this:

```
<p>Name: Andrew</p>
```

4. Name three benefits of consolidating redundant code.

    a. Files that share a common file are more likely to be consistent.

    b. Changes take less time.

    c. Files are responsible for fewer things, which reduces opportunities for errors.

5. List some places web user controls are used in DotNetNuke.

Skin files, Container files, Skin objects, Modules

Chapter 10

1. What type of animation is used on the Opacity property of a `<Rectangle>` shape?

The DoubleAnimation is used to modify decimal values.

2. What is the name of the file included in the Silverlight SDK that manages installation and injection into a web page?

The `Silverlight.js` *file is the JavaScript library available in the Silverlight SDK.*

3. What is the minimum syntax necessary to play a video in a Silverlight media player?

```
<MediaElement Source="MyVideo.wmv" />
```

4. How can a Storyboard animation be configured to start five seconds after it has been instructed to execute?

Configure the `BeginTime` *attribute on the* `Storyboard` *element or the* `animation` *element to the value of* `0:0:5`.

Chapter 11

1. What is the name of the CSS selector that will select all elements? Provide an example of its use.

The universal selector will select all elements.

```
*
{
    margin:0;
    padding:0;
}
```

2. Calculate the total width occupied by a `<div>` tag with the following CSS rule:

```
div
{
    padding:20px;
    margin:30px;
    width:40px;
}
```

```
(20px  times 2) + (30px times 2) + 40 = 140px
```

3. If the following two `<div>` tags were above and below each other, evaluate the margin between them:

```
div#top
{
    margin:30px;
}
div#bottom
{
    margin:60px;
}
```

Because vertical margins collapse, the larger of the two margins would prevail. Therefore, the margin value of `60px` *would be the distance between the two adjacent* `<div>` *tags.*

4. Write a shorthand CSS rule for all paragraphs following a `<div>` tag having an ID attribute of `sidebar` that will make the text appear in the Georgia font, 12pt, and bold. Instruct the browser to apply Verdana if the Georgia font is not available.

```
div#sidebar p
{
    font:normal normal bold 12pt Georgia, Verdana;
}
```

Chapter 12

1. HTML can be commented out on the client side using the following syntax:

```
<!--        -->
```

The browser ignores everything inside HTML comments, but it still exists on the page. How can you comment out something on the server side so it is not even sent down to the browser?

Using the following syntax will comment out everything in the middle so it is never sent on the wire to the browser.

```
<%--        -->
```

2. Consider a scenario where Page1 on a DotNetNuke site is standards compliant but Page2 is not. List some possible reasons that would cause the issues in the non-compliant page and how each potential issue can be addressed.

   a. *Page1 uses a skin with a doctype and Page2 uses another skin without a doctype. Adding a doctype to the second skin might fix the issue.*

   b. *Page2 contains different modules from Page1, which emit invalid markup. Testing the modules one by one on a third test page can help isolate the offending module.*

   c. *The HTML editor provider for the site allows an administrator to use non-compliant markup. Editing the HTML content using the online tools might resolve the issues with Page2.*

   d. *The skin used by Page2 contains non-compliant markup. Fixing the issues inside the skin might fix the standards compliance issue.*

3. Explain how DotNetNuke determines which HTML editor component to use inside the Text/HTML module.

DotNetNuke uses the provider module to select an HTML editor component. By default, the FCKeditor is configured to provide the features needed by the Text/HTML module. By adding the necessary files from a third party to a DotNetNuke installation and changing the web.config *file, you can instruct DotNetNuke to use an alternative HTML editor that provides the same required features — but implemented by a different third-party component.*

Chapter 13

1. If you don't have the authority to customize a container, how else might you envelop a module with a `<div>` tag and a unique ID attribute?

Use the header/footer fields in the module settings page to inject a `<div>` tag that envelops the module content.

2. What is the significance of the + characters in the following CSS selector?

```
table#sales td+td+td { background-color:#CCC; }
```

The plus sign indicates an adjacent selector; therefore the rule targets the <td> tags following the second <td> element inside an HTML <table> tag having an ID attribute value of sales.

3. What is the difference between RSS 0.9, RSS 1.0, RSS 2.0, and Atom?

These are various schemas that describe the expected XML elements of an XML news feed. Each of them provides similar information — just in slightly different formats and feature sets.

4. What happens if two style sheets in the same web page contain rules for the same CSS selector?

The lowest style sheet on the page has the highest priority and its rules will override any of the overlapping rules in the previous style sheets.

5. What is the lowest style sheet on a page in a default instance of DotNetNuke, and how can you edit it?

The Portal.css *file in the root of the given Portal is the lowest style sheet in a default instance of DotNetNuke. This file can be edited directly by loading the file in your favorite text editor, or using the browser-based tools in Admin, Site Settings using the Stylesheet Editor text box.*

Chapter 14

1. What are the four AJAX components available on http://ajax.asp.net?

This website contains downloads for (1) the ASP.Net AJAX Extensions, (2) the AJAX Control Toolkit, (3) The AJAX Library, and (4) the AJAX Futures.

2. What is the name of the Microsoft AJAX Extensions assembly that comes with a default installation of DotNetNuke?

The ASP.Net AJAX Extensions assembly is named System.Web.Extensions.dll

3. Suppose you added a register directive for the AJAX Control Toolkit inside a DotNetNuke module and dropped one of its components onto the page, but the component wasn't appearing in the browser. What might cause this behavior?

By default, the AJAX behaviors are disabled. To enable these features, the module must signal DotNetNuke of its intent to use them with the following code:

```
if( DotNetNuke.Framework.AJAX.IsInstalled() )
{
DotNetNuke.Framework.AJAX.RegisterScriptManager();
}
```

4. If you're reading JavaScript code written by another person, and you come across a variable named gbIsValid, what can you presume from the context of the variable name and common coding conventions?

You can presume, but not be guaranteed, that the variable is globally scoped and contains a Boolean value. Additionally, the variable name of IsSomething *or* HasSomething *is commonly used for Boolean variables.*

Chapter 15

1. Describe the two methods of calling `sIFR.replaceElement()`.

   One technique uses parameters based on position and the other technique uses named parameters so the order of the parameters is irrelevant.

2. What is a decoy style in sIFR?

   A decoy style is not shown to the visitor but it is used by the sIFR engine to evaluate an equivalent font to construct in Flash.

3. How does sIFR prevent a decoy style from affecting a page that does not have Flash or JavaScript enabled?

   The sIFR engine injects a CSS class attribute into the `<html>` tag of the page when sIFR is engaged. The attribute value is `sIFR-hasFlash`.

4. Suppose you want to use two distinctive fonts on a page with sIFR. How can this be accomplished?

   First, two separate Flash movies are prepared. Each Flash movie has one embedded font. Next, at least two calls to `sIFR.replaceElement()` are called. One of the arguments of the method call refers to a specific Flash movie file.

Glossary of Terms and Acronyms

ActiveX   Microsoft ActiveX controls can be installed into the Internet Explorer web browser and extend the capabilities of a website beyond cascading style sheets and JavaScript.

AJAX   Asynchronous Javascript and XML. AJAX technology uses JavaScript and the capabilities of modern web browsers to send and receive information from the web server in the background. AJAX libraries also include an array of features for enhancing and manipulating the HTML in a web page and bringing web applications closer to the experience seen inside a Windows client program.

API   Application Programming Interface. Some components expose methods of automating or customizing features. Developers write code to utilize the methods in the API.

ASCX   This is the file extension of an ASP.Net web user control. A web user control provides an independent feature that can easily be added or removed from a web page.

ASP.Net   The primary web development platform from Microsoft based on the .Net Framework, a managed platform for building Windows-based solutions.

Assembly   A compiled file for the .Net platform. Assembly files have a .DLL file extension. All .Net languages compile into DLL files that contain Intermediate Language.

Blog   A common term for a web log or online diary. The author writes posts on various topics for the public to read. Some blogs provide a feature for visitors to leave comments and enable a conversation.

C#   A common programming language in the Microsoft .Net Framework.

Cascading Style Sheets   A method for describing how a browser should display HTML. CSS standards are defined by the W3C.

Cassini   A lightweight web server that can be used in place of Microsoft Internet Information Server.

Classic ASP   Microsoft's predecessor web development platform. It consisted of files using the `.asp` file extension. The files contained a mix of HTML and interpreted server side code.

Container   A DotNetNuke wrapper around a module. Each module has only one container. Containers are responsible for features common to all modules such as the Module Settings button and the Module Actions menu.

Control Panel   A window displayed at the top of the browser window when the Admin or Host user is logged in. This window contains a number of commonly used functions to manipulate a DotNetNuke installation.

CSS   See Cascading Style Sheets.

CSS Rule   A combination of a CSS selector and the list of property settings that are applied to the selected HTML.

CSS Selector   The portion of a CSS Rule that identifies what HTML will be targeted with the given property settings.

CTP   Community Technology Preview. A classification of pre-release software distributed by Microsoft to the development community as a means to obtain feedback before it is officially released.

Directive   The top line in an ASP.Net page or web user control. These lines start with an angle bracket and the "@" symbol. Page directives, control directives, and register directives provide key information so the appropriate features can be configured by ASP.Net on the fly.

DNN   DotNetNuke. An open source web development platform based on ASP.Net.

DNN-Blue   The default skin applied to a DotNetNuke site.

DocType   The top line in the HTML source that identifies the HTML specification to the browser so the browser can operate in Standards Compliance mode. Without this signal, the browser will go into Quirks mode.

DOM   Document Object Model. HTML exists as a hierarchy of tags. Developers can use the DOM as a context for manipulating the web page with JavaScript.

FTP   File Transfer Protocol. Most hosting providers will give you FTP access to the web server you rent from them. You'll use an FTP client program to move files on and off your web server.

Google Reader   A popular web based client program used to read blogs.

HTML   Hypertext Markup Language. Web pages consist of HTML tags around text to give it some semantic meaning and a means to target specific sections with CSS. The W3C manages the HTML specification.

HTTP   Hypertext Transfer Protocol. Most of your web surfing occurs over an unsecure protocol for sending and receiving data from a web server. The data can be a text HTML file, or a binary file like an MP3 music file.

HTTPS   HTTP over SSL. A secure method of communication between a web browser and a web server. The data is encrypted between the two using Secure Sockets Layer and decrypted on both ends.

IE   Internet Explorer. The web browser from Microsoft.

IIS   Internet Information Server. The web server from Microsoft.

Image-Text   A png, gif, or jpg image file that contains text in a specific font that cannot be easily achieved with CSS. Although image-text files guarantee delivery of the design to visitors across multiple browsers, the search engines have a hard time reading the text inside an image file. Thus, they are a poor choice for search engine marketing.

Intellisense   A statement auto-completion technology in Microsoft Visual Studio. After typing a few keystrokes, a window appears with the possible commands that will complete the statement you started typing.

JSON   JavaScript Object Notation. An ECMA standard method of exchanging data. While XML uses tags to identify discrete data items, JSON uses a syntax related to JavaScript for marking up data. AJAX is a common place to see JSON in action.

localhost   The web server domain on your local development computer. A virtual directory can be added as a suffix to form a URL to a local site, for example `http://localhost/MyApplication`.

Module   A DotNetNuke module provides a single feature on a website, such as a list of documents. Modules provide their own feature management utilities such as adding and removing documents from the list. Modules are wrapped by a container file and are dropped into a pane inside a skin. Multiple instances of the same module can appear on a single page.

Module Settings   The standard page used to configure a given module. The container file includes a link to the module settings page.

Module Actions   The standard menu next to each DotNetNuke module that provides a list of common actions such as deleting the module or moving the module to another pane on the page.

Pane   A specific place in a DotNetNuke skin file where modules can be added. A skin can have one or more panes. A single pane can hold zero or more modules. The skin designer has no method of controlling which module or how many modules are added by an administrator at a later time.

Portal   A DotNetNuke portal is an instance of a website. A DotNetNuke installation can have one or more portals that share the same physical software while the content on each portal is maintained separately. Each portal can have its own URL, too.

Provider Pattern   A technology agnostic pattern that enables multiple providers to supply the same service but use different implementation details. For example, a database provider pattern can enable information to be stored in Microsoft Access or Microsoft SQL Server databases. The application layer doesn't care which one is configured, as long as it implements all of the features defined in the provider pattern.

Quirks Mode   A web browser display mode that can cause the same website to render differently, depending on the browser. This mode is best avoided with the use of a DocType at the top of the HTML source.

RSS   Really Simple Syndication. RSS is a format for describing recent updates to a website through XML. Visitors can subscribe to an RSS feed using an RSS reader. An RSS reader aggregates a list of several RSS feeds. The RSS reader tells the user when a given site has new content so the user knows when to return to the given site. Blogs are a popular implementation of RSS technology. Users don't have to waste their time coming back to a blog site that hasn't changed. Their RSS reader tells them when a new blog entry has been posted to the website.

SDK   Software Development Kit. Most software that exposes an API will include an SDK full of necessary files, documentation, and examples to fully use the API.

sIFR   Scalable Inman Flash Replacement. This technology uses JavaScript to replace selected HTML tags with a Flash equivalent. It's a good way to show specific fonts without resorting to image-text files.

Silverlight   A browser client technology from Microsoft that delivers Flash-like features and the text-based programmability of JavaScript and XML.

Sitemap   A plan or actual web page with links to every page on a given website.

Skin   A DotNetNuke skin delivers the ambient design around a set of modules on a web page. A page has only one skin. A skin has one or more panes, where modules can be added by an administrator. The skin designer has no control over type or quantity of modules inserted in a pane.

Skin Object   A skin object is a small feature injected into a skin. It's like a module but cannot be added or removed by an administrator like a module, and it usually provides a smaller feature than a module. The breadcrumb feature and the login hyperlinks are common skin objects on a skin.

SMTP   Simple Mail Transfer Protocol. A standard method of sending e-mail. DotNetNuke has a place to configure the SMTP server so it can send e-mail messages.

Standards Compliance Mode   A browser-rendering mode that helps ensure that the HTML appears in a similar manner across several browser types. The doctype at the top of the HTML source contains the specification that the browser should use to render the subsequent HTML text.

SWF   The file extension of a compiled Flash movie.

T-SQL   Transact Structured Query Language. Microsoft's proprietary version of the ANSI SQL standard used with Microsoft SQL Server database.

TTF   TrueType font. A font file format from Microsoft.

Universal Selector   The * character in CSS is the universal selector. It selects all elements in its scope. A selector of "*" selects all elements in the document. A selector of "#header *" selects all elements inside the element with the id value of "header."

URL   Uniform Resource Locator. A web address such as http://www.dotnetnuke.com

VB.Net   A managed language, similar to Visual Basic 6, and used to write code for the .Net Framework

VS   Visual Studio is an integrated development environment used for building solutions based on the .Net Framework.

VWD   Visual Web Developer Express. A free version of Visual Studio used to build ASP.Net websites.

W3C   World Wide Web Consortium. An international standards body. They define standards for HTML, CSS, XML, and several other items.

web.config   The XML configuration file inside an ASP.Net website.

Wiki   A website that permits any user to add or edit any content on the site. Some wikis are more permissive than others in this regard, but all of them are community focused.

XAML   Extensible Application Markup Language. An XML language for describing and building applications. Microsoft Windows Presentation Foundation and Microsoft Silverlight are two ways of displaying XAML files.

XCOPY   A command-line utility for copying files from one directory to another.

XHTML   An HTML file that conforms to the basic XML rules for a well-formed document. For example, every element must have an opening and a closing tag and all attributes values must have quotes around them.

XML   Extensible Markup Language. A human readable method of marking up data. XML files can be expressed as simple text files so they can be passed to any computer system. Before XML, files used rules such as comma delimiters or specific positions to indicate various fields in a data file. A well-formed document has just a few basic rules. For example, every element must have an opening and a closing tag and all attribute values must have quotes around them.

XSL   Extensible Stylesheet Language. A standard language for transforming an XML file into another format. XSL is expressed as an XML file itself. An XSL file can convert an exported XML file full of data into an XHTML file for visitors to browse.

Index

Z